Stilicho

Stilicho

The Vandal Who Saved Rome

Ian Hughes

Pen & Sword
MILITARY

First published in Great Britain in 2010 by
PEN & SWORD MILITARY
an imprint of
Pen & Sword Books Ltd
47 Church Street
Barnsley
South Yorkshire
S70 2AS

ISBN 978 1 84415 969 7

Printed and bound in the UK by
MPG Books

Pen & Sword Books Ltd incorporates the imprints of
Pen & Sword Aviation, Pen & Sword Family History, Pen & Sword Maritime,
Pen & Sword Military, Wharncliffe Local History, Pen & Sword Select,
Pen & Sword Military Classics, Leo Cooper, Remember When,
Seaforth Publishing and Frontline Publishing.

For a complete list of Pen & Sword titles please contact
PEN & SWORD BOOKS LIMITED
47 Church Street, Barnsley, South Yorkshire, S70 2AS, England
E-mail: enquiries@pen-and-sword.co.uk
Website: www.pen-and-sword.co.uk

Contents

For Joanna and Owen
For their patience and understanding

Acknowledgements

My first thanks must go once again to Philip Sidnell for his confidence in giving a second contract to an unknown author. I hope that this book repays that confidence.

I would like to thank Adrian Goldsworthy for again agreeing to read through early drafts of the entire book, a task which demanded a vast amount of patience and humour – mainly at my expense. For reading excerpted chapters I would like to thank Philip Matyszak, Robert Jones and Robert Vermaat for their time, encouragement and suggestions.

For helping me to secure otherwise impossible-to-acquire books, I would like to thank the staff at Thurnscoe Branch Library, Barnsley, and especially Andrea World of the Inter-Library Loans Department of Barnsley Libraries.

I would very much like to thank the following people for kindly allowing me to use their photographs in the plates: Beast Coins (www.beastcoins.com), Giovanni Dall'Orto of Wikimedia, Mario Ierardi (www.geocities.com), PHG of Wikipedia, and Majed Salem of Saudi Arabia.

From the website 'Flickr' I would like to thank: J C Cuesta, Dobersch, Tilemahos Efthimiadis, Erindipity, Fanaticissima, Sarah Gould, Keiron Hart, James MacDonald, MarkusMark, and Paul Murray.

I would like to express my gratitude to Assistant Professor Bret Mulligan of Haverford College, Pennsylvania, for his willingness to converse on the inscription to Claudian (Plate 3).

The book would not have been the same without the contribution of the members of both www.romanarmytalk.com/rat/ and www.unrv.com.forum. They have been exceptionally patient, especially with regards to questions about the availability of photographs.

I would also like to thank Patrik of Sweden (www.unrv.com) for his special efforts to secure high-quality pictures, and finally, Adrian Wink of Armamentaria (www.armamentaria.com) for once again allowing me to reproduce photographs of his excellent reproductions.

To all of these individuals, once again my heart-felt thanks.

However, most of all I would like to thank Joanna for her endurance in reading through yet another book about 'some bloke from ancient Rome'. For her patience and understanding I will for ever be in her debt.

And finally to my son Owen, I would like to apologize for all of the times when he has wanted to play and has been told, 'Sorry, Daddy is working'. Your patience will now bear fruit, as the work is finally finished …

List of Illustrations

Line drawings

Plate section

List of Maps

Foreword

It is a great pleasure to write this brief foreword to Ian Hughes' second book, following on from his earlier study of Belisarius as a general. Stilicho is in many ways the most fascinating of the succession of military strongmen who dominated the Western Roman Empire in the last few generations of its existence. He stands out in a period when few personalities register, and even fewer command any respect or admiration. Much of this has to do with the manner of his death, accepting arrest – and in fact execution – rather than leading his still-loyal troops in a war against the emperor. This single act, coming at the end of a long career, powerfully shapes our mental image of the man, and yet even this is surrounded in mystery. He may have acted through courage and a sense of duty to the state, feeling that it was better to accept the arbitrary judgement of an ungrateful and incompetent emperor rather than to start yet another internal conflict. Or perhaps he was just too tired to care, already mentally defeated, and rightly or wrongly believed that he could not hope to beat the Emperor Honorius. We simply do not know.

Indeed there is so much that we do not know about Stilicho's career and the broader history of these years. Details are often elusive, as is the broader context. From a military perspective, we not only lack full accounts of even the most important campaigns of this period, but also a wider sense of what the Roman army in Stilicho's day was like and how it operated. There is very little hard evidence for the scale of operations, the size of the forces led in the field by Stilicho, or the numbers of warriors following the barbarian leaders. Far less is also certainly known about the workings of the Roman state in these years than is often assumed. Stilicho's world is glimpsed only in scattered fragments of information. A few facts are known, other details are more or less plausibly guessed, while some remain elusive – no more than conjecture however confidently asserted.

It is a frustrating and intriguing challenge to write the history of this period. Ian Hughes sets himself an even more difficult task in writing a biography of Stilicho, where the central thread is the career of just one man. It is well worthwhile, for it is always good to remind ourselves that men like Stilicho, Honorius and Alaric were just human beings. Historians rightly concern themselves with wider social trends, where the successes and failures of individuals are seen principally as illustrations of broader patterns. Yet this is not how people actually live their lives, and it is very dangerous to remove this human element from history.

Biography has another advantage, in that it forces the historian to maintain a clear chronological narrative. In more general studies it is all too easy to pull fragments of information from diverse contexts to create an overall picture, which over time can often become so firmly entrenched that historians forget how it was first formed. In this book Hughes make sensible use of evidence from outside the period, but remains focused on the career of Stilicho himself. Simply looking at this in detail is highly valuable, as is considering such practical things as how quickly events could have occurred, and how fast information, individuals, armies or supplies could have travelled. Rapid summaries, and still more a thematic approach, all too often conceal serious flaws in the reconstruction of events.

Any historian working on this period will inevitably ask more questions than he or she can possibly answer with confidence. Hughes is very good at asking questions, and has a welcome willingness to challenge established orthodoxy on this period. He also has the honesty to let the reader know that there are some things we simply do not understand. His own suggestions are made clear as suggestions based on the available evidence, not facts, and the reasons for his conclusions explained. The best history encourages readers to follow the line of reasoning and decide for themselves whether or not to accept the ideas. The evidence for so many things is poor – perhaps poorer than is often understood – and this means that Hughes' discussion ranges widely. Apart from the study of Stilicho himself, there is much that is thought provoking about the wider history of this period and the nature of the army and empire. Agree or not, the reader cannot fail to be challenged.

As well as the problems over detail, Stilicho's career is significant for many broader questions. The Western Empire he served and for a while dominated would cease to exist by the end of the fifth century. Just two years after Stilicho's death, Alaric sacked Rome, making the execution of the Roman general assume even greater importance than most other political struggles between Roman emperors and their senior ministers. Stilicho had dominated the western empire for thirteen highly eventful years. During that time he managed to contain Alaric, but did not inflict a decisive defeat on him. It is quite possible that he never actually attempted to achieve such a victory, and may have judged that with the resources at his disposal, it was neither practical nor necessarily desirable. Alaric was not the only threat, and at times was a valuable ally. He remains famous for plundering Rome, but achieved little else of lasting importance.

It is hard to avoid hindsight, and prevent this overshadowing the debate, but Hughes manages this splendidly. All in all, this is a valuable and accessible addition to the histories of this dramatic period.

Adrian Goldsworthy
January 2010

Introduction

This book tells the story of one man, Flavius Stilicho. He is renowned as presiding over the Western Empire during the reign of Honorius, 'a rare period in which the cumulative effect of changes … over a long period combined with a series of crises to create a genuine turning-point in Western history.'[1] It was Stilicho that defended the West from the Goths under Alaric. It was Stilicho that was in control when the Vandals, Alans and Sueves crossed the Rhine in 406 and 'devastated' Gaul. It was Stilicho that had to defend Italy from the usurper Constantine III, who rebelled in Britain in 406 before crossing the English Channel and taking control of Gaul and Spain. Stilicho's death in 408 left the Emperor Honorius vulnerable and the West divided.

Stilicho was related by marriage to the Emperor Theodosius (379–395). When that emperor died he left Stilicho as guardian for Honorius, the young emperor in the West. Thanks to his semi-barbarian birth – his father was a Vandal, his mother a Roman – his motives and actions have often been questioned. Some historians have seen him as preferring to ally with Alaric and the Goths in an attempt to take control of the East rather than devoting his energies to the defence of the West. As a result, these historians have effectively laid the blame for the permanent division of the Empire and the collapse of the West firmly at Stilicho's feet.

At the opposite extreme, others have claimed that Stilicho the Vandal was the individual who saved Rome from the Goths, noting that shortly after his death Alaric led the Goths in the first sack of Rome since the fourth century BC – hence the title of this book. In this view, Stilicho valiantly fought to save Rome but in the end ran out of resources and was brought low by his political enemies.

The intention is not to follow either of these views, but to look afresh at Stilicho's career and attempt to reach a balanced conclusion as to his aims and motives and success or failure in achieving them. All of the available information will be analysed and modern viewpoints weighed before conclusions are reached. However, throughout it should be noted that all of the conclusions are open to question, as the sources are not conclusive, and that new theories are constantly being formed.

One other factor needs to be borne in mind. Stilicho lived and died 1,600 years before this book was written. In the intervening time the vast majority of information concerning his life and times has been lost. What remains is heavily biased either for or against Stilicho and needs to be closely analysed to determine how useful it is. As a consequence, it is impossible to form a clear picture of Stilicho as an individual and to gain a clear insight into his mental processes. All that is possible is an attempt to reconstruct the broad outline of his policies and personality.

The sources

The majority of the primary sources that cover the life of Stilicho are biased, either for or against him. As an example, Claudian wrote panegyrics (eulogies written in praise of individuals) for Stilicho and is definitely favourable to his regime, whilst Eunapius, a pagan, was hostile to Stilicho. Historians have tended to choose between these extremes, depending on their ultimate aim. However, this method is not really acceptable. Roman writers were extremely well-versed in their art and capable of writing very effective pieces of propaganda. Yet, as anyone who has studied the methods of propaganda will know, the aim is not to invent flaws, since invention can be disproved, after which the argument loses much of its force. Instead, wherever possible, actual events are manipulated until they fit the desired portrayal. As a result, whenever possible, when two different portrayals of events occur they will be analysed to determine whether they can both be seen as describing the same event but from different perspectives. In this way it is hoped that a more balanced view of Stilicho can be achieved, rather than one which relies on specific texts which are undeniably flawed. In the list of sources given, wherever possible their overall bias either for or against Stilicho is given and needs to be remembered at all times.

However, one other factor must be mentioned. Ancient historians were not writing 'modern' history. It is now believed that the best form of historical writing tries to present a balanced view of events, and includes all of the relevant information in order to build a complete picture of 'cause and effect'. This was not true in the past. Roman historians 'insisted upon personalizing events and on reducing complicated historical developments to a simplistic narrative'.[2] Therefore, each individual historian had an agenda, whether it was to promote a patron, to see all events as being acts of treachery, or some other variation on these themes. Therefore, anybody reading the ancient sources must always remember which theme the writer is developing and incorporate this into the analysis.

Secular sources

Ammianus Marcellinus

Ammianus Marcellinus (c.325–390) wrote a *History of Rome* covering the Empire from the accession of the Emperor Nerva (96–98) to the Battle of Adrianople (378). Although the first thirteen books have been lost, the work is valuable for its detail and accuracy when covering the events leading up to the Battle of Adrianople and the elevation of the Emperor Theodosius.

Claudian Claudianus (Claudian)

Claudian Claudianus (Claudian) (died c.404) was the 'best known of a long list of Egyptian poets from the fourth to the fifth centuries'.[3] Travelling from Egypt to Rome before 395 he wrote a panegyric to the brothers Probinus and Olybrius when they were elected as consuls by the Emperor Theodosius for 395. Shortly after, he accepted the patronage of Stilicho, for whom he wrote several panegyrics. He also wrote panegyrics on other occasions for the Emperor Honorius, as well as a 'History' in poetic form of the war against Gildo (see Chapter 8) and many other works. His works are the main source of information about the life and career of Stilicho. However, as they are panegyrics they must be used with extreme caution. Despite this, they are invaluable in attempting to unravel Stilicho's personal life and the policies he adopted with regard to 'ruling' the Western Empire.

Eunapius of Sardis

Eunapius of Sardis (Sart, Turkey: c.347 to early fifth century) wrote a continuation of the History of Dexippus which covered the years c.270–404. His work does not survive but is partially and indirectly preserved because Zosimus did little more than paraphrase Eunapius when recording events up to c.404. Eunapius was a pagan and was bitterly opposed to Christianity, a factor which affects his works. He was also hostile to Stilicho, which in one way is useful as it acts as a balance to the panegyrics of Claudian.

Gregory of Tours

See Renatus Profuturus Frigeridus

Jordanes

Jordanes (c.550) wrote two books. The *Romana* (On Rome) is a very brief epitome of events from the founding of Rome until 552. Due to the fact that it is extremely condensed, it can be useful but offers little that cannot be found elsewhere. He also wrote the *Getica* (Origins and Deeds of the Goths). This work is valuable in that it contains a lot of information that would otherwise be lost, especially those parts which may demonstrate a Gothic viewpoint. Unfortunately, due to its bias towards the Goths it must be used with extreme caution.[4]

Olympiodorus of Thebes

Olympiodorus of Thebes (born c.380) wrote *History of the Western Empire*, which covered events between 407 and 425, but this has been lost. However, like the works of Eunapius it has in a way been preserved due to it being used by Zosimus and Sozomen as the basis for events up to 410 and the sack of Rome by the Goths. A diplomat, he had good access to sources and so the *History* may have contained a lot of accurate information. Again like Eunapius, he was a pagan but, unlike Eunapius, he approved of Stilicho's policies. The early contradictions between Eunapius and Olympiodorus demonstrate that Stilicho's policies divided opinion.

Procopius

Procopius (c.500 to c.554) wrote the *Wars of Justinian*. In these he describes the wars fought by the general Belisarius on behalf of the Eastern Emperor Justinian. Included are many asides and brief entries concerning the history of the West and of the

Germanic peoples who had overrun the Empire. Usually he is assumed to be reliable but caution is needed where his work concerns events outside his own lifetime.

Renatus Profuturus Frigeridus

Renatus Profuturus Frigeridus (fl. fifth century) wrote a history that only survives in fragments. Fortunately, he was used as a source by Gregory of Tours, from which many items of value can be gleaned.

Salvian

Salvian (fl. fifth century) wrote a work known as *De gubernatione Dei* (On the Government of God: also known as *De praesenti judicio*) in which he describes life in fifth-century Gaul and contrasts the 'wickedness' of the Romans with the 'virtues' of the barbarians. Although written with a specific purpose, it can be used with care to furnish relevant information about conditions in Gaul after the invasions of 406.

Scriptores Historiae Augustae

The *Scriptores Historiae Augustae* was probably written in 395 by an unknown author or authors. Although too early to include information on Stilicho, many of the attitudes and assumptions upon which it is based can be used to interpret the views and beliefs of the Western Senate at the start of the reign of Honorius and the supremacy of Stilicho.[5]

Zosimus

Zosimus (c.500) wrote the *Historia Nova* (New History), which covers the period from the mid-third century to 410. He appears to have used two main sources for his information. Eunapius was used for events to 404 and Olympiodorus was used for the years from c.407–410. Zosimus was a pagan, writing in Constantinople, who was determined to show that Christianity was the reason for the disasters suffered by the Empire. He closely follows Eunapius and Olympiodorus, including in his work their biases towards Stilicho. This copying is so close that in the early part of the work he follows Eunapius and castigates Stilicho. Eunapius' work ends in 404 and at this point Zosimus is forced to turn to Olympiodorus. The transition is obvious, as in Book 5, Chapter 34, he stops castigating Stilicho, following Eunapius, and starts to praise Stilicho, following Olympiodorus. As it is obvious that he is not critical of his sources, although his work is useful it needs a great amount of caution when it is being used.

Church histories

Much of the information about Stilicho has to be gleaned from sources more concerned with ecclesiastical affairs. In some respects this can be interpreted as a negative aspect, but it is only their focus upon church history and the subsequent copying by churchmen that has allowed them to survive.

Ambrose

Ambrose (c.340 to April 397) was the Bishop of Milan during the early years of Stilicho's dominance. He wrote and delivered a eulogy on the death of the Emperor Theodosius in 395, the *De obitu Theodosii* and many of his letters still survive. His works are extremely useful in attempting to assess Stilicho's early policies and the workings of the bureaucracy, but unfortunately only a few items are relevant.

Augustine

Augustine (354–430) wrote many works, including *De civitate dei* (The City of God), which was written after the Gothic sack of Rome in 410. It includes information which is useful in reconstructing events concerning Stilicho, but the moralizing Christian nature of the work needs to be taken into account.

Orosius

Orosius (c.380 to c.418) wrote the *Historiarum Adversum Paganos Libri VII* (Seven Books of History Against the Pagans), which he completed in 418.[6] As Ororius was more concerned with defending Christianity rather than writing a true history the work is 'superficial and fragmentary'.[7] However, it is extremely valuable in that it includes a lot of detail concerning the years 395 to 410.

Socrates Scholasticus

Socrates Scholasticus (born c.380) wrote the *Historia Ecclesiastica* (Church History), which covers the years 305–439. It was written during the reign of Emperor Theodosius II (408–450). Written solely as a history of the church it contains much information on secular events, but mainly only where they impinge on church history. However, these items are otherwise unrecorded so they can offer unique insights into events.

Sozomen

Sozomen (c.400 to c.450) also wrote a *Historia Ecclesiastica* (Church History) sometime around the year 430. The section covering the life of Stilicho is in Book 9, which, like Zosimus, incorporates a lot of information from Olympiodorus. Therefore, it should be remembered that the two writers cannot be cross-referenced against each other as proof of events, since they both used the same source.

Theoderet

Theoderet (c.393 to c.457) wrote many works on Christian doctrine, but more importantly also wrote a *Historia Ecclesiastica* (Church History) which begins in 325 and ends in 429. He used several sources, including, amongst others, Sozomen, Rufinus, Eusebius and Socrates. Possibly due to the mixed nature of his sources, the work is chronologically confused and must be used with caution.

Letters

Many letters written at this time survive. Although most are obviously of a personal nature, some include snippets of information about Stilicho and imperial affairs. These can be valuable in filling in details but their accuracy in most areas remains unknown.

Amongst others, the letters of Saint Jerome (c.347–420), who also wrote a chronicle that ended in 380, Gaudentius (d. 410) and Paulinus of Nola (c.354–451) can help to illuminate otherwise unknown aspects of Stilicho's life.

Chronicles

The *Chronica Gallica of 452* is a continuation of the *Chronicle of Jerome* covering the years 379 to 452. The *Chronica Gallica of 511* also begins in 379 and continues to 511. Due to the similarity between the two, it is possible to see the *Chronicle of 511* as a continuation of the *Chronicle of 452*. Both of these works contain useful information but need to be used with care, since the dates given may not in fact be accurate.

Hydatius

Hydatius (c.400 to c.469) wrote a chronicle covering events from 379 to the middle of the fifth century. Although potentially valuable, his work contains many errors and must be used with extreme caution.

Marcellinus Comes

Marcellinus Comes (c. Sixth Century) wrote a chronicle which covers the period from 379 to 534 (an unknown writer continued the chronicle down to 566). Although mainly about the Eastern Empire, he included some information concerning the West, drawn mainly from Orosius.

Prosper Tiro

Prosper Tiro (Prosper of Aquitaine: c.390 to c.455) wrote a continuation of *Jerome's Chronicle*. *Prosper's Chronicle* finishes in 455.

Other sources

Notitia Dignitatum

The *Notitia Dignitatum* is an extremely important document. It purports to list the bureaucratic and military organization of both the Eastern and Western 'Roman' Empires. Thousands of offices are listed. Dated to c.420 for the West and c.395 for the East, it is potentially a mine of statistical and legal information. Unfortunately there are many problems. Probably originating with the Emperor Theodosius in the East, it may in theory have been intended as a full list of offices. Unfortunately, it was not kept strictly up to date and there are many omissions and duplications. Moreover, due to the fragmentation of the Empire during and immediately after Stilicho's lifetime, it is uncertain whether many of the army units listed existed in reality or only on paper. As a consequence, information taken from the *Notitia* should be accepted as possible rather than certain.

Collectio Avellana

The *Collectio Avellana* is a collection of documents dating from 367 to 553. Included is a letter from the Emperor Honorius to the Emperor Arcadius.

Codex Theodosianus

The *Codex Theodosianus* is a collection made during the reign of Theodosius II in the East of all of the laws since the reign of Constantine I. It includes many laws made either by or for Stilicho and so gives a window into aspects of his life and career that would otherwise be blank. As the laws are usually dated the *Codex* is also useful as evidence for the timing of events and can give insights into Stilicho's political and military policies.

As has already been noted, the detailed information that is available in the sources should not detract us from the knowledge that they were all written with a purpose. Even when this bias is openly declared it can easily be overlooked or forgotten. If this is the case with the major sources as listed above, it is even more the case with the multitude of minor sources not listed. The less important sources which are used are of varying accuracy and utility; however, where necessary, an analysis of these will be dealt with in the body of the text. However, if the source only gives us one or two snippets of information then it is possible that the source will not be analysed.

Abbreviations

In order to make the references more manageable, the following abbreviations have been used for ancient sources:

Saint Ambrose	Amb.
Ammianus Marcellinus	Amm. Marc.
Augustine	Aug.
Chronica Gallica of 452	Chron. Gall. 452
Chronica Gallica of 511	Chron. Gall. 511
Claudian Claudianus (Claudian)	Claud.
Collectio Avellana	Collect. Avell.
Eunapius of Sardis	Eun.
Gaudentius	Gaud.
Gregory of Tours	Greg. Tur.
Hydatius	Hyd.
Jordanes	Jord.
Marcellinus Comes	Marc. Com.
Notitia Dignitatum	Not. Dig.
Olympiodorus of Thebes	Olymp.
Orosius	Oros.
Paulinus of Nola	Paul.
Procopius	Proc.
Prosper Tiro	Prosp.
Renatus Profuturus Frigeridus	Ren. Prof.
Saint Jerome	Jer.
Salvian	Salv.
Scriptores Historiae Augustae	Scrip. His.
Socrates Scholasticus	Soc.
Sozomen	Soz.
Theoderet	Theod.
Zosimus	Zos.

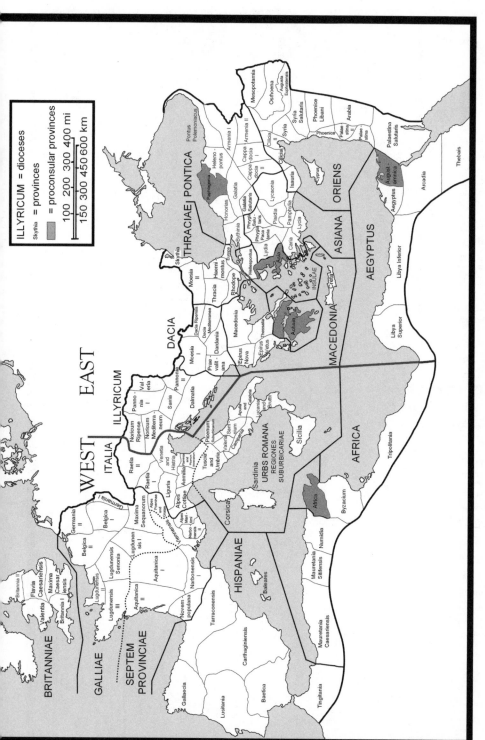

1. The Roman Empire on the death of Theodosius.

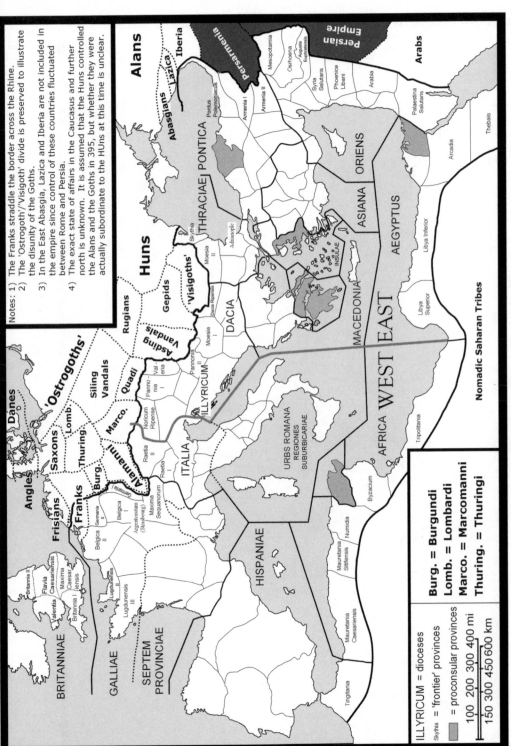

Notes: 1) The Franks straddle the border across the Rhine.
2) The 'Ostrogoth'/'Visigoth' divide is preserved to illustrate the disunity of the Goths.
3) In the East Abasgia, Lazica and Iberia are not included in the empire since control of these countries fluctuated between Rome and Persia.
4) The exact state of affairs in the Caucasus and further north is unknown. It is assumed that the Huns controlled the Alans and the Goths in 395, but whether they were actually subordinate to the HUns at this time is unclear.

ILLYRICUM = dioceses
Skythia = "frontier' provinces
= proconsular provinces

Burg. = Burgundi
Lomb. = Lombardi
Marco. = Marcomanni
Thuring. = Thuringi

100 200 300 400 mi
150 300 450 600 km

2. *The enemies of the Roman Empire, AD 395.*

Chapter One

The Roman Empire and its Neighbours

Rome

Stilicho was born sometime around the year 360. By this time the Empire had recovered from the rapid turnover of emperors and the barbarian invasions of the third century. Although civil war was still common and the threats of attack by 'barbarians' across the northern and eastern borders still remained, it was a period of relative peace after the chaos of the previous century.

The emperors Diocletian and Constantine are credited with major changes in the structure of the Empire, especially with regard to the bureaucratic, financial and military spheres. The details of these changes need not detain us here: where such detail is needed this will be covered at the appropriate point. However, certain trends need to be highlighted as they play a pivotal role in the life of Stilicho.

The first of these concerns the bureaucracy. The 'civil service' had greatly expanded following the reign of Diocletian and his inauguration of the Tetrarchy. In this the Empire had been divided and each half had been ruled by an *Augustus* (emperor). Each *Augustus* had his own *Caesar* (deputy and successor) to help run his half of the Empire. Each of the four co-rulers had a *Praefectus Praetorio* (praetorian prefect) to help with the administration of their 'quarter' of the Empire. Over the course of time the role of the *Praefectus* had changed from a military to a civilian post. However, each *Praefectus* still wielded great power and could influence military affairs as they retained control of the main logistical system of the Empire. Although abandoned on the death of Diocletian, the system of using four *Praefecti* was revived under Constantine. As time passed the position of prefect became more influential.

The second trend was a change in the nature of the army. The 'old', c.5,000-man legions were replaced by smaller entities numbering c.1,000 men, although some of the older formations may have continued to exist, possibly at the reduced number of c.3,000, on the borders.[1] This was for a variety of reasons, for example easing the logistical burdens by splitting troops into smaller formations and having them supplied from local areas to ease the difficulty of transporting goods over long distances. It was also in response to changes in the nature of Roman warfare. Large-scale battles were now becoming rare, with most conflicts being small-scale skirmishes and the repelling of limited border raids. Roman forays into barbarian territory rarely ended in battle, the tribesmen preferring to withdraw before the might of Rome. A further change was a policy of deploying troops either in or near to cities to act as garrisons, as described

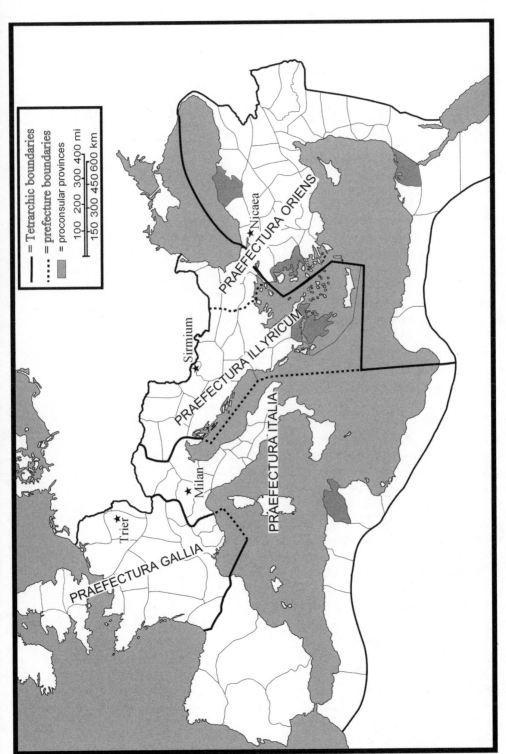

3. The tetrarchy and the prefectures of the Roman Empire.

PRAEFECTURA ORIENS

PRAEFECTURA ILLYRICUM

PRAEFECTURA ITALIA

PRAEFECTURA GALLIA

Nicaea

Sirmium

Milan

Trier

= Tetrarchic boundaries
= prefecture boundaries
= proconsular provinces

100 200 300 400 mi
150 300 450 600 km

in the *Notitia Dignitatum*. Although still often perceived as being 'mobile field armies', in practice they tended to remain stationary unless called on by the very highest military authority: either an *Augustus* or a *Caesar*.

As time progressed there had also been a change in the nature of the higher officers commanding the army. Although barbarian leaders were able to enrol in the army from an early date, they could not rise to the highest level earlier in the Empire due to being outside the '*cursus honorum*' ('course of honours'), the sequential order of public offices held by the Roman nobility. The granting of citizenship to the free population of the Empire by Caracalla in 212 and the crises faced by the Empire during the third century appear to have eroded traditional appointments. For example, senators had been barred from holding military office, probably in an attempt to restrict the number of revolts.[2] Subsequently, men of the equestrian class came to fill the posts previously reserved for senators. The barbarian nobles expected and received the status of equestrian and so gained the benefits that went with that status, including increasingly high posts within the army hierarchy. By the early fourth century Germanic officers were reaching the higher levels of military command within the Empire.[3] This trend would reach its pinnacle during the lifetime of Stilicho: by the end of the fourth century many of the top ranking officers were of Germanic extraction.

An often-overlooked development was in the financial sphere. Massive inflation had resulted in coins rapidly losing their value, partly as a product of debasement – the mixing of base metals with the gold or silver used to make the coins. The result was that lower denomination coins became increasingly worthless and only when Constantine introduced the *aureus*, a relatively stable gold coin, did the problem of inflation ease slightly. However, what is usually disregarded is that this would only help the rich and powerful, not the lower classes: the lower denomination coins continued to lose their value as they were continually debased. As a consequence, when Germanic invaders demanded gold for their peaceful cooperation, the burden tended to fall on rich senators who had political power. Consequently, any leader who gave away too much money in subsidies to barbarians would incur the hostility of powerful men who had the means to make their grievances felt.

Society

It is possible to see the later Empire as one in which the divisions within society contributed to the fall of the West. Over time the rich became wealthier. This was partly because many farmers were forced to sell their lands or their service to the rich in order to fulfil their tax obligations. Consequently, the rich greatly increased their holdings and wealth whilst many of the poorer people were forced into poverty. The outcome was that the wealthy came to hold power greatly disproportionate to their numbers. Once ensconced in their position, these same men tended to use their influence to protect their own interests rather than those of the state.

An example of their influence may be seen in the repeated elevation of usurpers in outlying provinces to the role of 'emperor'. These usurpers were supported by local magnates who felt that their own interests were at risk, and decided to support a man who promised to protect them. Usurpers could not have made such a bid without the support of the local magnates.

At the opposite end of the spectrum is the rise of the *bacaudae* in the West. The origin and nature of the *bacaudae* remains unclear, but it would seem that the phenomenon was mainly one of armed 'uprisings' by peasants in the less-Romanized areas of Gaul and Spain. The movement may have been enlarged, if not started, as a result of poorer peasants taking up arms to protect themselves and/or survive. Yet this is not the only example of peasant unrest in the West: there are numerous instances of local peasants helping invading armies, either by joining them or by guiding them to stockpiles of food and supplies.

Yet we must be wary of exaggerating the tendency of people to rebel against the Empire. Although it is natural for those with wealth to wish to safeguard it, there is a large difference between desiring a change of policy and actively becoming involved in supporting a usurper: if on the losing side, the magnates risked not only their own lives but those of their entire families. Likewise, the tendency amongst the poorer citizens was probably to see events as just one more burden that they had to bear in an extremely unjust world. The power of apathy amongst the poor should not be underestimated. The apathy may to some extent have been assisted by the rise of Christianity. The promise of rewards in the afterlife will have made many more tolerant of conditions in this life, as they were confident that their forbearance would be rewarded by God.

The fourth century

After the death of Diocletian there were further outbreaks of civil war. These continued until 324, when Constantine I gained complete control of the Empire. His dynasty continued to rule – in between fighting each other in yet more civil wars – until the death of Julian in 363 during his invasion of Persia. Jovian was made emperor on the spot to replace him and was forced to conclude a humiliating peace treaty to extract his army from Persia. Possibly as a reaction to the peace treaty, Jovian was killed in the following year (364) on his journey to Constantinople to accept the throne.

There followed the accession of Valentinian I and the beginning of a new dynasty. Valentinian, who was to reign until 375, quickly appointed his brother Valens to rule in the East. These two men were the emperors at the time of Stilicho's birth, and Valentinian's generalship and strength ensured that during this period the Germanic tribes in the West were contained and their invasions repelled, although the pressure on the borders of the Empire remained intense.

Valentinian I

After his accession, Valentinian spent time organizing his half of the Empire before travelling to Gaul to direct operations against the Alamanni, who in 366 had entered imperial territory. Forced to retreat, they regrouped before launching a further attack in 367. Valentinian and his army defeated them in battle, but the Romans also suffered high casualties. After negotiations, in 371 Valentinian made peace with their king, Macrianus and then spent time on improving defences along the Rhine.

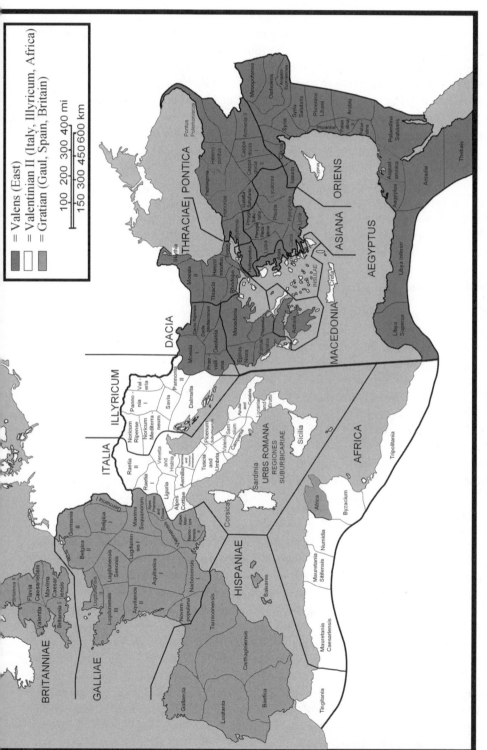

4. *The division of the Empire under Valentinian II, Gratian and Valens.*

Due to his personal focus on the activities of the Alamanni, when in 368 groups of Saxons, Picts and Scots raided Britain, Valentinian sent one of the *comes rei militaris* ('count' of the military), Theodosius, to recover and stabilize the situation across the Channel. In a similar manner, when in 372 a Moorish prince named Firmus rebelled in the province of Africa, in the following year Theodosius was again sent to restore the province to imperial control. Betrayed by some of his supporters, Firmus committed suicide rather than allowing himself to be captured. However, Theodosius was not to enjoy his reputation for long: in late 375 or early 376, possibly due to political intrigues at court, he was arrested and executed. His son, also named Theodosius, was spared and retired to live on his estates in Spain.

Unfortunately for Valentinian, the building of new forts along the Rhine resulted in increased tension. Following the death of one of their leaders, Gabinius, in 374, and claiming that the Empire had erected forts on their territory, the Quadi invaded Pannonia. Valentinian moved with an army to meet them. However, infuriated by the behaviour of their ambassadors, Valentinian suffered an apoplectic fit and died on 17 November 375.

Gratian and Valentinian II in the West

Valentinian was succeeded by his sons Gratian and Valentinian II, who were born of different mothers. Gratian had been acclaimed as *Augustus* as early as 367 at the age of eight but on the death of Valentinian in 375 the troops in Pannonia had acclaimed Valentinian II as co-emperor, although he was only around seven years old. Rather than fight a civil war Gratian acceded to their claims. Gratian chose to rule Gaul, Spain and Britain, leaving Italy, Illyricum and Africa to Valentinian II.

Gratian accepted his Uncle Valens' decision to allow the Goths to enter the Empire in 376. However, when the Goths rebelled against Roman rule in 378 Gratian was delayed as he was fighting against the Alamanni (being only ten years old, Valentinian was not expected to lead the army in the West). The delay meant that Gratian and the Western army missed the Battle of Adrianople.

Valens

Upon his accession in 364 the most pressing dilemma faced by Valens was the situation on the Eastern frontier. The Persians were intent on gaining the maximum benefits from the peace treaty of 363–4 and Valens' first task was to limit the extent of the damage to the frontiers. However, this was to be postponed for several years.

First, in 366 he was faced with the rebellion of Procopius, the last member of the Constantinian family. Valens had a shaky start yet managed to prevail and Procopius was defeated, but before Valens could head East he was faced with disturbing reports from across the Danube. He was informed that the Tervingi, a Gothic tribe north of the Danube, were planning to invade. Earlier in the century (332), Constantine I had defeated the Tervingi and made a treaty with them. They had kept to the treaty and had been preparing to support Procopius as the last descendant of Constantine's dynasty. When Procopius' attempt on the throne failed, their king, Athanaric, appears to have decided to act unilaterally.

In order to pre-empt their invasion, in 367 Valens crossed the Danube. The Tervingi retreated and Valens could not bring them to battle. Floods on the Danube the following year halted any attempt to repeat the invasion, but in 369 Valens crossed the Danube and defeated the Greuthungi (another Gothic tribe) before defeating the Tervingi. Athanaric was forced to sign a treaty, but was now hostile to the Empire and especially to the Arian Christianity supported by Valens and followed by many of his own people. According to some sources, as a result of his 'defeat' Athanaric began a persecution of those amongst his own people who had become Arian Christians.[4]

Sozomen and Socrates claim that the persecution resulted in a civil war amongst the Tervingi. The details are unknown, except that Valens appears to have supported Fritigern, the leading Arian Christian, against Athanaric. The precise chronology of these events is unknown, but this is unimportant. The vital information is that Valens and Fritigern had been allies prior to the events of 376.

The German tribes

By the fourth century many changes appear to have taken place within 'Germanic' society. These appear to have been partly the product of prolonged contact with Rome and a consequence of Roman interaction with German politics. The presence of an imperial power on their borders seems to have resulted in tribes being willing to form confederations far larger than those of earlier centuries, as their combined size made them more resistant to attack, either by the Romans or from other Germans. Yet one difficulty remained for these new confederacies: the individual tribes always had the option of forsaking the confederation and of acting on their own. An example of the complex nature of these tribal alliances can be found in the work of Ammianus Marcellinus. At the Battle of Strasbourg in 357 the Alamanni had two supreme kings, five subkings (*proximi reges*), ten princes (*regali*) and numerous lesser nobles.[5] The net result was that various leaders were always vying for power within each confederation.

Therefore, Germanic tribal groupings were not necessarily permanent, but dependent upon shifting loyalties and external influences. An illustration of this was the Goths. Until recently, it has been assumed that from time immemorial there had been two ruling 'dynasties', the Balthi and the Amals. This is far too simplistic a picture. Under pressure from the Huns they split into a myriad of smaller tribal entities. At different times some, but not all, of these smaller tribes attempted to enter the Empire.[6]

Another basic concept that has been challenged recently is the 'ethnic' nature of the various tribes. Tribal composition has usually been accepted as homogenous. For example, all Goths would be in tribal associations with other Goths, all Franks with other Franks and so on. An inspection of the evidence has led to this too being reassessed. Although groups such as the Visigoths, the Ostrogoths and the Franks had a core of eponymous tribesmen, they were often joined by neighbouring tribes in attacks upon the Empire. The most famous example of this is the crossing of the Rhine by a mixed force of Vandals, Sueves and Alans in 406. Yet it would appear from recent analysis that even where a single name is given to a large force, other tribes would be present. In fact, archaeology has shown the continuation of Dacian and Sarmatian cultures under Gothic rule, so there is a strong possibility that Sarmatian and Dacian tribes at least were represented amongst those that pleaded to be allowed to cross the Rhine in 376.[7]

The question then remains as to how well these tribes could communicate. Broadly speaking, it is now assumed by linguists that Franks on the Rhine would find it difficult, if not impossible, to communicate on a daily basis with Goths on the Black Sea. As a result, two possible models emerge.

The first is that different tribes tended to amalgamate only with those near to them. These peoples had the ability to communicate using a 'common language', possibly a simplified version of their combined languages using shared words and phrases. This model probably applies to the tribes which appeared on the Danube in 376, helping to foster the notion that they were all 'Goths'.

The second model is where the leaders of the tribes conversed, probably in Latin, but the rank-and-file members of the tribes failed to merge and so kept their separate identities. This would appear to be the case with, for example, the Vandals, Alans and Sueves that crossed the Rhine in 406, since once in Spain they separated into their tribal groupings and each took one of three distinct areas.

The amalgamation of large groups that could not converse with each other may have been helped by the Romans. During the course of the fourth and fifth centuries it became more common for at least some tribesmen, and especially the nobles, to spend some time in service in the Roman army. It is possible to suggest therefore that the leaders of tribes that did not share a language learned to use Latin to communicate, since by the end of the fourth century this could be understood by a large number of the nobles amongst the tribes.

One final aspect of Germanic culture needs to be addressed. Most of the tribes on the northern frontiers are grouped as 'Germani' by the majority of Roman authors and called 'German/Germanic' by modern historians. However understandable and useful, this simplistic approach can lead to false assumptions and biases that had no place in the fourth and fifth centuries AD.

A clear example of this comes in the discussions about Stilicho's Vandal birth and loyalty to Rome. Both ancient and modern writers wonder why he remained loyal to the Roman cause when fighting fellow 'Germans' such as the Goths. Such a question would be meaningless to Stilicho: of Vandalic descent, he shared neither a cultural bond nor a language with the Goths. Furthermore, the tribes of the fourth century did not have a 'shared cultural heritage': to the tribes of the Rhine those of the Danube were simply an alien group of warriors.

As a consequence, it should be remembered that when historians talk about 'The Goths' or 'The Huns' (and others), allowance must be made for the likelihood that included in these groupings would be tribes of different origin, and that many of the rank and file may have been unable to converse freely with each other. It should also be emphasized that due to the linguistic barriers there may not have been a shared sense of kinship and intrinsic loyalty to other members of the group.

Accordingly, it is extremely important to remember that there was no sense of political unity among the Germans: assumptions that the Germans would band together against the Romans is not reflected in the historical sources and does not reflect reality. It also explains why the Romans were willing to use German warriors when they had the option. The tribesmen that Stilicho hired or assimilated into the Roman army remained loyal to the end and had no qualms about fighting other 'Germans'.

The Huns and Goths

Although the Huns had little direct impact upon the life of Stilicho, a little explanatory note may be in order. In the pages of history the Huns appear out of the East like a whirlwind bent on destruction. Modern historians have tended to follow this catastrophic view of the Huns, emphasizing the sudden arrival of these fierce and irresistible tribes. Although recent research suggests that the picture is over-simplified, this is the image embedded upon the consciousness of the modern Western World.[8]

Yet there needs to be a full reappraisal of the Huns, although this seems unlikely given that the experts appear to differ on many topics within Hunnic studies. One thing that is clear is that, contrary to popular opinion, the Huns did not arrive driving all before them. There appears to have been a stout Gothic resistance under their leaders. King Ermanaric resisted the Hunnic advance 'for a long time', and his successor Vithimer 'died only after many defeats'.[9] This implies that the Goths fought long and hard against the Hunnic advance, suggesting that their impact was felt over several years – if not longer than a decade – before the Goths splintered and some headed towards the Empire. The impression is reinforced by the fact that, even after the defeat of the Goths, it took around ten years for the Huns to arrive on the Roman frontier in person. These are not the actions of an irresistible horde driving all before them.

It should also be noted that the Goths appear to have largely fragmented politically, with separate tribes wandering in exile and individually requesting entry into the Empire. There is also evidence that a large number of Goths remained in place and accepted the dominion of the Huns.

The split amongst the Gothic tribes also seems to be mirrored in the division inherent in Hunnic society. The Huns appear to have been a large collection of tribes slowly moving West in a combination of small groups and large armies. There is no evidence that all Huns owed their allegiance to a single political leader. In fact, there is even evidence to suggest that Hunnic mercenaries served under the pay of the Goths against the Hunnic invasions.[10] The modern concept of a centrally controlled, unified horde appears to have taken root due to the later kingship of Attila. Both before and after his rule division and separation would have been the norm, with individual Hun bands and tribes deciding their own fates and refusing to remain part of a large Hunnic nation. Therefore, despite their massive impact upon the policies and destinies of the West, the Huns will only be mentioned when individuals or groups appeared in the West, not as a major political force in their own right.

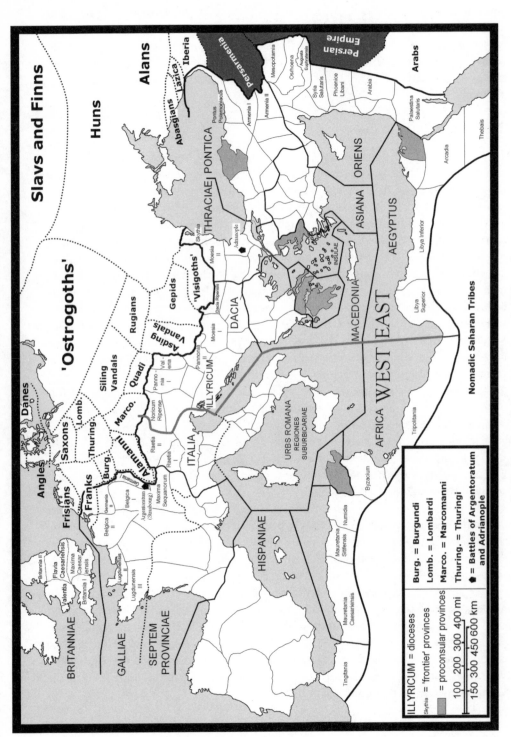

5. The Battles of Argentoratum and Adrianople.

Adrianople

In 376 a large number of tribesmen appeared on the banks of the Danube and petitioned the emperor to be allowed to enter the Empire. Shortly afterwards a second group appeared and made a similar request. Valens decided to allow the former to enter the Empire but refused access to the latter.

His decision may have been influenced by earlier dealings with one of the two leaders of the first group, Fritigern. The fact that there were two leaders of the Goths may represent the continuing religious divide amongst the Goths. Fritigern may have been elected to lead the Arians amongst the Goths, whilst the other leader, Alavivus, represented the pagan elements of the Gothic migrants. Ammianus claims that Fritigern was asked to become Christian before being allowed to enter yet this may represent confusion on the part of Ammianus, since it may be that the condition was that those not already Arian should convert.[11] It is interesting to note in this context that Alavivus soon disappears from the narrative, suggesting that he may have opposed the conversion and was removed partly in order to convince the Goths to convert.

Unfortunately for Valens, a complicated series of events resulted in the 'Tervingi' (as they became known) rebelling and defeating the local forces in battle. Furthermore, the second group, who were later labelled 'Greuthungi', had by this time also crossed the Danube.

Although these tribal names had been known for a long time it is unclear what relationship the tribes entering the Empire had with the tribes previously described as being 'free' in Germania. There now followed extensive raiding of the Balkans, a situation which forced Valens to gather an army and travel to the area to face the two groups, collectively known as 'The Goths'.

Valens finally faced Fritigern outside the city of Adrianople. Fritigern attempted to negotiate with Valens but, before anything could come of the talks, two Roman units attacked the Goths and battle was joined. A large number of Gothic cavalry arrived late on the scene and chased away the Roman horsemen.[12] At this point the Romans' fate was sealed. It was one of the worst disasters in Roman history, with up to 20,000 men being lost. Valens was killed by the victorious Goths in the pursuit at the end of the battle, allegedly being burnt in a cottage by Goths who did not realize the prize they were destroying. It is interesting to note that ancient sources see the defeat in terms of its religious significance: pagans see it as a punishment inflicted by the old gods for their neglect, whilst Christians see it as divine punishment for adherence to the pagan gods and the failure of Christians to adhere to God's laws.[13]

Some historians analysing the battle accept Ammianus' viewpoint that the Gothic attempts at negotiation were false and aimed at giving the Gothic cavalry time to reach the battlefield. Although Valens' indecision did allow time for these troops to arrive, there is every reason to believe that Fritigern was genuine in his attempts to reach a peaceful agreement. It should be remembered that Fritigern was not the sole leader of the Goths and that part of the difficulty the Goths faced was divided opinion about the best course to take to ensure their survival. Many would be against dealing with the Romans, arguing instead that they should fight rather than face the same betrayals they had already suffered. Yet the overwhelming belief would have been a recognition that the Goths could not defeat the entire Empire, and even a victory might leave the Goths so weak as to be defenceless against renewed attack. As a consequence, it is possible to see Fritigern's envoys as attempting to reach a real agreement rather than fighting a battle, with the result that the battle was actually a mistake for both sides.

Yet although this question is rarely considered, it is crucial in understanding the position of the Goths after the battle, and also after the peace treaty of 382 which followed. Attempting to negotiate, they had been treacherously attacked by a Roman army under the direct command of the emperor. From this point on, the Goths would be extremely hesitant to trust any Roman offers and would feel justified in breaking any terms agreed. Furthermore, not long after the battle Fritigern disappears from history, and it may be that as an 'appeaser' he was overthrown by those who had recommended fighting the battle.

On the Roman side there was a similar feeling of betrayal. Ammianus may have been following the line of an official Roman inquiry into the disaster when he pins the blame firmly on Fritigern's dishonest attempts to secure a peaceful settlement. Henceforward, the Romans would be unhappy to negotiate with the Goths except when absolutely necessary and would take every opportunity that arose to weaken their strength. The relationship between the Goths and the Romans would henceforward be one of mutual suspicion and distrust.

Theodosius I

Prior to the battle, and as the war against the Goths gained momentum, Gratian, emperor of the West, had a problem. He needed somebody to take charge of the Western army in the (Western-controlled) Prefecture of Illyricum. As a result, he called the younger Theodosius out of 'retirement' and deployed him to Illyricum.[14] Following the Battle, Gratian needed somebody to rule in the East, but a large number of important and capable military leaders had been killed at Adrianople. Theodosius would appear to have been the most obvious choice. Appointed as *Caesar*, Theodosius' first act was to defeat a Sarmatian attack on the Empire. He was quickly made *Augustus* and assumed supreme command in the East. To help in the war against the Goths and ensure that there would be no friction between the commanders on the spot, Gratian assigned the Prefecture of Illyricum temporarily to the East, ensuring that the passes from Illyricum to the West were securely guarded. Theodosius now had complete control of the war against the Goths.

Hastily conscripting fresh troops and assigning them to new units, Theodosius set about the task of restoring the situation in the Balkans. He posted as many of the new, raw troops as possible to peaceful provinces in the East, such as Egypt, and ordered the more experienced troops in these provinces to travel to the Balkans to face the Goths. His policy failed: in a battle with the Goths his 'Eastern' army was defeated and Theodosius retreated to repair the damage. Deciding to avoid facing the Goths in an open fight, Theodosius reverted to attacking isolated groups and the use of diplomacy to wean tribes away from the confederacy.

After Adrianople the Goths had formed a new method of surviving. This was to threaten to attack towns unless the towns supplied them with goods and provisions. Once this was given, the Goths moved on to the next town. In this way they maintained a steady supply of necessities – especially food – but did not devastate the countryside, meaning that they could repeat the tactic later.

Theodosius' response was to wait until the Goths had left an area and then garrison the cities they had threatened. When the Goths returned, the cities refused to supply them and the regular troops in the towns dissuaded the Goths from attacking. As time wore on, the Goths found themselves slowly being starved into submission.

Four years after the battle, in 382 the Goths capitulated. A peace treaty was signed and the Empire was seen as victorious. However, the gloss put on the treaty by the court panegyrists did not completely hide the reality of the situation. The Goths, far from being defeated and at the mercy of the Empire, retained their identity and their own leaders. Furthermore, although they were given lands in Thrace and northern Dacia, they were not given *conubium*, the right of intermarriage with Roman citizens. These tribes were not going to be integrated into the Empire. Instead, the treaty reinforced their isolation and helped to reinforce their identity as a people apart. This was a new departure for Romano–barbarian alliances: never before had the Romans allowed tribes to enter the Empire and also allowed them to retain their leaders and identity without attempting to assimilate them.[15]

Far from showing the superiority of the Empire, it shows that the Empire was stretched to the limit and needed a peace to help alleviate its problems. These included diplomatic manoeuvres with the Persians.

Once the treaty had been agreed, Theodosius sent ambassadors to Persia in an attempt to conclude the ongoing negotiations with regard to the status of Armenia. One of the leaders of the embassy was a young man by the name of Flavius Stilicho.

Chapter Two

Stilicho, Serena and Theodosius

As was stated in Chapter One, Stilicho was born sometime around 360*. Unfortunately, we cannot be more accurate as we are simply not told. The date fits in with him being described as 'young' by Claudian when sent on the embassy in 383, as this would mean that he was around twenty-four years old: still young enough to have it remarked upon but old enough to have the responsibility.[1]

His father was a Vandal who entered the Roman army and served as a cavalry officer under Valens; his mother was a Roman.[2] Neither is named in the sources. Much has been made of his Vandal ancestry yet no attempt appears to have been made to analyse his mother's status. Many nobles of barbarian origin were given high rank in the Roman army. However, there is no evidence that either they or their descendents were appointed to powerful posts at a young age. This suggests that Stilicho's mother was of a sufficient status to help promote his career. Moreover, Stilicho was soon to enter the emperor's immediate family by marriage. Although there is not necessarily a link between his mother's status and his marriage, it is likely that Stilicho's mother was of sufficient rank and influence to help counter the fact that his father was a Vandal.

He joined the army early, obeying the law passed by Diocletian stating that sons had to follow their fathers into the army. Thanks to his father's rank as a noble, along with his mother's possible high status, Stilicho began his career in the elite corps of the *protectores*. The *protectores* began in the third century and over time became a bodyguard unit, reserved for individuals who were earmarked for rapid promotion. Stilicho's talents were seen early and he appears to have been promoted to *tribunus praetorianus militaris* (praetorian military tribune), a tribune and notary on the imperial general staff, by 383.[3]

He is first mentioned by name when he was sent on an embassy to Persia in 383/4.[4] Thanks to the unsatisfactory peace treaty of 363 (following the death of Julian), there appears to have been an almost continuous procession of embassies between the two powers relating to the partitioning of Armenia. However, this particular mission had an additional agenda: in spring 383 Magnus Maximus, the *comes Britanniarum* (count of Britain), was proclaimed emperor in Britain. Maximus quickly crossed the English Channel into Gaul with his forces, and, surprisingly, little resistance was offered by the Gallic armies. When a little while later the Western Emperor Gratian arrived on the scene, Gratian's army abandoned him and he was forced to flee. Captured at Lyon, Gratian was executed. He was twenty-four years old. As a result, Stilicho's embassy to Persia was given the task of ensuring peace to allow Theodosius to prepare for a possible war against the usurper. What followed was a protracted period of talks,

* All dates are AD unless otherwise stated.

lasting for over three years, until in 387 a peace treaty was concluded and affairs in the East settled. Yet although Stilicho was one of the envoys, he did not lead the embassy: according to John Lydus the embassy was led by a man called Sporacius, who is otherwise unknown.[5]

This leads to a slight dilemma. On his return in 383/4 Stilicho married Serena, the niece and adopted daughter of Theodosius. Most historians still refer to Serena as Theodosius' niece. This is because, although Serena was adopted, it was not a full, formal adoption by Roman law: this would have placed her – and her husband and sons – in the line of succession. Theodosius did not want any complications when it came to his successors to the purple. Yet even so, by Roman custom the process of adoption superseded that of birth. With this in mind it should be remembered that, by law and by practice, Serena was Theodosius' daughter. As a consequence, the question must be asked of why Theodosius allowed his daughter to marry a semi-barbarous youth with little or no political influence. Unfortunately, due to the paucity of the sources, there is no way to answer this question with any authority. Claudian claims that Theodosius chose Stilicho for Serena because of his 'outstanding military achievements', however at the time of their marriage Stilicho was still young and had not had a chance to display any military ability.[6] In all likelihood the match was arranged by Serena herself.[7] It is probable that, as a member of the *protectores*, Stilicho was in the imperial presence enough to have been noticed and singled out by Serena. It is also possible that his actions in the diplomatic mission helped to elevate his status enough for Theodosius to accept the marriage, based upon the talent latent in the 'unknown' youth. Whatever the cause, one additional factor needs to be recognized: when Serena married Stilicho she was not marrying an 'uneducated barbarian'; she was marrying a man who, although his father was a Vandal, had been brought up and educated in the traditional imperial manner. Stilicho was not an outsider at the court but an integrated member of the imperial elite. Theodosius' complete acceptance of the marriage was later reinforced: when Serena gave birth to a son, Eucherius, Theodosius acknowledged the boy as his grandson.[8]

Yet in one way Theodosius was faced by a dilemma with the marriage of Serena and Stilicho. Stilicho was not of a suitable rank for his daughter. Therefore Theodosius immediately took measures to rectify the situation. Probably shortly after the marriage in 384, Stilicho was promoted to *comes sacri stabuli* (count of the sacred stables), a fact mentioned by Claudius in his *Laus Serenae* (In Praise of Serena), and this was quickly followed by his elevation to the post of *comes domesticorum* (commander of the household bodyguards).[9] Zosimus claims that when Stilicho died in 408 he had been a general for twenty-three years. This could in theory suggest that he was *magister militum* in 385, but this would be too rapid a promotion. Zosimus is clearly referring to Stilicho's appointment as *comes domesticorum*, so dating his promotion to 385, the year after his marriage.[10] These two rapid promotions were probably intended to raise Stilicho to a suitable status for his marriage to Serena, and should not necessarily be taken as indicative of superior talents: indeed, despite his rapid promotion through the military ranks Stilicho remained pre-eminently a politician.[11]

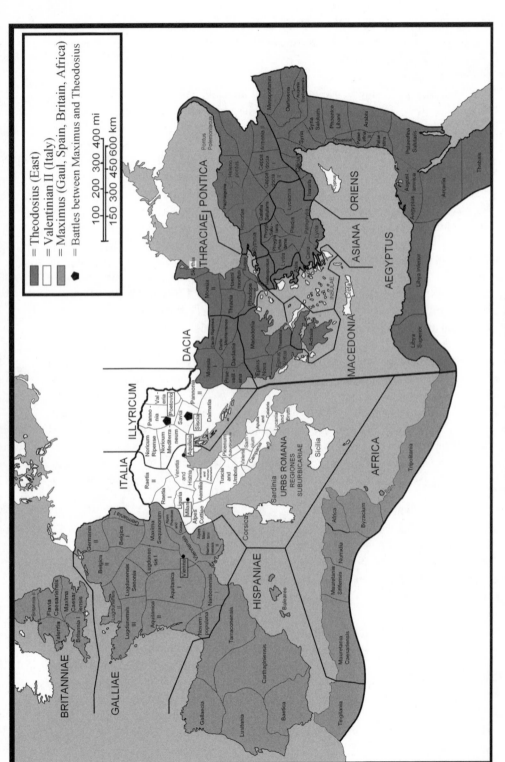

6. *Magnus Maximus and the Civil War.*

Magnus Maximus

As has already been noted, in 383 Magnus Maximus rebelled in Britain. He had served with Theodosius' father and may have played a political part in promoting Theodosius as the successor to Valens in 378–9. As a result, he may have expected a favourable reception from Theodosius. After Gratian had been deserted by his troops, captured and executed (23 August 383), Maximus was left in control of Britain, Spain and Gaul. At this point he sent envoys to Valentinian II at Milan and Theodosius in the East. Maximus' envoys demanded that Valentinian should accept Maximus as a 'father figure' and join him in Trier. The result would be that Maximus would become ruler of the West. Obviously, Valentinian could not accept such a subordinate status.

Maximus' envoys to Theodosius gave two options: either 'peace and alliance or civil war'.[12] Unfortunately, Theodosius was not in a position to oppose Maximus. Having only just concluded the Gothic War (in 382), he was also still in negotiations with Persia regarding the status of Armenia. Putting his difficulties to one side, in 384 Theodosius led a minor expedition to the West to demonstrate his support for Valentinian. Although little more than an exercise in public relations, it appears to have achieved its intended effect: Maximus made no military move against Valentinian, although diplomatic manoeuvring continued unabated.

Theodosius' weak position continued. Negotiations with Persia were protracted and in 386 a further group of Greuthungi appeared on the Danube and petitioned to be allowed to enter the Empire. Theodosius could not risk having more Germanic forces in the Balkans. Fortunately, they were opposed by Promotus, the *magister militum per Thracias*, and forced to retire.[13]

Finally, in 387, Theodosius was able to establish a conclusive peace with Persia. Although the terms were unfavourable to the Romans – with only one-fifth of the Armenian provinces remaining in Roman hands – at last troops were freed on the Eastern front for service elsewhere. Maximus was no doubt aware of these developments and decided to act quickly. In 387 he invaded Italy. Valentinian fled to Thessalonica and asked Theodosius for help. He was aided in the request by circumstances. Theodosius' wife Aelia Flaccilla had recently died and Valentinian's sister Galla was available. The marriage was useful to both parties: it secured the support of Theodosius for Valentinian II and at the same time embedded Theodosius firmly within the dynasty of Valentinian I. However, as Maximus had struck late in the season, Theodosius was forced to wait until the following year to act.

When the campaign season of 388 began, Theodosius acted with surprising speed. He used Thessalonica as his base and launched a two-pronged attack, with a naval invasion of Italy being sent at the same time as he led the majority of his troops in person by land into Italy. A large percentage of his forces appear to have been composed of Gothic troops serving under their own leaders, in accordance with the peace treaty of 382: these forces will feature prominently in the history of Stilicho. Alongside them were Huns and Alans, as well as a large force of regular Roman troops, including units from both the East and some that had followed Valentinian from the West.[14]

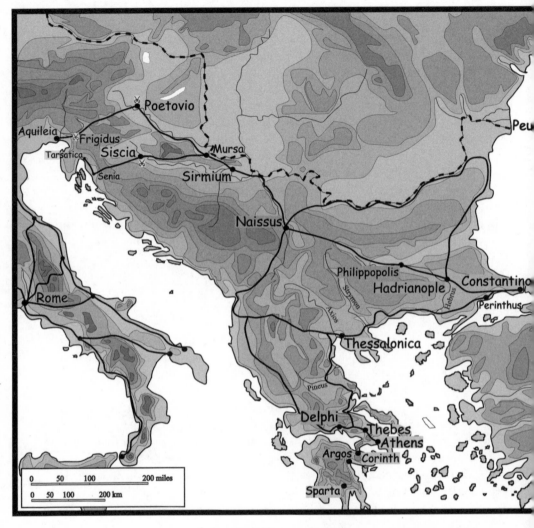

7. The Civil Wars in the Balkans.

The speed of the attack caught Maximus by surprise. Theodosius defeated Maximus' advance forces at the Battle of Siscia and then met Maximus' main force at Poetovio. After a hard-fought battle the Western armies were defeated. Maximus retired to Aquileia, perhaps expecting to withstand a siege, but the defeats had damaged the loyalty of his troops. When Theodosius' advance guard arrived at the city, Maximus was handed over to them. On 28 August 388 he was beheaded.

Whilst Theodosius was invading the West, according to Zosimus army units in the Balkans raised a rebellion after Maximus had bribed them to switch their allegiance.[15] It is likely that these were part of the regular forces that accepted the bribe from

Maximus and changed sides. Due to Theodosius' speedy victory, these men were forced to flee into the marshes around the mouth of the Axios (Vardas) near Thessalonica. From here they waged a guerrilla war from 388.[16] Theodosius sent Butheric, the Gothic *magister militum per Illyricum*, to pacify the area. After he had succeeded, he retired to the city of Thessalonica. However, by around 391 and possibly thanks to the events in Thessalonica (see below), the guerrillas had recovered a little and again began to raid surrounding areas.

Theodosius acted with clemency to the defeated West. Only a few individuals were executed and Maximus' immediate family – with the exception of his son Victor, who Maximus had promoted to *Augustus* – were allowed to live. However, Theodosius was left with a problem. Valentinian was clearly not yet ready to assume the full responsibility of *Augustus*. Previously, he had been well served by the Frankish general Bauto, but Bauto had recently died, and so Arbogast, another Frankish general trusted by Theodosius, was made *magister militum* and appointed to serve Valentinian.

After the defeat of Maximus, Theodosius stayed in the West for some time in an attempt to secure support for his new regime, and also used the time to reorganize the two armies which had been used against each other in the civil war.[17] During this time he made an effort to cultivate the support of the Roman Senate, going out of his way to placate them and ease their worries about the future. However, in 390 there occurred his famous conflict with Bishop Ambrose of Milan. At Thessalonica, the Gothic commander Butheric had arrested a charioteer who had allegedly committed a homosexual assault.[18] Angered by the arrest, a mob had killed Butheric and several other Goths in the city. As Butheric had been a favourite of very high rank, Theodosius ordered the garrison to enter the hippodrome when it was full and to massacre those inside in retaliation. Theoderet claims that 7,000 people were killed.[19] Theodosius regretted the act, but Ambrose refused to pardon him until he had spent several months as a penitent in Milan.

Alaric

The following year, 391, Theodosius began his journey back to the East. In late summer he reached the River Hebrus (Maritsa), where he was confronted by a Gothic force.[20] These were the same men that Butheric had earlier defeated, but following Butheric's death they had re-emerged as a nuisance in the area. Unwilling to risk his life in a small, meaningless skirmish, Theodosius immediately continued as fast as possible to Constantinople. According to Claudian, Alaric claimed to be the leader of the Goths who forced Theodosius to flee in fear.[21] However, the claim to being overall leader is open to question and may be the result of Alaric's propaganda later in his career. It is just as possible that Alaric was one of the leaders of a number of different groups that had joined to plunder the area. When Theodosius and his bodyguard refused to fight and fled to Constantinople, this allowed Alaric to later claim a victory over the emperor as part of his propaganda campaign to recruit fresh forces. Due to his 'victory' and thanks to the turmoil in the Balkans in the 390s, Alaric's army began to grow.[22] However, once back in Constantinople, Theodosius ordered Promotus, probably at this time the *magister militum per Thracias*, to deal with the Goths.

According to Claudian, Alaric was born on the island of Peuke in the mouths of the Danube – although this may have been a device to highlight Alaric's position between the Roman and Germanic worlds.[23] The similarity of his name to earlier Gothic 'kings' resulted in Jordanes being able to fit him into a supposed royal genealogy, where he was listed as a member of the Balt line, rather than of the Amals.[24] Although it is clear that this is a fabrication based solely upon the alliterative similarity of Alaric's name with Alaviv and Alatheus, Gothic leaders in 376, it is indicative of his importance in later history that Jordanes accords him such pre-eminence.[25] It may be that Alaric began his career as a high-ranking Goth who was part of the anti-Roman faction. He did not choose to serve Theodosius. He was forced to serve under the treaty signed with Rufinus or Stilicho in Thrace (see below), rather than the general treaty with the Goths made by Theodosius in 382.[26] This would help to explain why he revolted in 391. The death of Eriulf and the 'exile' of Fravitta (see below) may have left a political vacuum and Alaric was one of a number of potential candidates for the vacancies. His political and military abilities – especially his ability to steer a course between fighting and negotiation – would ensure that he rose in prestige and became the most prestigious 'anti-Roman' Gothic leader in the following decades.

Valentinian II

Freed from internal threats, Valentinian took up residence at Vienne in Gaul. Whilst he remained inactive in the city, Arbogast campaigned successfully along the Rhine. Distressed by his seeming captivity and the fact that Arbogast was earning glory while he remained idle, Valentinian complained to both Theodosius and Ambrose about his subordination to the Frank.[27] Eventually, he formally dismissed Arbogast from his post. However, Arbogast refused to retire, stating flatly that Valentinian had not appointed him and so could not dismiss him. He then tore the order into pieces in front of the young emperor.[28] It was now clear that Valentinian was no longer in control of his own court.

On 15 May 392 Valentinian was found hanged in his residence. Arbogast claimed that his death was suicide and ordered the body to be sent to Ambrose at Milan for burial. Ambrose's eulogy carefully avoided the question of foul play, and even now historians are unsure of whether the death was a suicide, brought about by Valentinian's humiliation at the court, or whether he was killed in order to leave the post of *Augustus* vacant.[29]

The East

Probably as part of his preparations for the war against Maximus, in 388 Theodosius reorganized the Eastern armies.[30] Such a restructuring was probably necessary after the confusion and disruption of the Gothic War, yet it is also possible that in part this was due to the fact that he needed to ensure that his position as emperor would remain unthreatened during his campaign in the West.

Accordingly, he created a system where there were five *magistri militiae* (masters of the troops) who were supposedly equal. There were two *magistri utriusque militiae praesentalis* (master of all troops 'in the presence of the emperor'), and one each of: *magister utriusque militiae per Thracias* (of Thrace), *magister utriusque militiae per Illyricum* (of Illyricum) and *magister utriusque militiae per Oriens* (of the East). Although these positions appear to have begun as equals, in reality the two *magistri praesentalis* soon acquired pre-eminence due to their proximity to the emperor.

As has already been noted, in the West he had appointed Arbogast as *magister militum* to supervise affairs with Valentinian II. No attempt was made to appoint a second *magister militum* in the West as a counterbalance to Arbogast. This is a surprise, given that he had expanded the number of *magistri* in the East. It would seem that Theodosius assumed that Arbogast's loyalty would ensure continued cooperation between East and West.

Stilicho

During Theodosius' invasion of the West in 388 Stilicho is not mentioned by any of the sources. However, his position as *comes domesticorum* suggests that he accompanied Theodosius and this is supported by two inscriptions found at Rome.[31] Consequently, it is highly probable that he fought in the Battles of Siscia and Poetovio. His actions during these battles may have been significant in some way, because when we next hear of him – in 392, after Theodosius' return to the East – he is being promoted to a higher position.

In late 391 Promotus, the *magister militum per Thracias*, was attempting to clear the Balkans of Gothic 'rebels' that included Alaric as one of the leaders. However, Promotus was killed in an ambush. The barbarians were allegedly acting on the orders of Rufinus, Theodosius' *magister officiorum* (master of ceremonies), with whom Promotus had recently quarrelled – although this is open to doubt.[32] From at least July 393 Stilicho had the title *comes et magister utriusque militiae*.[33] It is likely that his post was as *magister utriusque militiae per Thracias* as successor to Promotus, since this would most readily tie in with other events taking place at the time.

Details of his service in Thrace are extremely limited, mainly because our sources are focused on Arbogast and events in the West. However, Claudian describes Stilicho defeating the Goths, and, more importantly, avenging the death of Promotus.[34] Although only a very brief record, and certainly exaggerated by Claudian's poetic abilities, the episode does leave the impression that Stilicho was at last able to display his talent. Although the conflict appears to have ended without Stilicho winning a decisive battle, this should not be taken as demonstrating a lack of ability.[35] The situation for the East was improving, but a heavy defeat could easily tip the scales again and leave the Empire open to attack in the Balkans. In the circumstances, Stilicho followed the example set by Theodosius after Adrianople and used manoeuvre rather than battle to defeat the Goths. However, he was not left to negotiate the treaty himself: the talks were led by Rufinus, at this time probably newly appointed as Theodosius' *praefectus praetorio Orientis*.[36] Such a victory without heavy losses in battle would have been welcomed by Theodosius. The defeat of the barbarians, coupled with his actions in the next few months and his family relationship with the emperor, would help to establish his elevated position at Theodosius' court. It is noticeable that in the ensuing war in the West, Theodosius was not to be troubled by raids or rebels in the Balkans. As part of his agreement with Rufinus, and according to Zosimus in recognition of his military capabilities, Alaric was now forced to accept service in the Roman army as the commander of his own band of warriors, which became in effect a mercenary unit in the army.[37] The agreement may also be seen as part of Theodosius' plan to cultivate Gothic leaders, especially those who had shown military ability, and employ them for the benefit rather than the detriment of the Empire.[38]

Arbogast and Eugenius

With the death of Valentinian II Arbogast faced a dilemma. If he deferred to Theodosius then an inquiry would be held into the suspicious circumstances of Valentinian's death. Although it is unlikely that foul play was involved, it would be certain that the inquiry would find that Arbogast's actions had helped to drive the young emperor to suicide. Faced with this conclusion, Theodosius would have been prompted by his wife Galla – who was Valentinian's sister – to severely punish Arbogast. The only other course of action was to nominate a new emperor to fill the vacant post and then face Theodosius with the *fait accompli* in the hope of it gaining acceptance. Arbogast chose the latter option. On 22 August 392, only three months after the death of Valentinian, he made Eugenius, a former *magister scrinorum* well versed in grammar and rhetoric, *Augustus* in the West.

By promoting a native Roman and member of the senatorial class, Arbogast probably hoped to enlist the support of the Senate for the (almost inevitable) war with Theodosius. Eugenius immediately replaced Theodosius' men with his own appointees. However, although he was a Christian, in an attempt to maintain good relations with the Senate (which remained largely pagan) he allowed public money to be used for the rebuilding and rededication of pagan sites in Rome: for example he restored the 'Altar of Victory' within the Curia. Whilst this policy may have helped him internally, it increased tension between himself and the orthodox Theodosius. Meanwhile, Arbogast went on campaign along the Rhine. He attacked the Frankish kings Marcomeres and Sunno, who had taken advantage of the Roman civil war to raid Gaul whilst Maximus had been facing Theodosius. Arbogast quickly managed to pacify the region. The campaign also acted as a recruitment drive amongst the Germanic tribes on the frontier; many tribesmen now agreed to fight on his behalf.

In the meantime, Eugenius sent ambassadors to Theodosius requesting that he be recognized as emperor in the West. Although favourably received, it became clear that his elevation would not be accepted when in January 393 Theodosius promoted his son, the eight-year-old Honorius, to *Augustus*. According to Zosimus, Theodosius placed Richomeres, now *magister utriusque militiae*, in charge of the cavalry, but before the war could begin Richomeres died of disease.[39] After much thought, Theodosius appointed Timasius, the *magister equitum et peditum*.[40] He was tasked with organizing the army of invasion, with Stilicho, the *magister utriusque militiae per Thracias*, as his second in command. Theodosius was to retain overall control of the army.

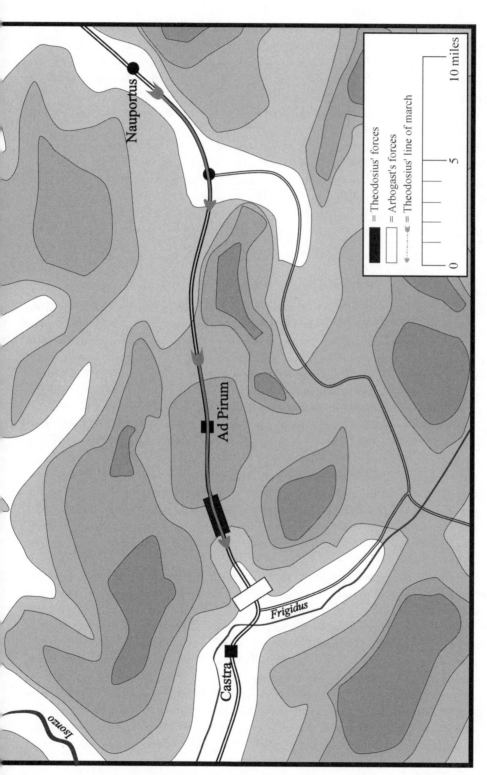

8. *Route of Theodosius and possible location of Arbogast.*

Finally, Theodosius recruited foreign mercenaries and once again called on the Goths to supply a large number of troops. This caused divisions amongst the Goths and a 'civil war' was avoided when Eriulf, the leader of the anti-Rome faction, was killed by his political opponent, Fravitta, at a banquet held in Constantinople, ironically organized by Theodosius to promote Gothic support for the war.[41] The political vacuum created by the death and flight of two of the Gothic leaders would be exploited later by Alaric.

Due to his actions, Fravitta was forced to accept service in the Roman army rather than risk retribution at the hands of Eriulf's friends and relatives. With the Goths now committed, and allegedly supplying 20,000 men for the upcoming campaign, command of these auxiliaries was shared by Gainas, Saul and Bacurius.[42] However, Theodosius' wife Galla seems never to have witnessed the downfall of her brother's tormentor; according to Zosimus, she died in childbirth before the army set out from Constantinople.[43]

The Battle of the Frigidus: 5–6 September 394

With the preparations complete, at some time in May, Theodosius led his army from Constantinople to invade the West. He left his son Arcadius in Constantinople, in the care of the *praefectus praetorio Orientis*, Rufinus. His plan was simply to invade Italy from the East. Arbogast, on the other hand, had decided not to emulate Maximus and divide his forces. Although this meant that he had to leave the passes across the Julian Alps undefended, he seems to have decided that defending the passes was secondary to keeping his army as a large single force under his personal control. As a consequence, Theodosius crossed the Alps unopposed and descended towards the city of Aquileia, so entering the valley of the River Frigidus. Here they encountered the army of Arbogast, encamped near the river.

The accounts of the battle that have come down to us are simple and do not enter into much detail.[44] However, as they are written by sources which tend to focus on the victor, they all describe the action from the point of view of Theodosius. The aims and actions of Arbogast are not usually considered, even by modern authors. This is strange, as without an understanding of Arbogast's strategy, the battle tends to make little sense.

Much like Theodosius' forces, Arbogast's army comprised a mixture of Roman and non-Roman troops. Alongside the regular Roman troops that he had concentrated from Gaul and Italy, Arbogast's army also included both Franks and Alamanni that he had recruited whilst campaigning on the Rhine.[45] Arbogast drew up his forces in front of the exit to the pass he expected Theodosius to use. Furthermore, he stationed troops on all of the strategic high-points surrounding the exit, so that when Theodosius emerged from the pass he would find himself partially surrounded.[46]

The only option open to Theodosius at that point would be a frontal assault, which Arbogast was confident of defeating. Later, when the assault had failed, Arbogast would send troops to the rear of the pass in order to block Theodosius' exits, so forcing him to surrender. Arbogast's strategy relied on predicting Theodosius' movements and on drawing him into a trap from which he could not escape. By accurately calculating Theodosius' movements and taking efficient steps to counter them, Arbogast proved himself to be superior militarily to Theodosius.

Theodosius acted in exactly the manner predicted by Arbogast. When Theodosius descended from the pass, he saw that Arbogast had deployed his forces so as to block the exit towards the river, and had simultaneously limited the space in which Theodosius himself could deploy. He also became aware of troops stationed on strategic heights blocking possible alternative routes down from the pass. These troops posed an additional threat to his flanks.

Realizing that he was in danger of being surrounded, Theodosius ordered the *foederati* and the other non-Roman auxiliaries to make a headlong assault in order to force Arbogast to at least partially withdraw and so give Theodosius room to deploy more troops.[47] After a ferocious assault – during which there was allegedly an eclipse of the sun[48] – both the *foederati* and the other units were repulsed with heavy losses; according to Orosius, 10,000 Goths lost their lives in battle.[49] Amongst the dead was the Iberian King Bacurius, who was possibly *magister militum vacans* (master of the troops of no particular region). As night fell the troops of the West celebrated a victory and, in accordance with his plan and in preparation for a continuation of the battle on the following day, Arbogast sent detachments of troops around the flanks of the Eastern army to secure the passes to their rear. In this way, when victory was won the Eastern army would be unable to retreat, bringing the war to a speedy end.

Theodosius' decision to send the *foederati* to attack first and so bear the brunt of the casualties is usually taken to be partly a ploy to weaken their power and so make it easier to deal with them after the battle had been won.[50] This is assuredly a mistake, as it assumes that Theodosius was confident of winning, which, in the circumstances, is impractical; if anything, he was in a very weak position facing a very strong foe. It is unlikely that he would risk his entire future – and that of his family – in an attempt to weaken political rivals. This is not really acceptable, being as it is an uncritical reiteration of the opinions of Zosimus, amongst others.

It is far more likely that Theodosius' strategy of all-out attack was forced upon him by circumstances. He would have been unable to deploy his own army fully thanks to Arbogast's skilful deployment, and the Eastern army needed space to descend from the narrow pass and time in which to fully deploy. As it was, Arbogast had ensured that this was impossible without fighting. Without the room to bring up troops from the rear, Theodosius had to attack with the troops stationed at the front of the army's column of march: the *foederati* and other *auxilia*.[51] Their failure to force the enemy back reinforced Theodosius' belief that Arbogast had the upper hand, since our sources now show him desperately praying to God for help.[52] This is not the action of a man so convinced that he is going to win that he will waste troops in an attempt to weaken their political importance. Although the end result would in reality weaken the Goths, it was not intentionally so.

With the repulse of the Goths, the armies settled down for an uneasy night, with the Eastern army's morale low due to the defeat and their poor circumstances. On the other hand, the Western army and Arbogast appear to have believed that the battle was won;

with the enemy unable to deploy properly the West was able to bring greater forces to bear on a limited front, so ensuring that there would be no escape – especially as Arbogast now sent troops to occupy strategic points in the pass to trap Theodosius where he was.

Overnight, the situation changed. The men Arbogast sent to cut Theodosius off instead deserted to the Eastern emperor, allegedly swayed by the emperor's persuasive arguments.[53] Seeing their defection as a good omen and a sign that God was with him, Theodosius renewed the battle on the following day. He attacked early in the morning, taking Arbogast by surprise, since he believed Theodosius to be surrounded and without hope.[54] Theodosius' confidence was to be further reinforced. After fighting had begun, a local wind, the Bora, began to blow from behind the Eastern forces towards the Western army. As the Eastern army advanced, large amounts of dust was disturbed and this was blown into the defenders' faces. Legend has it that the wind was so strong that it blew the defenders' missiles back at them, which is possible as it has been measured at around 60 mph. Confused and unable to see properly, the Western army wavered and broke. Punching through the centre, Theodosius' men reached the enemy camp, where Eugenius was captured and later executed. Seeing that he had lost, Arbogast fled. Realising that his position was hopeless, Arbogast finally committed suicide rather than be captured by Theodosius.[55]

The battle was over. It had lasted for two days of intensive fighting. Both sides had taken heavy losses, but for the West it was a disaster. It is likely that the losses suffered during the three battles of Siscia, Poetovio and Frigidus were greater than those suffered by the Eastern Empire at Adrianople. The need to rebuild the army in the following years would prove to be too great a strain for the Western Empire to bear. However, immediately after the battle such a conclusion would have been unthinkable. Theodosius had reunited the Empire under one ruler, who had now proved himself capable in war and a strong leader not afraid of reorganizing the Empire where it failed to meet his standards.

Ancient writers saw the battle as of tremendous importance. Obviously, given Eugenius' support for paganism and the presence of pagan standards in his camp, the victory was seen as a vindication of Christianity and showed God's support for Theodosius – especially when Christian writers wrote about the eclipse and the effects of the Bora.[56] After the battle it was clear that there would be no more pagan emperors and that paganism was on the decline. Slowly, the senators of Rome began to adopt Christianity and pagan religions and traditions were neglected and slowly fell from favour.

Stilicho's part in the battle is unknown. The sources do not mention him in any way or form, instead focusing upon Theodosius, the *foederati*, and the death of Bacurius. It is logical to assume that during the first day he played little part in the battle except in ensuring that the retreat of the *foederati* and *auxilia* did not break the army's morale. However, it is likely that during the second day he played a more effective role, leading his men and deploying some of the troops following Theodosius' orders. He may even have helped formulate the plan of attack along with Theodosius and Timasius. It is unlikely that the level of his involvement in the battle will ever be known with any certainty.

Prior to returning to the East, Theodosius made arrangements for Honorius to take over as emperor in the West. He had already been made *Augustus* prior to the campaign and it made sense for the boy to take command of the West. It would be unlikely for any further internal trouble to arise since the West had now suffered three defeats in rapid succession to Theodosius: possible usurpers would be wary of making the same mistake again. Furthermore, Ambrose, the powerful Bishop of Milan, wrote pleading with him to be merciful to the defeated.[57] However, the problem then became one of who to trust as 'guardian' for the youth until he became old enough to shoulder the burden of sole rule.

The individual would need to have experience of military command, since although internal threats would be small, the German tribes were still pressing on the frontiers and likely to invade, especially as they had contributed forces to Eugenius' and Arbogast's failed attempt to keep the West. If a single person was to be installed, he had to be trustworthy. He would be given the title of *magister militum*, and Arbogast had already shown how the individual could become so powerful that he could dominate the ruling emperor. Once he had made the appointment, Theodosius could think about returning to Constantinople. Before that could happen, he became seriously ill.

Chapter Three

Command in the West

Despite his illness, Theodosius did not intend to remain in the West. Groups of Huns had invaded Thrace and crossed the Caucasus, and a band of Marcomanni were devastating Pannonia, so his presence was needed in the East.[1] He fully expected to recover and return to Constantinople, and as a consequence he needed to arrange affairs so that his son Honorius, who was only eleven, would become secure in his position as *Augustus* of the West. Recent history had shown that placing a minor under the control of a military leader could result in complications, so Theodosius' decision could decide the ultimate fate of his son. Yet realistically his choice was limited. He would be unwilling to place his son in the hands of the Western generals he had just defeated. His options were restricted to Eastern generals.

9. Barbarian attacks on the East.

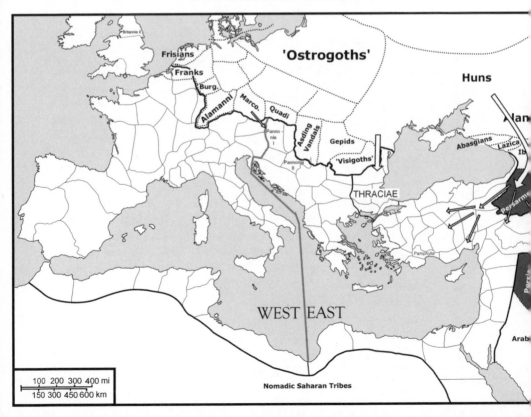

One option was Timasius, Theodosius' *magister equitum et peditum* during the campaign in the West. He was certainly an experienced and capable soldier – probably more so than Stilicho. However, he may have been seen as less trustworthy, especially as he is described as being 'an experienced soldier but insolent and proud and a heavy drinker'.[2] Theodosius did not need a leader who would arouse resentment in the West and result in the need for a third civil war.

It is possible that, had he lived, Richomeres would have been a possible choice. Beginning his career in the West, he had transferred East after surviving the battle of Adrianople and had been appointed *comites et magister utriusque militiae* in the East. He was placed in charge of the cavalry for the war against Eugenius but had died before the campaign began. Since he was the uncle of Arbogast he could be expected to sympathize with his nephew's predicament. Richomeres' appointment to lead the Eastern forces can therefore be seen as a sign of strong trust and an expectation of loyalty from Theodosius. Whether this would have resulted in him being installed as *comites et magister utriusque militiae* in the West is clearly a different matter, but remains a distinct possibility.

Richomeres' replacement for the war in the West was Stilicho, who had already shown in Thrace that he had at least some military capabilities. It is also possible, though unproven, that he had further displayed his abilities during the campaign against Eugenius. Yet above all there was his marriage to Serena and his inclusion within, and assumed loyalty to, the house of Theodosius. The nature of Serena's adoption meant that Stilicho would never be able to claim the throne for himself as a legitimate heir to Theodosius, and it is likely that Theodosius assumed that Serena, as his favourite, would keep a check on Stilicho's ambitions and continue to support her 'brother' during the coming years. In theory, Stilicho had the military ability to protect the West during Honorius' minority and was loyal enough to surrender the primacy when Honorius reached maturity.

As a result of his deliberations, there was only one choice and Theodosius made it: in October 394 Stilicho was installed as *comes et magister utriusque militiae praesentalis* in the West.[3] Theodosius sent Timasius, the *magister equitum et peditum*, back to the East to help deal with problems in Asia Minor, since he is next referred to as being in Pamphylia in 396. With him went the men rendered unfit by the battles they had fought.[4] At the same time Theodosius appointed the Goth Gainas as commander of the Eastern troops remaining in Italy.

Theodosius also used the time in the West to reorganize the civil appointments. He placed trusted men in positions of power, for example Basilius was made the new *praefectus urbis Romae*. He also made a symbolic gesture to the Roman Senate by appointing the young brothers Olybrius and Probinus, Christians of the house of Anicii, to be joint consuls. At this time the post of consul was still important and treasured, so the appointment of two very young men demonstrates the political awareness of Theodosius. It clearly demonstrated that members of the Senate were still important – as long as they were Christian.[5]

As he was making these new appointments Theodosius' health took a serious turn for the worse. An earlier bout of illness had alarmed the emperor and, in preparation for the worst, he reaffirmed Stilicho as '*parens principum*' ('parental guardianship') of Honorius. This was not as guardian or regent in the modern sense, but as the senior member of the imperial family with the moral right and responsibility to care for the young emperor.[6] Accordingly, the title *parens* will be used in order to avoid confusion with the modern terminology.

It should be noted that at no point was there doubt over the 'inheritance' of the Empire: Arcadius and Honorius did not succeed Theodosius.[7] Arcadius had been joint emperor since 383 and Honorius since 393. In theory, the three emperors had been equal. In reality, due to their youth, Theodosius had kept the reins of power firmly in his own hands.

The death of Theodosius

While still in Milan, on 17 January 395 he died of oedema (dropsy: the retention of fluid in organs), possibly a symptom of heart disease. He was forty-nine years old. Bishop Ambrose of Milan gave a panegyric on the man he had humbled, praising him for the suppression of both heresy and paganism. Finally, Theodosius was taken in pomp to Constantinople and buried on 8 November 395. He was to be the last emperor who, in effect, united both halves of the Roman Empire. From this point on the Empire would be divided between East and West.

Fortunately, once he had been victorious in his campaign against Eugenius and Arbogast he had summoned his daughter Galla Placidia, his adopted daughter Serena and his son Honorius to be with him in Milan. His eldest son Arcadius remained in Constantinople where he had been left as *Augustus*. All was ready for a simple transference of actual power from Theodosius to his sons, who would rule in name until they were old enough to rule in their own right.

Stilicho claims guardianship of the Empire

However, there was now a twist that has confused, baffled and intrigued historians ever since. Stilicho claimed that, on his deathbed, Theodosius called Stilicho to him and, without other witnesses, entrusted him with *parens* of both Arcadius in the East, who was about eighteen years old (born c.377), and Honorius in the West, who was ten (born 9 September 384).[8] In effect, Honorius was giving him control of the entire Empire, since the title of *parens* encompassed a power that surpassed that even of the title *Augustus*.[9] His claim was supported by no less a figure than Ambrose, Bishop of Milan, in his obituary for Theodosius as the emperor was lying in state in Milan.

> Theodosius is more glorious in this also, that he did not make a will in accordance with public law; he had nothing further to determine as regards his sons, to whom he had given everything, except to place them under the protection of a close relative, who was present.
>
> Ambrose, *de Obi Theod*, 5.

The truth of the bequest has been debated by historians, without any clear conclusions being reached. In itself this is not surprising, since the entire claim rests solely upon the testimony of Stilicho. In recent years historians have tended to avoid the question.[10]

It is possible that Theodosius may have made such a bequest. He would doubtless have been aware at the time of his death that his sons were not yet capable of independent rule. Apart from Honorius being too young, they had begun to show signs – especially Arcadius – of the lack of ability that was to be a hallmark of their reigns. In these circumstances, Theodosius desired a strong, dominant political figure that could be trusted to treat his sons in the appropriate manner: memories of Valentinian II would still have caused him anxieties.

However, having accepted that the bequest is a possibility, the nature of the bestowal is detrimental to the claim. There is absolutely no reason for Theodosius making the bequest to Stilicho without witnesses.[11] It is doubtless that Claudian describes Stilicho's claim accurately – there is no reason for Claudian to invent such a story and every reason for him to add witnesses. In fact, Claudian's panegyric on Honorius quickly turns into a defence of Stilicho's position.[12]

When they reached the palace the emperor bade all depart and thus unbidden addressed his son-in-law: 'Victorious Stilicho, of whose courage in war, of whose loyalty in peace I have made proof – what warlike feat have I performed without thine aid? What triumph have I won that thou helpedst me not in the winning? Together we caused Thracian Hebrus to run red with Getic blood, together overthrew the squadrons of the Sarmatae, together rested our weary limbs on the frozen Danube with our chariot's wheel – come, therefore, since heaven's halls claim me, do thou take up my task; be thou sole guardian of my children, let thy hand protect my two sons. I adjure thee by that marriage that makes thee kin with me, by the night that saw its consummation, by the torch which at thy wedding-feast the queen carried in her own hand when she led thy bride-elect from out the imperial palace, take on thee a father's spirit, guard the years of their childhood. Was not their sire thy master and thy wife's father? Now, now I shall mount untroubled to the stars for thou wilt watch over them.

Claud., *de III Cons. Hon.*

In a similar fashion, the support given by Ambrose, as quoted above, may have been simply a recognition of Stilicho's political supremacy in the West, rather than a belief in his appointment. Ambrose's acceptance of political and military reality was no doubt echoed by the court officials Theodosius put in place before his illness. They will have believed that retaining Stilicho, a known supporter of Theodosius' policies, was in their best interest. As a result, they too supported his claims to be *parens*, at least in the West.

Stilicho's claim to guardianship of the East will have reflected in part his desire to protect his nephew, since he would certainly have recognized that Arcadius did not have the political or personal strength to rule and that he was likely to be dominated by high-ranking court officials. When Theodosius had left to campaign in the West, affairs in the East had been left in the hands of his *praefectus praetorio Orientis*, Rufinus.

Rufinus was a skilful politician and capable of maintaining his power in the East, especially since he had been trusted by Theodosius and had been consul as early as 392. He was also a political enemy of Stilicho. His rapid rise to power had been resented by the military officers, especially Stilicho and Promotus. As a result, Rufinus had arranged for Promotus to be sent from court and made *magister militum per Thraciam*. It was clear that Rufinus would maintain control of Arcadius and the East unless Stilicho could lay a legitimate case for his own supremacy. The deathbed bequest was an attempt to put such a claim.

Yet in reality the claim was almost certainly false and based upon Stilicho's concept of what Theodosius would have wanted. It was also an attempt to remove his main political opponent, Rufinus, since an acceptance of Stilicho's claim would certainly lead to Rufinus' downfall.[13] As it was clearly of great political importance, the nature of the claim, with no witnesses involved, brought a reaction of disbelief in both East and West. Claudian's repetition of the claim between 397 and 400 may in part have been an attempt to counter the doubts that had arisen.[14] However, whether the claim was real or simply wishful thinking on the part of Stilicho is not as important as the effect that it had on his policies. Stilicho's focus was now to remain on the East.

The reason for Stilicho's claim is commonly accepted as being his desire to protect Arcadius. Yet there were almost certainly other factors involved. One of these is his experience as a commander under Theodosius. The victory in 388 and especially that of 394, in which Stilicho took part, probably resulted in him concluding that the West was weaker than the East and would struggle to survive without the cooperation and full support of the financially-viable East. The easiest way to arrange this was for Stilicho to become *de facto* leader of the whole Empire. Unfortunately the claim had the opposite effect; in the long run, the only result of the claim was to divide East and West, which resulted in a 'deterioration in relations between East and West that never entirely recovered'.[15]

Another factor in the claim was that, possibly from the start but definitely as time passed, it became clear to Stilicho that his command in the West was restricted by the increasing political and financial control of the Senate. Working within the limitations of his position as *magister peditum* rather than emperor, the constant need to refer to the Senate for agreement on policies and taxes became increasingly frustrating. There can be little doubt that this was to be a major reason for his continued claims to the guardianship of the East, since once in control of a united Empire, the financial support of the East would more than counter that of the Senate, so freeing Stilicho's hands to act in a more autocratic manner with regards to the West.

Stilicho's titles

The support given by Ambrose may have been vital in securing Stilicho's immediate position in the West. In the face of Ambrose's support, and even more because Stilicho was now in control of the combined Western and Eastern field forces that had fought at the Frigidus, the court at Milan accepted Stilicho's claim to be *parens* to Honorius.

Yet in reality his position was extremely insecure, and he now began the process of taking control of the military and political institutions of the West. With regard to Stilicho's military status, great care must be taken when analysing the titles he adopted, as they conform more to his political wishes than to a fixed military hierarchy (on military titles in general, see Chapter 4). He most often used the title *magister utriusque militiae*, but in reality he occupied the position of *magister peditum*, which in the West by this time had become dominant to that of *magister equitum*.[16] However, it is interesting that Stilicho did not use a single title throughout his career as the dominant figure in Western politics, and it has been argued that the vagueness of his titles reflects the fact that he was creating a completely new position for himself as the head of the Western government, whilst still remaining theoretically subordinate to the emperor.[17] However, Stilicho eventually came to use the terms *comes et utriusque militiae* to denote his military superiority and *parens principum* to highlight his civilian authority as head of the Theodosian dynasty, so when talking of Stilicho's position during the remainder of the book the title *comes et utriusque militiae* will be consistently used.[18] However, it was to be a long time before these titles were secure.

On the other hand, it should be noted that, his methods of securing his position notwithstanding, Stilicho was not an innovator. Theodosius is described as generally being quiet and cautious, almost to a fault, and totally without flamboyance: his civil legislation was finely balanced between the needs of the weak and the demands of the powerful.[19] Furthermore, his policies after Adrianople had allowed the Empire to recover its stability and slowly eroded the Gothic position to one where the Empire was the dominant partner, even if this was only just the case. Having such a strong role-model, it is not surprising that Stilicho adopted the majority of the policies and some of the traits exhibited by Theodosius.

Galla Placidia

Galla Placidia was the daughter of Theodosius. Whilst Honorius and Arcadius were borne by Theodosius' first wife, Aelia Flaccilla, Galla Placidia was the daughter borne by his second wife, Galla, daughter of Valentinian I. She was thus the sister of the adopted Serena and hence sister-in-law of Stilicho. Born in late 388 or early 389, her father had missed the birth, at the time being absent for the campaign against Maximus in Italy.[20] Shortly after her birth her mother Galla quarrelled with her stepson Arcadius, who was acting as the sole emperor in Constantinople in his father's absence in the West. She fled to join Theodosius in Italy, taking her young daughter with her. On their return in 391 Theodosius set Placidia up in her own household, despite her young age, possibly in an attempt to protect her from her jealous older half-brother.[21] When Theodosius fell ill in Italy in 394 she was summoned to Milan at the same time as Honorius, and so was present at her father's death in 395. After his death she was raised in the household of Stilicho and Serena, in the knowledge that her safety was in danger from Arcadius should she return East.

The Western Empire

The death of Theodosius in 395 is often seen as the date of the permanent division of the Empire into East and West. However, even a cursory inspection of the evidence demonstrates that this view is actually anachronistic. In the minds of contemporaries the Empire was a single entity. The political division was merely a military necessity, since one emperor would always have difficulty in countering the numerous threats on the borders of the Empire. This form of division was begun as early as the reign of Diocletian (284–305) – if not before – and Claudian's emphasis on the unity of the Empire and his portrayal of Stilicho's enemies in the East as agents of discord, intent on destroying the unity of the Empire, deserves greater emphasis than is usually given. Only after the life of Stilicho would the division into East and West become permanent, but even then a large proportion of the population would have seen the Empire as a single entity, as witnessed by the horror felt in both East and West when Rome was sacked in 410. As a consequence, it should always be borne in mind that the division of the analysis between East and West is simply to ease problems of investigation and understanding and should not be seen – as is too often the case – as an acceptance that East and West had been permanently divided following Theodosius' death.

Yet in one particular circumstance the division is actually relevant. In the West, when Stilicho was made *comes et utriusque militiae* he actually took the position recently vacated by Arbogast in which the focus of political power was the leading general, not the emperor. Therefore, when a major decision was needed Stilicho would assemble the *consistorium*, which had replaced the *consilium* of earlier emperors. The *consistorium* consisted of high-ranking officials such as the *praefectus praetorio*, the *magister officiorum*, the *quaestor*, the *comes sacrarum largitionum*, the *rei privatae* and any others whose opinions were thought to be valuable.[22] If a strong emperor ruled, he would manage the meeting, but with Honorius being a minor, Stilicho dominated proceedings. Honorius was simply a figurehead.

In the East, there was a slight difference that was to prove decisive as time passed. As in the West, the actual emperor, Arcadius, was a mere figurehead, but here the *consistorium* was dominated by civilian officers, usually the *praefectus praetorio Orientis* or, at other times, the *magister officiorum* or the *praepositus sacri cubiculum*.[23] The military officials, such as the *comites domesticorum* ('commander of the guard') and the two *magistri militum praesentalis*, were only ex-officio members, were very rarely summoned, and therefore failed to acquire the dominance that Stilicho was to enjoy in the West.

Gaul

In areas along the Rhine frontier defence had been entrusted to *foederati* or *laeti*: tribes who had previously been allowed to settle on Roman soil with the restriction that they help defend the frontier.[24] The main example of this was the Franks. During the troubles of the third and fourth centuries they had settled between the Meuse and the Schelde rivers. In 358 Julian defeated them but allowed them to remain in situ as *laeti* ('allies') on condition that they defended their new territory against other Germanic tribes and no longer attacked the Empire.[25] The Franks appear to have generally adhered to the terms of the treaty – even in the troubled year of 406 – which in many

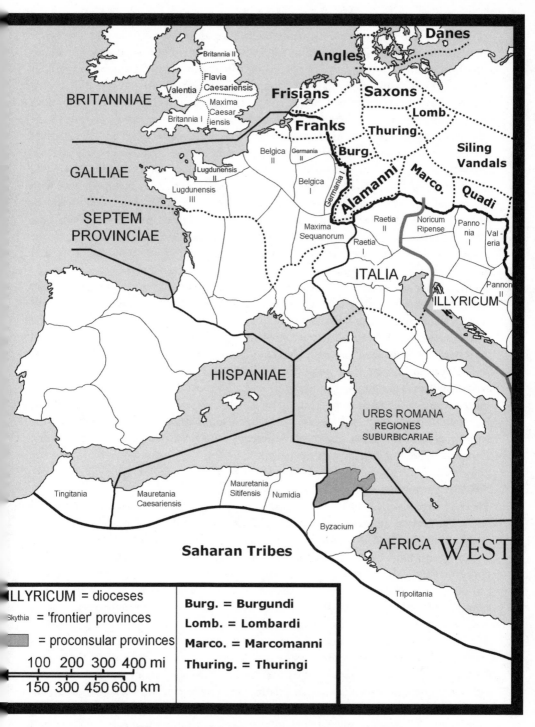

10. The enemies of the Western Roman Empire, AD 395.

ways is reminiscent of the earlier Client Kingdoms of the East. They remained independent but were subservient to Rome, helping to protect the frontier. No doubt the principle was that, like the earlier Client States, they would be absorbed at a later date. In a similar manner, smaller groups of tribesmen had been settled throughout Gaul and the Balkans, although these groups had not been allowed to retain their own leaders. Furthermore, constant victories over the Alamanni and other Germanic tribes allowed the Romans to leave the defence of the frontiers in their hands. As long as the Empire was perceived as being strong they protected the borders, but once the Empire was perceived as being in a weakened state the tribes had the tendency to make raids into Roman territory. On the whole, however, these developments allowed for the withdrawing of troops from areas protected by treaty – especially the agreement with the Franks – and their deployment elsewhere in the Empire. It is likely that the majority of the forces withdrawn by Maximus and Arbogast were taken from these areas. Unfortunately, these areas of the frontier were now only very lightly held by the Empire, and the allied tribes defending the frontiers would find it tempting to expand the territory under their control whenever the Empire appeared weak.

One further aspect of Stilicho's new guardianship needs attention. That is the effect that it had from the very start on politics within Gaul. Since the middle of the third century the capital of the West had been at Trier in Gaul. Rome was too far from the frontiers to act as a base for the emperor, whereas Trier was strategically positioned and from there the emperor was within reach of all of the threatened frontiers in the north of the Western Empire. As a result, the Gallic senators had accrued a large amount of influence, thanks to their easy access to the imperial court. Under Stilicho, the Western court became established in northern Italy. Relatively quickly, the Gallic senators lost their dominant position at the heart of the court to the Senate of Rome, although the senators of southern Gaul would retain some of their influence into the fifth century. This would have far-reaching consequences.

Britain

There is virtually no evidence for conditions in Britain. It is known that in 368 the *comes* Theodosius, father of the emperor, had restored order in Britain following the invasions and raids of 367. Despite their rescue, the provinces in the island remained unhappy with their treatment by the emperor and in 383 Magnus Maximus rebelled. Unfortunately for the island provinces, he then did what all pretenders to the throne had done before him and were to do after him: he departed for Gaul in an attempt to gain power on the mainland. To further his aims, he took many troops with him, so denuding the island of at least part of its defences.

With this rebellion in mind, it is probably best to see the island as slowly losing its image of Rome as the great protector of the Empire. Indeed, the fact that there were several rebellions during the rule of Stilicho (as will be seen) implies that the island was extremely unhappy with the state of affairs. On the other hand, it also suggests that, whatever else, Britain still saw itself as an integral part of the Empire, otherwise the islanders would have simply 'seceded', failing to obey orders from the emperor and instead organizing their own rule and defence.

The provinces' perception of their inclusion in the Empire seems to have been at least partially shared by the emperor and his advisors. The garrison of the island remains an integral part of the *Notitia Dignitatum* and there does appear to have been the appointment of officials by the emperor to govern the provinces. Unfortunately, when compared with Italy, Africa and Gaul, the returns from the provinces in taxes and trade appears to have been relatively low, even including the grain and other foodstuffs attested by the large numbers of villas being built or extended on a lavish scale in the island. As a result, Britain was not high in the priorities of the policy makers, embroiled as they were in maintaining imperial control of the core of the Western Empire. In these circumstances, it is not surprising that Britain was troubled by rebellion, with the population and local government being intent on pushing their claims for protection and security. It is unfortunate that the leaders they promoted quickly crossed to Gaul and laid claim to the Western Empire. In these circumstances, the problems of Britain were quickly subsumed in the fight for survival. Consequently, Britain was embroiled in a vicious cycle of rebellion and neglect.

Spain and Africa

These two areas were lucky in that they did not suffer from the threat of large-scale invasions, although the Moors were to prove a lasting nuisance, even invading Spain across the Straits of Gibraltar at times. Furthermore, they were at a distance from Italy and they were comparatively lightly held by Roman forces. As a result, they rarely appear to have suffered the difficulty of having troops withdrawn to face the enemies of the Empire in the fourth century. The net effect of this was that, although they remained central to the unity of the West – especially Africa, with its supply of grain for Rome and Italy – emperors were able to focus their energies on defending the frontiers in the north of Europe. However, it should be remembered that the *praefectus Africae* (prefect of Africa) was actually an extremely important individual, having control of the grain supplies to Rome. Care needed to be taken that he was loyal and liable to retain his loyalty in case of difficulties.

Italy

Due to its historic significance, along with the presence of many of the richest individuals in the Empire, the defence of Italy remained a priority for all of the emperors during the third century. Fortunately, the presence of the Alps along its northern borders helped to make the defence of the peninsula much easier than would otherwise have been the case. As long as the emperor had control of both sides of the Alps, Italy was safe, with the troops on the farther side providing warning of the approach of enemies, so allowing the passes to be defended and the enemy stopped from entering. However, if the emperor lost control of the far side, Italy was in peril. The Empire no longer had enough spare troops to man all of the passes, and without adequate warning the enemy was able to reach the valley of the River Po. Furthermore, there was political pressure from the Senate to maintain the defence of their homeland. The defence of Italy would dominate the policies of Stilicho during the time of his rule.

The political situation in the West

On the death of Theodosius Stilicho found himself in an unexpected and unusual position. Representative of an Eastern emperor who had defeated the West, upon Theodosius' death he instantly became the senior figure in the West without the military or political backing of either the Western Senate or the emperor in the East. In this context it is easy to see why Stilicho claimed the role as guardian of both Arcadius and Honorius: he would be able to use the court of Arcadius as a counterbalance to that of Honorius and vice-versa. As the pivotal figure upon which the two halves rested, he could use the other as a threat to reinforce his position.

Furthermore, despite being well-known to many of the most important figures in both halves of the Empire, he would be an unknown quantity to many. In addition, this was his first time in such a position of extreme power. He was used to working in the East as one of five *magistri* under a dominant emperor. He was now alone and no doubt many watched with trepidation, unsure how Stilicho would react to having so much power.

A further difficulty was that he was used to working alongside others who had gone through the same training in Theodosius' *protectores*. Now he would have to work with people who did not have that training and whose reactions to events he would have difficulty judging. This included the Senate in Rome.

Finally, there was the legality of his position and the possible reaction against him now that his protector, Theodosius, had been removed. His first action appears to have been to establish the validity of his rule. He did this by emphasizing his military position as *comes et magister utriusque militiae praesentalis* and by his use of the title *parens principum* to highlight his relationship with and the continuity of his service to the House of Theodosius. The use of the second of these titles would have given many individuals pause for thought; although not emperor, and therefore potentially open to political attack, Stilicho's position was actually highly unusual and theoretically superior to that of Honorius.[26] For the first time the guardian of an emperor in the West was related to the emperor but did not appear to be aiming to rule himself. The hesitation that these considerations caused and the continued support of the men placed in influential positions by Theodosius gave him time to act.

His first target appears to have been the Senate. From the time of Valentinian II (375–87) the Western court had been based in Milan. As a result, the Senate based in Rome had regained some of its lost power as Milan, unlike Trier, was within easy reach of Rome. Senators in Rome were able to make the relatively short journey to Milan, where they quickly gained and maintained their influence at court by means of *amicitia*, 'friendship between themselves and court officials'.[27]

Stilicho was unused to this milieu but realized that he could not dominate the Senate in the same way that the Senate in Constantinople had been dominated by Theodosius. In many cases Roman senators had managed to retain their influence even after involvement in the rebellion against Theodosius, showing their resilience and the emperor's recognition of their power and the effectiveness of their support.[28] Also, as an Easterner he would have been an unknown quantity to many. What he needed was an intermediary that could liaise with the Senate without Stilicho himself becoming personally involved. Fortunately, one such man stood out from the crowd.

Symmachus

Quintus Aurelius Symmachus was a major political figure and a committed pagan, who had already acted as the spokesman of a succession of emperors, such as Valentinian and Gratian, delivering speeches to the Senate on their behalf. Symmachus is now known mostly for the volume and literary content of his letters.[29] However, to his contemporaries his letters were not the most important facet of his activities: he was known as Symmachus *Logographos* ('the orator').[30]

In 382 Emperor Gratian ordered the Altar of Victory removed from the Curia, which housed the Senate. Symmachus, already a man of influence and power, led a delegation of protest, which the emperor refused to receive. In 384, some time after the death of Gratian in 383, Symmachus was made the *praefectus urbis Romae* (prefect of Rome), and he sent a letter to Emperor Valentinian II asking for the restoration of the Altar. Although the request was refused under the advice of Bishop Ambrose, it shows that Symmachus was still a focal point for the pagans amongst the Senate. Unfortunately for Symmachus, he also composed a panegyric for Magnus Maximus. When Maximus was overthrown, Symmachus had to deliver a speech of apology to Theodosius in order to obtain a pardon.[31] At some point, probably before 395, he became the *princeps senatus* ('First Senator'), becoming spokesman for the Senate. As such he was in a position to negotiate with Stilicho, giving him support in the Senate in return for concessions and influence. Furthermore, his position highlights that during the rule of Stilicho the Senate began to wield an influence that they had not had for many years.[32]

His influence quickly began to take effect. After a few false starts, Symmachus finally managed to secure Stilicho's patronage. Evidence for this can be found in the careers of two individuals who had been promoted to positions of power by Eugenius and Arbogast. Although few of those who had supported the usurpers had been executed by Theodosius, the survivors were ordered to repay the money they had earned whilst in office. Amongst them was Marcianus, who had been made proconsul of Africa under Eugenius. Likewise, Nicomachus Flavianus, who was *praefectus urbis Romae* (prefect of Rome) under Eugenius, was also ordered by Theodosius to repay his salary. In an attempt to secure support for his new regime and following the guidance of Symmachus, Stilicho acceded to the request for the cessation of the repayments.[33]

Symmachus' letters to Stilicho also demonstrate the novelty and main weakness of Stilicho's position. Since Stilicho was in effective control of the West, Symmachus always maintained a deferential tone in his letters: he did not want to alienate the man at the top. Yet at the same time the manner and style of his address would not have been appropriate for an emperor.[34] Stilicho could not demand the loyalty or claim the deferential treatment accorded to a ruling emperor. In all his dealings he would need to remember that the people he was dealing with would recognize his power but see themselves as potential rivals rather than loyal subjects.

The Senate

Yet the power and influence of senators such as Symmachus should not be surprising, although in many cases their patronage and influence may not have transferred to political influence at the highest levels.[35] As we have already seen, the military situation in the West was extremely precarious. Stilicho needed the support of the Senate, as they were the individuals whose goodwill would supply the tax revenue and provide the recruits and logistical support for the army.[36] After all, the Senate had a major social and political influence in Rome, central and southern Italy, Sicily and North Africa – especially Proconsularis (the area around Carthage) and Numidia (see Map 1).[37] Their wealth and influence mattered to a court stationed in north Italy. The Senate, however, had different priorities: 'Symmachus was speaking as a member of a class which, with quite unconscious selfishness, would preserve its economic interests and prejudices through the impoverishment and collapse of the Western imperial government'.[38] The net result was that Stilicho, who understood the needs of the army concerning conscription and pay, would have to perform a dangerous balancing act. He was opposed by the Senate's more traditional concept of success, the defeat of barbarians in battle and their elimination from the ranks of the army, whilst at the same time they resisted the conscription needed to make the employment of barbarians unnecessary and resented the need to pay the taxes.[39] Unfortunately, this was not in line with the policy of Theodosius, the befriending and using of barbarians, that he was attempting to maintain.[40] Throughout his time as commander in the West this issue would remain a potential danger for Stilicho.

In order to expand his links with the Western Senate, Stilicho was extremely careful in appointing men from the West as well as the East into positions of power, whenever possible maintaining Theodosius' policies of installing loyal supporters in positions of power in the West. For example, his first *praefectus praetorio Italiae* was Nummius Aemilianus Dexter, who had served under Theodosius as *proconsul Asiae* (proconsul of Asia) before becoming *comes rei privatae* (secretary to the emperor).[41] In the same manner, the first *praefectus urbis Romae* was Basilius, who like Theodosius, was probably originally from Spain and who was also loyal to the House of Theodosius. However, for unknown reasons Basilius was quickly removed and replaced by Andromachus on the recommendation of Symmachus, and Andromachus was later (401) made *praefectus praetorio Galliarum*.[42] Yet Basilius retained influence as he was later (408) chosen as part of an embassy to Alaric.[43] During the brief rule of Eugenius, Aemilius Florus Paternus, the *proconsul Africae* (proconsul of Africa), had remained loyal to Theodosius. He was rewarded with the post of *comes sacrarum largitionem* (count of the sacred largesse: chamberlain) in 396, as a result of which he was constantly petitioned by Symmachus.[44] The *vicarius per Hispania* from 395 to 397 was Petronius, brother of Patroninus, again probably on the recommendation of Symmachus. Patroninus himself was given the post of *comes sacrarum largitionem* in 401, also on the recommendation of Symmachus. In 396 Stilicho appointed Hilarius, another who had served under Gratian (in 383) as *praefectus praetorio Galliarum*. Aemilius Florus Paternus, who as *proconsul Africae* had held loyal to Theodosius in the civil war, was rewarded with the post of *comes sacrarum largitionem*.

Stilicho's most important appointment was to be made in 397 when Flavius Manlius Theodorus was selected as *praefectus praetorio Italiae*, whilst his son, also called Theodorus, was made *praefectus praetorio Gallias*. Theodorus remained in the post until 399, when he was elected consul – Claudian himself taking the time to write a panegyric for the occasion.[45] As a further honour for the family, Theodorus' brother Lampadius was to become *praefectus urbis Romae* in 398. The circumstances surrounding his appointment will be dealt with below.

These examples demonstrate that Stilicho was continuing to employ Theodosius' supporters who he assumed to be loyal to the Theodosian house and its policies. As he was continuing to use Theodosius' policies, he could assume their continued loyalty to himself as long as he maintained their goodwill.[46]

The above appointments all involved members of the Western aristocracy. Alongside these Stilicho made the Easterner Flavius Iunius Quartus Palladius the *tribunus et notarius*, and Hadrianus, appointed *comes sacrarium largitionem* in 395 and *magister officiorum* in 397 was, like Claudian, from Alexandria.

It may also be at this time that Stilicho began to introduce a system to control the appointment of all offices in the West. To that end, he now arranged matters so that appointments to the offices of *princeps* ('chief clerk') and the *commentariensis* ('registrar of public documents') on the judicial side, along with the two *numerarii* on the financial side, were men drawn from the offices of the *magistri praesentales*.[47] This resulted in Stilicho slowly bringing the reins of government into his own hands. It should be noted, however, that the dating of this reform is unknown, and rather than being a rapid change it may have been a slow process of transformation that took several years to complete. Whatever the date and longevity of the reform, slowly Stilicho began to personally dominate the legal and military processes in the West.

Yet in one aspect, Stilicho may have become restricted as time passed. The whole of Western imperial politics appears to have been played out within a framework of regional alliances and personal favour, and there is little doubt that Stilicho's policy of conciliation towards the Senate and the Western court, along with their proximity to each other, resulted in them drawing closer together in the early years of his control.[48] Unfortunately, Stilicho, as an outsider, is likely to have found the process increasingly frustrating. He had come from the Eastern court, where Theodosius dominated. Stilicho, on the other hand, was unable to dominate politics in the West to the same degree as Theodosius had in the East. Furthermore, circumstances created a situation which was to become ever more restrictive as time passed. However, in 395 this may not have been seen by Stilicho as a potential problem. He still had the major field armies of both East and West under his control: for the present, fear is likely to have restrained any opposition in the West.

Based in Milan, naturally the major influence on the emperor or his guardian was the continuous stream of petitioners arriving at Milan from Rome and southern Gaul. In fact, one of the first laws Stilicho issued was a restriction on the use of the public road system between Rome and Milan to those with proper authority, a clear sign of the large numbers of people using the system to petition the court.[49] As these were some of the most powerful, influential and rich individuals within the Western Empire, it is unsurprising that they managed to influence policy over the next ten years. The net result was that the main focus of Stilicho's policies was the defence of Italy and Southern Gaul. Needless to say, Africa ranked alongside Italy, as without its supply of corn Italy – and especially Rome – would start to suffer the effects of famine. Northern Gaul, Spain and Britain became less of an issue at Milan. Although this was to have dire consequences for Stilicho in later years, in 395 he seemed to have settled into his rule in a satisfactory manner.

Serena

In the story of Stilicho the activities of Serena, his wife, are sometimes lost. One example of her activities comes from 397. In this year the body of Saint Nazarus was (allegedly) found and it was decided to house his remains in the *Basilica Apostolorum* (Basilica of the Apostles), which had been commissioned in 382 by Bishop Ambrose in Milan. In honour of this the church was renamed the *Basilica San Nazaro* (Basilica of Saint Nazarus) and a new apse created to house the tomb. When Stilicho departed for the campaign in Greece against Alaric, Serena made a vow for his safe return.[50] When he arrived home safely, in accordance with her vow she not only donated the marbles for the *sacellum* housing the relics, but also gave money to have the rest of the church decorated, including the paving of the floor of the church.[51] Throughout the life of Stilicho she would spend money in the traditional Roman manner, although now it was for the building, decoration and upkeep of Christian churches rather than pagan temples. There is no doubt that her activities behind the scenes helped secure the position of her husband, especially with respect to many Christian doubters, since her activities ensured that Christianity was seen as the religion followed by Serena and Stilicho, despite his continued employment of pagans and heretics.

The political situation in the East

Rufinus

When Theodosius had left for the war in 394, he had left his son Arcadius in Constantinople in the care of the *praefectus praetorio Orientis* (praetorian prefect of the East), Rufinus. Rufinus was a Gaul, a fact that gives a clear indication that at this time there was no division in the Empire and that members from one half could easily cross and make a career in the other. Promoted during the reign of Theodosius, nothing is known of his career until he is noted as *magister officiorum* in 388. In 392 he was given the consulship, an event marking his rapid rise to power.[52] In the same year he managed to secure the dismissal of both Tatian, the *praefectus praetorio Orientis*, and Tatian's son, Proculus, the *praefectus urbis Romae*. Rufinus became the *praefectus praetorio Orientis*, and managed to engineer a trial for the two men, Proculus being executed and Tatian being condemned to death before being spared and exiled by Theodosius.[53]

The most notable aspect of his early career was an unwillingness to allow military affairs to be successfully concluded by the army. The most likely reason for this is that any glory claimed by a victorious general would undoubtedly undermine his own position. Therefore, as was already seen, when Stilicho had defeated the forces under

Alaric, Rufinus was the one who brokered the peace treaty and arranged for Alaric's forces to serve in the army as *foederati* with Alaric himself being given the rank of tribune.[54] Throughout his career Rufinus and his successors would attempt to use any means but deploying the army to keep barbarians out of the Empire. Although seen by ancient sources as 'traitorous', his example resulted in political affairs in the East remaining in civilian hands, so meaning that when a strong emperor emerged he was not dominated or overthrown by his leading general, as was to happen in the West.

When Theodosius led the campaign against Arbogast and Eugenius in 394 Rufinus was left in charge of the East. His policies and activities during the previous six years had alienated the army and created many enemies. Realising that he was in danger without the protection of Theodosius, Rufinus at some point managed to convince the emperor to allow him to recruit a bodyguard of Huns to protect him.[55] This may be the first example of a civilian gaining a military bodyguard that would later be called *bucellarii*, as a counter to the bodyguard of Stilicho, also formed of Huns, which appears to have been the first example of a general having a unit of *bucellarii* at his command.

Rufinus was obviously a skilled and ruthless politician, capable of holding his own at court. However, when Theodosius died all was suddenly in a state of flux. Although Rufinus appears to have been regarded by many in the East as the legitimate warden of Arcadius, Stilicho's claim to be *parens principum* of both of Theodosius' sons was a situation that Rufinus could not allow; given the hostility between himself and Stilicho, his life would be in danger.[56] Fortunately for him, Arcadius was weak-willed and easily influenced. He persuaded the young emperor to reject Stilicho's claim, possibly using the image of Arcadius being totally overshadowed by his older relative. It is also suggested that he planned to marry Arcadius to his daughter, in effect giving him a status comparable to Stilicho in the West of *parens principum*.

However, having managed to arrange for the rejection of Stilicho's claims, Rufinus still had political problems in Constantinople. Earlier in his career, as *magister officiorum*, he had quarrelled with the generals Timasius and Promotus. Promotus was shortly afterwards transferred to Thrace and then killed in an ambush, which some saw as being arranged by Rufinus.[57] Although the reference is late, it presumably had its source in rumours spread around court at the time.

Timasius had served in the campaign against Arbogast and Eugenius, but had been sent back to the East by Theodosius, probably to oversee military operations in Pamphylia in 396. Fortunately for Rufinus, the result was that at this moment of crisis Timasius was away from the capital and could be safely ignored.

Eutropius

The allegations concerning Promotus' death would also help the cause of Rufinus' major political rival at court, the eunuch Eutropius. A freed slave, Eutropius had entered service in the imperial palace and quickly risen to become a trusted supporter of Theodosius with the post of *praepositus sacri cubiculi* (imperial chamberlain).[58] A major rival of Rufinus, Eutropius quickly arranged to cooperate with Promotus' sons.

One of these had in his care a girl called Eudoxia, a woman of outstanding beauty.[59] She was apparently the daughter of a Frankish general named Bauto and after Bauto's death Promotus' son took care of her. As opponents of Rufinus, Promotus' sons were probably only too eager to help when Eutropius approached them with a plan to diminish the power of Rufinus.

Learning that Rufinus intended to marry his daughter to Arcadius, Eutropius took action: without the knowledge of Rufinus, Eutropius managed to arrange the marriage of Eudoxia to Arcadius, a marriage which took place on 27 April 395.[60] It is, unfortunately, unlikely that Zosimus' detailed story, although fascinating, is true. According to Zosimus, Rufinus was unaware of Arcadius' change of heart. Only when the wedding carriage collected Eudoxia did Rufinus realize that his plan had failed.[61]

The marriage blocked Rufinus' plans to become *parens principum* and also helped elevate Eutropius' standing at court, making him a serious rival to Rufinus. What measures Rufinus would have taken to block the rise of Eutropius will never be known, as in the same year events in Illyricum changed the balance of power in both West and East for ever.

Chapter Four

The Roman Army

Having discussed the military titles adopted by Stilicho it would now seem logical to analyse the military might of the Roman Empire. From the time of Diocletian onwards the size of units within the army appears to change. Modern research tends to limit unit strengths as follows:[1] guard units (*scholae* etc.) 500 men; *auxilia palatinae* 800 men; legions (*comitatenses*) 1,000 men; legions (*limitanei*) 3,000 men; *limitanei/riparienses* 300 men; cavalry (*limitanei*) 350 men. However, it should be remembered that these are modern estimates and therefore of uncertain reliability. Furthermore, long service on campaign or in battle would quickly reduce numbers to below these figures.[2]

Moreover, the army appears to have expanded to around 400,000 men from an original base of around 300,000 men.[3] To supply recruits for the new enlarged army, legislation was passed that the sons of soldiers were themselves legally obliged to follow their fathers into the army.[4] Furthermore, conscription was to remain a necessary evil for the remainder of the Empire, becoming annual at sometime around 365, at which time tough measures were announced for deserters and an attempt was made to enlist men currently avoiding service.[5] Maintaining the strength of the enlarged army was to be a problem for the emperors up to the battle of Adrianople in 378, after which it would become a major dilemma.

The new army was completely different to the old. The troops on the frontiers were reclassified as either *limitanei* (border defence, land) or *riparienses* (border defence, river) troops.[6] These troops had three main functions: to police the borders, to gather intelligence, and to stop small-scale raids.[7] The preferred Roman strategy for engaging barbarians was to use 'harassing warfare'.[8] The majority of this was conducted by the troops stationed in the interior provinces, in or near to strategic cities and fortifications. These were now designated as *comitatenses* (companions). Above these, with the emperor himself, was a further tier known as the *palatina* (palace troops).[9]

Army unit hierarchy

Yet the hierarchy was to become even more complex. At the top were the *scholae* who were now unchallenged as the elite bodyguard to the emperor. Below them were the *palatina*, with the *auxilia palatina* ranking above the *legiones palatina*. Below these were the *comitatenses*, and below them were the *limitanei* and *riparienses*. As time passed there grew an intermediate group known as the *pseudocomitatenses*, formed from border troops who were promoted to the ranks of *comitatenses* in order to fill gaps or take part in specific campaigns.[10] Finally, there were units whose status is either unclear or whose rank could differ between individual units, such as the *foederati, gentiles, dediticii, tributarii,* and *laeti.* However, the actual status of the troops at the lower end of the scale is vague. This is mainly because the sources use a wide range of terminology which is applied almost indiscriminately to a variety of units, usually of barbarian origin, and the application of titles need not necessarily follow a set pattern.[11]

The *gentiles* appear to have been composed of tribesmen, either recently settled within the Empire or recruited from tribes still living beyond the frontiers: with the sources available it is impossible to say for certain which of these was more prevalent.[12] Their exact status is unclear but *gentiles* are later listed amongst the *scholae* of Diocletian, and in the *Notitia Dignitatum* they are found in the *scholae* attached to both the Eastern and the Western *magister officiorum.*[13] Units of Sarmatian *gentiles* (*Sarmatarum gentilium*) are also attested as being stationed in Italy.[14] Due to the context, it is possible that they were settled as farmers throughout these regions with individuals then being enrolled in regular units.[15]

The *laeti* may have been different to the *gentiles.* They were formed from barbarians settled within the Empire who were obliged to provide troops for the army in exchange for land. The settlements were not self-governing, being administered either by a Roman military official or by the council of a local city.[16] However, there were units combining the two titles, such as the *laetorum gentilium* stationed in *Belgica Secunda,* which suggests that any differences between the two may be coincidental and more of a reflection of modern prejudices than of ancient custom.

Tributarii and *dediticii* appear to have been obtained from external sources. As their names suggest, it is possible that they were supplied as part of a treaty by tribes who had been defeated by the Romans.[17]

The *foederati* cause the greatest confusion to historians. This may be because the same title was given to troops recruited in several different ways. The name usually refers to barbarian troops serving under their own leaders as part of a Roman force. However, it may also refer to barbarian troops recruited directly into the army to either fill the ranks of normal Roman units, or instead to form their own, distinct, tribal units within the framework of the army. Furthermore, the name is given to barbarian troops of different tribes who were attracted to serve under one leader, either Roman or barbarian, who was part of the Roman hierarchy. Finally, as with the Goths, the name may be given to non-Roman troops serving the emperor as part of a treaty but who are not a part of the regular Roman army and do not serve under Roman officers. Due to the indeterminate nature of the *foederati* it is impossible to be clear on their nature and their status. As a result, each unit so designated has to be assessed solely using its own history.

There is also the problem of the emergence of the *bucellarii.* These men may have started as *foederati* serving under one leader, however they are generally accepted as serving under local magnates rather than generals. Only slowly were they accepted as part of the military hierarchy, serving as bodyguards to Roman generals. In fact, it is possible that Stilicho was the first Roman general to have had *bucellarii* serving as a bodyguard.[18] They would become increasingly important during the course of the fifth and sixth centuries.

Whatever their origin, wherever possible the Romans tended to employ barbarians, who may by now have composed nearly a quarter of the Roman army, away from the area of their origin.[19] In this way they would not be tempted to desert in the knowledge that they could easily find their way home, and, furthermore, coupled with their new training the distance from home would help to foster an esprit de corps with their unit, the only people they would know in a large and potentially unfriendly Empire.[20]

The above shows that, contrary to the expectations of modern authorities whose experience is dominated by rigid hierarchies and naming conventions, troop designation was not linked to specific methods of recruitment or use and appears to have been dependent upon the needs or whim of the emperor founding the units. As a consequence, the changes must be seen as 'organic and progressive, not wholesale or ordered'.[21] With this in mind, any attempt to analyse the titles of army commanders in an attempt to impose a rigid structure that lasts throughout the course of the later Empire is doomed to failure.

Training for command: the *protectores domestici* and the *protectores*

There were two sections of the imperial household whose function was to train and assess candidates for potential military command.

The lower of these was the *protectores*. Men who were recommended for the *protectores* spent time with their fellows under the supervision of the emperor or one of his deputies before being sent to command either single units or, when there were two stationed together, pairs of units.

The *protectores domestici* (household guards) were the successors to the *protectores divini lateris* ('observed guards of the divine emperor') of Gallienus (253–68). The title was originally given by Gallienus to his high-ranking officers, possibly as a visible reward for their loyal service, although it should be seen as a distinction, not a rank.[22] Over time the title and function changed and the group of men later known as the *protectores domestici* generally provided the army with its senior commanders. It was also possible for a member of the *protectores domestici* to become emperor on the death of the previous incumbent: examples include Diocletian (284) and Justin (518).

The *protectores* has been called a 'corps of officer cadets' and the *protectores domestici* a 'staff college'.[23] Both of these terms are misleading, prompting modern visions of men in uniform attending lectures on subjects such as grand strategy, battlefield tactics and logistics. This is unlikely to have been the case. It is more likely that they were ordered to read some of the military manuals that had been produced, observe more experienced officers in action, and then given commands of an ever greater nature to both build up their experience and observe their capabilities. There was no modern, written, 'theoretical' test prior to them being assigned a permanent rank. Only if they had the necessary qualities of command and control in the military sphere and if they were deemed loyal enough in the personal and political sphere would they be given a placement in a senior post. Especially in the case of the *protectores domestici*, these matters could only be decided through personal observation by the emperor, not by abstract written exams.[24] If the *protectores domestici* had in truth been a 'staff college', it failed in its purpose. The histories are replete with commanders who failed in their duty either through cowardice or inability: furthermore, the Emperor Valens was described as being unhappy with the quality of his subordinate commanders.[25]

Command hierarchy

An examination of the pages of the *Notitia Dignitatum* clearly shows troops commanded by officers, who in turn are subordinate to men of higher rank. This system appears to mirror the linear hierarchies of modern armies and so is assumed to work in the same way. Unfortunately, an investigation of the history of the various positions somewhat dispels the illusion.

Before an analysis can take place, two notes of caution must be applied. The first note is that ancient sources tend not to be interested in applying strict military rankings according to an accepted hierarchy. Therefore, the use of titles such as *magister peditum*, *magister equitum, magister utriusque militiae* and so forth may all actually represent the same post, depending upon the authority, accuracy and sources used by the author in question.

Furthermore, it is possible that in many cases these posts were short-lived under specific emperors or created for an individual and legitimately held but that they were then left vacant or abolished when the occupier left the post. Other uses of titles may have been caused by an author falsely 'promoting' his patron in order to gain extra patronage, or by his applying a later title to an earlier period in order to help his readers better understand events. Moreover, titles were liable to change without notice and they need not necessarily match the limits that are implied. Examples of this will be given below.

The second cautionary note is that the *Notitia* describes the standing army in time of peace. On campaign, the realities of warfare would have resulted in *ad hoc* command structures, rather than a strict adherence to the peacetime organization.[26] Although these changes may have been short-lived, their ramifications may have lasted longer than the campaign itself, with the individuals promoted for the campaign retaining their rank as a form of reward from the emperor. However, they subsequently did not fit easily into the command structure represented in the *Notitia*.

After his victory over Licinius in 324 Constantine (306–337) amalgamated his own troops with those of Licinius, so expanding the *comitatenses*. He then redeployed the troops around the newly conquered Empire to fit with his view of how the army should operate. Obviously, he also reorganized the command structure to accommodate the changes.

A major part of this reorganization was that the *praefecti* lost their military powers. These tasks were assumed by the *magister peditum* (master of the infantry) and the *magister equitum* (master of the cavalry). These *magistri* controlled the *comitatenses* and in theory had authority above the provincial *duces* (dukes). However, the *duces* retained the right to correspond directly with the emperor. The result was actually a division in the command structure, which could have severe and unexpected consequences. If a *dux* disagreed with the *magister* who was nominally his superior, he had the right to petition the emperor for alternative orders, leading to confusion and delay.[27] As a consequence, no *magister* could rely on his subordinates for unquestioning obedience.

Yet Constantine realized that the new powers given to the *magistri* were in some respects dangerous to his own authority, since they now commanded substantial forces in the field. Therefore, for his own security the emperor retained control of the elite *scholae* via the *magister officiorum*.[28] These troops would act as the nucleus for an army which would defeat any *magister* unwise enough to raise the standard of revolt.

It is possible that Constantine had two motives for the new, dual appointments of *magister equitum* and *magister peditum*. Firstly, it split the military command between two individuals, so making revolt more difficult. Secondly, it mirrored earlier dual institutions – especially the consulship – and so appealed to traditional values. It would now also be possible to send the two *magistri* to two separate theatres of war; with the addition of Constantine the Empire could now – in theory – fight a war on three fronts, or deploy multiple armies in the same war. Finally, it would allow Constantine to reward more than one man with the highest accolade short of being emperor.

Unfortunately, the system quickly changed, not least in the fact that differences emerged between the East and the West. In the East, under Valens I (364–378) there were at least two *magistri equitum*.[29] To differentiate between the two, one added the title *in praesenti* or *praesentalis* (in the presence). To ensure that the situation did not become unbalanced, the *magister peditum* also appears to have been given the suffix *praesentalis*. Over time the *magister peditum praesentalis* gained superiority, presumably due to his continued presence at court. In the West, the division between *peditum* and *equitum* slowly disappeared, with the change probably occurring later, possibly following the tenure of Merobaudes under the Emperors Gratian (375–83) and Valentinian II (375–392).[30] After this both commanders were nominally in control of equally sized mixed forces.

Below the various *magistri* were the *comes* and *duces*. As with the *magistri*, the two titles were not wholly distinct, with one serving above the other – although by the time of the *Notitia Dignitatum* this may have been the ambition. An example of the mixing of the titles dates from the reign of Constantine. He gave the title *dux Aegypti* to the military commander of Egypt. From about 384 the title of this commander changed to *comes rei militaris per Aegyptum*. The example shows that without more specific evidence the use of the *Notitia* to trace the development of ranks and titles within the army is fraught with danger. It seems likely that the designations *comes* and *dux* were given by different emperors depending upon the individual circumstances surrounding the appointment.

Having seen that there was little continuity in the use of the titles *dux* or *comes*, it is possible to look at other posts. On inspection, the same appears to be true of the title *praepositus*. It began as a temporary command, for example given to commanders in charge of detachments in transit. It then appears to have changed and become the title given to commanders of 'non-standard' Roman units, such as the *numeri* of the early Empire. In the later Empire the title was more widely used but there does not appear to have been any consistency in its use; for example, there were *praepositi* in the *scholae*, but also *praepositi legionis* and *praepositi cohortales* in the *limitanei*.[31]

In conclusion, it would appear that great care needs to be taken before deductions are made based on specific titles held by military commanders. We should not see the army's ranks as being a defined hierarchy that remained the same throughout the period. Instead, it should be seen as a fluid entity, changing its nature on the whim of emperors and/or as circumstances dictated. Both the date of the appointment, the actual nature of the appointment, and the predisposition of the emperor who appointed the post need to be taken into account before definitive statements are made. It may be possible to draw up a table showing the chain of command under one or possibly two consecutive emperors. To attempt to do the same for the entire fourth and fifth centuries would be impossible.

This situation can lead to confusion amongst historians. In a similar manner, the creation of new titles and the promotion of individuals to fill them is likely to have caused confusion in the military men serving at the time. As a consequence, in part at least the *Notitia* may have been an attempt to codify and organize all of the changes that had taken place in the previous century, primarily in an attempt to eliminate obsolete titles and functions and also to accord the recipients of posts their correct status in society. Yet although it should be accepted that, on the whole, the command structure of the *Notitia* may have been the goal for Theodosius, how far later emperors – especially in the West – maintained the progress towards that goal is a matter for debate.

Recruitment

There would appear to have been three methods of recruitment in the later Empire: the enrolment of volunteers, conscription and levies from 'barbarians' settled either as prisoners of war or as normal Roman farmers with a duty to provide troops for the army when a levy was demanded.[32]

Both volunteers and conscripts had to show that they were fit for the army. It was a long-standing tradition that many men were exempt from conscription. This included cooks, bakers, innkeepers and others whose jobs were deemed to be unsuitable as a background for service in the army. Slaves were also exempt for most of the time, only being conscripted in times of emergency when they were encouraged to fight by the promise of freedom and other rewards. On the other hand, the sons of serving soldiers were obliged by law to join the army.

Even following the army reforms of the late-third and early-fourth centuries, once the army had been enlarged the population of the Empire, notwithstanding losses from almost continuous warfare and epidemics, should have been able to provide the recruits necessary to maintain army strengths. Yet there were severe difficulties in maintaining the army's size.

The first of these was that a career in the army was unpopular. One of the main difficulties was that in the uncertain times of the fourth century joining the army could mean a recruit being posted to a province far from his home.[33] This could leave his family unprotected and so many men preferred to stay and defend their own homes.

Furthermore, there is some evidence for citizens being disillusioned with the government and its heavy taxation, and angry at the behaviour of troops (who may now have been billeted in homes in cities); there is even evidence of them siding with invaders in the expectation of better treatment and booty.[34]

Ammianus states that in some provinces – especially those such as Italy where conscription had become unknown in the previous centuries – some citizens preferred to cut off their own thumbs, so making them unsuitable for service, rather than serve in the army.[35] In 368 Valentinian I ordered that such men should be burnt alive as a discouragement to others.[36] However, this should not be overplayed. The cutting off of thumbs appears to have been restricted to provinces that had remained peaceful during the height of the Empire and so had no history of military service. Frontier provinces such as Gaul did not suffer from these habits; a law in the *Codex Theodosianus* merely shows that a problem existed, not the extent of the problem.[37]

Nor should it be thought that conscription was an ever-present feature of Roman civilian life. In times of war conscription would be needed to fill the gaps in the ranks, but in times of peace emperors had different agendas. When the need for men was not urgent, provinces were allowed to pay a tax – the *aurem tironicum* (gold for recruits) – instead of supplying men. As time went by this practice became more widespread, as emperors realized that they could use the tax to pay for mercenaries who were willing to fight and had less need of training. Yet the system was open to corruption. Emperors often found themselves to be short of money, since the income from taxes rarely covered the expenditure needed to maintain the Empire. When this happened, it was tempting to pass a decree calling for conscription simply in order to commute this to the *aurem tironicum* to boost the treasury.[38]

There can be little doubt that this had an effect on the attitude of the citizens being taxed. The provincials will have clearly understood the motives for the levying of such taxes, which will have caused discontent. Furthermore, there were naturally imperial officials who used the procedure to increase their personal wealth. The result was an increase in tensions, since the provincials felt they were being taxed for services that were not then being provided, and that dishonest officials were growing wealthy at their expense. In 375 the Emperor Valens passed laws attempting to curb the corruption, but the attempt seems to have had little impact before Adrianople in 378.[39]

Whether new troops were conscripts, volunteers or mercenaries, the *duces* were responsible for recruitment and for the assigning of individuals to units, which task also included the weeding out of men unsuitable for a military career.[40] Unfortunately we are not given any details as to how this took place. All that can be accepted is that the system appears to have worked prior to the battle of Adrianople.

Training

According to Zosimus, the training and discipline of the army was not as it had been in earlier centuries.[41] This is echoed by some authors, who maintain that the billeting of troops in cities had a detrimental effect on the army. Since the troops did not have a purpose-built training area such as those found in earlier forts, it is assumed that training must have declined and army efficiency deteriorated. However, the presumption does not allow for officer professionalism or troop needs. In all armies training can be undertaken in any open space of sufficient size. The predominant factor is the quality and enthusiasm of the officers. If the officers were of high quality, the troops would receive regular training; if not, they would not be trained.

The question of leadership is rarely raised in relation to the Late Roman Empire. It is generally assumed that the junior officers slowly lost the efficiency and skills that had helped the army achieve its peak. To a degree this must be accepted as the truth. There are indications in Ammianus that not all was well with the army's leaders. For example, when Julian was in the West a man called Dagalaifus was put in charge of troops with orders to attack marauding barbarians. Unfortunately, he delayed, claiming that he could not attack the barbarians as they were 'scattered over various places'. Shortly after, he was replaced by Jovinus, who promptly attacked and annihilated two separate groups, before fighting a drawn-out battle with a third force that later slipped away at night.[42] The episode reflects the situation in the army in the fourth century, with the army commanders varying widely in ability. The concept is reinforced, again by Ammianus, when he states that Julian removed commanders deemed incompetent and replaced them with 'men approved by long trial'.[43]

To a large degree training would also depend upon where within the Empire the troops were stationed. Troops deployed in Egypt, where their role was mainly of policing and crowd control, would likely need either less training or at least a different kind of training to those stationed on the Rhine or the Danube, where action against the enemy would be a daily possibility.

Questions have also been raised about the esprit de corps that was such an integral part of the early army. It has been argued that the billeting of troops on civilian households in cities would lead to the troops losing their unity because of continued interaction with civilians. However, it is possible to argue that the opposite may be true. The population often voiced its unhappiness with the situation, and it is likely that the troops in cities were faced with hostility and obstructions from the civilian population. In these circumstances, group loyalty could be reinforced, since the troops were in constant contact with people who did not share their aspirations or understand their problems. In short, the troops would not fit in with the civilians and remain isolated in 'hostile' territory. Such conditions probably resulted in greater esprit de corps, not less.

Although the poor quality of troops in the Later Empire has long been accepted as fact, analysis of battles – especially those of Argentoratum (Strasbourg) and Adrianople – has resulted in a reappraisal. It is now accepted that, to a large degree, Roman training methods continued into the fourth century: indeed, Ammianus affirms the esprit de corps and the survival of old skills in the *comitatenses*, such as the building of marching camps and permanent forts.[44] When properly led, and when training was combined with strict discipline, it can be seen that the Roman army was still a formidable fighting force.

Discipline

As with training, when analysing the discipline of the army historians have tended to focus upon Zosimus when he claimed that training and discipline had declined.[45] To reinforce this view, reference is also made to the variety of methods used by different emperors to punish undisciplined troops. Examples include Julian ordering such men to be hamstrung or to be paraded through camp dressed in women's clothes, or Theodosius ordering the amputation of hands.[46] It is usually implied that if such methods were needed, then the situation must have become severe.

Yet drastic measures against cowardice and poor discipline were a factor in Roman armies from the time of the Republic. It would be possible to use very early references to decimation, or the fact that on occasion troops who had shown cowardice were to sleep outside marching camps as signs that the armies of the early Republic were of poor quality.[47] Yet these armies conquered an Empire and are not assessed as being 'poor-quality' troops.

Again, the same analyses of the battles of the late Empire have shown that, on the whole, the troops were capable of beating any opponent that came against them. In fact, the best-known case of poor discipline was the cavalry at the battle of Argentoratum.[48] Yet even here the cavalry rallied and regrouped before rejoining the fight. In fact, historians are slowly coming to the conclusion that, at least in large, set-piece battles, the Roman army maintained its discipline and training, and that Zosimus' statement concerning the decline of the army is exaggerated.[49] In fact, there are few examples of defeat in large battles; most losses were on a smaller scale.[50]

Supply

Apart from the supervision of the recruitment process, the main duty of the *duces* was to liaise with the praetorian prefects, who by now had lost their military duties but had retained control of army logistics, the provision of food and military supplies such as weapons and armour. It is possible that the result was that the military function of the *duces* took lower priority than their bureaucratic and organizational role.

As with so much within the organization of the army, a lot depended upon the personal skills, efficiency and corruption of individuals. Two examples from Ammianus will suffice to show the distinctions. Both concern praetorian prefects. In the first, the *praefectus praetorio Orientis*, Rufinus, was forced to go before the troops and give them an explanation as to why their supplies had not yet arrived.[51] It should be pointed out that Ammianus gives floods and unseasonable weather as part of the cause of the failure, yet Rufinus is portrayed as inefficient in his logistical duties. In contrast, Anatolius the *praefectus praetorio Illyrici* (prefect of Illyricum) had gathered the necessary supplies ahead of time, with more continually arriving 'without trouble to anyone'.[52] Again, a note of caution is applicable: it should be mentioned that Anatolius is praised by Ammianus not only for his efficiency but also for his incorruptibility: the story may be biased.

Possibly in part as a response to these difficulties, supplies in kind slowly began to change to payment in lieu. In the early Empire, the government had supplied all of the requirements of the soldier, but had deducted the cost of these from the men's wages. By the time of Valentinian I the *limitanei* still received the supplies needed for nine months of the year straight from the government. However, for the remaining three months they were paid in gold and had to locate and purchase the supplies themselves.[53] Over the course of time the system had been extended until by 406 it included virtually all military personnel.[54] In such a situation, it would be easy for the troops to begin taking more than their money was worth. It is hard for military men to pay full price for goods from people they are protecting. Instead, they are likely to have expected a discount for any goods bought from the people they are protecting.

One final aspect is never assessed. Historians writing after the event have the benefit of hindsight and realize that the Empire would fall eventually. The Romans did not have this. It is likely that barbarian groups allowed into the Empire were not seen as the threat that they later became. This is due in part to Roman arrogance: why should the barbarians wish to overthrow Rome? In the preceding centuries all of the tribes and political entities that had been conquered by Rome had seen the benefits of inclusion and become members of the Empire: why should tribes such as the Goths or Franks be any different? Let them settle, allow them to have the benefits of rule and then they would lose their identity amongst the common Roman citizenry. This theory helps to explain why so many German leaders were accepted into service in the army. By serving the Empire they would gradually absorb the benefits and mentality of citizens – as had happened to the Gauls, the Britons and many other belligerent tribes.

Conclusion

Although the Roman army is considered by some to be the most efficient and modern army of the ancient world, these conclusions rest on very unstable foundations. Although much in the army appears to reflect modern practice, a large proportion of this is based more upon modern perceptions than upon reality. In the same way as today's armies are the product of centuries of development, so too were those of the later Empire. Yet an inefficient bureaucracy and the lack of rapid communications resulted in an army that resembles more those of the sixteenth century than of the twentieth.

The main difficulties faced by the army appear to have been caused by the reforms of the previous century. The army operating at a small scale could no longer rely on every aspect of its needs being supplied in an efficient manner, as this was now in the hands of a civilian bureaucrat. Furthermore, the division of the army into smaller commands resulted in the need for a larger number of military commanders. It is obvious that the increased demand resulted in some individuals being appointed who did not have the ability to fulfil their duties effectively. Yet in the mid-fourth century, when it was led by efficient officers the army retained its ability to defeat any enemy that challenged it.

Stilicho's army

Having examined the military capabilities of the whole of the Empire prior to the reign of Theodosius, it is now possible to analyse the condition of the forces that Stilicho became legal head of in 395. There will be no in-depth analysis of the Eastern army, since this was shortly to return to the East and so no longer be part of Stilicho's forces. All that needs to be remembered is that in 395 the Eastern army, as well as the Western army, incorporated large numbers of non-Romans, many of whom served for long periods in regular units whilst others formed distinct units led by their native commanders for single campaigns.

Prior to the battle of Adrianople the army of the West had maintained its integrity and had been employed to defeat the barbarian attacks that had caused Gratian to be delayed with such drastic consequences in 378. In contrast, the Eastern army had been severely defeated and lost large amounts of men and materiel at Adrianople.

By 395 the army of the West was in a perilous condition. After 378 the situation had turned on its head. Theodosius had managed to reform at least part of the Eastern army and by 382 had used it to force the Goths to capitulate and make the treaty in which they were given land in the Balkans. In a strange twist, their agreement to aid the emperor in his wars actually saved the East, as with the addition of their forces the East was stronger than it had been for quite some time.

Furthermore, whilst Theodosius had been engaged against the Goths, the West had dissolved into one of its many civil wars with the rebellion of Magnus Maximus in 383. When he had crossed the English Channel from Britain into Gaul he had taken with him a core of troops from the island. This had left the island's defences weaker whilst at the same time helping to secure Gaul for Maximus. The death of Gratian had obviated the need for the use of military force, but the balance of forces in the West had been changed to the detriment of Britain's defences.

Once it became clear to Maximus that he could not expect peace from Theodosius, he had collected a large army from the Western provinces, the core of it being the men that he had brought from Britain along with troops stationed in Gaul. When Maximus had invaded Italy Valentinian II had withdrawn with those loyal troops he could muster and travelled east to ask Theodosius for help.

Theodosius had mustered an Eastern army, including his Gothic *foederati*, and invaded Italy. At the battle of Siscia and then at the hard-fought battle of Poetovio, Theodosius had defeated Maximus and brought the rebellion to an end. Although many of the fallen were Western Germanic tribesmen recruited by Maximus for the campaign, the defeat weakened the Western army, and especially those units originating in Gaul and Britain. In contrast, the troops from Italy fought alongside Theodosius and so, presumably, their losses were comparatively light.

Following the defeat of Maximus, the remainder of the Western army were gathered by Arbogast and used in extensive campaigns to quell the barbarians across the Rhine and force them to come to terms with him – including the by now obligatory demand that they provide troops for his armies. Yet these armies too were to meet the fate of their predecessors. Gathered from Gaul and Italy, and including troops originally from Britain and the ever-present Germanic tribesmen, these men fought against Theodosius at the Battle of the Frigidus. Again, after a hard-fought contest over two days the armies of the West were defeated – this time with severe casualties – with the East escaping comparatively lightly, since the heaviest losses were suffered in the first day when the assault was led by the Goths.

The losses incurred by the Western army are all too often ignored by modern writers. Intent on discussing the Battle of Adrianople, the conflict at the Frigidus and its impact on the Western army is usually ignored. Even those who do acknowledge that the East's disaster at Adrianople was mirrored at Frigidus fail to recognize that the battles of Siscia and Poetovio were also major blows for the West.[55]

As a result of the defeats and the continuous demand for troops from Gaul and Britain to reinforce the army of Italy, Theodosius recognized the weakened condition of the Western army and employed the increasingly common method of bolstering the forces directly under imperial control. He upgraded units of *limitanei* to *pseudocomitatenses*. These units were given the title *Honoriani*, and can be found in the Western portions of the *Notitia Dignitatum*.[56]

Yet as usual these troops were probably drawn from the Rhine and/or British frontiers, so weakening these areas still further. Therefore, when Stilicho assumed command in the West, only the recently defeated Italian army was in condition to fight effectively.

It was clear that Stilicho needed time in which to recruit heavily, train and reorganize his demoralized army. The security of the West, at least for the present, was severely compromised. The field army led by Stilicho was depleted and its morale was at a low ebb. The traditional short term solution to the problem of army weakness was to recruit Franks, Alamanni and other Germanic tribesmen into the army. The West was already used to such service and had many Germanic leaders reaching high rank in the Roman army. A mini-campaign along the Rhine would both help to quell potential trouble after news of the defeat at Frigidus reached the tribesmen, as well as promoting a recruitment drive to build up the strength of the army. However, this would take time and until then the Western army was not in a condition to fight and win battles; it would be a while before Stilicho would be able to trust his new forces in open battle. Furthermore, the West was being forced to accommodate the Eastern army, probably with the result of constant minor frictions and the occasional more serious affray between the armies of East and West. The huge combined army in Northern Italy was one of Stilicho's first priorities.

In fact, one of Stilicho's first decisions concerned the Eastern forces that had been brought by Theodosius to the West. Desperate to cut down the need for supplies and eager to avoid at least some of the friction, Stilicho dismissed the Gothic *foederati* and other troops that had been recruited from tribesmen in the Balkans and beyond the Danube and sent them home. Amongst these forces were the troops led by Alaric, according to Socrates made *comes rei militaris* after the battle.[57]

However, it is possible that one group of barbarian warriors that had served under Theodosius and Stilicho remained in the West. It is known that at the end of his career Stilicho had acquired a bodyguard composed of Hunnic mercenaries. This is probably the first occasion when a Roman general formed a unit that was later to be known as *bucellarii*.[58] Although Stilicho was later to become concerned by the use of *bucellarii* by private individuals – especially as the size of these forces, which were in effect private armies, grew considerably – it is unclear at what date and on what scale they were first recruited by Stilicho himself.[59] It is possible that he brought with him a small force of mercenaries after he had served as *magister militum per Thracias* in the East, however this cannot be proved and remains a source of debate.

Army equipment

Unlike earlier periods in Roman history, the type of equipment used by the later Roman army is open to question. This is thanks to a combination of the statement in Vegetius that the army no longer wore armour, a lack of archaeological findings that can be specifically dated to the period, and the confusing picture painted by surviving monuments and funeral *stelae*.

It is worth quoting the passage from Vegetius:

> From the founding of the city down to the time of the deified Gratian, the infantry army was equipped with both cataphracts (body armour) and helmets. But upon the intervention of neglect and idleness field exercises ceased, and arms which soldiers rarely donned began to be thought heavy. So they petitioned the emperor that they should hand in first the cataphracts, then helmets.
>
> Vegetius, *1.20*

Up to the twentieth century the passage has been used as evidence that the later army was no longer equipped with metal armour. This was reinforced by details on sculpted columns, military arches, and other stonework which survives. In these, it was noticed that the troops seemed to wear 'moulded' armour formed to resemble human musculature. This was interpreted as being leather armour moulded to form the same shape as earlier breastplates as used by Greek hoplites.

However, more recent work has overturned this acceptance, and has, for example, shown that the sculptures in many cases have small holes drilled in them to make the appearance of mail armour. Furthermore, it is possible that Vegetius is describing an actual petition from the *scholae palatinae*, a guard unit, that they be excused from wearing armour.[60] In an attempt to emphasize the poor quality of the then–current army, Vegetius simply expanded the request to include the whole of the army, not just a single unit. On the other hand, the remains of copper-alloy scales found at Trier, along with remnants of mail at Trier, Weiler-la-Tour and Indepenta, the latter of which date to the late-fourth or early-fifth century, show that armour was still in use at the time, a point reinforced by Ammianus Marcellinus, who gives many references to individuals wearing armour.[61]

Finally, there is the evidence in the *Notitia Dignitatum*. The drawings that accompany many of the posts included in the document illustrate some of the equipment made in the imperial *fabricae* (factories). These include the items such as helmets and body armour, previously thought to no longer be needed. As a result of these insights, it is now generally accepted that the late Roman army wore heavy equipment equal to that of their predecessors. However, one more caveat needs to be remembered. In these days of mass-production, it is assumed that as soon as a new model of weapon or defence is introduced, the older one is classed as 'obsolete' and withdrawn. In the imperial *fabricae*, the process of production was time-consuming and expensive. As a consequence, items that were no longer 'fashionable' would continue to be issued until stockpiles were used. The overall result is that many items of equipment from earlier periods may have continued in use on a small scale and so remain invisible in the archaeological and sculptural records. This is especially the case with items such as bows, the manufacture of which could take over a year.

Missiles

The missiles used by the Roman army can be divided into long-range and short-range weapons. Long-range weapons included bows, slings, crossbows, and a variety of artillery, although larger equipment was usually reserved for use in siege warfare.

Bows

The most common form of missile weapon was the composite bow, as evidenced by the repeated use of the title *sagittarii* (archers) in the *Notitia Dignitatum*.

Slings (*fundae*) and staff-slings (*fustibali*)

Slings and staff-slings (slings attached to a 4 ft/1.18 m long stave) were also used. However, for whatever reason they were never to form a large proportion of the military establishment, being restricted to a few skirmishers supporting the combat troops.

Crossbows (*arcuballistae*)

A little-used weapon in military circles, although it is more commonly depicted in mosaics portraying hunting, is the crossbow, which may be the weapon described by Vegetius as *arcuballistae*.[62] Other versions of the weapon included the *cheiroballista* described by Heron, which was prepared by placing the end on the ground and pressing on the stock until the string was drawn and a bolt/arrow fitted into the weapon. As with the slings and staff-sling, the crossbow remained little-used by the army.

Artillery

Artillery had been used by the Roman army since at least the second century BC. Later variants included the *manuballista* (previously '*scorpio*' (scorpion)) of Vegetius, a torsion engine capable of accurately firing projectiles for a long distance.[63] The army also produced a version mounted on a cart for ease of transport, known as the *carroballistae*, which is shown on Trajan's column. There is little doubt that these weapons were used in the field, but the regularity and form of their deployment remains open to doubt.

Finally, there were the artillery used only for siege warfare, such as the *onager* (wild ass). These were used only in siege warfare, as they were large and difficult to set up.

Short range

Short-range missiles include mainly those thrown by hand prior to contact. Those with the longest range included a variety of darts, whilst for shorter ranges there was a variety of javelins of various weights and range.

Darts

Included amongst the darts were types called *plumbatae, mattiobarbuli/martiobarbuli, plumbatae tribolatae* and *mamillatae*. All of these weapons were meant to be carried by the infantry and thrown at the enemy as the range closed. In the case of the *plumbatae* the dart had a lead weight behind the head to aid in penetration, whilst the *plumbatae tribolatae* is claimed to have had three spikes emerging from the lead weight so that if it missed a target it still posed an obstacle by presenting a sharp point to an unwary foot or hoof.[64]

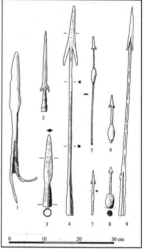

Javelins

There were a variety of thrown weapons that come under the loose category of 'javelin'. These include types called the *spicula*, the *hasta*, the *pila*, the *iacula*, the *verruta* and the *tela*. Despite prolonged investigation, it is clear that the differences between these weapons are unknown.[65] Vegetius suggests that

1. A selection of spear and dart heads. (after Bishop and Coulston/Stephenson).

each man should be issued one heavy javelin (*spiculum*) and one light javelin (*verrutum*).[66] However, it should be noted that these different names may be describing weapons that are almost identical. For example, it is known that the older *pilum* existed in a variety of forms, with some being heavier than others. It is possible, therefore, that Vegetius' report of a *spiculum*, which is usually accepted as the newer name for the *pilum*, actually describes the heavier variety, whilst the *verrutum* is referring to a lighter version of the same weapon.

As a result of these deliberations, it should be noted that although some writers refer to all of these weapons being derived from older variants, the new terminology might be different words used to describe the same thing.

Close-combat weapons
Swords

Earlier Roman infantry had been heavily trained in the art of using the short sword known as the *gladius hispaniensis*. On the other hand the cavalry had been issued with the *spatha*. For unknown reasons, over the course of time the infantry stopped using the *gladius* and by the time of the later Empire the whole army appears to have used the *spatha*. Vegetius also attests to the use of a shorter sword which he calls the *semispatha*.[67] There have been a variety of swords found in the archaeological record that are smaller than the *spatha* and so might in fact be the sword described by Vegetius. Unfortunately, apart from the name he tells us nothing about the weapon, so any correlation

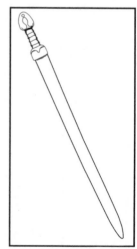

2. Late Roman sword from Köln (after Bishop and Coulston).

between archaeology and Vegetius remains speculation.

A long sword, usually thought to be of Germanic origin, the *spatha* had probably been used by the cavalry due to the need for a weapon with longer reach when fighting from horseback. The *spatha* was a long, double-edged sword which varied from between 0.7 to 0.9 m in length.[68] Although such weapons are usually described as being used in a 'slashing' motion, the *spatha* had a point that made it suitable for thrusting as well.

Spears

It is commonly assumed that hand-held, shafted weapons came in two types: those used as missiles and those retained for use in hand-to-hand combat. However, it is clear from ancient sources and modern re-enactors that there was little, if any, difference between the two types of weapon. This leads to the obvious conclusion that whether they were used as missile or hand-to-hand weapons was determined more by circumstances than by weapon typology. Therefore, any of the weapons described in the section on close-range missiles as 'javelins' could also be used in combat should circumstances dictate. Furthermore, spears such as the *spiculum*, which had a large part of its shaft encased in iron, would be ideal in combat as the iron would protect the wooden shaft from being sheared by enemy swords.

Yet alongside these variants are the types that would be classed simply as 'spears', used by both infantry and cavalry, ranging between 2 and 2.5 m in length (see, for example, Plate 26: the Stilicho diptych).[69] These weapons could either be thrown a short distance or retained for combat, and it is possible that their use can be interpreted as a change in fighting styles from earlier periods, as will be discussed below.

Others[70]

Alongside these weapons others were in use, although in most cases to a lesser degree. Many burials included a short, single-edged knife, which by this time appears to have replaced the earlier broad-edged dagger, the *pugio*. The change in the design of the dagger may simply have been a recognition that its use as a utility tool far outweighed

3. Detail from the sculpture at Gamzigrad. Note that the infantryman appears to have a ridge helmet and that the cavalryman is wearing a pilleus Pannonicus *and carrying an axe.*

its employment as a weapon. As a consequence, it became simpler and was only sharpened on one side.

Alongside traditional Roman weapons were others which were either of unknown origin or were Germanic imports. For example, there is evidence that some at least of the Roman cavalry used conventional axes, as mentioned by Ammianus and Procopius and shown in the *stela* from Gamzigrad and the Column of Arcadius.[71] Unfortunately, these are limited examples of the use of axes and so their distribution remains a mystery. There is also the use of maces, as mentioned by Theophylact.[72] Germanic imports included weapons such as the *seax* (a single-edged long knife) and the *francisca* (throwing-axe), which were slowly being introduced into the Empire, and attested later is the use of the lasso, following Hunnic practice.[73] Again, the extent of their use in the Roman army remains unknown.

Defensive equipment
Helmets

The earlier use of helmets with single-piece bowls spun from a single piece of metal disappears before the middle of the fourth century. Their place is taken by two new forms. The most common of these are the styles termed 'ridge helmets'. Possibly deriving from Persian helmets, they are first found in archaeological deposits dating to the early fourth century, possibly c. AD 325.[74] This date is confirmed by a coin from the reign of Constantine I (306–337) which appears to show Constantine wearing a 'stylized Berkasovo helmet', and by the sculpture found at Gamzigrad dating to the end of the third century (see figure 3).[75]

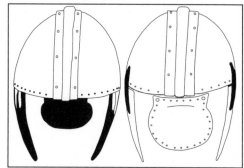

4. Front and rear views of a ridge helmet (after Stephenson).

There are several slightly different styles, all – as in the 'Berkasovo' example just cited – named after the place where they were found. There are many finds from around the Empire, but probably the most important were the up to

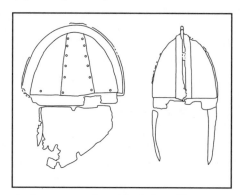

5. A more complex ridge helmet from Conçesti (after Stephenson).

twenty examples found at Intercisa (modern Hungary). There was a variety of styles involved, including the extraordinary version with an integral metal crest known as 'Intercisa 4'. Yet all of these were made using a similar technique, which was to manufacture the bowl as two separate pieces before joining them with a strip of metal along the crown, which gave them their distinctive 'ridge' appearance.

It would appear that many of these helmets had attachable crests, and it may be that the 'integral crest' of Intercisa 4 was either cheaper than buying a separate crest or may have been a way of distinguishing officers from other ranks.[76]

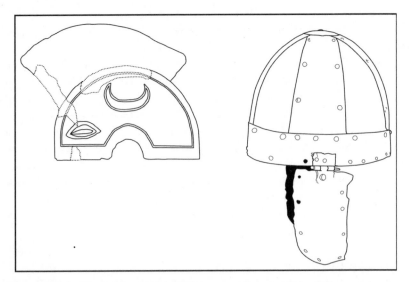

6. *The Intercisa 4 ridge helmet and the Leiden spangenhelm. The differences in construction and the large metal crest on the Intercisa 4 are clear.*

At some point in the fourth century, if not earlier, the Roman army adopted another form of helmet, the *spangenhelm*. Named after the *spangen*, the plates that joined the separate parts of the bowl together, they may be dated as early as the Tetrarchy (c.293–312), although this date is uncertain and they may only have been introduced in the fifth century.

The reason for the change from one-piece bowls to 'ridge' helmets (and possibly *spangenhelms*) is unclear. Earlier claims that this was due to the expansion of the army under Diocletian and the need to supply equipment that was cheaper and easier to make have recently been questioned.[77] It has been pointed out that the new manufacturing method required accuracy in order to join the two halves of the bowl properly, so making them difficult to manufacture. Furthermore, the fact that many of them have traces of silver, gilt and/or paste gemstones attached results in the end product actually being quite expensive.

These claims do not take into account the fact that the process of spinning iron can both weaken it and lead to irregularities in the bowl. This may account for the need to reinforce earlier, one-piece bowls across the brow. Furthermore, unless the manufacture was extremely well controlled, the ensuing bowl could be slightly off-centre and so weak down one half. This would have resulted in a high wastage of material as sub-standard bowls were returned to the forge for remaking. The new methods produced bowls that did not need brow reinforcement and were of a more uniform thickness and quality, since they are easier to work and toughen than the one-piece skull.[78] Although looking to modern eyes, with computer-driven accuracy, as if they are a step back, in production and quality they may actually have been an improvement on earlier helmets.

Although a little strange to modern eyes, there are artistic representations of troops wearing coifs.[79] These appear to be allied to extremely long coats of mail. How they were manufactured or what form they took in reality is unknown, as none have ever been found in the archaeological record.

A final piece of protective headgear was the '*pilleus Pannonicus*' (Pannonian hat). This was a round, flat-topped cap. The earliest depiction is from the coins of Constantine I and from the Arch of Constantine. When seen in detail it is depicted as being 'brown and furry' and was probably made of felt.[80] Of little defensive value in itself, its use amongst the military may have started due to its being used as a helmet lining. It may then have become a symbol for members of the army who were not wearing their helmets. In the porphyry sculpture of the four tetrarchs in Venice, the four emperors are wearing the '*pilleus Pannonicus*', possibly as a sign of their affiliation with the army.

Body defences

It is sad that due to decomposition or rust the vast numbers of helmets that were once common in the Empire have now been reduced to a mere handful. The case is even worse when it comes to body armour. Therefore, what follows is largely conjectural and could be supplanted at any time by new archaeological finds.

Mail

Simply put, mail armour was made by making lots of small rings of iron and joining them to make a flexible, but rather heavy, form of protection.[81] As has already been noted, there have been isolated finds of mail dating from Stilicho's era, enough to show that it was certainly still being made. Monumental evidence suggests that the mail came in two lengths: either a 'short' version covering the shoulders and coming down to around mid-thigh, or a 'long' version which reached to the elbow and the knee.

7. Details from the Arch of Galerius. The figure on the left, who might be the emperor, appears to be wearing a 'muscled cuirass', whilst that on the right appears to have holes drilled in the stone to represent ring mail.

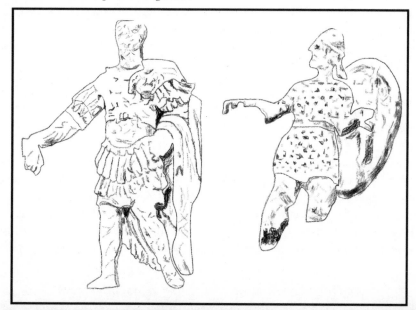

Scale

Scale armour is made by lacing small overlapping plates of metal onto a fabric or leather structure. The result is a form of protection roughly equivalent to that of mail, but without the large amount of flexibility that mail offers. It would appear that the shape of the scale 'shirts' took the same form as those of the mail shirts already described.

'Muscle cuirasses'

It is common for depictions of muscle cuirasses, reminiscent of the styles found in ancient Greece, to be represented on large monuments in this period such as the Column of Arcadius. Historians in the past claimed that these were made of leather, possibly '*cuir boulli*', mainly due to the style of the carvings appearing to depict movement in the cuirass, which would not be represented by metal.[82] There is no evidence anywhere else to support this theory, and there are technical difficulties with some of the proposed materials.[83] Therefore, unless further evidence comes to light, the use of leather remains a possibility, but no more than that.

There are difficulties with accepting depictions of muscle cuirasses on such monuments at face value. The most obvious of these is that the monuments probably owe more to traditional Hellenistic forms of carving rather than representing contemporary models. For example, on the Column of Theodosius troops with muscled cuirasses are also depicted with *pteruges* (sometimes spelled *pteryges*: the 'skirt' of leather which commonly covered the wearer from the hips down, as well as over the shoulders), attic helmets and hand-straps near the rim of their shields. All of these items refer back to ancient hoplite practices rather than reflecting what troops of the time actually wore.[84] Furthermore, a close analysis of the monuments has shown that some of these representations of muscle cuirasses actually appear to represent scale or mail armour. This would reinforce the theory that such monuments were carved with an eye more to the Hellenistic traditions of the past than to the accurate representation of contemporary armour.[85]

A further problem is the manufacturing process. Metal cuirasses needed to be tailored to fit the individual. As a result, the use of such armour is often dismissed by historians as it is extremely time-consuming and expensive to make. However, as many of the monuments no doubt depict senior officials and dignitaries that could afford such luxuries, it is likely that some of these representations may be accurate. Therefore, it is possible to claim that muscle cuirasses may have been worn by rich, senior officers but not by the common soldier.

Lamellar

A surprising absence during this period is that of *lamellar* armour. Made of longer strips of metal wired to a forming garment of cloth or leather, these long scales ran vertically in the armour producing a very firm but extremely stiff protection. Attested both before and after the period, it is curious that between c.350 and 425 there is no evidence at all for this armour, although it was present both before and after. The most obvious explanation is that it continued in use but that there is no written, architectural or archaeological evidence for it. However, the lack of evidence is puzzling.

Shields

The common form of shield used by the Romans was a large oval shape. However, the depiction of round shields on monuments has led to confusion. Some have seen this as evidence that the Roman army was being influenced by Germanic shields, whilst others have suggested that the oval shield was used by the vast majority of troops, with the round shields being used by guardsmen.[86]

Although it is certain that round shields were used by the Romans, their derivation remains uncertain, and we do not know how widespread their use was in the army. No doubt there were practical, regional or fashionable reasons for their distribution, along with their plausible use by guards units as a mark of distinction.

However, there is another form of shield that needs to be examined: the hexagonal shield (see figure 11). These shields appear to have developed first amongst the Germanic tribes, and there are depictions of them on the Arch of Orange, amongst other works. Testifying to their use in Roman settings are the wall paintings from Dura Europus. It is a sign of the adaptability of the Roman army that they were willing to use any item from their enemies' arsenals if they believed it gave them an advantage. In this case, the shield was probably suitable for use by riders with heavy mail coverings, possibly due to its shape and weight.

The *Notitia Dignitatum* lists many shield patterns and labels them as though they were associated with specific units within the army. Although the accuracy of the *Notitia* in this regard is open to question, it is interesting to note that according to Ammianus at the Battle of Strasbourg the Germanic tribesmen recognized Roman units by their shield devices.[87] Although the *Notitia* may be of dubious accuracy, the theory that units had specific shield designs appears to be correct.

Other

The use of segmented armour for the arms and legs of heavily armoured horsemen, the *catafracti* and *clibanari*, is attested and evidenced in the drawings of armour produced by the *fabricae* in the *Notitia Dignitatum* (see Plate 30). However, there is no evidence of its use by the infantry, although this should not be ruled out if the occasion arose.

The *catafracti* and *clibanari* also had armour for their horses. The exact nature that this took is unclear, although evidence from before and after this period suggests that it could be either linen, horn, copper-alloy or iron scales, or even possibly mail, though the latter would be extremely heavy.

Finally, it should be noted that greaves for troops' legs were now extremely uncommon, although again they are depicted both before and after this period, so it is possible that they continued in use.

Chapter Five

The Barbarian Armies

Our knowledge of the Roman army is based largely around conjecture and the interpretation of earlier and later sources. For the armies of the opposition, evidence is even more sparse. Although many writers described the nature of the Germanic forces, these descriptions are usually based more on literary themes and a desire to differentiate between the tribes than on reality. A major example of this is the descriptions of the *francisca*. This classic Germanic throwing-axe is portrayed as being used mainly by the Franks. However, archaeology has shown that it was distributed over a far wider area and so was used by the Alamanni, amongst others. As a result, it should be remembered that our descriptions of the various Germanic 'nations' conform more to ancient historiography and the desire to find a way of differentiating between the tribes than it does to reality. With these observations in mind, it is possible to investigate the German armies.

Organization

We know from later records that after the Germans had settled down in their own kingdoms within the former boundaries of the Empire they settled upon a decimal system for the organization of their armies.[1] This is a reasonable assumption, but it should be remembered that the Germans did not have formal, professional armies comparable to the Romans. Their armies were formed ad hoc based upon the nature of the forces available. Therefore, it is reasonable to assume that these armies were based upon a very informal adoption of the decimal system, with plenty of leeway allowed to take into account tribal and even village loyalties.

Most Western barbarians were farmers.[2] When called upon to serve the majority will have been equipped only with a spear and shield, and probably with missile weapons such as the *francisca* and the 'javelin'. These men will have been called upon by their political leaders, and here we do have some form of insight. The loyalty and service of a cluster of farms and villages were usually owned by one man. These are sometimes called *cantons*.[3] These groups may have been classed as individual tribes by Roman authors. The number of men that cantons could raise would vary, but it is estimated that the largest cantons would be able to muster at most 2,000 men, with the average more likely to be around 1,000.[4] This would tie in with the later 'official' the *thusundifath* (leader of 1,000).[5] It is possible that such men were in charge of 1,000 warriors since this was the number that would earlier have been raised by a single canton. Most of the men would be farmers, however each leader would have had a small retinue, his *comitatus*, maintained out of his own pocket, that served him in military matters. There can be little doubt that the majority of raids would be carried out by a single canton.

Command hierarchy

Each canton would hold a political alliance with a more powerful leader, who is likely to have dominated several such cantons. The larger armies had an even more complex hierarchy, with several layers of such leaders ending in the 'rule' of one or two leaders. Such a situation is described by Ammianus Marcellinus. It is worth quoting Ammianus when he describes the German forces at the Battle of Strasbourg (Argentoratum).

> Now all these warlike and savage tribes were led by Chnodomarius and Serapio, kings higher than all the rest in authority (*potestate excelsiores ante alios reges*) ... these were followed by the kings next in power (*potestate proximi reges*), five in number, by ten princes (*regalesque decem*), with a long train of nobles (*optimatum*), and 35,000 troops levied from various nations, partly for pay and partly under agreement to return the service.
>
> Ammianus Marcellinus, *16.12.23–27.*

As can be seen, Ammianus struggled to translate the German terms into Latin, with *reges* being the only word he felt was suitable. There can be little doubt that the ten 'princes' were the leaders of cantons, and that the 'nobles' were their '*comitatus*'. These ten leaders owed service, or at least some form of loyalty, to five men 'next in power' and these five followed the orders of Chnodomarius and Serapio. Yet although this system seems to follow to some degree the feudal system of the Middle Ages, this is not quite true. Any of the leaders from the canton upwards only owed loyalty to their 'superiors' out of common interests or fear. Each canton was its own political unit with its own, individual agenda. In theory, they could change allegiance whenever they desired. The Romans had in the past exploited these divisions for their own political purposes, and after Adrianople this factor had allowed Theodosius to slowly strip the Goths of men. Theodosius had negotiated with individual cantons and then moved them away from the Balkans. Political disunity was one of the major failings of the Germanic peoples at this time.

Training for command

This system left little room for formal command and control as practised by the Romans, and this must be seen as one of the main downfalls of the Germanic armies at this time. Obviously, the leaders of these groups gained experience from participating in inter-tribal or anti-Roman warfare and raids, but had no formal training, even of the rudimentary form available to Roman officers. Along with the lack of control over their forces, the fact is that the only commands most German generals had held was during raids and small-scale skirmishes. This is not an ideal preparation for leading troops in major battles.

Training and discipline

There were two elements to the composition of the German armies. The first was the *comitatus* of the individual leaders. The *comitatus* was a group of warriors who had sworn to protect their leader. In return, he provided them with food, equipment and entertainment. The main way he did this was to use them to raid either other tribes or the Roman Empire. In this way he collected booty (including slaves) which could be distributed as 'pay'. A successful raid would also attract more men, so enlarging the leader's *comitatus* and making him more powerful.

The men who formed the *comitatus* were retained on a permanent basis and so had plenty of free time in which to practise the art of warfare. Obviously, whether they did or not depended upon the status and nature of their leader. A powerful leader with a reputation for aggressive warfare may have encouraged military training: a less-aggressive leader may not have encouraged practice to such a great extent. Although as a consequence the quality of these troops could vary, potentially they formed a well-trained core of 'professional' warriors who in skill may have been able to match those of the Roman army. However, it is unlikely that they practised warfare on a larger scale, so the Roman legions tended to have the strategic and tactical advantage in large-scale battles.

It may be assumed that only the leaders and the *comitatus* would have had the finances available to buy horses. This would explain two stereotypes of Germanic cavalry. First, their paucity in numbers. Modern estimates suggest that a Germanic army would at the most have a third of its forces mounted. More often than not, the proportion would be lower, probably at around one-fifth.[6] The vast majority of the army were farmers relying on subsistence agriculture and could not afford to buy a horse.

8. A tenth-century illustration showing the overarm use of a spear (left) and (right) a drawing from the Stuttgart psalter showing a ridge helmet and a shield with a 'spiked' boss (after Boss).

The second stereotype is the quality of German cavalry. Vegetius himself comments that the Romans had progressed in their cavalry arm thanks to the example set by the Goths, Alans and Huns.[7] This suggests that the *comitatus* of the leaders did, in fact, spend time training at arms. However, it is noticeable that all of the nations attested as being worthy of emulation are from the East. Here, the cost of horses was lower and more individuals could afford to own one.[8] The nations of the West may have lacked suitable terrain for the rearing of horses and training of cavalry. From an earlier period, Caesar had sometimes had to supply his German mercenaries with horses, since their own were too small for the task.[9] The situation may have been improving over the intervening centuries, since later the Alamanni were renowned as a people 'who fight wonderfully from horseback'.[10] As a result, the armies faced by Stilicho need to be analysed in detail to determine the proportion of cavalry to infantry.

The other part of the army, and by far the largest number, was formed of the farmers who made up the bulk of the German population. The majority were equipped with spears and shields, although the better-off would be able to afford a sword. From the third century on, the deposition of swords becomes slightly more common in burials, although the finds at Ejsbøl North in Jutland has spearmen outnumbering swordsmen by a factor of three-to-one.[11] In contrast, thrown weapons such as axes and 'javelins' were relatively common. These men would have had some training, but mainly under the tutelage of fellow villagers who had seen service before. As a result, the quality of the massed forces of the Germans was variable. This helps to explain why the German warriors were renowned for their first fierce charge. They would attempt to intimidate and break the enemy as soon as possible. If the enemy were not broken, the German forces did not have the quality to maintain a long hand-to-hand battle and the chances were that they would break and run. This was especially the case in terms of the amount of equipment available.

Barbarian society had metalworkers of great skill and finesse. The quality of the goods they produced matched anything that could be made in Rome. However, there were not many of them. The result was that many items, such as swords, which were taken for granted by Roman soldiers, were available in Germania, but on a much reduced volume and at far greater expense. The majority of Germanic warriors could not afford a sword.

Still less could they afford protective equipment. It is interesting to note that a slightly later series of Frankish laws assessed a mail shirt as being equivalent in value to two horses or six oxen, and a helmet the equivalent of one horse.[12] This helps to explain why the Romans forbade the sale of weapons and armour to the Germans, and also why Germanic tribes were so poorly armed. Unlike the Romans, they simply couldn't afford the equipment.

Army equipment

Missiles

The majority of missiles used by Germanic troops appear to be of the hand-thrown variety. Although bows were in use, they were not composite bows as used by the

Romans, Alans, Sarmatians and Huns. Instead, they were simple bows made from a single piece of wood.[13] Archery does not appear to have been an important part of Germanic warfare, and so the evolution of the bow in the West was very slow when compared to the East. Agathias even goes so far as to claim that the Franks did not know how to use the bow.[14] Furthermore, unlike the Huns and the Alans, the Germans did not employ the bow as a mass weapon from horseback. Only individuals used the bow when mounted in the West.[15] Unfortunately, there is also little conclusive evidence for the carrying of more than one spear by the cavalry. Representations in art show only a single spear and ancient authors do not mention the use of javelins by German cavalry. As a result, it may be that German cavalry did not practise missile warfare, instead relying on advancing quickly to close combat and using the spear as a thrusting weapon. This is certainly the impression given by Procopius when describing the later warfare as practised by the Vandals and Goths.[16]

As with the bow, although there can be little doubt that the sling was known to the northern tribes, there is very little evidence for its use during the period in question. Therefore, although a possibility, whether or not it was used by troops in battle remains a mystery.

Alongside the variety of 'javelins' and their heavier equivalents (see below), the main missile weapon favoured by the Germanic tribes along the Rhine was the *francisca*. The *francisca* was a throwing axe carried by a large number of warriors. The axe was possibly first called the *francisca* by Isidore of Seville (c.560–636), who claimed that it was given that name by the Spanish because of its extensive use by the Franks.[17] It is notable that slightly earlier than this Gregory of Tours (c.538–594) called it either the

9. Franciscas. *These drawings show that the* francisca *did not follow a single design, but had variations ccording to when or where it was manufactured.*

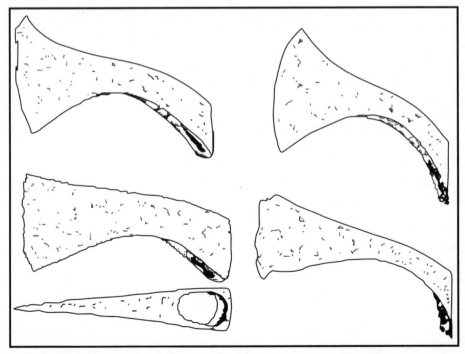

securis or the *bipennis*.[18] Therefore, only by the later time of Isidore was it used extensively by the Franks. Prior to this, it was used by many of the Germanic tribes, and examples have been found in Britain, Alamannia and further East.[19]

One area where the Germans were poorly served was in siege warfare. The tribes of the West did not know how to build artillery or other siege weapons with which to take cities. Instead, they were forced to rely on subterfuge and the betrayal of cities by sympathetic individuals within them.

Combat weapons

Swords

The sword used by the Germans was their own version of the *spatha*, the long, double-edged sword which varied from between 0.7 to 0.9 m in length.[20] Unfortunately, although the German smiths were adept at making these weapons, the results were expensive and so restricted their distribution among the poorer classes of warrior.

Spears

As was stated in the section on Roman equipment, it is commonly assumed that hand-held, shafted weapons were either used as missiles or retained for use in hand-to-hand combat, whereas in reality there was little difference between 'spears' and 'javelins'.

There was also little difference between many of the spears in use by the Romans and the Germans. For example, there seems to be a link between the Roman *pilum* and its derivatives, such as the *spiculum*, and the Germanic *angon* and its equivalents, as found in places such as Vimose and Illerup (third century), and Ejsbøl and Nydam (fourth century – see figure 1).[21] These items also appear to have been widespread and not the dominant weapon of a specific group. The *angon* is found as far apart as Britain and the upper Danube.[22]

However, as with the Romans, the most common item appears to have been a simple spear, which could be used either underarm or overarm by both the cavalry and infantry, and which was c.2.5 to 3.5 m in length with a variety of metal heads fixed to the top of the shaft.[23] These were the most common weapons used by the Germans, being found in large numbers throughout Germania.

Others

One item of equipment carried by German warriors was the *seax*, a 'short-sword' or 'dagger', depending on the dimensions of the individual weapon.[24] A single-edged

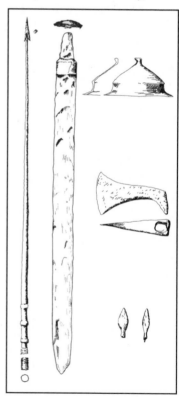

10. *A selection of the grave goods from a single grave at Krefeld-Gellep. The* angon *on the left, the* spatha *in the centre and the* francisca *on the right demonstrate that a single warrior could easily carry a variety of weapons that would later be associated with different 'tribes'. Note also the 'spiked' boss at the top right.*

blade of various lengths, as time passed it gradually became longer and turned into a short sword. However, in this early period it is probably best thought of as a dagger for when the primary weapon, either spear or sword, was lost or rendered unusable. Like the *francisca*, although later identified with a specific people, in this case the Saxons, in the earlier period it was found throughout *barbaricum*, not just in Saxony.[25]

Finally, as with the Roman army there were a number of other weapons that appear to have been used in limited numbers, according to the personal taste of the warrior. Amongst these are axes, clubs and 'warhammers', yet it should be remembered that none of these weapons were common.[26]

Defensive equipment
Helmets
Metal helmets were extremely expensive and beyond the means of the vast majority of warriors, being restricted to the wealthier nobles and *comitatus*. What little evidence there is suggests that they were similar to the *spangenhelms* and ridge helmets used by the Romans. As a cheaper alternative, Ammianus mentions the use of leather helmets which, whilst imperfect, would no doubt be an improvement on going bareheaded.[27]

Body defences
At this point in time it would appear that those few individuals who could afford armour wore either mail or scale styles. However, as mentioned above, these were extremely expensive; they are rarely found in burials, suggesting that they were considered valuable heirlooms rather than items for deposition.[28] However, it is possible that these items slowly became more common as time passed. Yet the process was slow; one of the greatest rewards for a German leader would be acceptance as a Roman officer, and the possible access to Roman arsenals for himself and his followers. This was to become an increasingly common occurrence.

Shields
The shields used by the German tribes appear to have been mainly round or oval in shape and could be anywhere from around sixty centimetres to one metre in height (two to three feet), probably based on personal preference.[29] The traditional hexagonal shape associated with the German cavalry employed within the Empire during the first centuries BC and AD was still in use, but this was to a lesser degree than the other styles. Although other styles of shield are depicted on monuments, in general they appear to be variants of the oval or octagonal styles and may have been relatively uncommon.

In the mid-to-late twentieth century and earlier there was a form of shield known as the 'coffin' shield that was traditionally assigned to the Goths. Although this is now firmly fixed, it has proved impossible to find any examples in either the sculptural or archaeological record. It is possible that some of the monumental evidence was interpreted as proof of the existence of these shields but that these examples have since been re-interpreted as stylistic conventions caused by the problem of perspective. As a result, although it is has proved impossible to determine whether these forms actually existed, the likelihood is that they did not.

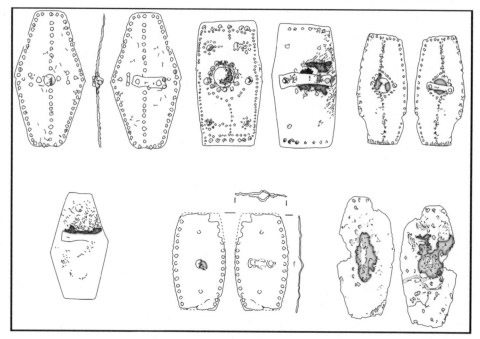

11. A small selection of Germanic shields, showing some of the shapes used other than round or oval (after Czarnecka: not to scale).

It is interesting to note that during this period there was a change in the shape of the shield-boss on Germanic shields. The metal 'boss' was used to cover the hole in the shield made by the hand-grip. Before and after the period of the 'migrations' the boss was usually a simple dome shape. During the migration period, although the dome shape persisted there was a change to a more pointed shape of boss (see figure 10). Warriors would always have punched with the shield when opportunity arose, but the earlier and later dome-shape of the boss implies that the shield retained a more important role as a defensive item. The change in boss shape to a 'point' suggests that the shields were now used in an offensive capacity for punching, implying that for a short period of time during the 'migrations' Germanic warriors adopted a more aggressive attitude to warfare.

Aims and the timing of attacks

It is difficult to judge the feelings of the German peoples towards the Empire. Obviously, with its standing army of trained troops it was a dangerous opponent that at any time could launch major assaults on tribes that had broken the peace or who were considered a threat. In effect, it was an armed camp full of warriors.[30]

However, when the Empire was weak, or when it was already engaged and its attention was focused elsewhere, it was tempting to launch an attack across the border with the intention of gaining plunder: to the subsistence farmers of Germania, the items that could be collected in a successful raid could have been far beyond their hopes of acquiring in peacetime. Furthermore, any leader who led a successful raid would gain a large amount of prestige, as well as having goods and captives with which to reward his followers. As a result, the neighbours of a canton that had launched a successful raid would be tempted to launch an attack of their own to maintain their social standing: should their neighbour become too powerful, he could easily lay claim to their own lands.

Yet this does not complete the barbarian vision of the Empire. The people of the Empire had a standard of living, especially amongst the higher echelons, that was unheard of in Germania. Furthermore, in the previous four hundred years there had been many examples of German warriors who had entered the Empire and risen to high rank, gaining along the way comparatively fabulous wealth. The Empire was 'a land of opportunity with great ease of living'.[31]

The availability of goods that they could not otherwise obtain accounts for the large number of raids and attacks launched against the Empire by German cantons. Yet there was always going to be the problem of when in the year to launch these assaults. The majority of Germanic raids appear to have taken place in winter.[32] Examples include the invasion of Italy by Alaric in 401 (see Chapter 10) and the invasion of Gaul in 406 (Chapters 13 and 14). It would appear that the Germanic tribesmen did not mind the harsh weather, since as farmers at this time of year they had little to do agriculturally. Furthermore, the harvesting of foodstuffs in late summer and autumn resulted in them having provisions to supply them during their attacks.

Strategy and tactics

The main strategy in Germanic warfare when attacking the Empire was the hit-and-run raid. These raids were intended to take captives and plunder before making as rapid an exit as possible from the Empire. There does not seem to have been any long-term strategy to Germanic attacks until after the Battle of Adrianople, and this concerned mainly the aims of the Germanic peoples already within the Empire. Therefore, the strategies these peoples followed will be dealt with on an individual basis when these events are covered in the text.

Germanic tactics were also limited, mainly due to the nature of their forces. With little training and little coordination, their tactics on the battlefield could not become too convoluted, as the troops would easily become confused. As a result, in battle the infantry formed a single line with the cavalry on the flanks. As at the Battle of Strasbourg, the cavalry could be supported by infantry and one flank could rest on difficult terrain, in this case a wood.[33] Furthermore, Strasbourg also shows ambushes were a possibility when the circumstances suited. In this case, the right wing was deployed in the wood, waiting for the Romans to advance before charging them in the flank.

However, the main attack was nearly always delivered by a mass infantry charge along the line. The bravery and physical strength of the German infantry could result in a breakthrough – again as happened at Strasbourg – but if the conflict became one of a long, drawn-out battle relying on attrition, then the Romans with their superior training, weapons and armour, usually had the advantage.

When defeated many of the Western Germans simply fled as best they could, but the Eastern Germans, such as the Goths, adopted the wagon laager of the nomadic peoples to the East. This gave them a secure place to which they could retreat. Furthermore, it acted as a military camp and could be used as a fortification if needed – as happened at Adrianople and later in Greece.[34]

As has already been noted, their inability to build siege engines resulted in their being unable to capture cities unless by stealth or treachery. As a result, they had to resort to blockade and threat. When circumstances were favourable, as after the victory at Adrianople, these tactics could work. If the circumstances were unfavourable, such as when cities were strongly defended, they tended to bypass them to reach softer targets, such as villas.

Conclusion

In conclusion, it would appear that there were very few changes in tactics or strategy between the first- and the fifth-centuries. However, the fact that many individual Germans took service in the Roman army no doubt had the effect of very slowly transforming their organization and outlook. Unfortunately, the nature of any such transformation is not documented by the Romans, who believed that they were facing the same type of foes as their ancestors had faced under Augustus and Marcus Aurelius.

Chapter Six

The Campaign in Illyricum, 395

According to Zosimus, when Stilicho took military command of the Western Empire he was in control of Italy, Spain, Gaul and Africa.[1] It is noticeable that Zosimus does not record him as having command over Britain or Illyricum. The omission of Britain is easy to explain. Zosimus, following Eunapius at this point, was writing after Britain had ceased to be part of the Empire and so, anachronistically, he omits Britain from the list of provinces allotted to Stilicho. The exclusion of Illyricum, however, is different. Until the battle of Adrianople, Illyricum was part of the Western Empire. Only after that defeat was Illyricum allotted to the East, in order that Theodosius should have an undivided command and so be better able to face the Goths. Although at first a success, the measure would prove to be a cause of dispute and increasing tension between East and West during Stilicho's lifetime. In theory, the region was the responsibility of the East, but it was unimportant when compared with the rest of the Eastern Empire. Therefore, whenever the East was threatened, the Prefecture of Illyricum became of secondary importance. This left the West open to attack across the Julian Alps by any enemy who crossed the Danube. As this was where the Goths had been settled, the issue was to remain of primary importance to the West.

Yet tension between Stilicho and the court in the East did not originate with Stilicho claiming Illyricum. When he had left on campaign Theodosius had apparently taken the imperial treasury with him, both in order to pay the troops and to help ease his way in the West once victorious. Claudian unwittingly shows that Stilicho had either kept, or had been accused in the East of keeping, this wealth for himself:

> All the wealth collected here by Theodosius or received by him after the war is Stilicho's alone, and he has small mind to restore what he has once acquired.
> Claud., In Ruf II, 156, a speech attributed to Rufinus

It is probable that Stilicho kept the money for as long as possible, and until the charge became widespread. Only then did he dispatch a large proportion of it to the East, ensuring that his acts were adequately publicized by, amongst others, Claudian.[2]

As was stated in the previous chapter, one of Stilicho's first actions as leader in the West was to dismiss many of the barbarian *foederati* who had fought for Theodosius at the Battle of the Frigidus. In many respects this was a sensible decision; Stilicho was in control of both the Western army employed by Eugenius and the Eastern army now led by Gainas. It is possible, although our sources neither confirm nor deny this, that there continued to be friction and sporadic outbursts of localized fighting between the two groups. It is also likely that any friction centred around the *foederati*, as these were not a part of the Roman disciplinary structure. Of more immediate concern, the presence in Italy of these two large armies was probably stretching the resources of the region to the limit. In the circumstances, disbanding the allied troops was a quick way of easing the logistical burden, as well as helping to reduce tension.

There can be little doubt that the majority of the *foederati* and other allies that were dismissed were unhappy with their treatment. Despite the heavy losses they had sustained during the first day of the Battle of the Frigidus, they had been released without any form of reward for their bravery. Coupled with the lack of rewards was the feeling amongst the *foederati* that they had been used. Roman sources claim that Theodosius had sent the *foederati* into battle first in a deliberate attempt to weaken them.[3] There can be little doubt that this theory was also common amongst the Gothic forces and as a result they were filled with anger and contempt for the Romans.

An added twist was the fact that Stilicho had disbanded the *foederati* in the middle of winter. They were ordered to take the direct route back to their homes. Unfortunately, this was the route that had previously been taken by Theodosius on his way to Italy and it is probable that most of the food in the area had already been consumed.[4] As their journey progressed their supplies began to run very low.

Alaric and his forces

Alaric was one of the leaders of the *foederati* making the journey back to the East. Unlike the majority of his troops, Alaric had been rewarded after the Battle of the Frigidus, probably being given the title *comes rei militaris* (count of the military), but this was not enough. Like most barbarian leaders, he desired a high rank in the Roman army which would give him command of regular troops as well as of his own followers.[5] This would bring him into line with other barbarian leaders serving in the army. No such appointment was offered.

As a consequence, Alaric decided to 'rebel', or at least make a nuisance of himself, by ravaging the surrounding countryside. This would have the dual purpose of putting pressure on the Eastern government to offer him a post and of allowing him to feed his hungry followers by plundering local Roman communities.

When analysing the course of Alaric's rebellion there are two related problems. One is that we do not know the source of his manpower and the other is that we have no idea of the size of his forces. Without knowing one it is impossible to know the other.

The main question concerning the origin of Alaric's army is whether the majority of the Gothic peoples who had been given land in 382 now joined Alaric. Unfortunately, no ancient source gives us specific information on which to base our theories. As a result, some historians see the bulk of Alaric's army as being a mixed force of no fixed origin that combined after the Battle of the Frigidus, whilst others see it as the warriors and families of the settlers of 382.[6] It is easy to sympathize with one modern authority when he states that the question is incapable of resolution.[7]

The 'mixed-force' theory is based upon the fact that once Alaric had declared a rebellion, he will have been joined by many non-Goths who were keen on opposing the

Roman Empire. As the army moved deeper into the Balkans, many disaffected individuals opted to join Alaric; the riot at Thessalonica – for which Ambrose had made Theodosius do penance – was still recent and may have been symptomatic of long-standing unrest in the area.[8] Furthermore, federates of other nationalities that had been released by Stilicho may also have opted to join Alaric. However, the core of the army remained those Gothic *foederati* who had decided to fight Rome again and it was they who gave the new group its tribal identity.[9] The difficulty with the hypothesis is that the relatively small number of Goths in the army should in theory have resulted in them losing their Gothic identity, which remained strong. Therefore, there must have been many Goths with Alaric from the beginning.

The opposite 'Goths of 382' theory is based upon the fact that Alaric's troops were almost invariably called 'Goths'. As a result, the hypothesis is that between 395 and 408 the majority of the forces commanded by Alaric was made up of the Goths who had been settled in 382.[10] This hypothesis suffers from two main problems. One is that he was joined later by federates settled in Pannonia, which may have included Goths settled either before or after 382.[11] The possible presence of Goths who were not settled in 382 weakens the proposition. Alaric's 'Goths' could be named after the Pannonian recruits, not the settlers of 382.

Furthermore, the proposition treats the Goths as a single body with a single aim. However, as was seen in Chapter 2, Theodosius' request for troops from the Goths in 395 had clearly demonstrated the deep divisions in Gothic society into pro- and anti-Roman factions.[12] Moreover, the sheer number of independent Gothic groups at large either inside or on the fringes of the Empire in the years 395–400 is hard to understand if all of the Goths settled in 382 had joined Alaric.[13]

The solution to the dilemma lies with Jordanes. He writes that much later there were tribesmen in Moesia who were known as '*Gothi Minores*' ('Lesser Goths'), possibly in an attempt to distinguish them from the 'greater' Goths of Alaric.[14] This leads to the conclusion that Alaric's rebellion split the Goths. It is almost certain that the main core of Alaric's forces were Goths that had settled in 382 and had opted to rebel. Yet Alaric was not followed by all of the Goths. Many, especially those with young families, opted to remain on the lands granted in 382 and became the *Gothi Minores* of Jordanes.[15] The increased size of the rebellion later attracted those non-Goths attested as being part of Alaric's forces, who were to remain a minority and allow the Goths to keep their identity.

As the size of his forces grew the rebellion quickly became a serious problem for the Roman authorities. Yet in an unforeseen twist, the increase in size now began to put pressure on Alaric. He desperately needed a high-ranking post within the Roman infrastructure in order to reward and protect his enlarged band of followers. However, given the context one point needs to be borne in mind: this was a revolt of a Roman military commander against the government in order to obtain concessions, not of a barbarian against Rome. Alaric was setting the trend for many of the later barbarian generals in Roman service

The new Gothic army was forced to rely on its military abilities to survive. The main hope for their survival lay with the political and military abilities of Alaric. Yet the

Goths were hampered by one major factor: being formed of disparate groups, it would be much easier for the Romans to use political manoeuvres to divide the Goths and so defeat them in detail. As a result, Gothic success or failure depended upon their cohesion and sense of solidarity. As time passed, a large part was played by their being – for the most part – Arian Christians. The fact that they were surrounded by Catholic Christians who thought of them as heretics and unbelievers meant that Arianism acted as a spur for them to retain their cohesion.[16]

Alaric's rebellion

Once he had decided to attack the Empire, Alaric moved towards Constantinople. In this he was acting with the knowledge that the majority of the Eastern forces usually stationed in the Balkan provinces and at Constantinople would be unable to defend the city, as they were currently in Italy with Stilicho. As a consequence, he advanced to the walls of the city unopposed.

The attack could hardly have come at a worse time for the East. There appear to have been bands of Huns and Marcomanni still at large in Thrace and Pannonia, and the Huns described earlier as crossing the Caucasus were now ravaging areas from Armenia and Mesopotamia to Syria (see Map 9). Moreover, with the main Balkan armies still in Italy with Stilicho, Alaric's arrival outside the walls of Constantinople resulted in the capital finding it difficult to defend itself.

However, it is unlikely that Alaric intended to mount an assault on Constantinople. Firstly, the walls were high and easily defended, even by the few troops remaining in the capital. Secondly, he did not want to capture the city but to pressure the government within to give him a legitimate, high-ranking post – which would be unlikely to happen if he had just attacked and sacked the capital.

In one respect, his arrival did have major repercussions. According to Zosimus, in an attempt to save the city (and himself) Rufinus had a personal meeting with Alaric and allegedly gave him permission to ravage the Balkans and Greece as long as he retreated from Constantinople.[17] Although the allegations of treachery are doubtless false, such a meeting is likely to have led to rumours of treachery. Furthermore, those estates in the area belonging to Rufinus remained suspiciously undevastated, although this is more likely a political ploy on Alaric's part than evidence of bribery and corruption from Rufinus. It is probable that Rufinus arranged to pay Alaric a subsidy to retire from Constantinople.[18] However, the idea that Rufinus and Alaric cooperated in order to oppose Stilicho, as is sometimes suggested, is extremely unlikely.[19] Alaric would only have collaborated if Rufinus had given him the post he desired.

Having been paid by Rufinus, it was not in Alaric's interests to remain stationary outside the city walls as it was clear that no command was to be forthcoming. Moreover, no doubt all of the available supplies had been taken into the city and so the area outside would not support his forces for long. Accordingly, he retired from the city and moved into Macedonia, a move which would maintain the pressure on Rufinus' government, since it was in no position to restrict his activities.

Stilicho moves against Alaric

With the East under attack from several different directions, it was clear that Stilicho had the only forces available to move against Alaric. Accordingly, early in 395 he made arrangements for the safety of the West, accepting the submission of the Franks on the Rhine and their continued defence of the area from attacks across the Danube.[20] He may not have needed to pacify the other Germanic tribes on the river at this time, since they had only recently taken part in the defeat at the Battle of the Frigidus and so would have been wary of attacking without evidence of weakness.

With matters on the borders satisfactorily concluded, Stilicho moved East, taking both armies to confront Alaric. The move has sometimes been seen as an early indication that Stilicho had designs on Illyricum, wishing to reverse the allocation of 379 when Gratian gave it to Theodosius to help in the wars with the Goths.[21] However, no such claims were made in the poetry of Claudian and nor do Stilicho's actions actually show any desire to control the prefecture. Only later in his career did Stilicho become aware of the importance of Illyricum and attempt to take it for the West.[22] Claudian's ten political poems between 395 and 404 all interpret events in Illyricum as problems for the Eastern government and fail to make any claim to Illyricum by Stilicho for the West.[23]

If Stilicho was not attempting to annex Illyricum, then his actions in chasing Alaric still need an explanation, and this can be found in Claudian's poetry and by analysing Stilicho's behaviour. It is highly unlikely that Stilicho was using Alaric's revolt as a pretext to moving close to Constantinople before marching into the city and ousting Rufinus. Given the time scale and the distances involved (approximately 1,000 miles between Milan and Constantinople), there is no clear evidence that he was even aware that Arcadius and Rufinus would not accede to his claims to the guardianship of the whole Empire.

Even had he known about their decision, it is more likely that Stilicho simply wanted to put pressure on Arcadius and the Eastern government. By defeating Alaric Stilicho would become the 'hero of the hour' in Constantinople and so gain immense political prestige. He would also highlight the inability of Rufinus and the Eastern government to protect itself in times of crisis. On the other hand, had he entered Constantinople with the combined armies, there was a distinct possibility that he would lose control of at least some of the Western troops, who would then go on to ravage the city as 'revenge' for the losses at the Frigidus. Such a loss of control would obviously weaken any influence he gained in the East due to the defeat of Alaric.

Furthermore, he could not be sure of the loyalty of the Eastern troops to his cause, since they were not under his direct command, instead being led by Gainas. As we shall see, Gainas had his own political agenda, quite separate from Stilicho's, and this may already have been becoming obvious.

One aspect of Stilicho's decision which has received little attention is the possibility that at least part of his decision to confront Alaric was because of Alaric's betrayal. Most historians have tended to forget that it was Stilicho that had 'defeated' Alaric when Stilicho was *magister militum per Thraciam*, and it had been arranged for Alaric to serve in the Frigidus campaign. Stilicho may have been influenced in his decision to march East by the desire to punish Alaric for repudiating the agreement of 393.

There are two final facets of the campaign that have not been considered. From a purely military point of view, the Battle of the Frigidus was a catastrophe for the West. Not only had they lost many men in the fighting, but the morale of the Western army had received yet another blow, now having lost three times in succession to the forces of the East under Theodosius. It made sense for Stilicho to lead the combined armies against Alaric. It would serve several different purposes. Firstly, it could help to unite the two forces were they to fight against a common enemy, so reducing the animosity between the armies of East and West. Secondly, the morale of the Eastern army was high. In contrast, that of the Western army would have been low following their defeat. Taking part in a victorious campaign would help restore the morale and fighting efficiency of the Western troops. A third factor is that faced by all Roman leaders throughout the history of the Empire: the need for a victory to help cement power.[24] Stilicho was attempting to run the Empire in the West, and here the traditional measure of success was defence of the frontiers and prevention of usurpation: political success could depend upon victory in battle over barbarians.[25]

Finally, one of Stilicho's aims was to bring the military system under his personal control.[26] There was no better way of achieving this than of leading the combined forces in a united and victorious attack against Alaric. Success would have helped cement the loyalty of all of the troops to Stilicho, resulting in any political opposition thus being weakened. At all times throughout the life of the Empire successful emperors had acknowledged that the loyalty of the army was paramount.

Therefore, those historians who claim that Stilicho was aiming to march in and conquer the East are almost certainly wrong, and are probably following Rufinus' belief that Stilicho was marching against him. For Stilicho, Illyricum belonged to the East. His reason for 'invasion' at this time was to defeat Alaric, to improve the morale of his army, and to put pressure on the 'ineffective' Eastern government to accede to his claim as *parens principum*.[27]

With some or all of the above considerations to the fore, Stilicho marshalled his forces and moved into Illyricum. As he passed through Noricum and Pannonia Stilicho left troops to act as garrisons to hold the frontier should barbarians on the Danube seek to attack whilst the Empire was in turmoil. Advancing deeper into the Balkans, he confronted Alaric in Macedonia and, when Alaric retreated, Stilicho pursued him to Thessaly. According to Claudian, somewhere in the valley of the river Peneus Stilicho managed to surround Alaric (see Map 11).

The recall of the Eastern forces

At this point yet another incident occurred that has aroused debate amongst historians. According to Claudian, Stilicho was on the point of destroying Alaric when orders arrived from Arcadius in Constantinople, demanding the return of the Eastern contingent of Stilicho's combined army.[28]

In the Claudian version of events, Rufinus persuades Arcadius that he does not need

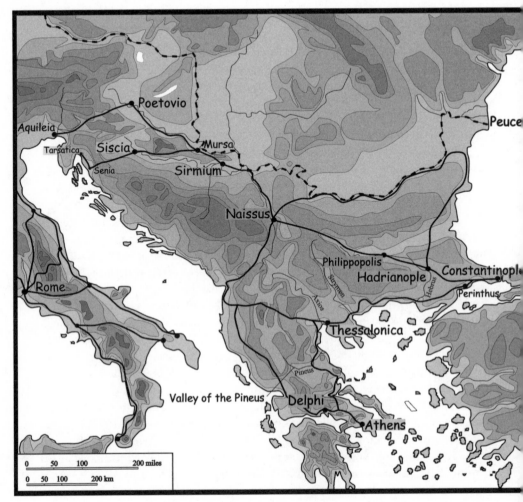

11. Stilicho's first campaign in Illyricum, AD 395.

Stilicho as his guardian, both because he is of age, and because Arcadius has Rufinus himself to guide him:

> Let him leave Illyria, send back his Eastern troops, divide the hosts fairly between the two brothers, and do not be heir to the sceptre only but to your forces.
>
> Claud. *In Ruf. II* 162–5.

In this way, according to Claudian, Rufinus arranged matters so that the Eastern army was recalled right at the point where victory was assured: Stilicho was frustrated at the very moment of his triumph and unwillingly dispatched the Eastern forces back to Constantinople before retiring to Italy. Consequently, Alaric was freed from attack and went on to ravage yet more territory in the East.

The quotation not only describes how Rufinus frustrated Stilicho's campaign against Alaric; it is possibly the source for the claim made earlier that Rufinus persuaded Arcadius that Stilicho had designs to take control of Illyricum.[29] However, this makes too much of the reference to 'Illyria'. It is much more likely that Rufinus used the argument that a refusal to issue the order would mean that Arcadius, although old enough to rule on his own, would always be a pawn to Stilicho's king. Furthermore, Rufinus was extremely afraid of Stilicho: Stilicho had claimed guardianship of both East and West and, according to Zosimus, gave every sign of being ready to accomplish his ends by force if necessary.[30] As a final note, it should be remembered that in this decision Rufinus would have had the backing of the Senate in Constantinople. The Senate in Rome possessed special privileges of long standing, many dating back to the period of the Republic. The Senate of Constantinople had no such connection with antiquity and so were prepared to defend their rights against domination by Stilicho and the West.[31]

Many historians have accepted the story more or less at face value. They have gone on to note that although Stilicho did not have the right to keep the Eastern forces once they had been recalled, he should be blamed for not destroying Alaric prior to returning the troops to the East. Others have claimed that the story is a fabrication, made by Claudian to cover Stilicho's failings as a general.[32] However, these theories tend towards the extremes, either accepting all of the Claudian version or none of it. Yet there would appear to be a middle way.

To analyse the last point of view first, it is unlikely that the story is a literary device to cover Stilicho's inabilities. As was seen earlier, there was probably friction between the troops of the East and West.[33] Accordingly, Cameron claims that Stilicho was losing control of his troops and this is why he could not mount an attack on Alaric.[34] In order to prevent loss of face, Claudian then invented the story of Arcadius' demand for the return of the troops.

This is highly unlikely. The military commanders of the combined armies would expect such an order to be common knowledge. If the order was an invention, then the whole military establishment would have been questioning the legitimacy of the claim. Such doubt would have seriously undermined Stilicho's credibility and it is highly unlikely that he would have countenanced such a risk. Therefore, it is probably safe to assume that the order was actually issued by Arcadius.

On the other hand, although the order was issued, this still leaves areas of uncertainty.[35] These revolve around the continuing problem of using Claudian as the source for events. There are parallels between the claim here and the similar claim used to explain why Stilicho did not bring the barbarians to battle in 393.[36] There is also the need to explain why, if he was on the verge of doing so, Stilicho did not defeat the Goths before sending the Eastern troops to Constantinople.

The major factor is that the composition of Stilicho's forces may have made him cautious about forcing a battle. It is almost certain that many of the regular units of the Roman army at this time included Goths. To use these in a strategy of manoeuvre is one thing: to force them to fight against troops they had recently fought alongside and who were also probably their kinsmen was quite another matter. Furthermore, both the Eastern and the Western forces may have been unhappy at being forced to fight alongside each other having so recently faced each other as enemies. As a further point, this division might have been encouraged by Gainas for his own purposes.

As a consequence, it is unlikely that Stilicho was preparing to launch an attack against Alaric as he did not have either the troops willing to fight Alaric or the confidence in his men to launch such an attack. It is more likely that he was using manoeuvre and the threat of battle as a way of inducing Alaric to negotiate another treaty. It is during these manoeuvres that the order from Arcadius arrived.

Stilicho did not have any option but to obey Arcadius' written orders. Not only did Stilicho not trust his troops to face Alaric in battle, but even if he did it would have taken too long to launch an attack. Any long delay would play into Rufinus' hands, as it could easily be interpreted as a hostile move by Arcadius. Furthermore, Stilicho wanted to become the guardian of both East and West. If his first act for Arcadius was to disobey a straightforward command, there would be little chance of the emperor bowing to his wishes.

It is with this in mind that a little-known piece of evidence from Zosimus needs to be assessed. According to Zosimus (following Eunapius) Stilicho persuaded Honorius to allow him to return the troops to the East, ostensibly to help with the invasions that had happened since he had travelled West with Theodosius.[37] Although the text is confusing and conflates the campaigns of both 395 and 397, there is enough evidence to suggest that Stilicho was aware of the distress of the East and recognized that Arcadius had need for the troops Stilicho had under his command. As a consequence, when the order arrived, he immediately dispatched the troops as required.

As a last point, it would appear that his wife, Serena, and the rest of his family were still residing in Constantinople following the funeral of Theodosius. Although not as pressing as the other reasons already outlined, part of Stilicho's decision to return the troops may have been based on fear that his family may be seized and held as hostages.

On the other hand, the return of the troops may also have been a political gamble on Stilicho's part. He would have known that Rufinus had little military ability and therefore would have known that Alaric would not be faced by the Eastern army led by Rufinus. Moreover, if Rufinus did not trust Stilicho, still less did he trust those military men of ability still in the East, since he had already argued with both Timasius and Promotus. Therefore there would be no military attempt to defeat Alaric and the perception of the Eastern government as weak and ineffectual would be increased.

It is also likely that Stilicho knew of Gainas' ambition, and he may also have known that Gainas would remove Rufinus at the earliest opportunity. Yet Gainas did not have the political support to take the place of Rufinus. Once again there would be political chaos in the East, and this would leave a political vacuum that Stilicho could hopefully use to his advantage.

Stilicho could wait, both in the knowledge that the political situation in the East was extremely unstable, and also that at a later date he would probably still be obliged to deal with Alaric on behalf of the Eastern government and so be seen as the saviour of Constantinople. He may also have hoped the gesture would help his position, as Arcadius could interpret it as Stilicho being willing to act as a supporter rather than an overbearing leader.

As a final point, part of the difficulty with modern interpretations of Stilicho's decision to return the Eastern forces is the inability of modern historians to recognize that their perceptions of ancient warfare may be false. The assumption that 'victory' was founded on 'total defeat in battle' is anachronistic. Although valid earlier in the Empire, the method was no longer the *modus operandi* following the defeat at Adrianople. One of the foundations upon which Stilicho was to build his rule (see below) was that he continued to follow Theodosian policy, militarily as well as politically. Although Theodosius had attempted to fight a pitched battle in 379, he had been defeated. After that he had resorted to manoeuvre and blockade to defeat the Goths. Accordingly, Stilicho had spent the majority of his adult life following the concept of avoiding defeat in battle.[38] There were only going to be two exceptions to this, and in both of them the quality of the forces he deployed was high and the quality of the opposition was relatively low – especially when compared with Alaric and his men.

Despite the (equally anachronistic) claims of Claudian, there was never really any likelihood of Stilicho utterly defeating Alaric in 395. Stilicho would have been extremely reluctant to risk everything by committing himself to the uncertainties of battle. At best, Alaric would have been cornered and forced to negotiate.

Stilicho withdraws to Italy

With only the demoralized army of the West Stilicho would not have felt confident in his ability to defeat Alaric in battle. After all, although the *foederati* had been defeated and taken heavy casualties at the Battle of the Frigidus, they had been on the winning side. In contrast, the forces he now controlled had suffered a heavy defeat at the same battle. In the circumstances, Stilicho may have felt it unwise to risk battle. Also, if Claudian's wording of the order is anywhere near to being accurate, he had received a direct command to leave Illyricum and return to Italy. Stilicho's first response to any imperial order was to obey. Throughout his career he appears to have always followed the legitimate commands of the ruling emperors, relying on persuasion to ensure that those commands followed his own wishes.

The assassination of Rufinus

As Stilicho retired with the Western army back to Italy, the new *magister militum per Thracias*, Gainas, led the Eastern forces back to Constantinople. As they approached the city, the Emperor Arcadius and his *praefectus praetorio Orientis* Rufinus came out of the city to greet them at Hebdoman. Obviously, in the presence of the Emperor Rufinus was unable to deploy his bodyguard of Huns. During the speeches the troops slowly surrounded the imperial entourage. Suddenly, they struck; without warning Rufinus was torn apart by the troops.

Once again the cause of the attack has been widely discussed by historians, although without any consensus being reached. Some have gone with Claudian's account, where he claims that Stilicho was working behind the scenes to eliminate his main rival. In this version, Stilicho was responsible for giving the orders for Rufinus' death. As part of the scenario it is sometimes assumed that Eutropius was in a political alliance with Stilicho at this time, since he took the reins of power from Rufinus and there followed a short period of cooperation between the governments in Milan and Constantinople.

Yet on reflection this would seem unlikely. The only situation in which it would work would be where Stilicho knew Theodosius was about to die and also knew that Rufinus would be a major obstacle in the path of his ambition to control the whole Empire. He would have needed to have known that Arcadius would recall the troops. He would even have needed to know in advance who he could trust in the fast-changing world of imperial politics. Even then, the political arrangements would have had to have been extremely swift, since there was a limited amount of time between Stilicho's claim to be *parens principum* of the whole Empire, his marching West and the request by Arcadius that the Eastern army be returned to Constantinople.

The main beneficiary of Rufinus' fall was Eutropius. As a consequence, it has been suggested that Eutropius was the man who arranged for the troops to kill Rufinus, having as his agent the Gothic general Gainas. Yet, as we shall see, the nature of Eutropius' fall would seem to preclude the possibility, as Gainas does not seem to have been a willing ally. The nature of politics in the imperial courts resulted in ever-changing alliances, as will be seen below.

Others have proposed that Stilicho made arrangements with Gainas to assassinate Rufinus, holding Rufinus responsible for the recall of the troops and Alaric's survival in the Balkans.[39] The concept has merit: when the order arrived it is likely to have made both men angry and frustrated. Obviously, Stilicho would have now become aware that Rufinus was going to block his attempt to become sole guardian of the Empire. Gainas is likely to have been annoyed, since the order blocked the attempt to force Alaric to battle, a battle in which Gainas was likely to have gained a large amount of credit in the East.

All of these accounts, however, fail to take note of two vital pieces of information. The first is found in Claudian. In his attack on Rufinus, Claudian does not actually claim that Stilicho gave the order to either the troops or their commanders to kill Rufinus. Instead, he states that the troops did it on their own out of a sense of loyalty to Stilicho.[40] The concept that the assassination was not undertaken for political motives is reinforced by Philostorgius, who states that Rufinus was killed by the troops partly by the orders of Stilicho, partly in indignation at his scornful treatment, since 'he had been caught sneering at them'.[41] Although it must be accepted that Philostorgius might be following in the footsteps of Claudian, it is interesting that no other individuals are mentioned in connection with the assassination.

As a consequence, it is most likely that the assassination of Rufinus was carried out without overt political motives, except possibly on the part of Gainas. Instead, it should be seen as a reaction by the troops to Rufinus' treatment of them, possibly exacerbated by the superior treatment they had received under the leadership of Stilicho.[42]

The political situation in the East quickly clarified and settled down. The *praepositus sacri cubiculi* Eutropius now benefited from his support of Arcadius.

Having earlier supplied Arcadius with a wife, Eutropius was able to step into the vacuum created by Rufinus' death. He assumed all of Rufinus' powers and slowly began to extend his influence at court.

Gainas was maintained as the *magister militum per Thracias*. Although this was probably a step forward in his career, he may have been given the title but no actual troops to command, these being taken by Eutropius for a campaign against the Huns in the East.[43] Eutropius provided a staff, but it would seem that Gainas had to raise fresh troops himself. Being given such a nominal command is unlikely to have been appreciated by one of the leading military commanders in the East.

Chapter Seven

The Rhine and the Greek Campaign, 396–7

Stilicho

At the end of the campaigning year of 395 Stilicho arrived back in Italy. It was obvious that he did not have the resources to deal with Alaric, although this remained one of his top priorities. Yet in some ways this may have been a relief, as by this time he must have been aware that tensions on the borders along the Rhine were becoming high. A campaign on the Rhine frontier would be advantageous in three respects. The first is that he would be able to secure the frontier against attack, a necessity for when he reopened hostilities against Alaric in the East. The second is that a successful campaign would allow him to recruit troops from submissive kings, so reinforcing the army that had been weakened by the West's successive losses in civil wars to Theodosius. The third is that it would give the army a successful campaign and so begin the process of restoring the morale damaged by previous defeats.

The East

Either before the end of 395 or early in 396 messages arrived in Milan from Constantinople. We have no clear indication of the extent or precise nature of the diplomatic exchanges that took place at this time. It is clear that both Stilicho and Eutropius agreed on many things. In some ways Eutropius may have been a better political and strategic leader than Stilicho. He may have realized eight years before Stilicho that the Prefecture of Illyricum was vital to the defence of the West.

Illyricum, and especially the Diocese of Pannonia, was extremely important to the defence of Italy.[1] Cassiodorus goes so far as to state that Raetia and Noricum were the 'bars and bolts' of Italy.[2] By the fourth century the *Claustra Alpium Iuliarum* (Fortifications of the Julian Alps), which had probably been founded under Constantine, had been extended to secure both the defences into Italy and the logistical land links into the Danubian provinces.[3] Furthermore, if enemies were at large in the Balkans, Illyricum was vital to the defence of Italy as it allowed the defenders to garrison and patrol both sides of the Julian Alps. This was essential in that it resulted in the Alps being the second line of defence, so any defeated troops could fall back and defend the passes against pursuing enemies. Furthermore, knowing that the Alps would be defended would act as a deterrent to further attack. As a final point, control of both sides of the Alps would enable the defenders to monitor the line of approach of enemy forces and so allow them to mount an ambush as the enemy crossed the passes

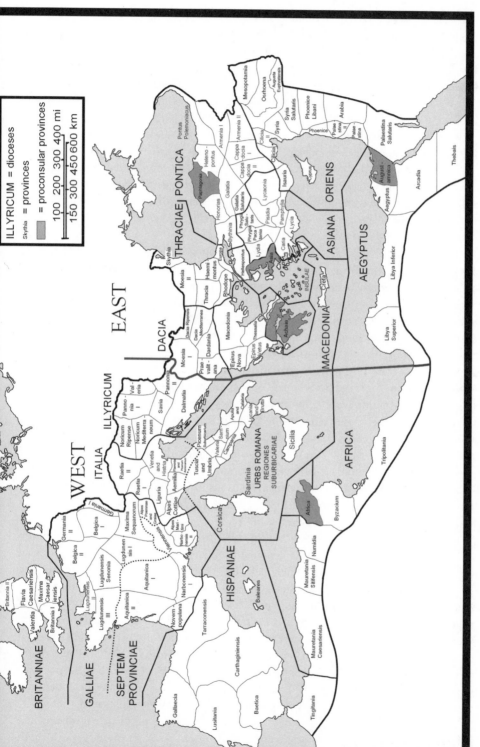

12. *The return of the Diocese of Illyricum (previously Pannonia).*

– as evidenced by Arbogast's ambush of Theodosius at the Battle of the Frigidus.

As long as the Empire was united and the East was strong, the control of Pannonia was irrelevant. The East would, in part, be using the resources and revenues from Illyricum to defend the diocese from external attack. However, once the East was no longer able to control the provinces – as had happened following the Gothic War of 376–82 – Italy suddenly became a frontier province that was exposed to fast attacks across the Julian Alps, and had little defensive capability with which to repel them.

In addition, there was the obvious fact that it supplied taxes to whoever governed it. Finally, and much more importantly, Illyricum was a valuable source of recruits. Without control of the prefecture, which was renowned for its men and horses, the Western army had major problems recruiting enough quality troops for the army.[4] Eutropius may have come to the conclusion that when Stilicho had attacked Alaric in 396 at least part of his actions was determined by the need to protect Milan and Italy from Alaric.

These considerations may have affected Eutropius in his decision to give part of Illyricum back to the West. However, there was another pressing reason for Eutropius to cede the provinces to the West. By transferring responsibility for their defence to Stilicho and the West, the provincial garrisons that were in place to protect against attack, both from Alaric and across the Danube, could be withdrawn and employed by Eutropius in his projected campaign against the Huns in Asia Minor, or at least be used to garrison Constantinople whilst he was away.[5] Archaeology suggests that after 394 the Alpine passes were no longer systematically defended, possibly as the garrison was withdrawn to the East and Stilicho was only sporadically able to man the defences due to other commitments keeping his troops employed elsewhere.[6]

As a consequence, Eutropius came to a formal agreement with Stilicho which transferred the Diocese of Pannonia (Pannonia, Noricum and Dalmatia) from the East to the West. Now Stilicho had a buffer-zone between the heart of his Empire and Alaric. By ceding Pannonia to Stilicho, Eutropius might have been hoping that Stilicho would overlook his claims to the East and focus instead upon the problems of the West. In this, at least for a short time, Eutropius appeared to have been successful, as Stilicho was to spend all of 396 campaigning in the West.

Eutropius may also have hoped that this concession would remove Stilicho's desire to face Alaric in battle: the East had enough problems with both internal and external difficulties, without including Stilicho and the Western Empire amongst them. The Huns were still ranging without check through the East and Eutropius seems to have seen them as a far greater danger than Alaric, and there were ongoing problems in negotiations with the Persian Empire. He may also have decided very early that a sure way to cement his position in power would be to lead an army against the Huns and secure a victory in person. Yet this could only be achieved with both Stilicho and Alaric removed as threats. By giving Stilicho the Western provinces of Illyricum, he may have hoped to pacify the head of the Western government. The only way he could gain control over Alaric would be by giving him the military position he craved.

In some modern works covering this period there is a problem concerning the perceived discrepancy in the allocation of the title of *praefectus praetorio Illyrici* by both

East and West. In the West, at some time either late in 396 or early in 397, Stilicho appointed Theodorus as *praefectus praetorio Italiae, Africae et Illyrici*.[7] Simultaneously, beginning in June or July 397 until 12 November 399, Anatolius was appointed as *praefectus praetorio Illyrici* in Constantinople.[8]

This has been interpreted as a response to Stilicho being declared *hostis publicus* (public enemy) in the East and is further used as evidence that even at this early stage Stilicho wanted to control Illyricum; his designation of Theodorus is seen as a counter to that of Anatolius and is interpreted as a sign of increasing tensions between East and West.[9] Yet a close scrutiny of events shows that this is not the case.

The first fact that is usually overlooked is that Theodorus' appointment dates to before the Greek campaign of 397 and the declaration of *hostis publicus*.[10] The appointment does not appear to be a response to the declaration in the East, and so should not be seen as having ulterior motives.[11]

Furthermore, the post of *praefectus praetorio Italiae, Africae et Illyrici* (praetorian prefect of Italy, Africa and Illyricum) is a traditional post in the West, as evidenced by the insignia within the *Notitia Dignitatum*. As a consequence, the appointment should simply be interpreted as Stilicho allotting a traditional post to Theodorus. This was necessary as there was now a need to administer the Illyrican Diocese of Pannonia that had been returned to the West by Eutropius. The Eastern Prefect Anatolius remained in control of the remainder of Illyricum, but it should be acknowledged that Anatolius was the only one of the two allowed to pass laws, and these laws applied throughout the prefecture as long as they did not interfere with Western control. All known laws concerning Illyricum of this period are rendered in Constantinople.[12]

The Army

Before Eutropius could exert any control over Alaric he needed to stamp his authority on the East, and especially on the army. When Eutropius assumed control after the fall of Rufinus he had a major dilemma. The East once more had a large army to either protect the Balkans or to attack the Huns, yet it was stationed in Constantinople. As a consequence, any individual given control of this large force could immediately use it to gain more influence in the governing of the Empire. This situation needed to be avoided and any general's potential influence minimized.[13] To do this Eutropius would have to act immediately as any delay would play into the hands of the military administration.

The immediate outcome was that Eutropius continued to employ Rufinus' method of using non-military means of solving military problems. The main danger to his authority was Timasius, the *magister equitum et peditum* who had served Theodosius in the Frigidus campaign alongside Stilicho. Early in 396 Eutropius arranged for allegations of treason to be brought against Timasius, and he was exiled before, allegedly, dying whilst trying to escape. At the same time another leading general, Abundantius, was also convicted and exiled. The latter case shows that Eutropius had little time for sentimentality, as it was Abundantius that had gained him his place in the imperial household.

Having removed the two leading military men in the East, Eutropius was now able to fill the ensuing vacancies with men of his own choosing. Furthermore, his actions in removing military leaders also removed military opposition to another plan that he had. It would allow him to open negotiations with Alaric concerning his desire for a post in the army.

At the same time as dealing with the problems caused by the army, Eutropius was certainly promoting men of his own choosing to senior positions within the civilian bureaucracy. Alongside these appointments he had some of the duties of the *praefectus praetorio Orientis* transferred to the *magister officiorum* in order to weaken the power of the prefect and ensure that the successors to Rufinus' post did not succeed to his level of influence.

Unfortunately for Eutropius, the trials of his opponents and the overhaul of the bureaucracy and the positioning of his own men took time. It is probable that he was not securely in control until late in 396, so any negotiations with Alaric were opened either late that year or early in 397.[14] In the interim, Alaric had not been idle. He had moved his forces into an area little-touched by barbarian attacks across the Danube.

396

Alaric

With Stilicho busy elsewhere and the Eastern army focused upon the Huns rampaging through the East, Alaric appears to have been left with a virtually free hand. He realized that any attempt upon the West would only provoke Stilicho into another major campaign, so a foray into Italy was out of the question. Yet although he must have appreciated that he had no chance of taking Constantinople, he still needed to maintain pressure on the Eastern government to assign him a command. Alaric decided to lead his men into an area long untouched by war, and so rich in the booty and supplies his followers needed.

Taking the defenders by surprise, he marched through the pass at Thermopylae and entered Greece. Zosimus claims that Alaric was allowed to move through the pass due to treachery on the part of Antiochus, *proconsul Achaiae* (proconsul of Greece) and Gerontius (commander of the garrison at Thermopylae). Both of these individuals had allegedly been appointed specifically for the purpose by the treacherous Rufinus. This should not be taken at face value; in Zosimus most reverses are described as being due to treachery.[15] It is more likely that Gerontius was appointed to command the pass at Thermopylae with only a small force, either detached from Stilicho's army or direct from Constantinople. Although certainty is impossible, it may be that he had the forces described by the *Historia Augusta* as being given to the future Emperor Claudius II in the third century. If so, he had command of two hundred infantry, one hundred heavy cavalry, sixty other cavalry, sixty archers and one thousand raw recruits.[16] With so few troops, and with the majority being raw recruits, it is obvious why Gerontius did not attempt to stop Alaric and his larger force of seasoned veterans.

Alaric quickly terrorized Greece: the only major cities left untouched were Thebes and Athens. However, the nature of these 'attacks' is uncertain. The behaviour of his forces in Greece does not imply that they wanted land distant from the Hunnic threat, but that Alaric was still hoping for a post in the Roman army.[17] As a consequence, it is likely that he did not attack and slaughter the inhabitants of Greece. It is more likely that he followed the same policy as that adopted by the Goths between 378 and 382, where they threatened to attack cities unless they were provided with goods and provisions. The theory that Alaric intended to remain in Greece is certainly possible, but unfortunately it is impossible to prove, either one way or the other.[18]

Stilicho

When Alaric moved south, Stilicho would have been certain that Italy was, for the present, secure from attack. According to Paulinus, early in 396 Stilicho was in Milan.[19] He had two main concerns. One was to cement his position as head of the Western government. This was actually to be relatively easy. Alongside his control of the army, Stilicho was surrounded by men like himself, the protégés and appointees of Theodosius. After Theodosius' victory at the Frigidus Theodosius was determined to maintain control of the Western half of the Empire. Accordingly, he had appointed trusted individuals to positions of power in the West. Stilicho continued the policy of appointing men who had been involved in Theodosius' councils and who, like Stilicho, could be relied upon to continue the policies of Theodosius. He simultaneously appointed individuals from Italy in order to maintain the support of the Senate. In these appointments he was helped by Symmachus, who continually provided suggestions and recommended individuals from the Western court to serve in specific posts.[20]

Stilicho managed to achieve a balance between men that he knew and who had served under Theodosius and new appointments made from within the Senate in order to maintain the goodwill of that body. It further helped to integrate the Senate at Rome, which consisted of many of the richest men in the West, with the court at Milan.

Stilicho's second major concern was the poor state of the army.[21] Between 387 and 394 the Western army had suffered three major defeats at the hands of Theodosius, two against Magnus Maximus and one against Arbogast and Eugenius. As if that was not enough, in 388 – when Magnus Maximus had taken large numbers of Gaulish troops to Italy to face Theodosius – the Franks had invaded across the Rhine. They had attacked the provinces of Germania and Belgica before retiring across the frontier. A Roman counter-attack had defeated some Franks who had remained at large in the Empire, but when the army had crossed over the Rhine it had been defeated by Marcomeres and Sunno, the leaders of two Frankish cantons.[22] The cumulative effect of the repeated defeats will have seriously eroded Roman morale and confidence.

Shortly after these defeats Arbogast had become head of the Western government and he had agreed a treaty with Marcomeres and Sunno, who may also have had hegemony over other tribes in the area. Early in his rule Arbogast had led the Western army into Frankish territory to ensure their cooperation and loyalty, and then prior to the civil war in 394 Eugenius had also led a campaign along the Rhine before he faced Theodosius in battle. Again, this had been to ensure that fear restrained the Franks from attacking whilst Eugenius and Arbogast were facing Theodosius.[23] The military displays may have been a success, since there is no evidence of an attack by the Franks in 394 or 395. However, the overall result of the campaigns of Arbogast and Eugenius was an increase in tension on the frontier. If the frontier was to remain stable, this could not be allowed to continue. When he was free from the threat of invasion by Alaric, Stilicho gathered his army and led a campaign along the Rhine.

Details of the campaign are sparse, but, according to Claudian, the attack was effected at maximum speed, possibly in order to catch the tribes unawares:

> Descending from the river's source to where it splits in twain and to the marshes that connect its mouths he flashed his lightning way. The speed of the general outstripped the river's swift course, grew as grew Rhine's waters.
>
> Claudian, *Stil I*, 198–200

The impression is reinforced by the claim that Stilicho set out 'with the moon yet new' but returned 'or ever it was full'.[24] There is further a description from Orosius, as outlined by Gregory of Tours, which has Stilicho 'crushing' the Franks and travelling around Gaul 'as far as the Pyrenees'.[25]

Although no doubt the descriptions are embellished, it would appear that Stilicho's movement was surprisingly swift: the speed of the campaign caught the tribesmen by surprise. There is no evidence in any of our sources for fighting between the Romans and the tribesmen, yet Marcomeres was 'arrested' and exiled to a villa in Tuscany. Sunno escaped, but then reappeared amongst his own tribe, claiming sole rule and declaring that he wanted vengeance against his brother's captors. Unfortunately, his people did not agree and killed him.[26] As a final piece of evidence for the quality of the campaign, according to Claudian the tribes along the Rhine offered their children as hostages and begged for peace.[27]

For Claudian, the main aim of the campaign was securing recruits.[28] Stilicho's shortage of recruits is supported by the laws issued against deserters.[29] There is no doubt that this was – probably – the major purpose of the campaign. One of the overriding factors in the last decades of the Western Empire was the shortage of recruits. However, as he was still insecure, Stilicho was unwilling to antagonize the Roman senators and major landowners by ordering them to release men from their estates for the army. Instead, the senators gave money and this was used to levy German recruits. In fact, Claudian was able to profit from this, using it as a way of winning support for the recruitment of barbarians from a conservative class who were, as a whole, unhappy with using 'barbarians' in the army.[30] Yet to a competent general, there would be other considerations to be taken into account.

Stilicho still wanted to defeat Alaric in battle. In order to achieve this he would need to muster as many troops as possible. As a consequence of these deliberations, Stilicho concluded that a successful campaign along the Rhine would intimidate the barbarians into submitting and make it less likely that they would attack across the frontier. As a further result, Stilicho would be able to withdraw extra troops from the Rhine frontier for the coming campaign.

The claim that Stilicho was 'desperately scraping together armies of half-trained, half-reliable Germanic troops to counterbalance the Visigothic "allies"; denuding frontier defences well below the danger level; and ignoring the fears and miseries of many provincial populations' may apply to his later years, but is not yet appropriate.[31] He had ensured that, for the near future at least, there would be no trouble along the borders with the Germanic tribes.

One other factor may have been included amongst the reasons for the Rhine campaign. In the previous decade the army of the West had suffered many defeats. One of the lessons learned by the Romans was that if your army was defeated in a major battle, one of the best ways of restoring morale was to win a series of lesser skirmishes and so get the men used to achieving victory again. Stilicho was confident enough in his abilities to lead such a fast campaign in the West. Although the campaign did not include any fighting, the mere fact that a threat was enough to overawe the barbarians would have been a welcome change to the troops. This morale boost was especially needed as it is certain that Stilicho still wanted revenge on Alaric for his 'desertion' of the Roman army. To face Alaric, who appears from his early reputation to have been considered a formidable foe, Stilicho would need his men to be confident of victory.

397

At the start of the campaigning season of 397 Stilicho gathered his army, which was now composed of his regular forces plus the Germanic troops recruited in 396, on the Adriatic coast – probably at the main fleet base in Ravenna.[32] At the same time, ships were ordered to assemble to transport the force across the Adriatic. In a short space of time Stilicho was ready to move, but was held back by personal considerations. Bishop Ambrose was mortally ill and Stilicho was concerned enough about the welfare of his most powerful supporter to wait on developments before moving.[33] When Ambrose finally passed away in early April 395, Stilicho was finally free and set sail for Greece.[34]

There have been claims in the past that Stilicho was intent from the first upon annexing the whole of Illyricum at least from the East, and that the invasion of Greece was an 'attempt to wrest territory from the East'.[35] There is no validation of this theory in the sources, nor in an analysis of Stilicho's actions. He was simply following his primary instincts, attempting to protect both halves of 'his' Empire from the ravages of Alaric as well as putting pressure on the government in the East. If he could defeat Alaric he could show that he was more effective than the ministers in Constantinople and this would show to Arcadius that he would be better off with Stilicho as guardian. Furthermore, he still had not forgiven Alaric for his 'treachery' in rebelling in 395, and he accordingly sought to re-establish his supremacy over the Gothic leader. Finally, a quick victory would enable Stilicho to enrol Alaric, or at least the troops he commanded, in the much-depleted Western army.[36]

The invasion

Stilicho set sail with the fleet and landed at Corinth, which Alaric had already sacked.[37] It is probable that Stilicho expected and received a welcome from the Greeks, since he was coming to save them from barbarian oppression. Upon his arrival, Stilicho wasted

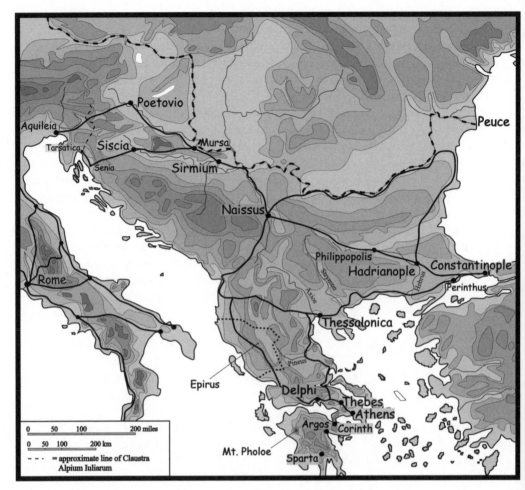

13. Stilicho's campaign in Illyricum, AD 397.

little time and advanced on Alaric. Alaric quickly withdrew. Unlike the campaign of 395, Claudian attests that this time there was fighting between the forces of Stilicho and Alaric.[38] The fact that Alaric was forced to withdraw suggests that Stilicho's men had the better of these encounters, although the claim by Claudian concerning the large numbers of Goths killed in battle is doubtless an exaggeration to flatter Stilicho. Within a short time Alaric had been trapped on Mount Pholoe in Arcadia.[39]

It is at this point that the situation once again becomes blurred by contradicting sources. There are two major variations on what happened next. Claudian claims that Stilicho was – for the third time – on the verge of defeating Alaric when he was ordered to leave Greece, this time by Arcadius following Eutropius' advice.[40] However, there is a different tradition as reported by Zosimus (quoting Eunapius) of Stilicho once again losing control of his troops and so allowing Alaric to escape.[41] Added to this there is one further, minor, complication: there is the need to account for Eutropius'/Arcadius' decision to declare Stilicho *hostis publicus* (public enemy). This final piece of evidence is obscure but vital.

In the main, historians have tended to follow one of these two traditions.[42] Yet a close examination of the debate suggests that both traditions contain an element of truth. Furthermore, it is possible to amalgamate the two traditions into a single version that includes the key elements of the story. This allows acceptance of both traditions, and indicates that the ancient sources are merely giving a version of events that reinforces their own, prejudiced, view of Stilicho. Any evidence that is contrary to the story they want to tell is simply ignored – a sin of omission rather than an outright falsification.

As a result, what follows is an attempt to fit the different accounts into a single chronological narrative, explaining the political actions and the relevance to the sources as the story unfolds. However, it should be remembered at all times that this chronology is not secure and the events described are thus open to different interpretations.

The campaign

In early 397 Stilicho landed in Greece. Unfortunately, this was not part of his jurisdiction and by acting in this way he was certain to arouse the enmity and fear of Eutropius in Constantinople. In fact, it is probable that this sort of event is exactly what Eutropius may have been guarding against when he ceded Western Illyricum to Stilicho early in 396. Once he had learned of Stilicho's landing, Eutropius knew that Stilicho was intent on fighting Alaric again. This would seriously damage the ongoing negotiations to bring Alaric into the mainstream of the Roman military command structure in the East. Therefore, Eutropius played on Arcadius' fears and so secured an order for Stilicho to leave the area and return to his own 'dominions'. The idea that Arcadius could be coerced into sending such an order is not surprising; after all, there were centuries of imperial tradition which demanded that 'internal' politics should take precedence over 'external' enemies. Even though Alaric was inside the Empire, he was not as yet part of the bureaucratic and military inner circle. Therefore, it is highly likely that Arcadius, under the prompting of Eutropius, actually did send an order telling Stilicho to leave Greece. Claudian might be exaggerating on some aspects of the order, but the claim is not entirely a fabrication.[43]

However, there was now a major difference between events in 395 and those in 397. In 395, Stilicho accepted the order to return the Eastern army to Constantinople and himself returned to Italy. With his new, entirely 'Western' army to support him, Stilicho must have decided that, this time, he would force Alaric to submit before returning to Italy. As a consequence, his forces attacked Alaric and, in a series of small-scale battles, forced him to retire northwards. Again, in describing the number of Gothic dead Claudian exaggerates the facts, but there is no falsifying of evidence.

When it became clear that Stilicho was not following the emperor's orders, fear and tension grew in Constantinople. Apart from ruining the ongoing negotiations with Alaric, Eutropius would have interpreted the attack as part of a long-term plan whereby Stilicho would first defeat Alaric and then arrive in Constantinople expecting to be installed as the *parens* of Arcadius. Furthermore, Eutropius had recently organized the dismissal of two Eastern generals, both of whom may have been allies of

Stilicho.[44] He simply could not afford to allow a victorious Stilicho to enter the city.

Accordingly, Eutropius again worked on Arcadius' doubts and fears. This time, Arcadius was persuaded to declare Stilicho *hostis publicus*.[45] This ensured that there would be a hostile reception for Stilicho in Constantinople should he advance on the city having defeated Alaric. Again, this followed in the tradition of seeing internal rivals as the major threat to an emperor's rule. The theory also gives a plausible reason for such a drastic pronouncement. It instantly put pressure on Stilicho to leave Greece, as well as indicating clearly to Alaric that Stilicho's attack was not endorsed by the Eastern government. As a final note, Stilicho lost the houses, goods and lands that he held in the East, since as an enemy of the state they were forfeit. They were probably confiscated by Eutropius.[46]

The declaration created a major obstacle for Stilicho. Apart from everything else, it was probably expected that the declaration of *hostis publicus* would be shortly followed by a declaration of war.[47] He would be unable to claim to be acting in Arcadius' best interests if his actions caused the opening of hostilities between Honorius and Arcadius. Unfortunately, his plans now received a second setback. Having blockaded Alaric and begun the act of starvation he appears to have settled down to await the inevitable. In fact, Zosimus goes further than this, claiming that:

> He forced the barbarians to flee to Pholoe, where he could easily have starved them out had he not devoted himself to luxury, comic actors and shameless women ...
>
> Zosimus 5.7.2.

The delay gave Alaric time to act. He used a portion of the spoils taken in Greece to bribe some of Stilicho's troops to allow him and his men to escape. This concept also helps to explain the reference in Claudian to Alaric's attempt 'to corrupt the Roman army with gold'.[48] Furthermore, once it was perceived that Alaric's camp was deserted, Stilicho lost control of his forces, who attacked and pillaged the now empty camp.

Such a loss of control is not in itself surprising. Stilicho's regular forces were being supplemented by contingents of northern barbarians, raised following his expedition along the Rhine in 396. It is easy to forget that the troops supplied would not be serving as regular troops in the Roman army under Roman discipline. They would tend to serve *en masse*, in separate units under their own leaders. This allows us to accept Zosimus' account that Stilicho lost control of his troops, although the suggestion that this was due to his own lax habits is probably a device to show him in as bad a light as possible.[49]

Stilicho had now received a double blow. Firstly, he must have realized that his federate troops were not as loyal as he would have hoped and could not really be trusted in a pitched battle. As a result, his confidence in victory over Alaric would have been severely damaged. Furthermore, he had now been deprived of a major reason for the campaign by being declared *hostis publicus* in Constantinople. There was little chance of his being accepted into the capital as a hero and so being able to take control of the East. As a result, Stilicho decided to leave the East to deal with the problem of Alaric and retired to Italy.

The declaration of *hostis publicus* by the East immediately had severe repercussions for both Stilicho and Illyricum. As they retired, Stilicho's troops plundered those areas of Greece through which they passed.[50] Although perceived as Stilicho losing control, there are two actual motives for these attacks. By declaring Stilicho *hostis publicus* Eutropius as a by-product also declared all of Stilicho's followers to be *hostis publicus* at the same time.[51] Although possibly an attempt to undermine the loyalty of his troops, the declaration backfired.[52] When this information reached the Western troops, they immediately felt aggrieved that the government they were trying to support had instead turned against them.

The second factor was the manner in which Stilicho had launched the campaign. By mounting a rapid seaborne assault, he no doubt hoped to take Alaric by surprise, allowing him to quickly achieve contact with the Gothic forces and so catch them unprepared for either battle or siege. Unfortunately, to do this Stilicho had relied – quite naturally – on political support from the Eastern government and on the territories in Greece for supplies. It is unlikely that he had transported enough provisions across the Adriatic to maintain a prolonged campaign. As a result, when he was declared *hostis publicus* the Greek cities which had been supporting the war withdrew their aid. He quickly began to run short of supplies. Naturally, the troops, already aggrieved at being declared enemies, were only too willing to take the supplies needed from the country through which they passed en route back to the fleet, before sailing for Italy.[53] In the meantime, taking with him the majority of the spoils captured in Greece, Alaric retreated to Epirus, where he continued his depredations.[54]

The interpretation given here gives a clear and understandable reason for the end of Stilicho's campaign in Greece without the need to interpret Stilicho's decision to retire as being made after the conclusion of a treaty with Alaric.[55] Furthermore, neither is there the need for Stilicho to have learned about Gildo's rebellion in Africa and so been compelled to return to Italy to deal with the situation, a claim which is chronologically difficult to maintain.[56] Instead, the proposed explanation gives a reasonably simple passage of events that takes into account all of the known factors and sources.

The aftermath

On his arrival back in Italy Stilicho assessed his options. It was clear that he needed to rebuild the army as an efficient fighting force – especially as Gildo, the *comes et magister utriusque militiae per Africam* (count and general of all troops in Africa), had declared for the Eastern court (see next Chapter). In order to do this, what he needed above all were Roman recruits that could be trained to perform under orders whilst maintaining strict discipline. He needed to act to strengthen the army, and he needed the support of the Senate to achieve his aim. At this time the weakness of his own position would have been infuriating to someone who believed himself the rightful *parens principum* of the unified Empire.

Eutropius

Stilicho's campaign had probably lasted as little as eight or ten weeks from start to finish, yet it had badly upset Eutropius' plans. Fortunately, the decision to declare Stilicho *hostis publicus* appears to have appeased Alaric. Following his escape from Stilicho, Alaric had crossed the Corinthian Isthmus – again aided by the treachery of Gerontius, if Zosimus is to be believed – and had moved on to Epirus where, freed from the threat of attack, he was busy stripping the countryside of its resources.[57]

With half of Illyricum now being administered by the West, Eutropius continued with his plan to promote Alaric to be *magister militum* of the much-lessened Prefecture of Illyricum. The plan fulfilled two complementary functions. By allocating Alaric only part of Illyricum, Eutropius could limit the amount of power Alaric would wield. At the same time, placing Alaric and his troops in Illyricum made him a military buffer to the political ambitions of Stilicho. With Alaric an official member of the Eastern military hierarchy, an attempt by Stilicho to attack him again would be a declaration of war on Arcadius. On the other hand, the apparent enmity between Alaric and Stilicho would ensure that they would not combine their forces in an attempt to oust Eutropius from power. At the end of 397 Alaric was made *magister militum per Illyricum* and probably settled in Macedonia and Thrace. The pay of a *magister militum* 'must have been beyond the wildest dreams of avarice for a Goth'.[58] In addition, the post may have entitled his followers to the pay and benefits of regular Roman troops.[59] Between 397 and 401 Alaric was to retain a low profile in his new post.

At around this time envoys arrived in Constantinople from the Western province of Africa. The governor, Gildo, offered to change his allegiance from Stilicho and the West to Eutropius and the East. Although this would involve a possible war with Stilicho, Eutropius appears to have agreed to Gildo's proposal. The acceptance ensured that Stilicho would now definitely not be leading an army into the Balkans for a third time: the food supply to the city of Rome was severed when Gildo changed allegiance and Stilicho would be forced to cope with events that did not include Alaric. With Stilicho's attention focused on the West, Eutropius was free to act in the East.

Accordingly, Eutropius led the Eastern army in person to face the Huns in Asia Minor. Within a very short time they had been forced to withdraw back across the Caucasus. Indeed, the campaign was so effective that the Huns were not to threaten the Caucasus again until 425. Eutropius had shown that, despite his political opposition to Rufinus in Constantinople, he was in fact a successor to Rufinus' policies. He had dealt with affairs in the Balkans without recourse to deploying an army under a general who may gain prestige for defeating Alaric. Furthermore, when he had realized that the Huns could only be forced out of the Empire by a military campaign, he had led the campaign in person. The military hierarchy would not be allowed to gain prestige and power by conducting a successful operation on their own. From this point on he would allow the army to slowly run down.[60]

Chapter Eight

Gildo's Revolt and the African Campaign, 398

Gildo and his family

To understand the nature of Gildo's revolt it is necessary to trace his family's history back prior to the reign of Theodosius. His father, Nubel, was the King of Mauretania and probably a Christian.[1] He had several brothers, including Firmus and Mascezel. Around the year 373 Firmus had led the revolt in Africa that was suppressed in c.375 by *comes* Theodosius, the father of the future emperor. Firmus committed suicide rather than allow himself to be captured. During Theodosius' campaign Mascezel supported Firmus, whereas Gildo was part of the forces of Theodosius.

Gildo is not mentioned again until 385, when he was made *comes Africae* as a reward for his loyalty to the Emperor Theodosius.[2] The trust shown was misplaced, and on the outbreak of civil war between Theodosius and Magnus Maximus in 387 Gildo threw in his lot with Maximus. However, even though he had supported Maximus, following his victory Theodosius left Gildo in control in Africa. Partly this was certainly due to Theodosius' policy of forgiveness for those who had joined the revolt, but there will have been an element of politics in the decision, since Gildo's status as a 'prince' of the Moors will have helped in controlling the rebellious Moorish tribes.[3] As a guarantee of his actions, Theodosius took Gildo's daughter Salvina back to Constantinople with him. At first she was a hostage. Later she married Nebridius, the nephew of Theodosius' first wife Flaccilla, as a reward for Gildo's continued loyalty.[4] In this way Theodosius may have hoped to secure Gildo's ongoing support. Part of the agreement between Theodosius and Gildo may have been Gildo's acceptance of his brother Mascezel's presence in Africa, even though the two men had been on opposite sides in Firmus' rebellion.

When Theodosius went to war against Arbogast and Eugenius, Gildo did not cut off supplies of grain to Rome, since this would have provoked great resentment against Theodosius in the West. Although it is possible to interpret his actions as being out of self interest, simply waiting to see who was victorious, it is interesting to note that his decision to join neither side nor to cut off supplies to Rome was later applauded by Theodosius; either shortly before, during the course of or shortly after the war, he was made *comes et magister utriusque militiae per Africam*.[5] It is possible that the negative interpretations of his inactivity were related more to the later propaganda of Claudian than contemporary politics.

Before his death Theodosius arranged matters in the West to his liking. Stilicho was given command of Britain, Gaul, Spain and Africa. It is very likely that Gildo was unhappy about the change in his status; he had gone from being the trusted minister of a distant emperor to being bound to the rule of a man in nearby Italy. In many ways the change was likely to curb the amount of power and freedom of action he had in his province. Moreover, Stilicho was not an emperor and Gildo may have disliked the enforced subservience to a mere 'soldier' and fellow official.

The rebellion

The evidence for the whole episode is poor, and heavily reliant on Claudian. What follows is an attempt to piece together the fragments in a logical order, paying particular attention to establishing a chronology. Vital to this is an understanding of the slow pace of communications, as one aspect often overlooked when discussing imperial diplomacy is travel times for messengers and the delay in receiving information. Delays in communication placed 'fundamental limitations ... on the ways in which the Empire could function'.[6]

The dissemination of news

The *cursus publicus* (imperial post) had a normal speed of approximately 80 kilometres (just over 49.5 miles) per day. If it was an emergency, this could be increased to 320 kilometres (just under 199 miles) per day, but this would use fresh messengers on each leg of the journey. If it was necessary for the messenger to arrive in person, the rate would be very much reduced and rely upon the stamina of the individual.[7] An example of the speed of news occurs during the rebellion of Procopius in 365. The rebellion was declared in Constantinople on 28 September 365 but it was not until late October or the beginning of November that the news reached Valentinian in North Gaul. Messengers sent by the land route from Antioch to Rome would take not less than one month to cover the 3,000 miles.[8]

A further difficulty is that of travelling across the Mediterranean. The winds that affect the Mediterranean can be extremely strong and tend to blow in cycles. As a result, for example, news travelling from Constantinople to Carthage might travel quickly thanks to the prevailing winds, but when a response was needed the same winds would hamper the return journey. Furthermore, strong and violent winds would halt all sea journeys, since the galleys in use at the time could not traverse rough seas. One example of the problems that could ensue concerns a letter sent by the Emperor Gaius (Caligula) to Petronius, legate of Syria. The ship on which it was carried was storm-bound for three months and only arrived at its destination a full twenty-seven days after messengers which had been sent carrying the news that Gaius had been assassinated.[9] Therefore, it should be remembered that although according to Pliny the trip from Puteoli to Alexandria could be expected to take nine days, this may have been in ideal conditions.[10] Despite the image normally conveyed, the Mediterranean 'did not provide a medium of speedy and reliable internal communications for the Empire'.[11]

Finally, it should also be noted that there is no clear evidence that the imperial navy was used for transporting messengers; the task was usually assigned to a trader heading in the right direction.[12] In these days of powered ships and instantaneous transmission of news, such delays are often overlooked, yet in the past by the time news arrived it could be completely out of touch with events at the source.

Events

After Theodosius died, Gildo's daughter Salvina appears to have remained at court in Constantinople, since her husband was a relative of the emperor and well-placed in the court. The speed of the developments between East and West, especially in relation to Rufinus, resulted in Gildo being slow to act, but once he realized that there was no longer any threat against his daughter, Gildo seems to have slowly begun to assert his independence.

The first sign of Gildo's new-found freedom was an attempt to assassinate his brother Mascezel. Unfortunately for Gildo, his brother escaped the attempt and fled to the court at Milan. However, Mascezel's two sons were not so fortunate and both were killed on Gildo's orders.

Gildo immediately recognized that the main source of danger was Mascezel appealing to Stilicho for aid.[13] However, by this time he had probably been made aware of the estrangement between Stilicho and the Eastern court following the Greek campaign. Accordingly, Gildo sent envoys to Eutropius in Constantinople offering his service to the Eastern emperor.[14] This fulfilled two separate functions. Firstly, by associating his revolt with the Eastern court, Gildo dramatically raised the stakes. Any military attempt by Stilicho to overthrow him could now spark off a civil war between East and West. Secondly, by pledging his personal loyalty to Eutropius he ensured the safety of his daughter, who still lived in Constantinople.

He sent further messengers to Stilicho in an attempt to forestall the West giving aid to his brother and informing them of his change of allegiance. The messengers arrived in Milan in early winter 397.[15] Possibly in an attempt to put pressure on Stilicho, Gildo seems to have reduced the amount of grain being exported to the city of Rome.[16] He may have hoped that this expression of his power would deter Stilicho from either helping Mascezel or resisting his attempt to change allegiance.[17]

The legal aspects

At this point it is necessary to investigate some of the legal and political arguments concerning the legality of Gildo's transfer of allegiance from East to West, since this underpins many of the assumptions made about his motives. It has sometimes been assumed that Gildo was acting within his rights when he offered to exchange his loyalty from Milan to Constantinople, since he had been appointed by the Emperor Theodosius and Theodosius was based in Constantinople.[18] Superficially plausible, this actually makes little sense. Before his early death Theodosius had installed Stilicho as *parens* of Honorius, and entrusted to him the rule of Italy, Spain, Gaul and Africa.[19] It is clear that in Theodosius' opinion Gildo was now subordinate to Stilicho.

At no point after the appointment of Stilicho was Gildo officially appointed in

Africa by Arcadius in Constantinople.[20] Therefore, to suggest that Gildo had the right to change his allegiance is unreasonable: the natural consequence of such an assumption is that all governors had the right to change allegiance when an emperor died. There is no evidence of any earlier governor changing his allegiance from West to East or vice versa without the approval of the relevant emperors – unless it was during the course of a civil war or of the rise of an usurper. Both Arcadius and Honorius were legal rulers in their respective halves of the Empire, so Gildo's attempt must be seen for what it was – an attempt to save himself from the retribution of his legal superior, a man known to be following the policies of the deceased Theodosius. This would almost certainly include a continuation of the status quo in Africa, but this had been shattered by Gildo's attempt to kill his brother.

Constantinople

When Eutropius received the emissaries from Gildo proposing the change of allegiance, it would appear that the overtures were welcomed, at least in essence. By the time that they arrived Stilicho had already been declared *hostis publicus* and had retired from Greece; negotiations were continuing with Alaric for a peaceful settlement of his desire for an army post, and Eutropius was preparing to lead an expedition in person against the Huns wandering around Asia Minor.[21] It was clearly impossible for the East to send any physical reinforcements to Africa, since these were badly needed elsewhere.[22] As a result there would appear to have been an agreement whereby Eutropius would send quasi-legal orders to Gildo accepting Africa as part of the Eastern dominions, but Gildo was left to deal with the situation unaided.

It is possible that Eutropius was quite happy to stir things in the West without actually committing himself to any action; after all, with Africa in revolt and the grain supply to Rome cut, Stilicho would be unable to take any further action in the Balkans or against Constantinople itself. Eutropius could lead the army East in the knowledge that all would be secure for his return.

Furthermore, there remained the possibility that Stilicho would be toppled from power in the West, in a similar manner to Eutropius' assumption of Rufinus' powers. The loss of the African grain supply to Rome was certain to cause political upheaval. The possibility of the removal of such a powerful figure as the joint-emperors' brother-in-law must have been a serious temptation to Eutropius. He was willing to take the (possibly minor) risk of starting a civil war in the hope that the affair would damage Stilicho in the West.

In one respect the fact that the East did not take part in the African affair was extremely fortunate. Stilicho's quick response resulted in the situation being settled before Eutropius could return from his campaign and act upon Gildo's offer, and an open breach – and probably civil war – was prevented.[23]

Rome

At the beginning of autumn 396 news of the rebellion reached the population of Rome. Reports of Gildo's defection were quickly followed by a reduction in African exports of grain and the population rapidly became alarmed at the possible consequences of Gildo's actions.[24] Stilicho reacted to the situation with commendable speed, organizing for supplies of food to be transported from Gaul and Spain to compensate for the shortfall.[25]

Earlier, in 395, Stilicho had made an ally of Symmachus. An immensely gifted and talented politician, Symmachus, although a pagan, had continued to thrive in 'Christian' Rome, being, amongst other things, *praefectus urbi Romae* (prefect of Rome, 384) and consul (391). Renowned for his honesty and character, he became Stilicho's voice in the Senate, making speeches and demands that may not have succeeded had Stilicho made them himself. In return, Symmachus could count on Stilicho to reward his clients with valuable offices when he recommended them.

As the crisis deepened Stilicho made an extremely intelligent political move. He offered to restore the right of *senatus consultum* to the Senate.[26] The *senatus consultum* was an ancient privilege whereby the Senate was allowed to pass laws. Obviously, during the course of the Empire, this right had been abrogated by the emperors, much to the dismay and annoyance of the Senate.[27] Although it was obvious to the Senate that in return their first act was expected to be that they condemn Gildo, they could hardly refuse to accept the return of such an ancient privilege. However, politically it changed the balance of power dramatically in Stilicho's favour.

Yet there was a further factor in their decision. The senators themselves had large estates in Africa that would be under threat should Gildo be allowed to transfer his allegiance to the East. Fiscal interests alone made Stilicho and the Senate allies. Yet the concession ran much deeper than at first appears. Being seen as a restorer of the Senate's ancient privileges, Stilicho made allies of many of the senators. Yet when he had Symmachus convince the Senate to declare Gildo *hostis publicus*, in effect the responsibility of declaring war upon Gildo moved away from Stilicho and fell upon the Senate.

The result of this shrewd manoeuvre was that when Gildo began an embargo in late autumn of the supplies needed by Rome, as he did instantly upon hearing of the declaration, the citizens blamed the Senate rather than Stilicho. One further consideration was that Stilicho would need the help of the Senate during the crisis, since the cost of moving and billeting his army in Italy and of preparing for the upcoming campaign would be large.[28] Furthermore, it was now clear that an army would have to be sent to Africa to restore the rule of the West. History shows that wars in Africa could be long, drawn out affairs.[29] Should this happen again, Rome would be brought to the brink of starvation and Stilicho wanted to be absolved of any blame by the citizens should the war be protracted – or even turn into a further civil war with the East.[30] Also, should the army be defeated again it would be seen as the fault of the Senate, not himself. In this context it is interesting to note Claudian's claim that Stilicho did not lead the army in person out of fear that Gildo would simply retire into the interior and so prolong the war.[31] Although usually ignored as being a device simply to excuse Stilicho staying in Italy, it is probable that a major invasion led by Stilicho would have, in truth, resulted in Gildo withdrawing into the interior and signalled the beginning of a long, drawn-out 'guerrilla' war, which would be greatly to Stilicho's detriment.

Finally, the move helped Stilicho with regards to his greatest worry at the start of his guardianship: by having the Senate declare war, the Senate would then be placed in a difficult position to refuse to supply recruits for the army. Despite the fact that calling for recruits would be likely to upset the Senate, since the burden of supplying large numbers of men would fall primarily upon the aristocracy due to their huge landholdings, on 17 June 397 Stilicho issued a law enforcing conscription.[32] Symmachus details some of the negotiations which took place between Rome and Milan.[33]

Predictably, once the law was passed in Milan, embassies were immediately sent from the Senate in Rome asking that the call for recruits be commuted to a tax payment. The embassies proved effective and in two laws, issued on 24 September and 12 November, the conscription was cancelled and commutation for gold was declared, with the rate being assessed at 25 *solidi* per recruit.[34]

However, Stilicho remained extremely anxious about the situation and the repeal was reversed. A second series of conscriptions followed. When Florentius, the *praefectus urbi Romae*, was deemed to have shown insufficient energy in implementing the conscription he was dismissed and replaced by Lampadius, brother of Theodorus (*praefectus praetorio Italiae*) and uncle of the younger Theodorus (*praefectus praetorio Galliarum*). Although further petitions from the Senate again resulted in the cancellation of the legislation, they were instead compelled to donate large amounts of grain for the good of the city during the war with Gildo.[35]

The second cancellation betrays Stilicho's awareness of his own weakness; he could not afford to alienate the Senate, since he would need their support to maintain his position in the years ahead. Although the increase in tension could have led to widespread opposition to Stilicho's government, he appears to have balanced the pressures and emerged virtually unscathed from the incident.

However, he had now alienated a number of senators with his policies and one factor that now began to further tell against him was his employment of pagans and heretics (such as Symmachus, who was a confirmed pagan). The more militant Christians amongst the elite in Rome began to stir in opposition to his rule.

On the wider political stage, Stilicho greatly raised the stakes by having the Senate, on behalf of Honorius, declare Gildo *hostis publicus*. Firstly, this highlighted that the East's involvement in Western affairs had strengthened rather than weakened Stilicho's position, and therefore any interference in the hope of destabilizing Stilicho's position would be unprofitable. Secondly, the involvement of the Senate would make Eutropius more wary of supporting Gildo, since supporting Gildo in opposition to the wishes of the Senate in Rome would have greatly raised the probability of the outbreak of civil war.

The timing of the declaration could hardly have been better, as it was at around this time that Eutropius' envoys arrived and indicated that, although Eutropius had gone East to face the Huns in person, when he returned he was in favour of accepting Gildo's desertion of the West. With the backing of the Senate, Stilicho rebuffed Eutropius' claims, and although several embassies arrived from the East, thanks to his strengthened position Stilicho was able to give them all the same, short reply.[36]

Since the rift between East and West was growing greater as time passed, Stilicho realized that speed was of the essence; not only did he need to restore the food supply from Africa to Rome before the supplies in Gaul and Spain were exhausted, but he needed to act before Eutropius returned from the East and was put under pressure to reinforce Gildo against attack.

Command against Gildo

It was obvious that Stilicho could not take command in person. In the first instance, he was still *hostis publicus* in the East and he needed to maintain a low profile in order not to damage relations any more than was strictly necessary, as he still had pretensions about becoming Arcadius' *parens*.[37] Moreover, defeat or delay would damage his authority in the West and leave him vulnerable to political attack.

And delay was the most likely outcome. Gildo was still the *magister militum per Africam*, in at least nominal control of the regular Roman forces in Africa and so in command of a formidable force. However, his main power base was amongst the Moorish tribes and so his army was likely to include large numbers of relatively low-quality troops unsuitable for large-scale battles. However, these troops were excellent for 'guerrilla' warfare. Unless Gildo was overcome quickly it was certain that he would retire to the interior and the support of the Moorish tribes. In that case, the conflict would become a drawn-out guerrilla campaign which would have severe political implications for Stilicho in Italy.

In addition, the political situation in Rome and Milan was tense and Stilicho was unwilling to leave a political vacuum by taking command in Africa. Should Stilicho leave the thirteen-year-old Honorius in the care of others, the half-expected delay in the retaking of Africa would lead to opposition politicians in Rome seizing the initiative and claiming power. As a consequence, the possibility that Stilicho would lead the army in person was never likely to be a reality.[38]

Mascezel

As a result of his deliberations Stilicho now needed to appoint someone to lead the expedition. The obvious choice, for a variety of reasons, was Mascezel, the brother of Gildo. Having survived the attempt on his life, Mascezel had fled to Milan in aid of support, and Gildo's decision to kill his sons meant that there was little chance of Mascezel joining Gildo against Stilicho. Furthermore, by sending Mascezel, Stilicho could downplay the gravity of the situation, changing it from one that was the concern of the two imperial governments to one that was the outcome of a local family feud. In this way, he could send Mascezel without it being seen as an all-out attack on an imperial province that had been potentially claimed by the court at Constantinople. By removing himself from command, the result was that any action from Constantinople would result in them being perceived as the aggressor and, if that happened, this would help him in dealing with the Senate and the population of Rome.

Yet there are two further aspects to be considered. In 373 Mascezel had sided with his brother Firmus during the latter's revolt against the Empire. Thanks to his loyalty to Firmus, it is probable that Mascezel remained high in the affections of those local tribes who had also supported Firmus. This may have been one of the reasons for Gildo being compelled by Valentinian I to retain Mascezel in the country during his time as governor: his presence would act as a check on Gildo's influence and so reduce the risk of a new revolt. Furthermore, he appears to have been a strict Catholic, a fact which Stilicho may have been counting on to secure support from fellow Catholics in Africa. In contrast, Gildo was a Donatist.[39] If Mascezel was as popular as suggested, then he could claim the support of the majority of the tribes against Gildo, so reducing the need for Stilicho to send large forces and also – hopefully – reducing Gildo's power base and so making his quick defeat more likely. Finally, unlike Stilicho, Mascezel had already fought over the African terrain and this experience could prove vital in a battle with Gildo, who would have a similar knowledge.[40]

Mascezel's ability to count on local support seems to be supported by the nature of the forces Stilicho organized for the attack. We are not given an exact breakdown of the troops sent to Africa by Stilicho. The little information we have comes from Claudian and Orosius. According to Orosius, the army under Mascezel comprised some 5,000 men.[41] Claudian includes a list of units, and when this is compared to the units listed in the *Notitia Dignitatum* it becomes clear that these were all units of the elite *palatina*. Therefore, these units could reasonably expect such a mention, but obviously there is no guarantee that forces from 'lower-ranking' units were not also included in the army and were not mentioned by Claudian as being of little note.[42]

The following table gives a list of the forces listed by Claudian and attempts to link them with units in the *Notitia Dignitatum*.

Table 1: a possible derivation of the list given by Claudian: *Bell. Gild*. 418–23

Description in Claudian	Possible unit name(s)	Reference in Not. Dig. (Seeck)	Unit type
Herculean Cohort	*Herculi*	Oc V 3	*Legio Palatina*
Jovian Cohort	*Iovi Seniores/Iuniores*	Oc V 2/23	*Legio Palatina*
Nervian Cohort	*Nervi*	Oc V 25	*Auxilia Palatina* (archers)
Felix Cohort	*Felices Seniores/Iuniores*	Oc V 31/32	*Auxilia Palatina*
Legion ... Augustus ... the Unconquered	*Octaviani* (?) (Possibly the old *Legio VIII Augusta*, named after Octavian/Augustus *and* the number eight)	Oc V 10	*Legio Palatina*
Regiment of the Lion	*Leones Seniores/Iuniores*	Oc V 26/27	*Auxilia Palatina*

Given the speed of muster, it is reasonable to assume that these units formed at least a large proportion of the forces placed under the command of Mascezel. Although in theory Roman fleets were maintained as part of the army, in practice these were not kept in continuous commission, probably due to cost.[43] Furthermore, the speed was such that it is unlikely that with such short notice many vessels could be gathered that were suitable for the transport of horses, which were carried in specially designed vessels.[44] Yet this may not have been of major importance to Mascezel; he could rely on support from his own people when he arrived back in Africa, and the Moors were famous for their light horsemen. As a consequence, it would appear that Mascezel was sent to Africa with little or no cavalry support, these instead being supplied by allies joining him upon his arrival. Whilst Mascezel prepared for the upcoming campaign, Stilicho arranged for the billeting of the remainder of the Italian army throughout Italy. If the war went badly, Stilicho would quickly be able to gather them together and lead a second expedition to Africa.[45]

Mascezel and the Christians

Mascezel is a shadowy figure who has been relegated to practical obscurity by the sources. The little we know suggests that his alliance with Stilicho would be less than easy. As was already noted, he was a Catholic and during his brief stay in Milan he appears to have attached himself to the powerful Catholic party at court. By doing this he allied himself to a group that was at odds with Stilicho, since they were strongly opposed to his policy of leniency towards heretics and pagans (such as Claudian and Symmachus).[46] An example of his piety is given in Orosius, where he is shown as holding up the expedition by stopping en route to Africa at the island of Capraria while he fasted and prayed with the resident monks.[47] It was clear that he would join the opposition to Stilicho's rule, a situation that Stilicho would find hard to tolerate.

It should not be thought that the division between Christianity and Paganism was simply one of religion, although it is possible to perceive it as such. The conflict was one of the loyalties and customs accorded to the old gods of Rome as against the 'brash, intolerantly aggressive newcomer' that was Christianity.[48] The pagans in the Senate saw themselves as the '*pars melior humani generis*' ('the better part of the human race').[49] They were men of wealth, breeding, influence and culture who were defending the pagan past which had raised Rome to Empire against the Christianity that seemed to be attempting to erase that past. As part of the conflict, the pagans interpreted the downturn in the Empire's fortunes as being caused by the rejection of the old gods and the adoption of the new. The accusation and counter-accusation resulted in the production of many literary works defending the differing faiths. Those Christian works that survive form the basis of much of the historical interpretations on the life of Stilicho who, as an Arian and an employer of non-Christians, was denounced by most 'good' Christians as bringing about the fall of the Empire.

The African campaign

The expedition against Gildo set sail from Pisa in November 397.[50] They passed

Liguria on the right and Etruria on the left, before they stopped at Capraria to allow Mascezel to pray with the monks.[51] Upon leaving the island they avoided Corsica but were scattered by a storm as they passed Sardinia.[52] The various parts of the fleet landed as far apart as Sulci, Olbia and Caralis before they finally gathered together at Caralis for the rest of the journey.[53] From Caralis it is certain that the expedition sailed to Sicily, as sailing direct to Africa from Sardinia was too long a journey for the available vessels.

Africa

We have no clear idea what Gildo was doing in Africa as these events unfolded. It is likely that throughout the crisis he remained in or near to Carthage. Here he would be available to receive ambassadors from both East and West and be ready to dictate a prompt reply to be taken to Constantinople or Milan. There is no doubt that Mascezel had informers in Africa ready to tell him where Gildo was located. It is most likely that these informed him of Gildo's whereabouts while he was in Sicily.[54]

Having learned of his brother's position, Mascezel sailed to a nearby location and quickly disembarked the troops. Moreover, he was allegedly certain of victory as the spirit of the recently deceased Bishop Ambrose appeared to him in a dream and foretold his victory.[55] Mascezel must have known that Gildo was unaware of his arrival and was unlikely to have maintained many of his troops near to his location – if only to ease any problems of supply. What happened next remains unclear. Zosimus writes that after disembarking near to Gildo, Mascezel 'so thoroughly worsted him in a sharp battle' that Gildo lost hope and hanged himself.[56] This is not the complete story. Gildo had many troops and supporters so the loss of one battle is not really enough to account for his despair. It is more likely that upon hearing of Mascezel's advance many of

14. Mascezel's route to Africa.

Gildo's supporters deserted him and joined his brother.[57] The much-reduced force was then defeated in battle and Gildo attempted to escape. In his second poem against Eutropius, Claudian claims that Gildo's flight was hindered by winds: 'those same winds which hindered Gildo's flight may seek to drown thee in the sea'.[58] This suggests that Gildo attempted to escape by sea, but adverse winds confined him to harbour – possibly at Carthage. Realising that he could not escape, and was certain to be captured, Gildo lost hope and committed suicide.

Stilicho

Unaware that the expedition would be such a rapid success, once it had left Stilicho took steps to further establish his position as head of the West. Obviously, one part of his strategy was to accept the involvement of the Roman Senate by restoring a certain amount of power to that body. This had the beneficial repercussion that the Senate now became involved in difficult political decisions, which allowed Stilicho to ascribe blame elsewhere and so allow him to take a backward step and be seen merely as one of the top men, rather than as the supreme leader.[59] He also began to change the leadership of the army, placing men of his own choosing in important positions. This had the very important consequence that only Stilicho could now rely on the army for support: any attempt to remove him would likely provoke a vicious response from the army.

However, Stilicho does not appear to have considered these measures enough in themselves to secure his position as *parens* over Honorius. Possibly echoing the political move made earlier by Eutropius, Stilicho decided that he needed to marry his daughter Maria, who was now about twelve years old, to the young emperor. Accordingly, Maria was married to Honorius, probably in February 398.[60]

Yet politically there was also a need for the marriage: as Mascezel had found, there was continuing opposition – especially amongst Christians – to Stilicho's status as *parens principum*. By marrying his daughter to the emperor, Stilicho reinforced his claim to be *parens* to Honorius. Claudian supported the marriage. In January 398 he produced '*Quarto Consulatu Honorii Augusti*' ('Panegyric on the Fourth Consulate of the Emperor Honorius'), which made no mention of the ongoing war, although there are allusions to the previous conflict between c.372 and 375 when the *comes* Theodosius had defeated Gildo's brother Firmus.[61] For the ceremony itself he composed the '*Epithalamium de Nuptiis Honorii Augusti*' ('Marriage of the Emperor Honorius' often referred to as 'Epithalamium of Honorius and Maria'), a propaganda tool in which Stilicho is lauded as the 'guardian of peace with honour'.[62] What may be just as important is the unusual practice of placing the main speech in the *Epithalamium* in the mouths of the army; this was against tradition and may have been a way of reminding the audience that Stilicho's main claim to power remained his command of the army.[63]

Any opposition to this arrangement will have been muted; after all, Honorius was only fourteen and clearly not capable of running the affairs of the West. Moreover, with every passing day Stilicho was becoming more secure and there was little anyone could do to stop the marriage. On the other hand, it is possible that many in court were dismayed by the wedding, realizing that by this act Stilicho had reinforced his relationship to the young emperor: *parens principum*, adopted brother-in-law, and now father-in-law.

When news of Mascezel's triumph reached Rome there would have been much rejoicing and relief; the threat of the blockade was removed and the citizens could rely once again upon a regular shipment of food from Africa rather than worrying about how soon the stocks in Gaul and Spain would run out. For Honorius there was an extra bonus. As was the rule in such cases, upon his death Gildo's lands were confiscated and given to the emperor. These were found to be so extensive that a new post had to be created, the *comes Gildoniaci patrimonii* (count of the patrimony of Gildo), to administer them.[64]

Mascezel returned in triumph to Milan. His glory was to be short-lived; according to Zosimus, he was crossing a bridge in company with Stilicho and a group of imperial guardsmen when, on a pre-arranged signal, he was pushed into the river and drowned.[65] Although this may be little more than Eastern propaganda, the fact that Mascezel had allied himself with the Catholic opposition to Stilicho, plus the fact that he had returned a hero after an exceptionally fast victory, means that, if an accident, it was an extremely fortunate accident for Stilicho. It is more likely that, on this occasion, Stilicho did indeed arrange for his potential rival to be eliminated.

Not content with Mascezel's death, it was clear that, politically, Mascezel would not be allowed to gain the credit for the campaign. In his poems Claudian ensured that Stilicho received the credit, with Mascezel's contribution to the war being minimized.[66] Yet this is not really surprising: there was a long tradition throughout Roman history of emperors claiming the responsibility for victories achieved by their subordinates. The main difference between these examples and Stilicho is that Stilicho was not, in fact, the emperor, although his power at this point was actually probably greater than some previous emperors had wielded.

The war was now over. Its importance is difficult to overstate: Stilicho had come close to leading the Western Empire into another civil war with the East – as later admitted by Claudian.[67] Only by accepting that Mascezel needed to lead the expedition and by dispatching it as fast as possible had Stilicho pre-empted any serious claim to Africa from the East. Furthermore, by quickly dashing the designs of Eutropius Stilicho managed to inflict a political defeat on him that would help those who were determined to undermine his power in the East.

There still remained the problem of controlling the newly retaken territory. Theodosian policy was to keep power in the hands of local nobles, in the hope that in return they would be loyally served. Stilicho no longer had this option. Instead, he opted for a new solution to the problem. He combined the forces of Africa and Tingitana, including the *limitanei*, and placed them under the command of a single individual who was given the post of *comites* (count).[68] Although this placed a lot of power in the hands of one man, as long as the man could be trusted this would not be a problem.

Aftermath

Once the war was over, and after Eutropius' death (see below), Claudian changed the tone of his claims. In '*de Bello Gildico*' ('The War Against Gildo') Honorius is credited with the initiative for the war, yet in the later '*de Consulatu Stiliconis Liber Primo*' ('On the Consulship of Stilicho Book One') it was Stilicho that was acclaimed for the victory. Although it is possible that this was a device to clear Stilicho of any connection with the war – after all, at the time he was *hostis publicus* and so involvement in a province claimed by the East could create political difficulties – it is more likely that this was simply a means to magnify Stilicho's achievements.[69]

Claudian also took the opportunity of shifting the blame for the war away from Gildo and placing it on Eutropius, who was by then dead and discredited even in the East. The change in emphasis in Claudian's work is usually explained as an earlier need to pin Eutropius' actual guilt for the war on Gildo in order to avert a new civil war; Eutropius was actually responsible but Claudian could not say this at the time as it would have caused a heightening of political tension.[70] Yet this need not necessarily be the case.

The change can be explained by political expediency. In his earlier works Claudian correctly blamed Gildo for the war Gildo had actually started. At this time Stilicho was still hoping that his claim to be *parens principum* would be accepted by Eutropius. As a result, any part played by Eutropius is downplayed in order to avoid conflict. Furthermore, with Stilicho declared *hostis publicus* in the East Claudian took a soft line with regard to Eutropius in his early works in an attempt to minimize the crisis brought about by the war.

Once Eutropius was dead, Claudian switched the blame away from Gildo in an attempt to further damage Eutropius' reputation. In this way he could magnify the deeds of Stilicho in resisting the foul acts of Eutropius and promote his patron as acting wisely in resisting Eutropius' political machinations. In this manner it may have been hoped that the East would see their mistake in appointing Eutropius and instead accept the wise and loyal Stilicho as *parens principum*.

Yet when the war ended such considerations were still in the future. At the time, all that mattered was that the grain supplies to Rome had been restored and a potential threat to Stilicho's regime removed. Yet there was a further benefit to the campaign in Africa; although the successful conclusion to the war had enhanced Stilicho's reputation and position in the West, in the East Gildo's speedy defeat and death damaged Eutropius' standing, since he had been unable or unwilling to give physical support to a governor who had specifically asked to join his regime. Opposition to Eutropius in the East began to stiffen.

Chapter Nine

Consolidation, 398–400

When news arrived in Rome and Milan of the victory in Africa, Stilicho's place as the head of the Western government was assured – at least for the present. Although he had been ruling since 395, Stilicho had focused more on his claim to *parens principum* of the East and on opposing Alaric than on ruling the West. Accordingly, his reaction to events between 395 and 398 was more one of improvisation to meet the current needs than that of long-term strategy. For the first time he now had both the incentive and the time to begin to put into place those measures that would enable him to defy rivals for the next ten years.

With Mascezel's death Stilicho was able to claim the victory in Africa as his own, and Claudian immediately set about composing works to that effect. Yet although he had removed a rival who could have risen to become a powerful figurehead, influential opposition remained in the form of militant Catholic senators opposed to his use of pagans and heretics. To counter this, Stilicho had to take steps to ensure that the army was strong and loyal. As a consequence he put in process measures aimed at enlarging the army in Italy and at bringing the military establishment under his personal control.

The condition of the army was to remain his major challenge, a problem to which he would never find the answer. Stilicho was in command of the last substantial army in the West. Over the course of the previous ten years the others had been denuded to supply recruits for the *praesental* army in Italy, especially for the civil wars against Theodosius. Heavily defeated, they had remained in Italy as part of the army of the *magister peditum*. The defeats had further resulted in a loss of morale in the army, although the procession along the Rhine frontier in 396 may have restored confidence to some degree. Nevertheless, the events of 395 and 397, where the army, or sections of it, displayed a lack of discipline and loyalty towards its new leader showed that Stilicho was not yet secure in his position.

Army reforms

The dating and precise nature of Stilicho's changes are not specified in the sources and are as yet poorly understood and open to interpretation. It is extremely unfortunate that the main evidence for the army comes from the *Notitia Dignitatum*. Although a valuable resource, the *Notitia* raises more questions than it answers. One of these is the date that the army units listed were raised. The dating of changes has to be inferred by close scrutiny, especially of the titles of units. As is to be expected, controversy about the ensuing theories continues.[1] All that can be said is that it is probable that Stilicho began at least part of the process of strengthening the army and ensuring its loyalty early in his rule, during the campaign along the Rhine in 396. However, the Western command structure shown in the *Notitia Dignitatum* almost certainly reflects Stilicho's recognition that he would not be accepted by the East, which only really became apparent after the Greek campaign and the revolt of Gildo. Therefore the majority of the changes were probably implemented once he realized that he would only rule in the West and so had to consolidate his position by bringing the Western military establishment under his personal control.[2]

Needing to augment the forces at his personal command, Stilicho followed the policies used by Theodosius. He removed units designated as *limitanei* and *riparienses* from the frontiers and upgraded them either to the position of *comitatenses* or to the lesser status of *pseudo-comitatenses*.[3] As an additional effect, the move would advance these troops in seniority and privileges and probably increase their loyalty to their commander. The units so upgraded are assumed to be those named *Honoriani* after the Emperor Honorius in the *Notitia Dignitatum* (see below).[4]

Those units who had suffered heavy losses received an infusion of new recruits built around the core of the old units.[5] The newcomers were men enlisted from inside the Empire and recruits from barbarian tribes or from the Goths still inside the Empire. Stilicho slowly began to augment the strength of the army of the *magister peditum* in Italy, although it should be remembered that he preferred to use other titles for his rule.[6]

The gaps created by the withdrawals may have been filled by newly recruited *foederati* from across the frontier, especially where these were cavalry.[7] In this he followed another of Theodosius' policies: that of the conciliation, management and, above all, employment of barbarians.[8] After all, Stilicho needed troops and it was easier to recruit readily available Germans than antagonize the Senate by attempting to enforce conscription. In this context it is important to note the issuing of a law which pressed into service 'any *laetus* (sons of *laeti*), *Allamannus* (Alamanni already in the army), *Sarmatians* (probably any trans-Danubian barbarian), vagrant, son of a veteran or any person of any group subject to the draft'.[9] On the whole, however, any new forces under their own leaders were not recognized as part of the formal structure of the army and so were not included in the lists of the *Notitia Dignitatum*.[10]

What is also clear is that the financial straits surrounding the early years of Stilicho's tenure suggest that few if any troops were raised before the African campaign against Gildo. It was only with the defeat of the revolt that the Western coffers were replenished; as has already been seen, the victory allowed Stilicho to confiscate Gildo's land in Africa for the emperor, and released so much money that Stilicho may have been able to add ten new bodies of troops to his forces and begin the fortification of those imperial frontiers on the Rhine and in Britain that required it, a task that continued until 401.[11] Furthermore, he now felt relatively secure and was confident enough to promote Jacobus to be *magister equitum*, alongside but inferior to himself who remained *magister peditum*. The experiment may not have been a success, since in a short poem Claudian reprimanded Jacobus for attacking his, Claudian's, poetry.[12] By late 402 Jacobus was out of office, carrying relics from the West to Constantinople.[13]

Comes rei militaris

Another of Stilicho's reforms is harder to pin down. Study of the *Notitia Dignitatum* reveals that he created new posts in Africa, Britain, Italy, Illyricum and Spain in order to defend the Empire.[14] In the East, Theodosius had created five *magistri militiae* to defend imperial territory. In the West there were only three: the *magister militum per peditum*, the *magister militum per equitum* and the *magister militum per Gallias*. Two *magistri* were not enough to defend the West; Stilicho would be willing to appoint a *magister militum per Gallias*, but rarely felt secure enough to appoint anybody as *magister militum per equitum*, since they would have practically equalled his own position.

As a consequence, he appears to have created five new posts of *comes rei militaris*. These posts are evident in the *Notitia* and can be dated to Stilicho's rule, but the lack of other information makes it impossible to date the appointments precisely. Although it is possible that they were all appointed simultaneously as part of a 'grand strategy', it is more likely that each one was appointed on an ad hoc basis as they were deemed necessary.

The first of these appointments was seen in the last chapter. Following Gildo's defeat, Stilicho created a new post of *comes rei militaris* to control the provinces of Africa and Tingitana. Once it was seen that this was a success, Stilicho appears to have extended the idea to further areas where military control was becoming a problem. It is likely that the next *comes* appointed was in Spain. Although the provinces in the peninsula were some of the most peaceful in the West, it is probable that inactivity had caused a weakening of imperial forces, both in terms of recruitment and morale; when danger threatened the frontiers, troops from Spain were rarely called upon. A new commander could instil discipline and return the forces in Spain to the peak of efficiency. This would have the additional benefit that, should they be required, they would be able to match the regular forces serving in Italy.

Further commands were created in Britain, Illyricum and Italy. The circumstances surrounding the creation of the other posts will be dealt with at appropriate moments in the text rather than being outlined here. However, it should be noted that these new commands contained forces that were similar in size and location to the positioning of the legions earlier in the Empire.[15]

The *Notitia Dignitatum* and the *Honoriani*

Within the *Notitia*, units with the word '*Honoriani*' in the title are assumed – almost certainly correctly – to have been raised during the reign of Honorius. Yet the date and manner of their recruitment remains unknown; they may have been completely new units made from Roman and/or barbarian recruits, or they may have been created by using the remnants of existing units as a core around which new recruits could learn combat skills and discipline.[16] We simply do not know.

Realistically there are only two generals who could have had such a major impact on the army during Honorius' reign: Stilicho and Constantius (c.410–21). However, the fact that there is a large time span for either Stilicho or Constantius to raise the troops results in any theories being conjecture. On the other hand, since units are listed in the

Notitia in order of seniority, and since new units or possibly even renamed units would be lower down the list, it is more than likely that the troops at the top of the following list were raised by Stilicho during his time as head of the Western government. Furthermore, it is possible that the units were named for a specific reason.[17] The following table lists the units and suggests reasons for their names.

Unit name	*Notitia* reference	Comments
Honoriani iuniores	Oc V 67 / VI 17	Almost certainly the earliest troops raised by Stilicho due to their seniority
Honoriani seniores	Oc V 68 / VI 36	
Honoriani Gallicani	Oc V 72 / 220	
Honoriani Atecotti Seniores	Oc V 197 / VI 74	
Honoriani Marcomanni seniores	Oc V 198	
Honoriani Marcomanni iuniores	Oc V 199	
Honoriani Atecotti iuniores	Oc V 200	
Honoriani Mauri seniores	Oc V 203 / VI 51	Possibly raised/named following the victory over Gildo?
Honoriani Mauri iuniores	Oc V 204	
Honoriani victores iuniores	Oc V 215	
Honoriani ascarii seniores	Oc V 216 / VI 79	
Honoriani felices Gallicani	Oc V 247	
Honoriani victores	Oc VI 48	
Mattiarii Honoriani Gallicani	Oc VI 52	
Equites Honoriani Taifali iuniores	Oc VI 59	
Equites Honoriani seniores	Oc VI 60	
Equites Honoriani iuniores	Oc VI 79	
Felices Honoriani iuniores	Or V 21 / 62	
Felices Honoriani seniores	Or VII 37	Brigaded with *Felices Arcadiani seniores* (Or VII 36): suggests may have been raised prior to the death of Arcadius in May 408, possibly during the short period of collaboration in 402–3.
Equites felices Honoriani	Or XXXI 40	
Equites felices Honoriani Illyriciani	Or XXXVI 22	Raised prior to/following the abortive attempt upon Illyricum in 407?

Having to rely on the money released by internal warfare meant that Stilicho could not count upon similar funds becoming available again in the near future. Stilicho could not afford to squander his resources. The army needed to be husbanded and nurtured, not risked in battle, since finding recruits was becoming a major difficulty.[18] In fact, it was only the need to restore the grain supply to Rome that had prompted Stilicho to risk sending troops to Africa in 397. Fortunately, they won without incurring significant losses.

Federates

To augment the army in time of war Stilicho relied more and more on recruiting ad hoc bodies of barbarian troops to serve when needed. Given the financial condition of the West this was an extremely useful method of recruitment, since these troops could be hired for single campaigns or campaign seasons. This reduced costs since they would only be hired for a limited period and so would not need paying after the campaign had finished – unlike regular troops. Furthermore, by hiring these mercenaries a smaller standing army was needed, so there was less need to pay for the training of new recruits. Moreover, the hiring of foreign mercenaries reduced the number of regular troops reaching retirement age, which had the additional benefit of lowering the number of troops retiring and equally of lowering the amount of money needed to pay for retirement benefits.[19]

Interestingly, Olympiodorus claimed that the title 'federates' was first given to non-Roman units in the reign of Honorius.[20] This was almost certainly during the guardianship of Stilicho. It is possible that although he was not the first individual to raise such troops, Stilicho was responsible for regularizing and formalizing the recruitment of wholly barbarian units serving under their own leaders into the army.[21] The system was attractive to the barbarians. Their leaders were eager to gain a foothold in the Roman command system because it could give them wealth they could not expect in their own countries. Furthermore, in return for the protection of a strong leader their followers would look after them and be willing to demonstrate for their promotion, leading to their achieving greater wealth and power. Examples of such leaders include Gainas and Tribigild.

However, there were inherent dangers in hiring large numbers of 'barbarians'. The most obvious was that this would antagonize the Senate, who traditionally wanted the army to be 'Roman' and place less reliance on barbarians. Although both Stilicho and his predecessors had raised foreign auxiliaries, for the most part these remained stationed on the frontier in Gaul and Germany. The result was that the army in Italy contained mainly Roman troops who had been freed from service on the frontiers by the employment of barbarians. This method of recruitment allowed Stilicho to maintain the fiction that the Empire was being defended by troops who were almost wholly Roman. Later, Stilicho was forced to maintain a greater number of barbarian troops in Italy, with an associated rise in opposition from an aristocracy infuriated by his use of non-Roman troops.

Yet such recruiting practices were to prove harmful to the Empire. By allowing ever-more Germans to enter the army, with many attaining high rank, Rome lost some of her military prestige. This is not because the use of Germanic mercenaries 'tainted' the army itself, but because the Roman military machine which had so long terrorized the barbarians now became intimately known to their enemies. Once a process is understood, not only can the fear factor become lessened but successful counter-measures can be put in place to deal with them.[22] With the increased use of mercenaries, a larger percentage of the German tribes became immune to the fear previously caused by the Roman military machine. Furthermore, at the same time as Roman armies began to look more and more like their Germanic opponents, so the Germans began to look like and use their own forces in the Roman manner. Wars which had once been of Roman efficiency against barbarian inefficiency now became more akin to civil wars, especially in the number of losses inflicted. This may help to explain the increasing reluctance of Roman generals – including Stilicho – to face Germanic warriors in open battle; the losses were now becoming prohibitive and hard to replace.

On the other hand it is possible that Stilicho was looking at the larger picture and attempting to use the example of the Franks as a model. The Franks had been allowed to settle on Roman territory earlier in the century on condition that they guard against further intruders. This had worked well since the Franks had – by and large – kept to their promise. Their part of the frontier had stabilized, with the added benefit that emperors in need of Roman troops had been able to withdraw garrisons freed by the Frankish occupation. By involving other tribes on the frontier in the garrisoning of that frontier, Stilicho may have been hoping to both stabilize the border and allow the withdrawal of ever more Roman forces.[23] This would help explain the diplomatic activity on the Rhine, culminating in a treaty in late summer 398 with both the Franks and the Alamanni, which 'secured the Rhine border in an impressive way'.[24] In this way he could further strengthen his army with 'Roman' troops without weakening the frontiers against attack.[25] It is also possible that Stilicho was consciously trying to emulate the pattern seen in the early Empire, where existing kingdoms in Asia Minor and the Middle East had first been employed as 'Client Kingdoms' that acted as buffer-states and sources of manpower. Only later were these absorbed into the Empire.

But it must not be forgotten that there were difficulties with his methods. Stilicho ordered troops to be withdrawn from Raetia at least twice between 395 and 401. The effect of these changes has been highlighted by a study of their impact in Raetia.[26] The portrayal of small garrisons – sometimes as little as fifty men – in a 'decaying landscape that had once been a prosperous Roman countryside' is dramatic and highlights the fact that in some provinces Roman power was now withdrawing from the periphery and focusing upon preserving the core. The net result was the withdrawal of the wealthy individuals who owned villas and had earlier set the example of the benefits of Roman life. Furthermore, life in Roman towns also went into a steep decline as both towns and villas were abandoned as defensive sites in favour of hilltop defences.[27] In Raetia, the new garrisons of barbarian forces had no Roman example to follow, instead remaining culturally Germanic. In contrast, there is the continuity of Roman life in Noricum, yet the reasons for the differences between the conditions in the different provinces remain unclear.[28]

The fact that the process of reinforcing the central army relied almost entirely upon the loyalty and trust of the tribes on the frontiers was also extremely risky. It is probable that Frankish loyalty was partly due to internal political stability that may not have been present in other tribes at this time. There was also the major problem that in senatorial circles Stilicho's actions could be interpreted as abandoning the frontiers to barbarians. Should these tribes prove disloyal and attack the Empire, opinion against Stilicho would automatically harden.

Bucellarii

> In the time of Honorius the name *bucellarius* was given not only to Roman soldiers but also to certain Goths.
>
> Olympiodorus, *fr. 7.4.*

The evolution of the *bucellarii* is not wholly clear and is based mainly on this one quote from Olympiodorus. From this it is apparent that *bucellarius* began as a nickname for Roman troops, although whether it was applied to specific forces, for example those acting as bodyguards, is unknown. However, by the time of Stilicho it was becoming a name given to some of the non-Roman bodyguards being adopted by high-ranking Romans. Such troops may have begun as 'private forces' enrolled at the instigation of the government but actually commanded by civilian magistrates for 'police' duties, for example in Egypt.[29] The *bucellarii* appear to have entered a patron/client relationship with their employer, a status that could be inherited by the client's son. This relationship could be ended by mutual agreement, by a government decree disbanding the *bucellarii*, by the redistribution of the *bucellarii* after the disgrace of their client, or possibly by the *bucellarius* alone.[30]

An early example of the employment of *bucellarii* is that of Rufinus, who had a small bodyguard of Huns, permission for which must have been granted by Theodosius before he went on campaign in 394, probably to give Rufinus protection whilst the emperor was away. Obviously, they were not allowed in the presence of the emperor and so were unable to prevent Rufinus' assassination in 395.

Stilicho made use of the growing employment of *bucellarii* by personally recruiting a large force of Huns to act as a personal bodyguard. Furthermore, he allowed some of the high-ranking officials he had appointed to recruit and maintain their own small body of troops. He probably recognized, even at this early date, that in so doing he actually created a small force that he permanently had access to in times of trouble.[31] Although at first the concept appealed to him, especially as he was faced with opposition and the possibility of rebellion, over time these 'bodyguards' became increasingly large until, in 406, he was obliged to pass a law severely limiting the size of the forces allowed to private officials.[32]

However, there was one major flaw in the increased employment of 'barbarians' of which Stilicho was unaware. The greater use of non-Roman *bucellarii* as bodyguards, which was reflected in their conditions of service and especially in their privileges, began to be resented by the troops in the regular army, who saw their own position being usurped by 'foreign interlopers'. As Stilicho increased the number of barbarian troops in the army, agitation amongst the regular forces began to grow.

There was also a need to ensure that the army was loyal only to him. As was highlighted earlier, using his position as *comes et magister utriusque militiae* Stilicho began to slowly appropriate the right to appoint the principal administrators to all of the offices of the *comites* and *duces*. By the end of his regime he had taken control of all of the military administration.[33] This was vital to his survival. The measures allowed him to maintain a tight control of the *comites* and *duces* he appointed in the West and to monitor their actions to a high degree. The presence on their staff of officials loyal to Stilicho would ensure that the men in command of troops would be extremely cautious about becoming involved in any opposition to Stilicho.

Political developments

Throughout the period 395 to 400 Stilicho maintained his claim to *parens* of the entire Empire. There is no doubt that his claim was sincere; after all, he was the senior member of the House of Theodosius – especially since the marriage of Honorius and Maria – and believed himself to be the best-equipped to look after the interests of the two young emperors. Yet he was not naïve politically. The claim was also an internal weapon that he used in the West to shore up his position and maintain control.[34] After all, it was unlikely that anyone would wish to supplant him and inherit the political divisions that the claim had created between East and West. Indeed, if Claudian is to be believed, the conflict between East and West continued to escalate and now involved attempts at assassination.[35] Instead, opponents would be more likely to wait and see what the outcome would be, probably in the hope that one of the assassination attempts would succeed.

The marriage of Maria to Honorius was not the only dynastic link that Stilicho attempted to arrange in his early years in power. In early January 400 Claudian recited his two latest poems, *de Consulatu Stilichonis Liber Primus* and *de Consulatu Stilichonis Liber Secundus* (On the Consulship of Stilicho, Books One and Two).[36] In the second of these it is announced that Stilicho's family will be united for the third time with the House of Theodosius.[37] Stilicho's marriage to Serena was the first, the second was Honorius and Maria, and the third would appear to be the betrothal of Eucherius, Stilicho's son, with Galla Placidia, Theodosius' daughter. In this way the marriage ties between Honorius and Stilicho would be cemented to the maximum of Stilicho's ability. Yet, although the betrothal was announced, the two never married. Partly, this may have been due to Stilicho's desire to avoid resentment and undesirable rumours in the Senate.[38] Another marriage between his offspring and the children of Theodosius would undoubtedly cause feelings of disgust and unrest; after all, Galla Placidia was biologically the second cousin of Eucherius, but by adoption was his aunt. Yet it is also possible that Stilicho was keeping her in reserve. There was a chance that the marriage between Honorius and Maria would prove to be childless. If the emperor died without an heir, Eucherius, acknowledged as his grandson by Theodosius, would be a serious contender for the throne. Being able to marry Theodosius' daughter would obviously boost Eucherius' claims to the throne. In the meantime, Galla Placidia would be useful if kept unmarried, since the possibility of a marriage tie with the royal family would keep many of Stilicho's supporters in line.

Yet the main obstacle faced by Stilicho remained the obstinate refusal of the aristocracy to participate in the defence of their own Empire. Although they accepted Stilicho's rule, they stubbornly clung to the privileges accorded to them in the past. They resented paying tax, using any means possible to limit the amount they paid to the government. As a result, the government attempted to enforce conscription as it couldn't afford to pay for 'mercenaries'. The aristocracy opposed these attempts to enforce recruitment as they wanted to keep able-bodied men to work for them on their vast estates. Accordingly, the government demanded payment *in lieu* of recruits with which to pay for mercenaries. This was resented by the aristocracy who clung to the ideal that Rome should be defended by a 'Roman' army, not by outsiders. This vicious cycle was one of the main factors that restricted Stilicho's ability to deal with the crises that would soon arise.

The Pictish war

During the course of 398 the Picts may have attempted to attack across the northern frontier of Britain, possibly as a result of news arriving of Gildo's rebellion.[39] The attack appears to have been defeated and news sent to Italy of the assault. In response, in 400 Stilicho seems to have ordered the forces in the north to withdraw to Hadrian's Wall and also ordered repairs and upgrades to the wall and other structures – the work being paid for with the money raised during the African campaign. Although unsupported except possibly by archaeology, the story suggests that Stilicho was working to maintain the structure of the Empire from an early stage in his rule.[40] It is likely that it was at this time that Stilicho first appointed a military *comes* in Britain to coordinate local defence. However, priorities were to change as time passed. Britain was again allowed to fade into the background as he came to focus more and more on one area, to the detriment of others.

Affairs in the East

Alaric

In his new position as *magister militum per Illyricum*, Alaric controlled regular Roman forces as well as his own tribesmen. It would appear that Alaric and his men were billeted in cities according to normal Roman practice, although Claudian's claim that they retained the captives taken in Greece as slaves remains doubtful.[41]

In his new post he was able to exercise jurisdiction as a regular Roman officer, which no doubt enhanced his reputation amongst his followers.[42] More importantly, he also took control of the imperial *fabricae* (arms factories) at Thessalonica, Naissus, Ratiaria and at Horreum Margi in Moesia Secunda.[43] Using these factories he was able to extensively equip his men with Roman-made equipment. The result was that they became a much more effective military machine, being able to face the Roman troops

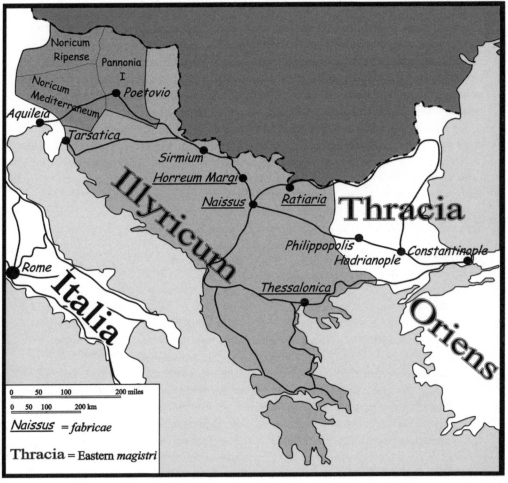

15. Alaric as magister militum per Illyricum *with associated* fabricae.

at near parity.

Furthermore, it is possible that Alaric was able to improve the quality of his cavalry whilst in Illyricum. Although never very numerous, it is almost certain that the proportion of cavalry in Alaric's forces was, for a Germanic army, relatively high. This was due in no small part to his access to the Thracian herds. It is clear that he would not be allowed to vastly increase the number of horsemen under his control, as the leaders in Constantinople would have been wary of making Alaric too powerful and the emperor retained personal control of the distribution of the horses.[44] On the other hand, it is likely that he was allowed to replace many of the weaker mounts. Being composed largely of nobles and their *comitatus*, the cavalry were already a formidable force; with more powerful horses, the quality of Alaric's cavalry now became exceptional for a barbarian army.

Yet it was not only the cavalry that was improved by the stay in Illyricum. Both the cavalry and the infantry were able to acquire armour and helmets from the Roman *fabricae*. Furthermore, freed from the necessity of finding food, the troops were also free to train and improve both their drill and their fighting techniques. Since Alaric could now command Roman troops, it is possible that he gave orders that the Goths be trained by Roman officers. Yet although they were now becoming the equivalent of the best-trained Roman troops, their major drawback remained: they were only united behind Alaric whilst he was successful.

Yet this did not really matter. Alaric had achieved what he wanted: a regular Roman command and comparative wealth for his followers. It may not have been on the scale of Stilicho or Arbogast, but it was enough to keep him and his followers content for a little while. From 397 to 400 he was able to relax a little and reap the rewards of his actions. Only at the end of this period did the situation begin to deteriorate.

East–West Relations

Understandably, a serious deterioration took place in East–West relations following Stilicho's expeditions to Illyricum. The major difficulty lay with the fact that power no longer lay with the emperors. Instead, it was held by individuals who did not have the legal standing of emperor. As a result, they needed to be constantly on the guard against enemies who now only had to control the emperor, not attempt to overthrow him.[45] Understandably, trust became secondary to suspicion in their dealings with others.

In the West, part of the opposition to Stilicho was based on the rebellion of Gildo. It was acknowledged that in large part Gildo's defection was due to the Eastern government's hostility to Stilicho and Gildo's attempt to turn the division to his own advantage. This turn of events was unacceptable to many in the West.[46] It would appear that Claudian's poem '*de Bello Gildonico*' ('The War against Gildo') was written to counter the reaction of a growing Western opposition. In the poem Claudian declares that Gildo was the 'third tyrant', coming after Magnus Maximus and Eugenius.[47] In this manner the poem fulfils two functions. Firstly, it separates the actions of Gildo from the political quarrel between Stilicho and Eutropius; in effect, separating the rebellion from the problems faced by East–West relations. Secondly, the poem endorses Stilicho as the continuator of Theodosian policies, since he has now taken Theodosius' place as the defender of the West. In this way Claudian and Stilicho will have hoped to quieten unrest and encourage the concept that Stilicho was actually in the right, following as he did Theodosian policies throughout the crisis.

With regards to East–West relations, Stilicho's status as *hostis publicus* emphasized his removal from Eastern politics and resulted in him adopting a low profile in relation to Eastern affairs, although an attempt at reconciliation in Claudian's poem '*de Bello Gildonico*' was ignored in Constantinople.[48] A good example of Stilicho's restraint, possibly linked with his attempt at reconciliation, is in the Western nomination for consul for the year 399.[49] As Stilicho was still *hostis publicus* in the East it was certain that his nomination would be rejected, so for 399 the West's proposal was Mallius Theodorus, a gifted Milanese lawyer. There is no evidence at this time that Stilicho was attempting to provoke discord in the East. He did not need to, thanks to the actions of Eutropius.

Eutropius

Eutropius' position as leader of the Eastern government seemed assured. Secure in the affections of Arcadius, not least because he had organized Arcadius' marriage to Eudoxia and so frustrated Rufinus, he had also personally led the forces that had evicted the Huns from Asia Minor.[50] His reputation could not have been higher. If his rise had been rapid, his fall was to be spectacularly swift.

His feelings of security resulted in a mistake of catastrophic proportions. Following his victorious campaign against the Huns, he secured the nomination to be consul for 399. The Senates of both East and West were appalled at the thought of a 'eunuch-consul'. Such a thing had never happened before and the action was felt to be an insult to the dignity of the Empire. The post of consul was still held in high regard and was seen as a legacy from the past; the holders could be traced back over 900 years to the foundation of the Republic.[51] The move was viewed with shock and horror, especially in the more conservative West. Although the move was accepted by Arcadius in the East, in the West it was rejected. In the West the consuls for the year are listed as either Mallius and Theodorus or as Mallius Theodorus alone.[52]

With the announcement all attempts at conciliation between Stilicho and Eutropius appear to have ceased. The poet Claudian was now given permission to attack Eutropius in his poems. Furthermore, Claudian was a friend of Theodorus and had accepted a commission to write a panegyric on Theodorus' nomination as consul. The situation provided a perfect opportunity for Claudian to show his talents. In '*Panegyricus de Consulatu Flavii Manlii Theodori*' ('Panegyric on the Consulship of Flavius Manlius Theodorus') he was able to highlight Theodorus' manly pursuit of legal matters as an honest and upright family man.

> Thou art as deaf to the prayers of injustice as thou art generous and attentive where the demand is just. Pride, that ever accompanies office, has not so much as dared to touch thy mind. Thy look is a private citizen's nor allows that it has deserved what it thinks to have but grown; but full of stately modesty shines forth a gravity that charms because pride is banished. What sedition, what madness of the crowd could see thee and not sink down appeased? What country so barbarous, so foreign in its customs, as not to bow in reverence before thy mediation? Who that desires the honeyed charm of polished eloquence would not desert the lyre-accompanied song of tuneful Olympus? In every activity we see thee as we see thee in thy books, describing the creation of the newly-fashioned earth or the parts of the soul; we recognize thy character in thy pages.
>
> Claud., *Pan. Man. Theo.* 241f.

In contrast, throughout '*In Eutropium, Liber Prior*' ('Against Eutropius, Book One')

Claudian depicts Eutropius as the 'non-man' who owed all he had to deceit and dishonesty. The result was a 'savage, hysterical flood of invective' from which all attempts at reconciliation had been removed.[53]

> His passion for gold increases — the only passion his mutilated body can indulge. Of what use was emasculation? The knife is powerless against reckless avarice. That hand so well practised in petty thefts, accustomed to rifle a cupboard or remove the bolt from the unwatched coffer, now finds richer spoils and the whole world to rob. All the country between the Tigris and Mount Haemus he exposes for sale at a fixed price, this huckster of Empire, this infamous dealer in honours. This man governs Asia for the which his villa has paid. That man buys Syria with his wife's jewels. Another repents of having taken Bithynia in exchange for his paternal mansion. Fixed above the open doors of his hall is a list giving the provinces and their prices: so much for Galatia, for Pontus so much, so much will buy one Lydia. Would you govern Lycia? Then lay down so many thousands. Phrygia? A little more. He wishes everything to be marked with its price to console him for his own fortune and, himself so often sold, he wants to sell everything. When two are rivals he suspends in the balance their opposed payment; along with the weight the judge inclines, and a province hangs wavering in a pair of scales.
>
> Claud., *In Eut. I.* 190f.

To add to Eutropius' problems, he made a major miscalculation. His claim to sole responsibility for the defeat of the Huns had repercussions closer to home. Although his military abilities may have been great, it is clear that without the aid of his military leaders – who probably acted as advisors during the campaign – he would not have been successful.[54] In spite of their support during the campaign, Eutropius continued with his policy of marginalising the same military leaders.

If that did not infuriate the generals, in direct contrast to his treatment of them he now appeared to reward Alaric for his pillaging of Greece by giving him a major military post, that of *magister militum per Illyricum*. It should not be forgotten that in the East the posts of *magister militum* were, theoretically at least, equal.[55] By his actions Eutropius had made a rebel the equal of loyal, long-serving soldiers. This was obviously an insult of the highest order.

If the aristocracy in Constantinople were dismayed by his nomination for the consulship, they were also apprehensive concerning a further mistake Eutropius made. It was a long-standing tradition that the senior minister could charge citizens for access to the emperor to present petitions. Eutropius appears to have taken this to a greater degree than ever before, allegedly even charging Eudoxia for access to her husband during the day.[56] Although probably a later invention to accentuate his greed, the story does highlight his growing reputation for avarice.

Furthermore, Eutropius had differed in his appointment practices from Stilicho in the West. Whereas Stilicho had continued to appoint men of standing who had served under Theodosius, as well as men of traditional families who would expect such advancement, Eutropius had promoted 'new men'. As a result, and much to their infuriation, the old, powerful families had been disassociated from the running of the Empire.

As the senators and citizens of Constantinople began to view their new leader with unease, and with the army leaders becoming impatient with their exclusion from power, Eutropius' hold over Arcadius received a devastating blow.

Gainas

In 397, in company with Stilicho, Gainas had led the Eastern army against Alaric. Upon their recall, he had led his troops back to Constantinople, where he had engineered the death of Rufinus. As a *comes rei militaris* his powers were limited and he undoubtedly felt slighted by Eutropius' failure to reward him adequately for his services. He was probably made *magister militum per Thraciam*, but this may have seemed a hollow prize as he does not seem to have been given any troops, instead being forced to raise his own once he was in position. This would have been galling, especially when Eutropius made the rebel Alaric *magister militum per Illyricum* and gave him Roman troops to command.

According to Sozomen, Gainas was forced to recruit Germanic warriors from across the Rhine, promising their leaders the rank of tribune.[57] This would accord with him being given few – if any – troops to command. He was attempting to create a new army for himself. Yet it is likely that most Germanic recruits would be enrolled in the army following normal measures; the rank of tribune would only go to his friends and relatives from beyond the Rhine. These were coming under pressure from the Huns, and Gainas was simply promising to use his influence to try to get them influential posts in the Roman army. At this time Hunnic power across the Danube was growing and it is probable that Hunnic leaders did not want potential warriors crossing the Rhine to serve in the Roman army against them. Incentives would be needed to ensure that the German leaders who crossed would not be forced to return and face Hunnic wrath for their 'desertion'.

Annoyed at not being given an appointment suitable to his service and seniority, Gainas would have felt very insecure. After all, one of his predecessors was Abundantius, the general who had used his influence to promote Eutropius' career. His patronage had not saved him from Eutropius and he had been disgraced and exiled. If Eutropius could banish a patron, there was no doubt that he could do the same to a Goth from across the Danube.

Tribigild's revolt

Following the campaign of Eutropius against the Huns in 397, Tribigild, one of Gainas' relatives, had been promoted to *comes rei militaris* and had been sent to Phrygia to command the Gothic troops stationed at Nacoleia.[58] During the summer of 399 he had been in Constantinople, before leaving to rejoin his troops. During his stay in the capital he may have expected to receive a further promotion to a more senior position, in a similar vein to Alaric, or he may have had his subsidies cut, or both.[59] Whichever one is correct, in retaliation when he arrived back in Phrygia he revolted, immediately losing his post as *comes*.[60] A native of Selge in Pamphylia led resistance to Tribigild and, gathering a force of local farmers and slaves, almost trapped Tribigild in an ambush.[61] Forced to withdraw from Phrygia, Tribigild began to ravage Lydia, Pamphylia and Pisidia (see Map 1).[62]

Alarmed at this turn of events, Eutropius offered high rank to Tribigild if he would stop the rebellion.[63] Tribigild refused the offer and the revolt continued, Tribigild's forces being swollen with the arrival of 'slaves and outcasts'.[64] In the face of stiffening opposition it would appear that Eutropius, after disbanding much of the military staff and replacing them with his own, inexperienced nominees, was forced to turn to Gainas for assistance. It seems that in the emergency all available troops were gathered, including raw recruits who were Goths.[65]

In a position subordinate to Gainas, Eutropius appointed his own close friend Leo as *comes rei militaris* in the East.[66] Leo was first sent to defend the Hellespont before being dispatched to take control of Pamphylia. In the meantime, Gainas was ordered to defend Thrace and the Hellespont against attack, though whether the attack was expected to be made by Tribigild or whether Gainas was to guard from the possible threat of rebellion by Alaric in Illyricum is unclear.[67] Fravitta, the *magister militum per Orientem*, remained at his HQ in Antioch.[68] Once in Pamphylia Leo was allegedly attacked by barbarian troops sent by Gainas to help him.[69] Confused and threatened, Leo was easily routed when Tribigild advanced against him, dying in the rout.

With Leo dead, Eutropius had no choice but to order Gainas to cross into Asia Minor and defeat Tribigild. Once in Asia Minor, however, Gainas remained inactive and allowed the revolt to continue, probably encouraging Tribigild in his actions. It is unclear whether Gainas and Tribigild were acting together from an early stage or whether Gainas only later encouraged the revolt.[70] It seems likely that Tribigild was at first acting on his own initiative, and that only later did Gainas realize that he could use the situation to his advantage. This he now did, as he complained to the Emperor Arcadius that he could not face Tribigild as it was far too risky and he faced a possible defeat.[71] He also pointed out that Tribigild's main reason for rebelling was Eutropius. Therefore, he would only risk facing Tribigild if his demands were met and he could attempt to negotiate a treaty with Tribigild. Obviously, part of these demands included the ultimatum that Eutropius be removed from power.

Eudoxia

Back in Constantinople opposition to Eutropius had begun to focus around Arcadius' wife Eudoxia. Eutropius seems to have continually reminded her that she owed her place to him, and the constant reminders and accompanying insults resulted in her turning against Eutropius. She was joined by other ministers who were in opposition to Eutropius and the movement began to build.

When the message from Gainas arrived Arcadius initially refused to dismiss Eutropius, a man for whom he felt considerable affection. However, at this point Eudoxia intervened and convinced the emperor that Eutropius had to be removed from power. Reluctantly, Arcadius complied; in autumn 399 Eutropius was arrested and sent into exile in Cyprus. The news of his fall was received with relief in the West, and Claudian responded by writing '*In Eutropium, Liber Posterior*' ('Against Eutropium, Book Two'), which denigrates his failure to deal appropriately with Tribigild's revolt.[72] At an unknown later date Eutropius was to be recalled and tried for treason before finally being executed.

Eutropius' legacy[73]

Eutropius is represented in our sources as an evil eunuch, filled with avarice and willing to use unscrupulous methods to attain his desires. Although it is likely that some of this reputation is well deserved, there exists a valid reason for his greed. Although he doubtless retained a percentage of the money he raised for himself, the remainder was used to replenish a depleted treasury. Theodosius' wars had been costly and Rufinus had not had the time to raise much money. Therefore, it was left to Eutropius to fill the unpopular role of money-gatherer. Using his popularity with the Emperor Arcadius, Eutropius forced the rich to pay taxes and the East managed to maintain a healthy reserve of cash. His legislative activity clearly illustrates this.[74] In contrast, Stilicho in the West could not afford to treat the Western senators in such a cavalier fashion, as he needed their support. The cash supplies dwindled as he was forced to use what cash he had to pay for mercenaries.

Furthermore, Eutropius continued to implement the policies of Rufinus by refusing to use the army unless it was an extreme emergency. This resulted in the generals being deprived of ultimate power. Again this can be compared favourably with the West, where the growth of military power ultimately led to the overthrow of the last emperor. Although the end result was Eutropius' fall and exile, the example he and Rufinus had set continued in use and ensured that when strong emperors did arise, they were able to retake control of both the army and of the East.

The coup of Gainas

Eutropius' place as 'head' of the *consistorium* was taken some time before August 399 by Aurelian, a respected individual of a traditional family, who had previously been *magister officiorum* and prefect of Constantinople.[75] Seen as the leader of those opposed to the employment of Germans in the Empire, his appointment was not what Gainas expected as the result of his intrigues. However, Aurelian's appointment was popular in the court as it was viewed as a return to traditional practices after the rule of Eutropius. As such, he was elected consul for 400 in Constantinople, although this was not recognized in the West.

Yet Aurelian's command of the East was to be short-lived. Gainas was now the undisputed leader of the army, yet following Aurelian's appointment he was still excluded from councils and only on the periphery of government. Using the example of Stilicho as his benchmark, Gainas was unhappy with his subordinate position. Gainas joined his forces to those of Tribigild and advanced to Chalcedon. There he demanded and received a meeting with the emperor.

Arcadius was forced to submit to Gainas' demands. Aurelian and his supporters were sent into exile. He was replaced by the pro-German Eutychianus. Gainas was finally made *magister utriusque militiae in praesentalis*.[76] He was now the equal in the East of Stilicho in the West. He entered Constantinople and assumed his position as head of the government. Tribigild, however, did not live to gain the fruits of his victory: he died shortly afterwards of an unknown cause.[77] Of all of the commanders of Theodosius I in the East, only Gainas, Fravitta and Alaric now remained.[78]

Fall of Gainas

Unfortunately, Gainas did not have the ability to cope with his new-found power. Conditions in the capital quickly deteriorated. Against his will, Eudoxia was crowned as *Augusta* (empress) on 9 January 400 and, aware of his fast-deteriorating position, Gainas feigned illness and left Constantinople. He arranged for his followers to meet him outside the city, but, in an unprecedented move, as they left they were attacked by the population of the city. Some 7,000 were alleged to have been trapped in the city and slaughtered, and Gainas was quickly declared *hostis publicus*.

In response, with the remainder of his followers Gainas moved to Thrace and devastated the area before attempting to cross to Asia Minor.[79] Fravitta, earlier the *magister militum per Orientem* although he may have been declared *magister militum in praesentalis* by this time, moved to block the attempt and heavily defeated Gainas. The victory was so resounding that a column was built by Arcadius depicting Gainas' defeat, although a statue of Arcadius, not Fravitta, surmounted the column. Gainas headed back north through Thrace and, prior to crossing the Danube, killed the Roman troops still with him out of fear of betrayal.[80] After he had left Thrace, the province was further plundered by runaway slaves and deserters claiming that they were Huns.[81] Fravitta followed Gainas north and was able to restore order in Thrace as he moved. Once outside the Empire Gainas was attacked and killed by the Hunnic king Uldin, who was rewarded for his act by being given the title *comes*.[82] Upon his return from the successful campaign, Fravitta was nominated for the consulship in 401.

Gainas' legacy

Aurelian and his fellows were recalled from exile and reinstated, with Eudoxia now in firm control of the government. By coincidence, Synesius of Cyrene was present as an ambassador for his city at the restoration and he made a speech, *De Regno* (On Kingship), which called for the elimination of barbarians from all positions except as slaves. Although superbly timed for the downfall of Gainas, the speech should not be seen as echoing popular opinion and government policy against barbarians; it is more of a local reaction against the actions of the barbarians over the previous two years and, as such, reflects a temporary state of affairs.[83] In fact, when seen in context it is probable that Synesius was voicing support for his friend Aurelian. Aurelian had been exiled in part for his stand against the appointment of Alaric and Gainas. Synesius was voicing his support. Later, in an unconnected letter Synesius actually praised the *foederati* for their service.[84]

However, echoing Synesius' speech, the fall of Gainas is usually seen as the defeat of the 'barbarian' element in the East, which allowed affairs to be kept under imperial rather than 'barbarian' control. This is compared with the West, where a succession of 'barbarian' army leaders presided over the end of the Empire.

This is unjustified: after an interregnum in the East there once again arose powerful generals of barbarian birth. The difference between the East and the West is only minimal but essential. After the fall of Gainas the civilian ministers were determined that never again would they be dominated by individuals whose only claim to power was the support of the army. The result was that, unlike in the West, when a strong emperor reappeared he could more readily enforce his decisions on the council, removing members obstructing him and once again personally taking control of the army. In the West, the emperors remained subordinate to the *magister militum* until, finally, they were perceived as unnecessary and the Empire quietly faded away.

Chapter Ten

Alaric and the Invasion of Italy, 401–402

Reconciliation

The Western court was confused and alarmed at the news coming from the East.[1] The confusion in the Eastern capital would have been almost indecipherable in the out-of-date reports reaching Stilicho in the West. However, one thing quickly became clear: Eutropius had fallen. In response Claudian wrote his two invectives attacking Eutropius. The second of these was written in September 399, after the fall of Eutropius but before the coup of Gainas in March 400.[2] This poem contains the last mention of the claim to guardianship of both halves of the Empire:

> There now shone forth but one hope of salvation — Stilicho. Him the expectation of whose visits the consciousness of deeds ill-done had ever rendered bitter and unpleasant, him whose approach even as far as the Alps afflicted the Byzantines (*Byzantinos* (*sibi*)) with fear of death and punishment, all now wish to come, repentant of their former wrongdoing. To him they look as to a star amid this universal shipwreck of war; to him innocent and guilty alike address their prayers.
>
> Claud, *In Eutropium, II* 502f.

The claim is aimed specifically at Aurelian, demanding that he relinquish his position and accept Stilicho in the East. Furthermore, with Eutropius gone, Stilicho's status as *hostis publicus* ceased.[3] As a result, in 399 Stilicho arranged to be nominated for the first time as the consul for 400; Symmachus was to travel to Milan to be present for the festivities.[4] This was Stilicho's reward for the reconquest of Africa. Due to the confusion in the East, however, Stilicho refused to acknowledge Aurelian as the East's nominee for the consulship.[5]

In the meantime the level of confusion continued to grow. Aurelian was removed by pressure from Gainas in December 399 and replaced by the pro-German Eutychianus. Eudoxia was crowned *Augusta* (empress) on 9 January 400, possibly as a reward for her support against Eutropius, before Gainas organized a coup in March and took control in Constantinople.[6] However, Gainas himself was overthrown in July and his troops massacred. Aurelian and his followers returned, but it was Caesarius, not Aurelian, who became the new *praefectus praetorio Orientis*. Stilicho and the Western Senate must have been wondering what was going to happen next.

However, contrary to the experience of the previous year, the situation now settled in the East, although tension between the two courts remained high. As messengers travelled between East and West it soon became clear that Stilicho's claim to be *parens principum* of the East was effectively invalid. The claim had not been based upon Arcadius' age, since he had long been old enough to rule, but on his inability to rule effectively without guidance. As the senior member of the Theodosian house, Stilicho saw it as his duty to safeguard the two emperors against unscrupulous guardians, hence his claim in 399.

It slowly became clear that the ministers leading affairs in the East were in reality colluding with the Empress Eudoxia. As a capable individual in her own right, she had the capacity to guard Arcadius from harm and she would ensure that the East would be passed to her children – by 400 she had two, Flacilla and Pulcheria. In early 400 she gave birth to a third daughter, Arcadia, and in 401 to a boy, Theodosius. The continuation of the Eastern Empire in the hands of the Theodosian house now seemed assured. Stilicho allowed his previous claims to *parens principum* of the East to lapse, instead adopting a policy of family loyalty. Slowly, East–West relations thawed, as shown by the presence of both emperors on the base of the Column of Arcadius and the fact that the two emperors were declared joint consuls for 402.

On the other hand, claims that relations had thawed to such an extent that the East now returned all of Illyricum to the West are unfounded; Illyricum remained divided.[7] However, it may have been at around this time that the Diocese of Pannonia, which had earlier been transferred to the West, was renamed 'Illyricum' – possibly to aid clarity in the West concerning the title of *praefectus praetorio Illyrici*.[8] The actual prefecture, however, remained part of the Eastern Empire.

The improvements in relations were slow and not universally accepted. One of Eudoxia's councillors – and allegedly the father of her son Theodosius II – was called John. At some point, probably in 404, he was accused by Fravitta of deliberately trying to wreck the unity of the Empire by opposing the renewal of friendly relations with the West.[9] Fravitta was quickly arrested and executed.[10] Although a later phenomenon, the episode illustrates that the understanding between East and West remained fragile.

Alaric

As the talks between East and West continued, one person was left on the periphery. Alaric, the *magister militum per Illyricum*, is not mentioned in any of these events, although the outcome would have a grave impact upon his political position, especially with regard to his location between East and West. Furthermore, many of these recent events would have directly affected his personal standing.

In 400 Fravitta, the *magister militum in praesentalis*, had pursued Gainas through Thrace, restoring order to the troubled province. In the following year Fravitta had remained either in Constantinople or in the Balkan region. His destruction of Gainas had shown that there was to be no unity between the last survivors of Theodosius' military commanders in the East. Alaric was on his own.

The rapid fall of Gainas also illustrated that the civilian government had regained control of the East. Although his position as leader of his people was now assured, thanks to the long sojourn in Illyricum, things were beginning to look bleak for Alaric: he had lost Eutropius, the man who had initially given him the position, and the East was, paradoxically, becoming stronger now that Gainas had been evicted.[11] Furthermore, the rising of the population in Constantinople against Gainas had shown that, however temporary, the mood in the East was anti-German and anti-Eutropius. This is shown by the reading of Synesius of Cyrene's treatise, *De Regno* (On Imperial Rule), in which he attacks the employment of 'Skythians' (Goths) and criticizes the employment of high-ranking barbarian officers.[12]

Although for the time being Fravitta adopted a low profile – after all, he was a Goth – he was still a capable general and a formidable foe.[13] The East now had an efficient army available which it was willing to use and a general capable of using it. Should the government turn against Alaric, he would be hard pressed to survive.

Taking all of these considerations into account, it was clear that Alaric's position was at best insecure. With Gainas' flight through Dacia and Fravitta's subsequent campaign, it is likely that supplies dwindled in the Balkans. Furthermore, it may be that the Eastern government chose this time to cancel Alaric's *annona* (subsidies).[14] However, although it is possible that this helped to formulate his decision to move, with the resources of a large part of Illyricum to call upon the loss of the *annona* should not have caused a long-term problem.

There is also the suggestion that Uldin the Hun and his followers had been accepted as *foederati* as a reward for killing Gainas. It is possible that Uldin used his new position to threaten the Goths in Illyricum in an attempt to force them to leave.[15] Yet there is no evidence in Claudian for such a suggestion; instead, he places all of the blame for what happened next on Alaric.

Overall, although it is unlikely that the East took any action regarding Alaric, he must have realized that in the near future the army would be turned against him, at which point he would be forced to return to a nomadic existence. He was also aware that there was resistance in the Gothic ranks to his continued dominance of Gothic affairs, although at this time only Sarus, a Goth of high standing, was willing to stand up to him.[16] As a result of all of these events, Alaric took the only course open to him: he offered his services to Stilicho.[17]

Unfortunately, Stilicho was not in a position to offer him a post. The Senate in Rome was steadfast in its disapproval of the use of even limited numbers of barbarians; to enrol Alaric and his forces was to invite political disaster. Furthermore, there was nowhere that they could be stationed.

The East could leave them in Illyricum, since this was a relatively isolated position from which they could cause relatively little damage to the East. There was no such backwater in the West. Maintaining Alaric in the Diocese of Illyricum (Pannonia) was not an option. The position would give him easy access to Italy and allow him to place too much pressure on the Western government. Giving Alaric a command in Gaul or Spain was also out of the question; his forces would settle in relatively peaceful and prosperous areas and, once settled, they would be unwilling to move at a later date. Furthermore, being settled in any of these places would greatly strengthen the Goths' political position. Stilicho did not have the military strength to both control the Goths in the West and defend Italy against attack from the north.[18] Alaric's offer of service was declined.

As the situation in Constantinople stabilized, and as the possibility of an agreement between East and West grew, Alaric must have felt that all he had worked for was under threat. The army under Fravitta was nearby and precluded any advance on Constantinople, as he had done in 395. The East was now secure from danger. Moreover, it was possible that the army would be sent to attack him, either to destroy him, to force him out of the Empire, or at least remove him as a threat by eliminating a significant proportion of his forces. This could take the form of defeat in battle or by military pressure forcing the tribesmen to change allegiance. Possibly in response to his weakening position, Alaric appears to have decided to raise the stakes a little: in either 400 or 401, for the first time he took the title '*Rex Gothorum*' ('King of the Goths').[19] Although at this early date it was probably a political manoeuvre to emphasize the unity of his people and so send a clear warning against attack to the East, the title of *Rex* (Gothic '*reiks*') showed that he was the sole leader of the Goths and could now be styled '*Tyrannus Geticus*' by Prudentius. However, it was still inferior to the title of '*Thiudans*' which was applied only to the ruling emperor of Rome.[20] The net effect was that the gradual centralization of power and the curbing of independent Gothic authority had begun.[21] The elevation of Alaric as '*reiks*' was the first step in creating a unified Gothic 'kingdom'. By giving the Goths clear leadership, it began the process of eliminating the situation where separate and equal Gothic leaders led groups that could, as a consequence, do what they wanted. However, at this early stage the Goths still relied on Alaric's ability to withstand Roman pressure to conform and merge with the rest of the Roman population.[22]

Yet as his feelings of insecurity grew Alaric realized that his time as an Eastern general was now running out. Stilicho had turned down his offer of service, yet with the East secure there was nowhere else he could go. Learning that Stilicho was busy dealing with the situation in Raetia and Noricum, Alaric decided to act.

The invasion of Raetia and Noricum

As the negotiations continued between East and West and between Stilicho and Alaric, in early autumn 401 news arrived of an invasion of Raetia and Noricum by Vandals and Alans.[23] Quickly gathering his forces, including the troops guarding the passes over the Julian Alps, Stilicho set out on campaign to defeat the invaders.[24] Unfortunately there are no details of the campaign: Claudian tells us simply that the enemy were quickly cowed and agreed to furnish new recruits.[25]

The information given is far too sparse. The campaign itself, spread over two distinct provinces, almost certainly lasted well into the new year. This would have been expected by Stilicho. He would, therefore, have known that shortly after he had crossed them the passes over the mountains to Italy would have been difficult to traverse, as they would have been blocked by winter snows.[26] Anticipating a successful conclusion to the campaign, Stilicho would have expected to remain in the area with

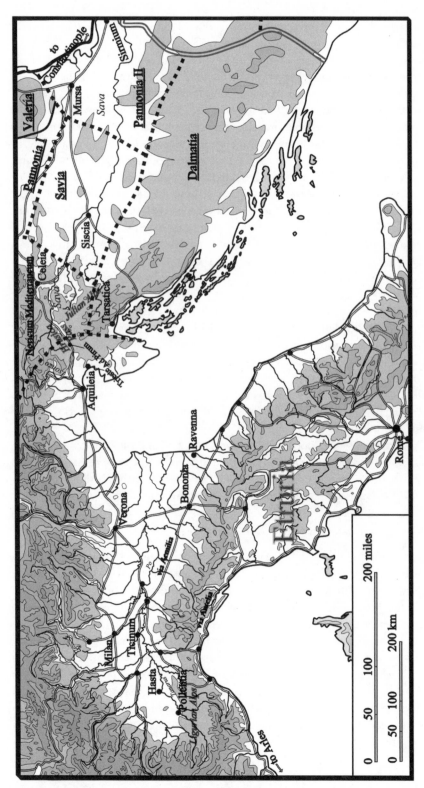

16. *Alaric's invasion of Italy.*

the army to supervise the peace treaties and organize the integration of the new recruits. He will also have wanted to spend some time in the new year parading the army along the Danube frontier to ensure there would be no further invasion, as he had on the Rhine in 396.

Yet from one section in Claudian it is clear that Stilicho was beginning to come under pressure from the Senate. Given the recent disturbances against the use of Germanic troops in the East, there seems to have been a similar reaction against their use in the West. The circumstances and events are unclear, however Claudian emphasizes that the numbers of barbarians being enrolled were 'adequate' for the task, not overwhelming.[27] Traditional senatorial expectations were once again coming to the fore. In the circumstances, it was lucky for Stilicho that he managed to secure recruits from the recently defeated tribes; whilst he was still in the north word reached him of an unexpected attack.

The invasion of Italy

In clear breach of his agreement with the East to be *magister militum per Illyricum*, Alaric gathered his forces and in late autumn 401 he invaded the West. He was aided by the good fortune that the Alan and Vandal raids on Raetia and Pannonia had come when the harvest was still being gathered; once in Italy supplies would not be a problem, at least for a short while.[28]

Stilicho was completely taken by surprise.[29] There have sometimes been claims of collusion between the Eastern government and Alaric in the latter's decision to invade Italy.[30] Given the attempts at rapprochement between East and West this is doubtful. It is far more likely that Alaric was reacting to political developments within the East and in response to the newly found concord between East and West, and was coming to the conclusion that at some point he would be attacked and forced out of Illyricum. Furthermore, whenever Stilicho had attacked him, Stilicho had first led a campaign on the frontier to pacify the area and recruit fresh troops. Although the campaign in Raetia was obviously a reaction to invasion, it was certain that Stilicho – if victorious – would use the campaign to enlarge the Western army.

Any attempt to force the passes across the Julian Alps against a newly reinforced Italian army was unthinkable. Alaric had taken part in the futile assaults by the *foederati* during the first day on the army of Arbogast and Eugenius at the Battle of the Frigidus in 395; he would not want a repeat of the ordeal. Stilicho's absence in the north was the only real chance that Alaric would have of invading Italy. As a result, Alaric quickly took his army over the mountain passes and was in Italy before Stilicho could return with fresh troops and re-establish the Alpine defences.

The move placed Stilicho in extreme danger. Alaric's army was now a far more formidable force than they had been under Fritigern a generation earlier. They had benefitted from long service both alongside and against the Roman army, and thanks to their long sojourn in Illyricum they had been completely re-equipped at the Empire's expense with arms and armour lacking in earlier armies.[31] Furthermore, it is also likely that during Alaric's time as *magister militum* he was able to attract many individual warriors and small family groups, both from inside and outside the Empire, so enlarging his forces.

The invasion

Alaric entered Pannonia near Sirmium (see Map 16).[32] From there he marched swiftly north upstream along the Sava, crossing the Hrusica Pass into Italy on 18 November 401, not long before the passes became blocked by winter snow.[33] It is interesting to note that the garrison of Ad Pirum on the pass did not cause him any delay, probably because the majority of the garrison was with Stilicho in the North. En route he would have passed near to the Goths that had earlier been settled in Pannonia, and a large number of these Goths may have joined his expedition.[34] Descending onto the coastal plains north of Trieste, Alaric was faced with small-scale opposition at both the Isonzo and Timavo rivers, but these were easily brushed aside and he headed for the north of the peninsula.[35] The first major city he came to was Aquileia, which he placed under siege.[36]

The reaction in the West was, unsurprisingly, one of complete shock. The cities of Italy had walls, but the vast majority of the Italian army was in the north with Stilicho. At the same time as the Goths descended into Italy, Claudian reports the appearance of portents and omens predicting dire calamities.[37] Honorius contemplated moving the court to Arelate (Arles) in Gaul, and it is possibly at this early stage that Flavius Macrobius Longinianus was sent to Rome to oversee repairs to the Walls of Aurelian, since they were in a state of disrepair and it seemed obvious that Rome was a potential target for the advancing Goths. The situation in Italy was confused and the raids of small bands of Goths widespread. North Italian bishops were unable to attend the dedication of a new church by Gaudentius of Breschia, and Symmachus, on a mission from Rome to Milan, was forced to detour via Ticinum to reach the imperial court.[38] Once there, he was forced to await the return of Stilicho from Raetia.

Quickly realizing that Aquileia was too tough a nut to crack, in early 402 Alaric raised the siege and passed into the Plain of Venetia, taking control of many of the minor cities in the area. However, as Stilicho was trapped in Noricum by the weather, Alaric decided that, as when he had first rebelled against the East, the best way to pressurize the Western government into acceding to his demands was to advance towards the imperial court in Milan. Accordingly, within a short space of time Milan was placed under siege.

Although Stilicho was unable to organize the logistics for a very quick return to Italy – especially as many, if not all, of the passes were blocked – he was able to take other actions in order to secure the safety of Italy. To that end, he sent messengers to Britain and the provinces of Germany ordering a muster of troops and their despatch to Italy at the earliest moment.[39] At the same time, he oversaw the assembly of the new Alan and Vandal recruits that his successful campaign in Raetia and Pannonia had furnished. Finally, he passed an edict inviting slaves to volunteer for service, a measure which, more than any other, highlights the fear and desperation felt in Italy.[40]

As his orders began to take effect, and as the weather moderated, at the beginning

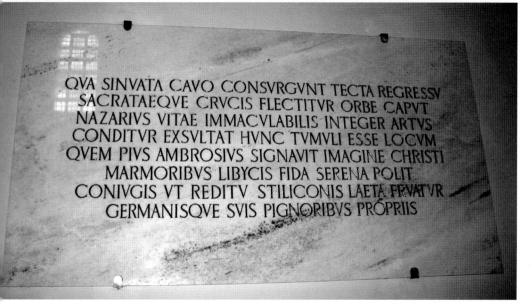

QVA SINVATA CAVO CONSVRGVNT TECTA REGRESSV
SACRATAEQVE CRVCIS FLECTITVR ORBE CAPVT
NAZARIVS VITAE IMMACVLABILIS INTEGER ARTVS
CONDITVR EXSVLTAT HVNC TVMVLI ESSE LOCVM
QVEM PIVS AMBROSIVS SIGNAVIT IMAGINE CHRISTI
MARMORIBVS LIBYCIS FIDA SERENA POLIT
CONIVGIS VT REDITV STILICONIS LAETA FRVATVR
GERMANISQVE SVIS PIGNORIBVS PROPRIIS

1. Plaque of Serena in the Basilica of San Nazaro, Milan. The church was heavily embellished by Serena in thanks for the safe return of Stilicho from the campaign in Greece. (*Courtesy, Giovanni Dall'Orto*)

2. Monument in the forum in Rome dedicated to Stilicho. After his death Olympius declared a *damnatio memoriae* on Stilicho, and as a result inscriptions dedicated to Stilicho were located and his name erased from them. In this case, the two lines that have been chiselled away were the dedication to Stilicho. (*Courtesy of G. Dobersch*)

Statue base dedicated to Claudian, Museo Archeologico Nazionale di Napoli. (*Courtesy, Berliner Brandenburgische Akademie der Wissenschaften*)

4. Mosaic from Faenza, Italy, showing a 'heroic', 'nude' Honorius seated on his throne along with Stilicho, who is standing on the left. (*Courtesy, Nic Fields*)

5. The Bas Relief of the Obelisk of Theodosius, from the Hippodrome in Constantinople. The children flanking Theodosius are Arcadius and Honorius. (*Courtesy, Erindipity, Flickr*)

6. The Colossus of Barletta. Although the identity of the emperor is disputed, it may be Honorius. (*Courtesy, Fanaticissima, Flickr*)

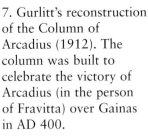

7. Gurlitt's reconstruction of the Column of Arcadius (1912). The column was built to celebrate the victory of Arcadius (in the person of Fravitta) over Gainas in AD 400.

8. The Colonne di San Lorenzo, Milan, one of the few Roman remains from the period of Stilicho's rule still extant in Milan. (*Courtesy, Paul Murray, Flickr*)

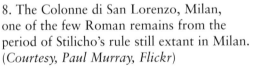

9. A *cheiroballista* from Trajan's Column. Although nearly three centuries earlier than Stilicho, these catapults remained in use in the Late Roman Army.

10. Detail from the Arch of Galerius, showing the emperor and his retinue wearing what appear to be classical 'muscled' breastplates depicting human musculature, as worn by earlier Greek hoplites. (*Courtesy, Tilemahos Efthimiadis, Flickr*)

11. Another section of the Arch of Galerius, showing troops wearing ring mail. Although it looks a little like 'scale mail', the ring mail is clearly depicted with small, drilled holes at the centre of the 'scale'. (*Courtesy, © Lorraine Kerr, caeciliametellaphotography.info*)

12. Coin from the reign of Constantine I, showing the emperor in a 'pilleus Pannonicus' (Pannonian hat). Possibly the earliest representation of this form of headgear. (*Courtesy, Beast Coins*)

13. Coin from the reign of Constantine I, showing the emperor in what may be a ridge helmet. Although in some ways unsatisfactory as a dating technique, the depiction of emperors wearing 'new' styles of helmets is one of the few methods we have of determining when these were introduced. (*Courtesy, Beast Coins*)

14. Coin from the reign of Honorius. Again, the emperor is depicted wearing what appears to be a ridge helmet, this time with an attached crest. (*Courtesy, Beast Coins*)

15. Gold Aureus issued by Constantine III. The four 'G's demonstrate that the coin was produced early in Constantine's reign, since they represent Constantine himself, along with Honorius in the West, and Arcadius and Theodosius II in the East. Shortly after this issue Arcadius died and Constantine consequently produced coins with only three 'G's. (*Courtesy, Beast Coins*)

16. Gold Aureus issued by Honorius. In contrast to that of Constantine III, this coin only has three 'G's displayed: for Honorius, Arcadius and Theodosius II. Honorius would only accept Constantine III as a colleague under extreme pressure. (*Courtesy, Beast Coins*)

18. A reconstruction of the helmet found near Koblenz. Despite the oft-assumed belief of deterioration in the quality of late-Roman equipment, the helmet shows that Roman craftsmen could still produce splendid defensive equipment. (*Courtesy, www.armamentaria.com*)

17. The Intercisa 4 helmet. The exact purpose of the large metallic crest is unknown. It may have been to designate the wearer as an officer, or it may simply have been a matter of personal taste. (*Courtesy, www.armamentaria.com*)

19. A reconstruction of the Intercisa 1 helmet, which demonstrates the simplicity of the design when compared to the earlier, 'imperial' styles of helmet. (*Courtesy, www.armamentaria.com*)

20. A reconstruction of Intercisa 2, which again shows the simplicity of design, although this time with simple decoration. (*Courtesy, www.armamentaria.com*)

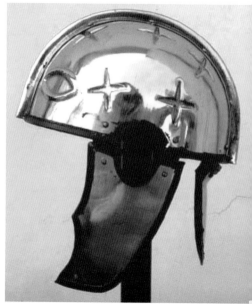

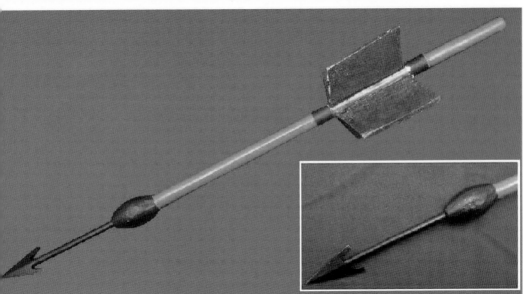

21. A reconstruction of a *plumbata*. The weight would help to give extra penetrative power to the dart, so making it a very dangerous weapon in the hands of men trained in its use. (*Courtesy, www.armamentaria.com*)

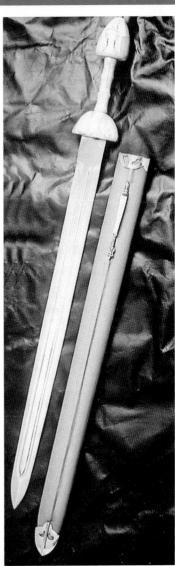

22. A reconstruction of a Roman *spatha*. This 'longsword' had replaced the earlier, shorter, *gladius* by the time of Stilicho. The reasons for the change are unknown and still a matter of some controversy. (*Courtesy, www.armamentaria.com*)

23. 'The Burial of Alaric in the Bed of the Busentinus', by Leutemann. Although the imagery used bears little resemblance to the realities of the fifth century, the burial of Alaric in the bed of a temporarily diverted river has aroused the imagination of artists and historians throughout the ages, and is a testament to the hold that Alaric and his Goths have on the image of the 'noble barbarian' that still exists to this day.

24. Consular diptych of Probus Anicius, consul in 406, depicting Emperor Honorius. (*Photograph from Ludwig von Sybel, Christliche Antike, vol. 2, Marburg, 1909*)

25. The Symmachi-Nicomachi Diptych, produced around the turn of the fifth century to celebrate the marriage alliance of these two powerful Senatorial families.

26. The Stilicho Diptych. On the left is Serena, wife of Stilicho and adopted daughter of the Emperor Theodosius. With her is their son, Eucherius.

On the right is Stilicho. His shield carries a depiction of two children, thought to be the emperors Arcadius and Honorius. If the attribution is correct, the diptych, usually dated to c.395, could be a representation of his claim to be 'parens principum', and so the 'shield' of the two young emperors. (*Courtesy, © Majed Salem, Saudi Arabia*)

27. A beautiful Gothic Eagle, dating to c.500.

The exquisite artwork clearly shows that Gothic leaders had talented craftsmen in their following. However, the cost of such craftsmanship would have placed such items far out of the reach of the average Gothic warrior/farmer.

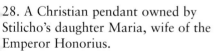

28. A Christian pendant owned by Stilicho's daughter Maria, wife of the Emperor Honorius.

The words are formed in the shape of the Christian *Chi-Rho* symbol. The shape of the 'Rho' is formed from a vertical line reading HONORI, with the name of Maria herself forming the top of the symbol. The '*Chi*' is from the names STELICHO and SERENA. The whole is finished with a horizontal line formed from the word VIVATIS. (*Musée du Louvre, Courtesy, PHG, Wikipedia*)

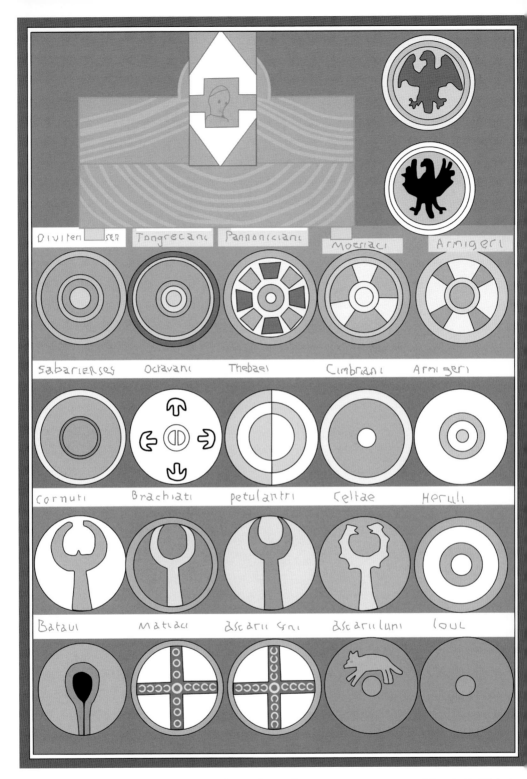

29. The insignia of the *magister peditum* from the *Notitia Dignitatum* (Oc. 5.1). This is the insignia that would have been adopted by Stilicho upon his taking control in the West in 395. Although his titles changed throughout the course of his career, it is likely that this was the only insignia of his rank that was ever used.

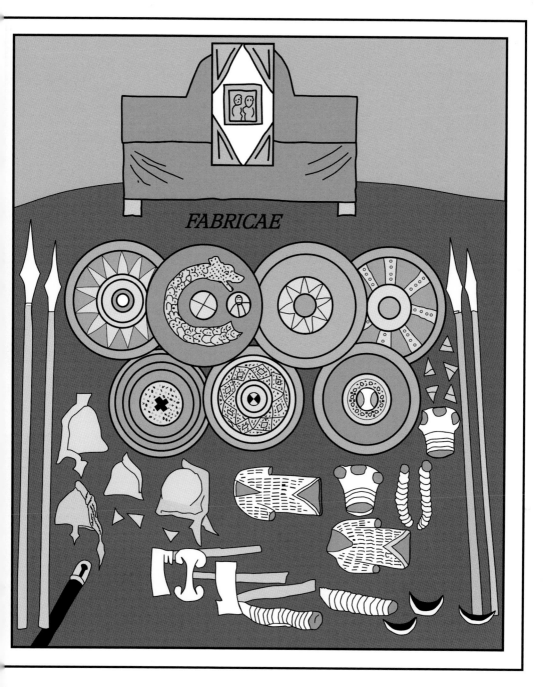

FABRICAE

30. Insignia of the *magister officiorum* from the *Notitia Dignitatum*, Oc.9.1. Despite Vegetius' claims to the contrary, the insignia clearly demonstrates that the imperial *fabricae* were producing a wide range of military equipment, including shields, helmets, body armour, and weapons.

31. The Basilica di Sant' Ambrogio, Milan, is the location of 'Stilicho's Sarcophagus'. Although the sarcophagus almost certainly does not contain the body of Stilicho, this demonstrates the affection with which Stilicho's memory is generally held. (*Courtesy, Keiron Hart, Flickr*)

32. Detail of the central panel of the Sarcophagus. (*Courtesy, Giovanni Dall'Orto*)

33. The sarcophagus itself is heavily decorated and ornamented. The level of detail shows how highly esteemed Stilicho was in the centuries after his death. (*Courtesy, Giovanni Dall'Orto*)

34. Built in the late fourth/early fifth century by Bishop Ursus, this is all that remains of the Neonian (Orthodox) Baptistery, Ravenna. Built during the period of Stilicho's supremacy, it is likely that Stilicho watched this structure being constructed.

35. Santa Agata Maggiore, Ravenna. Founded in the late fourth century, possibly when Stilicho was in control in the West, the fact that the main surviving buildings are churches demonstrates the increasing power of the Catholic church from the time of Theodosius I. (*Courtesy, J C Cuesta, Flickr*)

36. The Basilica di San Nazaro, Milan. Originally built as the Basilica Apostolorum by Bishop Ambrose, when the body of Saint Nazarus was discovered a new apse was built in the church to house it and the church was renamed. Serena, wife of Stilicho, vowed to donate to the church if Stilicho returned safely from the campaign in Greece. After his return, she fulfilled her pledge, donating the marbles for the *sacellum* and also embellishing the rest of the church. (*Courtesy, MarkusMark, Flickr*)

of March Stilicho led his troops over the mountain passes and back into Italy. Advancing with his army on Milan, uppermost of the fears in his mind would have been the political dilemma he would face if Honorius was captured or killed. Deciding that speed was essential, he split his troops, himself leading an unknown proportion ahead of the main body. Arriving in the early dark of night, he found the bridges over the River Adda to be held against him. Deciding that he needed to reach the city as soon as possible he led his small force in a night attack, breaking through the Goths' defences and entering the city.[41] Stilicho entered Milan amidst much rejoicing and relief.[42] Once inside he persuaded Honorius not to go to Gaul. Instead, preparations were made for the court to move to Ravenna, a coastal city protected by marshes with only one means of access from land. The move was completed before the end of the year.[43]

The move to Ravenna is in some respects a surprise, and defines that change in status of the emperor from ruler to figurehead. Previously, the court had been located in a strategically important location, one from which the emperor could lead his troops to defend the Empire. The move to Ravenna does not signal the 'preoccupation of the imperial government with the defence of Italy from the north-east'.[44] The move highlights the change from warrior-emperors to emperors who had no connection with the army and so needed to be easily defended by a few household troops should the enemy break through the frontiers. Never again would Stilicho have to face the possibility of losing Honorius to enemy attack. Seen in this context, it is possible to discount claims that the move was prompted by the imperial government becoming preoccupied with the defence of Italy. Although the preoccupation is correct, the emphasis is not.[45]

Stilicho's arrival and fast entry into the city will have dismayed Alaric, who now realized that when the rest of the Roman army arrived he could easily be pinned against the city and be forced to face the Romans from both front and rear. Accordingly, he raised the siege and moved West, upstream along the northern bank of the River Po. It would appear that the Goths were heading for Gaul.

However, before he reached the mountain passes he veered south, crossing the Po and heading for the Ligurian Alps. According to the ancient sources this was due to the fact that he wanted to either threaten or even capture Tuscany and Rome, but despite these claims there is no evidence that Alaric ever thought he could take Rome and set up a kingdom of his own.[46] If he had wanted to head to Rome or Tuscany, he had taken the wrong route. He should have earlier attempted to take either the *via Aemilia* towards Bononia, from there crossing the Apennines, or have headed towards the *via Aurelia* and taken his forces directly to Etruria and Rome. As a consequence, it is almost certain that, as he approached the mountains, he heard of the impending arrival of the Rhenish and British forces earlier ordered to march to Italy by Stilicho. Being pursued by Stilicho, and afraid of being trapped between the two forces whilst in the mountain passes, Alaric altered the route of his march yet again.

Yet there is no hard evidence to suggest that he had altered his strategic plans. He still planned to enter Gaul, but the arrival of fresh troops blocking his preferred route forced him to change direction. The plan now was pass to the south of the Alps and so enter Gaul from the south-east. Accordingly, Alaric marched along the river Tanarus and assaulted the walls of the town of Hasta (Asti).[47] Here he was defeated and forced to retire, going upstream in order to avoid the pursuing Romans.[48] He finally set up his camp approximately two kilometres below Pollentia, near to a local river called 'Urbs' ('city': now the Orba), according to Claudian fulfilling a prophecy:

'Away with delay, Alaric; boldly cross the Italian Alps this year and thou shalt reach the city. Thus far the path is mine. Who so cowardly as to dally after this encouragement or to hesitate to obey the call of Heaven?' So he spake and made ready his army to take the road, exhorting them to combat. Prophecy serves to augment his vain pride. Ah! for the grudging oracles ever dumb with mystic utterance; 'tis the event alone that (too late) discloses the true meaning which the seers themselves could not read. Alaric reached the farthest confines of Liguria where flows a river with the strange name of the City.

Claud., *de Bello Getico*, 546f.[49]

It was at the River Orba that Stilicho finally caught up with Alaric.

The Battle of Pollentia

The Roman forces approached the Goths on Saturday 5 April 402. Unfortunately, we have not been left with a clear description of events surrounding the battle, instead again having only three main narratives from two separate writers – the *Panegyricus de Sexto Consulatu Honorii Augusti* and *de Bello Getico* of Claudian (Panegyric on the Sixth Consulship of the Emperor Honorius and The Gothic War), and the *Historiarum Adversum Paganos Libri VII* (History Against the Pagans in Seven Books) of Orosius – from which to piece together a narrative of events.

Claudian, as is to be expected, claims a victory as further evidence of Stilicho's superiority. Orosius, on the other hand, states that the result was inconclusive because the leaders were being punished for fighting on a holy day.[50] Although the two would appear to be contradictory, there is, as usual, a way of combining the accounts into a single, coherent version of events. However, most of the details are unclear and have to be drawn from the relatively vague writings that have survived. Thanks to this, and again as is usual in the history of Stilicho, the information is open to interpretation and it is possible to draw entirely different conclusions from the same records.

It is certain that the battle was fought on Easter Sunday, 402. It is also clear that the Goths were Arian Christians and were set upon following the religious observances of such a holy day. Furthermore, they were not expecting attack from the Orthodox Christian Roman forces, who they expected to also follow the requisite religious practices.

On a more personal level, Alaric had by now a long acquaintance with Stilicho and would know of his desire not to stain the holy day. He also knew that Stilicho was a cautious general and would most likely resort to using manoeuvre and blockade rather than pitched battle – especially since he had not yet been reinforced by the troops approaching from the West.[51]

Yet the Romans attacked. Orosius states, without giving adequate explanation, that Stilicho handed over supreme command to the Alan Saul.[52] At first glance this seems odd, since the Alans that Stilicho had with him are usually assumed to have been those added to his forces following the recent campaign in Raetia and Noricum. Yet this is not the case. At least some Alans had been serving for far longer in the Western Roman army; Saul himself had had joint command, with Gainas and Bacurius, of the barbarian troops deployed by Theodosius at the Battle of the River Frigidus. He had escaped in flight early in the engagement, and it is this episode that may account for the allegations of treachery which Claudian implies were laid against him.[53] Therefore Saul should be seen as a long-standing imperial officer – he appears to have been either a *comes rei militaris* or a *magister militum* – who appears to have served with Stilicho from his installation as *parens* of Honorius.[54] In this context, his appointment to command the troops in Stilicho's stead is actually a natural occurrence – especially as Stilicho may have felt uncomfortable fighting on such a religious day. Saul was a pagan.

Part of the reason for the opening of hostilities was the fact that the Roman troops were eager to fight, despite the religious demands of Easter Day. It would appear that the successful campaigns on the Rhine and in Raetia had had a positive effect on morale. This was not part of Stilicho's nature, and accordingly he handed command of the army to Saul, a far more aggressive commander who was eager to dispel the claims of cowardice and treachery which had been laid against him after the Battle of the Frigidus.

His rapid advance took the Goths by surprise.[55] The Goths were forced to retire after suffering relatively heavy losses. The Alans who led the Roman attack appear to have been in the centre of the assault, and it was here that the Goths were routed. It was during this phase of the battle that the Goths suffered the most losses, and it is clear that these were mainly the infantry. No doubt the Gothic cavalry, who had only suffered light casualties, retired faster than the infantry and reformed relatively unhindered.

However, once the Gothic cavalry had reformed they looked to turn the tables on their pursuers. The Alans were counter-attacked, Saul was killed and the once-pursuing troops now fell back towards the main body of the Romans. However, Stilicho took control of the army and stabilized the situation. The Gothic assault petered out and, after much fighting, it was clear that Alaric had suffered a military defeat. He had lost his camp, the vast majority of his baggage, many of his prisoners and large numbers of the Gothic wives and children – including his own wife – had been captured by the Romans.[56] He withdrew towards the mountains and prepared a defensive position.

The aftermath

Claudian was able to announce to the Roman world that the Goths had finally been defeated. There is little doubt that when Alaric invaded Italy the inhabitants feared another Adrianople, dreading that the Goths would defeat Stilicho's army and turn to ravaging the Italian countryside, demanding payment for their forbearance. Instead, the army had defeated the Goths and much of the spoil from Adrianople, as well as Greece, had been retaken. The humiliation had been avenged. Furthermore, a multitude of Roman prisoners had been released and many Gothic family members had been captured, including Alaric's wife. It is in this context that Claudian compared the battle to those against Pyrrhus, Hannibal, and Spartacus.[57] This is usually interpreted as mere poetic licence, but when it is interpreted within the context of the times, it more than likely expresses the feelings in Milan and Rome when news arrived that Alaric had been defeated.

Alaric retires

Having finally managed to inflict a defeat on Alaric, and having captured many of the family members of his warriors, plus the fact that Alaric was now firmly on the defensive and entrenched in the Apennines, Stilicho was in a strong bargaining position. Accordingly, he opened talks with Alaric and persuaded him to leave Italy and settle instead in Pannonia (Illyricum).[58] With his greatly weakened force, Alaric was no longer the threat he had been and so sending him to Pannonia (Illyricum) was not as dangerous as it had been even the year before. The direction which Alaric now took implies both that he had been defeated and that he had been forced to accede to Stilicho's demands that he leave Italy. As Claudian noted, Alaric always had the ability to change direction – both before and after he had crossed the Po – and could at any time have headed for Rome, but he did not do so.[59]

However, Stilicho was no fool; despite the agreement, he tracked Alaric as he led his troops back towards the Julian Alps. This was just as well, as the withdrawal was not straightforward. Hindered by floods, Alaric had repeatedly to stop before crossing rivers.[60] Finally, he crossed the Po and headed towards Venetia.

What followed is a mystery. For some reason Alaric halted near to the town of Verona. One possibility is that Stilicho had decided that he needed a firm victory to bolster his regime and so advanced to battle. Or maybe Alaric decided to stop in order to put pressure on the government in order to receive a more favourable deal – according to Claudian, his men were suffering from the heat and bad food, implying that Stilicho had refused to give him access to Italian food supplies as he retired.[61] It may even be that Alaric was still intent on crossing the Alps to reach either Raetia or Gaul and changed direction in order to cross the mountains, forcing Stilicho to react.[62] The exact reason is unknown.

In the circumstances, it is most likely that Alaric attempted to force the crossing of the Alps.[63] Politically he was in a cul-de sac. He had broken his treaty with the East and so could not expect a welcome upon his return. In the West he had been defeated – albeit narrowly – by Stilicho and would not be given the senior military post he needed in order to reward his followers for their loyalty. In the circumstances, it is most likely that he decided to strike out for the Alps. If he could achieve a crossing he could either gain land for his people in Gaul despite the Roman resistance, or at least force the Romans to come to an agreement whereby he gained the status he needed. The claim by Claudian that Stilicho had lured Alaric over the Po and so ensured that Rome was safe before attacking him does not stand up to analysis. Any defeat, anywhere in Italy, would once again leave Italy open to Alaric; the fact that he was beyond the River Po, which has many crossing points, is irrelevant.[64]

Stilicho had been following shortly behind Alaric. When Alaric made his move, Stilicho was ready for him. It is almost certain that by this time Stilicho had been joined by the troops from Gaul and Britain. Furthermore, the Battle of Pollentia had shown that Alaric's forces were not invincible, and the Roman troops would have had superior morale compared to the recently defeated Goths. In the circumstances, Stilicho did something that he had never done before. He led his troops in a concerted attack upon the Goths.

The Battle of Verona

Unfortunately, as is usual with this era, we have no actual details of the battle that took place outside Verona in summer 402. Despite the fact that Alaric was still strong in cavalry and that the terrain was ideal for their use, Alaric was undeniably defeated by Stilicho, at one point almost being captured.[65] According to Claudian only the failure of the Alans to follow Stilicho's tactical plans allowed Alaric to escape, although there is no reason to accept the claim at face value.[66] Once the battle was lost Alaric attempted to break out to Raetia, but was blockaded on a hill before he could reach the mountain passes.[67] At this point, many of the troops that Alaric had led over the Alps into Italy lost faith in their leader; large numbers now began to desert to Rome.[68] Amongst these was Sarus, a Goth of some standing, who along with his brother Sigeric (also known as Sigerichus and Segericus) were vehement opponents of Alaric.[69] Also taking service with Stilicho was Ulfilas, who later rose to high rank in the Roman army.[70] Although Claudian doubtless exaggerates the scale of the desertions, there were undoubtedly many who felt that Alaric could no longer command the respect and fear that he once had and they decided that secure employment with Stilicho was preferable to an unknown future with Alaric. A large proportion of the deserting troops were the Gothic cavalry.[71]

Aftermath

Alaric was no longer in a position to intimidate Stilicho. Before the end of the year he crossed the Julian Alps and settled in Pannonia (Illyricum). Although his precise destination is unclear, there is no indication that he attempted to resettle in Eastern Illyricum. He was no longer *magister militum per Illyricum*, instead being simply an intruder, and he would have feared being attacked by the Eastern army under Fravitta.[72] It is almost certain that he negotiated with Stilicho and was allowed to settle with what remained of his forces on the borders of Dalmatia and Pannonia, most likely in Pannonia II (see Map 12), as otherwise he would have been forced to mount yearly campaigns in Illyricum to support his men, which is nowhere indicated in our sources.[73]

Although the exact circumstances are unknown, Sozomen suggests that Alaric was allotted *annona* as part of the settlement.[74] It is also possible that Stilicho gave hostages to Alaric at this point, rather than as usually claimed in 405, although the dating is debatable.[75] As a consequence, it is possible that Alaric was made *dux Pannoniae secundae*, or possibly was the first *comes rei militaris per 'Illyricum'*, as claimed by Orosius, in this way gaining power similar to that enjoyed by the *comes rei militaris* of Africa, or Britain, or Spain.[76] Whatever the case, for the next three years he caused few problems for Stilicho.

Stilicho and Alaric

Different interpretations

Even in modern works there remains confusion and doubt over Stilicho's failure to 'destroy' Alaric when he had the chance at both Pollentia and Verona. Various interpretations have been advanced for Stilicho's failure. These range from: his being a poor military commander and so not taking his chance when it was there; his being hampered by his inability to control his troops – especially at Pollentia; his having a secret agreement with Alaric; to his not wanting to destroy Alaric, but to keep him as a threat with which to subdue the Senate. All of these are valid, in that they fit the information that has come down to us and explain the seemingly inexplicable fact that Stilicho had Alaric at his mercy on two separate occasions and failed on both to destroy Alaric.

Many of these interpretations have been heavily affected by the conflicting views that even the ancient sources held. Claudian and Prudentius consider the battles to be Roman victories.[77] Conversely, both Cassiodorus and Jordanes consider them to be Gothic victories.[78] Finally, Prosper of Aquitaine, Orosius, and Jerome consider them to have been drawn battles.[79]

The claims of Cassiodorus and Jordanes are of doubtful legitimacy, since both were writing for later Gothic kings and are so unlikely to have risked their patron's wrath by commenting negatively upon Alaric's deeds.

The claims of Claudian and Prudentius deserve attention, since they appear to fit the facts: Alaric withdrew after Pollentia, and following Verona he did not attempt to put pressure on Stilicho for several years, even failing to take advantage of the invasion of Italy by Radagaisus (see next chapter). In these circumstances, it is clear that the victories lay with Stilicho, and that the defeat at Verona was significant and reduced Alaric to virtual impotence.

The comments of Prosper, Orosius and Jerome, however, deserve more recognition. It is clear that they believed that Stilicho could not have defeated Alaric, since Alaric's forces remained a threat after the battle. According to traditional Roman values a defeated foe lost all ability to act on their own initiative apart from the ability to flee. It is clear that Alaric had not been forced to flee Italy after the battle. These writers – and the modern authorities that have followed them – adhere to the traditional aristocratic manner of their predecessors: all enemies of Rome were to be instantly defeated in battle, using all of the forces necessary.[80] Where they were not defeated, the Romans themselves had obviously lost and so the emperor (or whoever was in charge) immediately gathered greater forces with which to avenge the defeat. To put it simply, the purpose of the Roman army was to fight and win decisive victories, not to be defeated or to delay.

However, in attempting to fit Stilicho's actions within a specific political framework, most writers have overlooked the military consequences of the victories in 402. Especially following the loss at Adrianople, the army adopted the policies soon to be described by Vegetius and later written down by Maurikios in his *Strategikon*.[81] Examples in Maurikios include: 'it is well to hurt the enemy by deceit, by raids, or by hunger, and never be enticed into a pitched battle, which is a demonstration more of luck than of bravery';[82] or 'if an enemy force, superior in strength or even equal to ours, invades our country, especially at the beginning of the invasion, we must be sure not to engage it in pitched battle'.[83] Many historians, both ancient and modern, are anachronistically applying the methods and principles of the earlier Empire to the fourth century and later. This is due to the ancient sources being members of the Roman aristocracy who wanted to uphold the traditions of their forbears whilst failing to understand that circumstances had changed and that the methodology of the earlier Empire was now inappropriate. Modern writers have tended to follow their lead. Over the preceding 200 years the manner of battle had changed. Long gone were the days when the Romans put in the field thousands of legionaries and attacked the enemy. Politics, economics and manpower shortages had changed the ethos of the Roman army.

Stilicho and others of his generation – including Theodosius – had followed the new methods of fighting wars. These were by their nature less likely to give a fast, decisive result. The more politically inclined and conservative senators were unaware of this profound shift of emphasis and continued to hold the examples of their predecessors – especially individuals such as Caesar, Trajan and Septimius Severus, with their fast, decisive campaigns – as military role-models. However, the potential losses in such military campaigns were no longer tenable, since the Empire no longer had access to willing recruits except from outside the borders. The conservative senators were unwilling to accept that this was the case. Prosper, Orosius and Jerome were part of this tradition and did not understand that it had passed. Some members of the Senate, however, may have held a different view. Despite doubts about the level of the victory, a monument was erected in the forum to celebrate the defeat of Alaric at Pollentia and Verona (see Plate 2), and Stilicho and Honorius marched under a triumphal arch built to commemorate the victory. Although this may have been erected in large part due to political pressure from Stilicho and/or Symmachus, the fact that it was built suggests that in a large part of Italy there was simply relief that the Gothic threat had finally been removed.

Conclusion

With these considerations in mind it is possible to formulate a theory that covers all of the existing evidence. This assumes that the circumstances after every battle were different and assumes that Stilicho was reacting to a different situation after each of the two battles. To understand why he acted as he did, it is necessary to deal with each battle in isolation, rather than judging the campaign of 402 as a single entity.

First, it is necessary to assess the tradition that Stilicho, having won at Pollentia, wasted the opportunity to reduce Alaric's position even further by not following up and defeating his forces again. This repeats the error of anachronistically expecting Stilicho to behave as Caesar or Trajan and attack the enemy regardless of the strategical necessities; and the strategical necessity in question was that Stilicho could not afford even a small defeat. The Senate were unwilling to allow him to conscript men from their estates, nor did they want him to continually 'dilute' the Roman army with barbarian troops. In the end he was to take the only option available to him: he was to open negotiations with Alaric.

Up to the Battle of Pollentia Stilicho was adhering to the methods of his time, using manoeuvre and blockade to defeat the enemy, rather than risking all in a pitched battle.[84] Not only did this accord with his military experience, but he also knew that a heavy defeat would be disastrous for the Empire since there were now only a limited number of recruits available for the army. In all of his life Stilicho had only ever taken part in one decisive battle, when Theodosius led his forces over the Alps and faced Arbogast and Eugenius at the Battle of the Frigidus in 394. In this battle losses had been heavy, especially on the first day, and, although the casualties were mainly amongst the *foederati*, the experience illustrated how easily things could go wrong. Stilicho did not have the resources of Theodosius, and especially he did not have the sheer volume of *foederati* that Theodosius had had in 394. As a consequence, any losses were likely to come from his own troops, and these would be extremely difficult to replace.

Furthermore, Stilicho did not have the need to win a quick battle. Theodosius knew that he had to have a decisive victory at the Battle of the Frigidus in order to neutralize Eugenius. Eugenius was a political opponent in a civil war, and should Theodosius not act decisively support in the East could easily waver and switch to Eugenius. In contrast, there was no point at which Alaric would begin to gain support in the Senate in Rome.

Yet it is possible that something else was at work here. As has been noted, Stilicho had received accelerated promotion due to his marriage to Serena. As a result, his military experience was extremely limited. In the fighting against Alaric in 395 and 397 he demonstrated that he was adept at using manoeuvre and blockade. On the other hand, his actions during the Gildonic War (where he placed Mascezel in command) and at Pollentia (where he placed the army under the command of Saul) suggests that when it came to leading an army into a standard, set-piece battle, Stilicho was almost totally lacking in confidence. This helps to explain why Claudian took such pains to promote Stilicho's martial ability; he knew that Stilicho was not comfortable leading an army into battle and so had to exaggerate his feats in order to boost Stilicho's confidence, as well as simply supporting his patron.

It is also usually claimed that Stilicho followed the long-standing Roman tradition of deploying the *foederati* in such a way that they bore the brunt of the fighting at the

Battles of Pollentia and Verona – a similar claim to the use of the *foederati* by Theodosius at the Battle of the Frigidus.[85] The claim concerning Theodosius has already been analysed and found to be at fault (see Chapter 2). As with Theodosius, the later claim originates from a contemporary account of the Battle of Verona, in this case Claudian:

> If the soldiers flag with wearied ranks he throws the auxiliaries into the line heedless of their loss; thus he cunningly weakens the savage tribes of the Danube by opposing one tribe to another and with twofold gain joins battle that turns barbarians against themselves to perish in either army for our sake.
>
> Claudian, *VI Cons. Hon.*, 223f.

Modern writers have tended to accept the concept of the Empire using allied troops in this way practically at face value.[86] Yet at the Battle of Pollentia, the Alan Saul deployed the army, and the Alans did not suffer many casualties during the initial attack. It was only when they were counter-attacked by the Gothic cavalry that the Alans suffered significant casualties. As a consequence, it is plain that the Alans were deployed where they were most effective, not where they would absorb casualties. In fact, Claudian makes no mention of the Alans at Pollentia being used to absorb casualties, merely noting that Saul was heroically killed and his men would have fled if not for the timely intervention of Stilicho.[87]

The quotation above refers to the Battle of Verona. The phrase 'If the soldiers flag' implies that the Roman troops were in the front line and were only replaced by the allies when the Roman troops became tired. Contrary to popular belief, it would appear that the Alans did not fight in the front line on this occasion. The losses appear to have been mainly suffered by the regular Roman forces.

Claudian could not report that casualties amongst the Romans had been high. Instead, Claudian introduces the claim that the barbarians had been used to kill barbarians. This downplays the losses incurred by the Roman army and emphasizes the skills of Stilicho as a general by comparing him to Theodosius. Furthermore, the claim acts as a counter to the traditional senatorial demand that only Roman troops should serve in the Roman army. If an army was composed only of Romans, all of the casualties were suffered by native troops. On the other hand, by employing barbarians the losses were suffered only by barbarians on both sides, to the greater glory and security of the Empire.

Claudian was in part following literary traditional when he exulted in 'barbarian fighting barbarian'. This is seen, for example, in Tacitus, who states that:

> He (Agricola) arrayed his eager and impetuous troops in such a manner that the auxiliary infantry, 8,000 in number, strengthened his centre, while 3,000 cavalry were posted on his wings. The legions were drawn up in front of the entrenched camp; his victory would be vastly more glorious if won without the loss of Roman blood, and he would have a reserve in case of repulse.
>
> Tacitus, *Agricola*, 1.35.

Yet this is not the only reason for Claudian's claim. Claudian was also attempting to use it as a lever to encourage the Senate to allow Stilicho to recruit more non-Roman troops into the army; after all, if the army used barbarian troops in this way, it was to the greater benefit of the Empire. Furthermore, dead mercenaries did not need paying and using them in this manner saved Roman lives. Although later Claudian blames the Alans for letting Alaric escape, this is part of his balancing act of endorsing Stilicho to the Senate; the barbarians are useful in that they save Roman lives in battle, but Stilicho had to have an excuse for allowing Alaric to escape again.[88]

There is one final factor relating to the argument of whether or not Stilicho would use the Alans in order to weaken them. Throughout his military career in the West Stilicho's main difficulty was in obtaining recruits for the army in the face of stiff opposition from the Senate in Rome. With limited manpower, he is unlikely to have risked weakening the Alans, part of his own army, by sending them in first.

Having discounted some of the traditional claims, it is possible instead to interpret the Battle of Pollentia as a turning point for Stilicho. Having saved the army from disaster following Saul's death and the defeat of the Alans, Stilicho seems to have gained in confidence. He followed the Goths back across northern Italy and when they attempted to change their route of march in order to cross the Alps, he did not hesitate in launching an assault on their forces. The ensuing victory, although not as crushing as Claudian claims, ended Alaric's threat to the West. Realizing that their leader was no longer in a strong position and was now running from the Western Army, many of the Gothic troops – especially the cavalry – began to defect to the Romans.

On the other hand, although Stilicho had gained confidence and defeated the Goths in battle, there still remains the question of why he did not finish the job and eliminate Alaric after Verona. It is quite likely that some of the claims made previously, especially that of Stilicho wanting to retain Alaric as a threat to intimidate the Senate, remain valid. After all, a former ally was always a potential future ally.[89] Yet one aspect has always been overlooked: the composition of Stilicho's forces.

The army had taken losses at both Pollentia and Verona, but the gaps were now being filled by the Gothic 'deserters'. The result was that Stilicho's army became relatively more powerful. Ironically, however, it was now no longer a tool with which to complete the destruction of Alaric. To ask the new Gothic recruits to attack men that less than a week before had been their comrades-in-arms was to invite disaster. It would be impossible to tell Gothic 'friend' from Gothic 'foe', and it would be hazardous in the extreme to assume that the Goths recently enrolled would not change sides half way through the battle. Such an occurrence would be a catastrophe.

Instead, Stilicho had to revert to using threats and political pressure to force Alaric to retire. Fortunately, the recent defeat and the loss of manpower meant that Alaric was no longer in a position to resist and he retired to Pannonia (Illyricum). As an added bonus for Stilicho, once Alaric had been defeated and been forced to withdraw to a small area under Roman jurisdiction, the loss of face meant that he had little chance of receiving reinforcements for his depleted forces. It was clear that Alaric now needed Stilicho more than Stilicho needed Alaric.[90]

On the other hand the fact that Alaric was settled in Pannonia and Noricum is also usually overlooked. As was noted in Chapter 3, Pannonia and Noricum were crucial for the defence of Italy.[91] The fact that Stilicho felt secure enough to allow Alaric to settle there as a Western official attests to his belief both that Alaric had been severely defeated, and to the fact that Alaric could be trusted. Over the next five years Alaric repaid this trust by refusing to take advantage of Stilicho, even during the invasion of Italy by Radagaisus.

There is one more aspect to the nature of Stilicho's victory that is usually glossed over. The fact that Stilicho had allowed Alaric to escape resulted in 'passionate undercurrents' in Roman society.[92] The traditions of the Empire declared that barbarian generals were to be fought and crushed completely, not allowed to escape and then employed as military officials. Furthermore, Stilicho's victory would have been compared unfavourably with events that had occurred only two years before in the East. In 400 the East had expelled Gainas and massacred his men in traditional Roman fashion. When contrasted with Alaric's escape, Stilicho's victory lost a little of its sheen. Furthermore, it will have been at this time that doubts began to be expressed concerning his methods of dealing with barbarians, doubts that were to grow in the succeeding years.

Chapter Eleven

The West and the Invasion of Radagaisus, 402–406

Conditions in the West

Throughout the late-fourth and early-fifth centuries the nature of many areas of the Western Empire changed dramatically. The main source for these changes is archaeology, but unfortunately archaeology does not provide exact dates which can be tied into a chronological narrative, merely outlining changes that evolved over a period of more than a century. As a result, it is impossible to connect events in the archaeological record directly to Stilicho, yet it is necessary to comment upon them so that a clearer understanding of Stilicho's difficulties and resultant policies will emerge.

Over the previous centuries the Empire had admitted large numbers of barbarians to the Empire, dividing them amongst interior provinces and slowly absorbing them into the citizenry. During the course of the late-fourth and early-fifth centuries a process that had begun long before began to accelerate; barbarians were admitted to the frontier provinces and allowed to settle there in return for military service. The detail of the process need not concern us here, but the impact that it had upon the nature of the Empire needs clarifying.

The 'Germanic' frontier

From an early date emperors began to look at the possibility of employing Germanic tribes already in situ to defend the Empire. As an example, Constantine (306–37) had enrolled Burgundians, Alans and possibly Sueves as federates.[1] Furthermore, large numbers of Franks had entered the Empire during the confused period prior to Julian's appointment as Caesar in the West in 355. It would appear that Julian recognized their occupation of previously Roman territory on condition that they remained within the allotted areas and defended these against attack from outside the Empire.[2] It is likely that this decision had the added benefit of releasing at least some of the troops defending the area for service during Julian's impending civil war. He almost certainly retained these men under his personal command for the ill-fated attack upon Persia.

The precedent was followed by Stilicho. After the campaign of 396 along the Rhine it would appear that the Frankish tribes again acknowledged Roman authority and agreed to maintain the peace, guarding the northern frontiers and allowing Stilicho to remove yet more troops to reinforce the Italian army. In this manner conditions on the lower Rhine and sections of the upper Rhine and Danube in effect ceased to function as traditional frontiers and meaningful boundaries. As more Germans were admitted or simply moved in, it is likely that the sense of insecurity amongst the Roman population grew. The result was that those who could migrated into the interior, so leaving more land untilled and untaxed.[3] The protection for those citizens still living in these areas was the Germans living in their villages nearby.[4]

The changes were easily justifiable and included a realistic assessment of the modest threat posed by the Germanic tribes in situ on the Rhine.[5] Yet despite the fact that the change was a sensible short-term measure, the effects were, despite their gradual nature, dramatic. The Roman troops that had previously defended the frontiers were withdrawn, being sent to defend weak frontiers or, more commonly, swell the armies of the emperors during the invasions and civil wars of the later fourth century.[6] The villa economy along the frontiers, however, had relied upon the demand for goods from the army. The withdrawal of the army resulted in the villas losing their main market. Archaeology shows villa agriculture to be on the retreat along the upper Rhine and Danube from as early as the mid-fourth century.[7] As the process of troop relocation accelerated, the economic damage to the frontier regions grew.

It was not only the villas that suffered from the economic loss of the army. The Germanic tribes living along the frontiers would have augmented their incomes, when circumstances allowed, by trading their surplus food with the imperial forces. Furthermore, the more affluent army officers would have provided an ideal market for the Germanic craftsmen who at this time were producing ornamental items such as brooches of intricate design (see Plate 27). Without these sources of income, and in the knowledge of why they had been lost, it is possible that the Germanic tribes not settled as *foederati* saw the opportunity for small-scale plunder across the frontier. Although not severe enough to merit attention at court or mention in the sources, these raids will have helped to reinforce the feeling that the border regions had been forgotten by the Empire. As an added difficulty, Stilicho's concentration on events in Italy and Illyricum may have resulted in his neglect of the traditional Roman policy of subsidy and alliance in the territories immediately behind the frontiers. As a consequence, these areas became unsettled, and demonstrate 'considerable change and instability' in the archaeological record.[8]

Not only did the frontiers lose their economic viability as time passed, they also lost the secondary function of villa life: the imposition and example of Roman values that had earlier transformed 'barbarian' territories into Romanized provinces. As a result, not only were the frontier provinces now defended by Germanic settlers with little loyalty to Rome, the Empire had lost the main means of Romanizing the new settlers.

Gaul

There was to be a further blow to the provinces of northern Gaul. It is probable, but by no means certain, that during Stilicho's regency fundamental changes took place in Gaul that lasted until the end of the Empire. These involved the movement of the capital of the *praefectus praetorio Galliarum* from Trier in the north to Arles in the

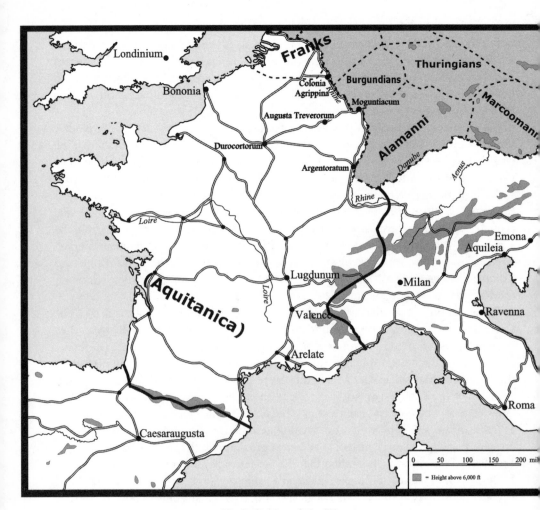

17. Stilicho and the West.

south, a change prefigured by the court of Valentinian II (375–392) being based at Vienne, south of Lyon.[9] The change is known to have happened at some time between 395 and 418, and included an intermediate stage when the *praefectus praetorio Galliarum* returned to Lyon, the old capital of Gaul. Although it is certain that the mint at Trier closed shortly after the suppression of Eugenius in 394, this does not necessarily mean that the capital moved at the same time.

If the change was made during the regency of Stilicho, the most likely date for the change would be following the expulsion of Alaric from Italy in 402.[10] The episode had shown that Italy was now vulnerable and it was clear that the routes between Milan and Trier were becoming less and less secure. As a result, it would have suited Stilicho to have the *praefectus praetorio Galliarum* relocate to a place nearer to Milan. It is possible that Stilicho recognized the potential difficulties arising from the move, since it would appear that he also created a 'Gallic Council' – possibly a deliberate recreation of the 'old high-imperial council of the Three Gauls' that had represented all of the northern Gallic provinces and which had also been based in Lyon. The move didn't have the morale effect required, since the council was not called to meet much before 407, after which events ensured that the council withered away.[11]

The effect of the change on northern Gaul will have been slow to show itself, but have become increasingly dramatic over time. In a similar manner to the presence of the army, the court had had an economic and cultural impact, especially upon the areas around Trier – as was also the case with all of the imperial capitals. Now that the praetorian capital had moved, taking with it the attendant bureaucrats, local produce would have had a diminished market, so reducing the need for large-scale supply by local villas around Trier.

As villas became economically redundant, their owners removed to the south of Gaul where markets were still to be found.[12] These changes tie in with the archaeological record, which shows that around this time most towns and rural centres in northern Gaul (north of the Loire) were in decline, especially to the east of Paris. Furthermore, the same downturn is echoed in trade patterns and in the quality and variety of pottery production.[13] However, this decline varied in intensity, with larger, more important centres such as Trier remaining viable longer than other urban centres.

Politically, the move was extremely damaging to northern Gaul. As the court of Honorius and Stilicho remained in Italy from 395, it is clear that the senators of the north would slowly lose much of their power as the Senates of southern Gaul and Rome gained influence in Milan. Yet the blame for the process should not be laid entirely at the feet of Stilicho and his successors. Gratian's tutor Decimus Magnus Ausonius of Bordeaux gained much influence and prestige at court from the mid-360s. From this time at the latest the court became dominated by men drawn from Aquitania and southern Gaul.[14] Therefore, the removal of the capital from Trier to the south should also be seen as a natural consequence of their domination.

As an unfortunate by-product, these changes demonstrated that northern Gaul was no longer central to the politics of Rome. There is no doubt that to the aristocracy of northern Gaul – and of Britain beyond – the move reinforced the idea that they were unimportant in the eyes of the emperor and that they were becoming increasingly marginalized when it came to political and military inclusion within the Empire. The result was the beginning of a change of loyalties. Local landowners began to realize that they were paying their taxes to an emperor who did not then provide for their defence. Many began to ask for protection from local Germans rather than the distant emperor. It was easier, more effective and probably cheaper for the landowners to pay a sum to the local German 'king' than their taxes to the emperor, since in many cases the Roman army was either not present or had insufficient numbers to fulfil their role of local defence. Loyalty to the emperor began to decline and new loyalties, either to local magnates or to the German tribesmen who actually defended the Empire, began to be formed.

The *bacaudae*[15]

Nowhere can the change of loyalty be seen more clearly than in the rise of the *bacaudae*. The sheer volume of uprisings in Gaul and Spain, possibly from as early as the second century onwards, is surprising, and is often overlooked by historians analysing the Fall of the West.[16] The first uprising under the name *bacaudae* was c.283–4, when Gallic peasants rebelled against their treatment.[17] The ferocity of the uprising is implied by the fact that the new emperor, Diocletian (284–305), was compelled to appoint Maximian as his co-ruler with specific responsibilities for putting down the revolt. Although repressed – both on this and on later occasions – the *bacaudae* would re-emerge throughout the course of the late Empire and remain a factor in imperial control of Gaul and Spain.

Originally, it would appear that the *bacaudae* were risings of peasants in Gaul and Spain against the excessive taxes they were being forced to pay. This would especially be the case at times such as 283–4 when the Empire was unable to defend them from outside attack. As time passed the uprisings began to include men of higher class, such as doctors and the lower gentry. They also began to spread, with *bacaudae* even being found in the Alps between Gaul and Italy. This latter may have been a further factor in the decision to move the seat of the *praefectus praetorio Galliarum* from Trier to Arles.

Although probably still focused upon grievances over taxes, the fact that later risings included men from the middle classes reinforces the idea that in some areas of the West loyalty to the emperor and the Empire was eroding and that local allegiances were beginning to evolve as a replacement.

Yet these dramatic changes in loyalty were slow to evolve and are only easily perceived in hindsight. Despite the negative, long term effect of the changes, it made sense both for Stilicho and for the Gallic senators to move the Gallic capital nearer to Milan, where each would be able to exert more influence on the other. Despite Symmachus' influence and his endorsement of Italian individuals, under Stilicho the aristocracy of Aquitania and southern Gaul maintained a strong presence at court. As these individuals included most of the richest men in the West, the change in location of the capital of the prefecture was a necessary evil as without their support Stilicho would be hard pressed to survive.

Britain

The difficulty with the defence of Britain would always be one of access. It was always a relatively straightforward task to march an army to the channel, but the logistics of transporting a sizeable force across the sea was a rather daunting affair, especially when transporting horses. Therefore, the defence of the island remained, for the most part, in the hands of troops permanently stationed there. Yet when the need arose, it was still feasible to send troops to help the islanders, as when Theodosius the Elder was sent to restore order in the province in the fourth century.

Fortunately, the same logistical difficulties applied to Germanic raiders. The need to rely on boats resulted in overseas attacks being raids of various strengths rather than attempts to secure land for settlement. Therefore, the only serious threat would come from the tribes to the north of Hadrian's Wall. As a consequence, on the whole the island was left to defend itself.

This relative security enabled the British to undergo something of a 'golden era' in the fourth century, with large, expensive villas being built. Unlike the situation in Gaul, although a proportion of the army was withdrawn to the continent, the majority appear to have remained in the island, supplying a market for the goods produced by the villas. Yet even here there appears to have been a decline in the late fourth century. This was probably due to the removal of one very large market for goods produced in the province: the garrisons along the Rhine. It was actually easier to transport goods, especially grain, along the rivers of England, across the Channel and then up the Rhine, rather than to use overland continental routes to supply garrison troops along the frontier. This was a long-standing contract with the merchants supplying the ships and therefore not the same logistical problem as transporting troops. When troops began to be withdrawn from the Rhine frontier, and especially when their place was taken by Germanic tribes who relied on growing their own food, the markets withered and the villas ceased to be economically viable.

As the markets slowly collapsed it became obvious that the emperor was no longer greatly concerned about the safety and defence of Britain. The withdrawal of troops and their failure to return resulted in the aristocracy in the island questioning whether the Empire was fulfilling the functions for which Britain paid its taxes. As a consequence, throughout the fourth century there is a history of governors and generals being acclaimed emperor in the island and crossing to the continent to make good their claim. Unfortunately, the majority of them lost their wars and the troops that they had taken with them were either killed or absorbed by the victorious emperor. Either way, again the defences of the island were weakened. Despite the fact that Stilicho appears to have repulsed a Pictish invasion in the early years of his rule, the transferral of the court from Milan to Ravenna and the removal of the *praefectus praetorio Galliarum* from Trier to Arles almost certainly left the British feeling isolated and unprotected. Frustration again began to grow in the province.

Other areas

The decline in villa and urban life outlined above is echoed in the archaeology of the Prefecture of Illyricum, including Noricum and Pannonia, with one distinct difference: overall, the process was much slower than in the West, although some areas seem to have declined quicker than others.[18] This is almost certainly due to some areas giving easy access to Italy, and so being maintained by the Western emperors as one of the main defences of their dwindling regime, whilst others helped to supply the new-built city of Constantinople with the goods and services it needed. However, in Spain and Africa the old system appears to have continued unaffected. This is mainly due to the fact that Spain was practically untroubled by outside threat. More importantly, Africa remained the main supplier of foodstuffs to Rome and so maintained high economic output with a concomitant adherence to the Roman lifestyle that was to last beyond the Vandal conquest until annexation by Islam in the seventh century.

Conclusion

The Roman frontiers in the West underwent a profound change in nature that is not always described by historians and rarely shown on maps. The Empire continued to claim the territory up to and across the Rhine and Danube, but some of the frontier provinces should probably no longer be described as 'Roman', since a large proportion of the population living there now had little or no real loyalty to the emperor in Italy.

With Britain and northern Gaul in economic decline, the Empire was forced to rely more and more on the revenues from Spain, southern Gaul, Africa, Sicily and Italy. The senators of southern Gaul ensured that they maintained a presence at court to defend their rights and privileges and to demand protection from external threat. The province of Spain appears to have been maintaining its position thanks to its comparative safety. However, the majority of the large landowners in Italy, Sicily and Africa were members of the Senate at Rome. Once it is recognized that the policy of 'withdrawal' from the frontier provinces resulted in the Empire becoming more dependent on a very limited number of people as its main tax base, Stilicho's relations with the Senate and his dependence upon their revenues and manpower becomes easier to understand.

In this context it is possible to support claims that Stilicho's policy towards the Senate may have been partly one of conciliation, but to a very large degree it was based on 'common concerns, vested interests and political and military pressures'.[19] Without the support of the Senate, the declining tax revenue of the West could no longer support the armies that were needed to defend it against attack, and without the Senate's reserves of manpower, the armies of the West did not have the numbers with which to repel invasion. As imperial control of the West declined, reliance came to be placed more and more on the senators of Southern Gaul and Rome.

Symmachus

One event in 402 is usually mourned by classicists and passed over by historians as being interesting but of little real import. During the course of Alaric's invasion of Italy in 401–2 Symmachus travelled on a mission from Rome to Milan.[20] This is the last mention of him in the sources and it is clear that he died soon after completing his mission. With his passing Stilicho lost his voice in the Senate. It is hard to estimate the damage that this loss did to Stilicho. When Symmachus died Stilicho was almost at the height of his prestige: Africa had been recovered, the tribes on the Danube had been cowed into supplying troops and Alaric had been defeated in Italy, with much of the plunder the Goths had taken during and after the battle of Adrianople being recovered. At first Symmachus' death would have had little effect on events.

Yet slowly his loss began to be felt. Obviously, he had helped to promote Stilicho's policies, but his presence had probably been far more effective that that. As the dominant figure in the Senate, he had helped reduce opposition. There can be little doubt that his seniority, oratory and *auctoritas* (a combination of the authority, influence and esteem in which an individual was held) had helped to overawe resistance to Stilicho. Apart from his ability to convince his audience, his influence and force of will ensured that opposition remained within containable bounds. With his death, and the lack of any replacement of equal standing and ability, opposition – especially amongst the strongly orthodox Catholics – began to grow. Fortunately for Stilicho, as yet he still had enough personal *auctoritas*, thanks both to his previous actions and his relationship to Honorius, that opposition remained muted.

Yet increasingly as time passed Stilicho came to rely on a small number of officials to run the Empire. During the final years of his rule a tendency to give repeated tenures to powerful officials becomes apparent. In many ways this can be seen as natural, since individuals who are gifted and willing to serve actually need to serve, otherwise they become obstructive and their petulance can damage their patron. Yet it is possible that the nature of his appointments illustrates that support was narrowing and opposition growing in strength.[21]

Alaric

There is no direct information in the sources concerning the activities of Alaric from 402 to 405. The sole evidence for affairs in Illyricum comes from the *Collectio Avellana*. In a confusing passage in a letter from Honorius to Arcadius, dated after 20 June 404, it is clear that Eastern Illyricum had recently been devastated by barbarians.[22] The letter is difficult to translate, and has been taken as Honorius sincerely apologizing to Arcadius for the depredations of Alaric in Eastern Illyricum, or of Honorius accusing Arcadius of not informing him of barbarian depredations in Illyricum.[23] The specific meaning is unknown, but is of vital importance. If Honorius is apologizing for attacks by barbarians upon Eastern Illyricum, it means both that Alaric had disturbed the peace and that he was in official employment of the Western government. If the letter is an accusation that Arcadius had withheld information, it is unlikely that Alaric was the culprit and we may instead be seeing an otherwise unrecorded attack upon the Empire.

Both of these hypotheses suggest that Stilicho had settled Alaric in Illyricum (Pannonia) with a fixed command. In the first, Alaric was employed by the Western government and invaded Eastern Illyricum, demonstrating that he had come to an agreement with Stilicho in 402 and settled on the border between East and West. In the second, he was not involved in the conflict at all and his presence may have helped deter attacks on Pannonia and Noricum. On the other hand, there must have been a compelling reason for him not to join his forces with Radagaisus in order to invade Italy again. After all, this was likely to put him in a better position to issue demands. The only explanation must be that Alaric had already been given an official post by Stilicho which was better than anything Radagaisus would have to offer; it is unlikely that fear of Stilicho would have been the motive.

The sources

Unfortunately our knowledge of events from 404 is clouded both by the death of Claudian and the ending of the history of Eunapius. Claudian's last poem is '*Panegyricus de Sexto Consulatu Honorii Augusti*' ('Panegyric on the Sixth Consulship of the Emperor Honorius'), which was written in early 404 and does not display any hostility to the East (see below). Therefore, his death occurred in early to mid-404.

The result of Claudian's death and the ending of Eunapius' work is that we are left with a very large gap in our knowledge concerning the actions, outcomes, and motives of Stilicho in relation to the Eastern court and the events that were to unfold from mid-404 to 408. The loss is irreplaceable and we are forced to rely instead upon the fragments of Olympiodorus that are left, and the histories of Sozomen and Zosimus.

Relations East and West

The thaw in relations between the courts at Ravenna and Constantinople was not destined to be permanent. From the start there was doubt in the East about Stilicho's motives and aspirations. After all, he had always laid claim to be *parens principum* of the Empire; many of the leading men of the East would always regard him as a threat.

This is clearly illustrated by events already alluded to. In 404 Fravitta spoke against John, the *comes* of the treasury and allegedly the father of the younger Theodosius. Fravitta accused John of opposing the concept of imperial unity, after which John arranged for Fravitta to be tried and executed.[24] Fravitta's death may have seriously damaged relations, since it is possible that Fravitta was an ally of Stilicho. Even at this early stage the accord between East and West was clearly fragile and soon to be destroyed again. The breach was opened wider by two further events in the East.

John Chrysostom ('the Golden-mouthed')[25]

The first of these surrounded John Chrysostom, Bishop of Constantinople. He had earned his epithet due to his blistering sermons against abuse of authority by secular and ecclesiastical authority, especially on the part of Eudoxia. Chrysostom had been summoned to the capital from Antioch and made bishop by Eutropius in 398. When Eutropius was overthrown in 399 he fled to Chrysostom. Not only did Eutropius claim sanctuary, but he reminded Chrysostom that he owed his position as bishop to Eutropius' patronage. However, Chrysostom had not wanted to be bishop and hence the claim of patronage was not acknowledged. Yet Chrysostom actively defended Eutropius' right to sanctuary and gave him shelter in the church. Although Eutropius was exiled and later executed, Chrysostom had earned his reputation as a fearless protector of morals in the capital.

Throughout this period Chrysostom was in dispute with Theophilus, Bishop of Alexandria. There was a major disagreement over which bishopric was to be paramount in the East, in the same manner as Rome was paramount in the West. Theophilus believed that he, as the Bishop of Alexandria, should be dominant over Chrysostom, the bishop of Constantinople. Unfortunately for Chrysostom, he had allegedly made comments supporting the teachings of Origen. Origen, who lived in the third century, had suggested that Jesus was subordinate to God, rather than following the orthodox Catholic teachings of the equal trinity of the Father, the Son, and the Holy Ghost. Obviously, this was unacceptable. However, nothing more was made of it until after his death, when some of his more fervent followers took his teachings to their extremes. This resulted in these views being declared anathema by the church in the sixth century. Yet even before this his views were being attacked and, by being seen to defend Origen, Chrysostom left himself open to criticism.

In 403 the dispute between Chrysostom and Theophilus reached its height. The Empress Eudoxia exploited the allegations as an excuse to depose Chrysostom and send him into exile. That night there was an earthquake and rioting in Constantinople. Eudoxia interpreted the earthquake as a sign of God's displeasure at the deposition and Chrysostom was quickly reinstated.

Three weeks later there was an inauguration ceremony outside Chrysostom's cathedral for a silver statue to Eudoxia. Chrysostom claimed that this interrupted his services and again denounced the *Augusta*. As a result, at a synod in the following spring Chrysostom was condemned and debarred from his church. Unfortunately, shortly afterwards at Easter two thousand people arrived to be baptised by Chrysostom. Having no church in which to carry out the procedure, he reverted to using the nearby Baths of Constantine. The event quickly turned into a protest. The government ordered troops to be sent to restore order and they subdued the uprising with much bloodshed.

Eudoxia could no longer tolerate Chrysostom's presence; on 24 June 404 Chrysostom was exiled again and sent to Armenia, despite the fact that on the same evening Santa Sophia was destroyed by flames. However, before his departure he sent a letter to Pope Innocent in Rome demanding a formal trial. The pope arranged for a Western synod, which declared the earlier Eastern synod invalid and letters were sent by Innocent and Honorius to Arcadius to organize a joint synod in Thessalonica to finally settle the question.[26] Arcadius appears to have ignored the letter – or at least no response survives. Unfortunately, the ambassadors sent to convey the letters from Honorius, Stilicho and Innocent were poorly treated. There is little doubt that Honorius was as angry as Pope Innocent and Stilicho over the blatant insult.

The Empress

The Western intrusion into specifically Eastern affairs was undoubtedly one of the main causes of increasing tension between the two courts. The other occurred at some time in mid-404, after the death of Claudian, who does not mention the event. At some point in the year Arcadius paraded statues of Augusta Eudoxia alongside his own throughout the East. The conservative West was deeply affronted by this constitutional innovation, and saw in it yet more evidence that the East was in political and moral decline. As a consequence of these events, Stilicho refused to recognize the Eastern nominations for consul for either 404 or 405.[27] Tensions continued to grow between the two courts.

The claim to Illyricum and the problems of dating events

It is extremely frustrating that Claudian died in 404, as events between 405 and 407 are possibly the hardest to unravel of any during the life of Stilicho. According to the most commonly accepted theory, faced with the worsening relations between East and West

Stilicho now decided to put into action his long-held designs on Illyricum. However, as has already been noted, there is no evidence whatsoever that Stilicho had any long-term plans to annex the prefecture. Furthermore, it is extremely difficult to impose a chronology on events and without a precise chronology it is impossible to decipher Stilicho's motives with any degree of certainty.

It has to be acknowledged that the sources state specifically that Alaric was promoted to *magister militum per Illyricum*, and sent by Stilicho to Epirus, which was undoubtedly still under the jurisdiction of the Eastern Empire.[28] Some authorities have dated this to 405 using Zosimus, some to 406 using Olympiodorus and Sozomen.[29] Dating the event to 405 using the history of Zosimus is fraught with danger. The text at this point is very confusing and worth quoting in full:

> After ravaging all of Greece, Alaric retired, as I have already described, from the Peloponnese and the Achelous valley and stopped in Epirus to await the fulfilment of his agreement with Stilicho, which was this: seeing that Arcadius' ministers were alienated from him, Stilicho intended with Alaric's help to add the whole of Illyricum to Honorius' Empire and, as a result of their agreement about this, he soon expected to put his plan into action. While, however, Alaric was standing by ready to obey Stilicho's orders, Radagaisus gathered four hundred thousand Gauls and Germans from over the Danube and the Rhine and started to invade Italy.
>
> Zosimus, *New History, VIII. 26.* 1–2.

In this account eight years is omitted from Alaric's life in the East, as Zosimus has him ravaging Epirus in 397 before waiting for Stilicho in 405–6. The confusion is caused by the ending of Eunapius' history and the subsequent switch by Zosimus to using Olympiodorus. Eunapius ends with Alaric in Epirus and Olympiodorus begins with Alaric in Epirus. Consequently, Zosimus connects the two without accounting for the intervening years.[30] Accordingly, whatever the merits of Zosimus, on this occasion his testimony must be viewed with extreme caution and not necessarily be taken at face value.

It is also worth quoting from Sozomen's *Ecclesiastical History*, 8.25:

> Stilicho, the general of Honorius, a man who had attained great power, if any one ever did, and had under his sway the flower of the Roman and of the barbarian soldiery, conceived feelings of enmity against the rulers who held office under Arcadius, and determined to set the two Empires at enmity with each other. He caused Alaric, the leader of the Goths, to be appointed by Honorius to the office of general of the Roman troops, and sent him into Illyria; whither also he dispatched Jovius, the praetorian prefect, and promised to join them there with the Roman soldiers in order to add that province to the dominions of Honorius. Alaric marched at the head of his troops from the barbarous regions bordering on Dalmatia and Pannonia, and came to Epirus;

and after waiting for some time there, he returned to Italy. Stilicho was prevented from fulfilling his agreement to join Alaric, by some letters which were transmitted to him from Honorius. These events happened in the manner narrated.

Translation: http://www.ccel.org/ccel/schaff/npnf202.iii.xiii.xxv.html

(March 2009)

It would appear that Sozomen has a better understanding of events at this time, and it is interesting to note that he does not ascribe Stilicho's failure to join with Alaric to Radagaisus' invasion, but rather to 'letters from Honorius'. It is almost certain that if Stilicho's plans had been thwarted by Radagaisus' invasion of Italy, Sozomen would have openly declared it. Furthermore, Sozomen also states that Jovius was appointed *praefectus praetorio Illyrici* and sent with Alaric to Epirus, an appointment that is attested to 407 but may have been given in late 406.[31]

As a consequence it is almost certain that in 405 Alaric remained in situ in the Diocese of Illyricum (Pannonia) and that Stilicho made no move to attack the East or annex the Prefecture of Illyricum. On the other hand, it is possible that Stilicho had, at last, recognized the strategic, financial and military importance of the prefecture. It is plausible that, either before relations began to deteriorate or just as they began to fail, Stilicho realized that his claims to be *parens* were going to be rejected again. Stilicho instead decided that he might succeed with a lesser claim. Therefore, he alleged that Theodosius was planning to return the whole of the Prefecture of Illyricum to the West before he died.[32] It was possible that the ministers in Constantinople would see this as a small price to pay in return for his dropping the claim to being *parens*. Obviously, on the negative side this was likely to accelerate the decline in relations between the Ravenna and Constantinople.

It may also have helped intensify opposition in the West to his policies. Up to this date there is little evidence for any resistance to Stilicho, but it would appear to have been steadily growing. According to Rutilius Namatianus in the '*de Reditu suo*' ('A Voyage Home to Gaul'), opposition to Stilicho was mounting and was using the prophecies in the Sibylline Books, a collection of oracular sayings kept in the Temple of Apollo in Rome, to throw doubt on Stilicho's actions. As a result, possibly in the year 405, Stilicho had the books burned.[33] Although the story may not be true, it does suggest that Stilicho's enemies were becoming more vocal in their opposition to his rule.

The death of Eudoxia

Before the end of 404 circumstances once again intervened to cloud events. Probably brought on by the religious and political strains of the year, the *Augusta* Eudoxia had a miscarriage. It was to prove fatal for herself as well as the child; on 6 October 404 Eudoxia died.

A passage from Zosimus suggests that her death resulted in political turmoil in the East, possibly reflected in the removal of Eutychianus from office as *praefectus praetorio*

Orientis and his replacement by Anthemius.[34] With this in mind, Stilicho may have used the change of regime to make one last attempt to reassert his claim to be *parens* of Arcadius, or at least demand control of the whole of the Prefecture of Illyricum. Without Claudian's poems, we have no way of knowing.

The potential dual claim to Illyricum and acceptance as *parens* did have one major effect. It caused relations between the two imperial brothers to reach breaking point. Before anything further could be done, Italy was once more invaded by Germanic tribesmen, this time led by the Goth Radagaisus.

Radagaisus

The origin of Radagaisus is clouded in mystery. Called 'King of the Goths', it is likely that he was the leader of a Gothic tribe that had remained north of the Danube under Hunnic control.[35] It is possible that as the Hunnic king Uldin extended his power he claimed suzerainty over Radagaisus. It is also possible that in part Radagaisus was unable to counter Hunnic power due to Stilicho's policies. Stilicho's absorption with events in Italy and Illyricum may have meant that Radagaisus, and other leaders like him, lost their subsidies and so struggled to maintain large armies with which to counter the Huns. As a result, the level of control wielded by Uldin appears to have grown to an unacceptable level and Radagaisus decided to invade the Roman Empire rather than remain under Hun rule. His goals are unclear, yet it is possible that he was hoping to emulate Alaric and obtain land and a title for himself in the West. It is highly unlikely that he believed that he could overthrow the might of the Empire.

According to Zosimus Radagaisus gathered together his followers, along with others who also no longer wanted to be under Hunnic rule, and crossed the Danube and the Rhine into the Empire. The passage deserves closer attention.

> While, however, Alaric was standing by ready to obey Stilicho's orders, Radagaisus gathered 400,000 Gauls and Germans from over the Danube and the Rhine and started to invade Italy.
>
> Zosimus, 5.26.3

The phrase 'Gauls and Germans' was, by this date, simply traditional literary terminology for non-Romans across the Rhine and Danube. However, the use of both terms strongly suggests that Radagaisus did not lead only his own tribe, but that he was joined by others also willing to risk entry to the Empire in preference to remaining under Hunnic rule.

Furthermore, the statement that he crossed both the Rhine and the Danube is important. It suggests that he did not pass through Illyricum or Pannonia as is sometimes claimed.[36] Instead, he probably crossed the border and ravaged Raetia in the summer before crossing the Alps at the Brenner Pass, entering Italy towards the end of the year before the snows fell.[37] This would help explain why Alaric took no part in the events that followed.[38] The invasion did not pass near him and he preferred to maintain his position as a Roman commander than risk all again by joining an invasion led by a

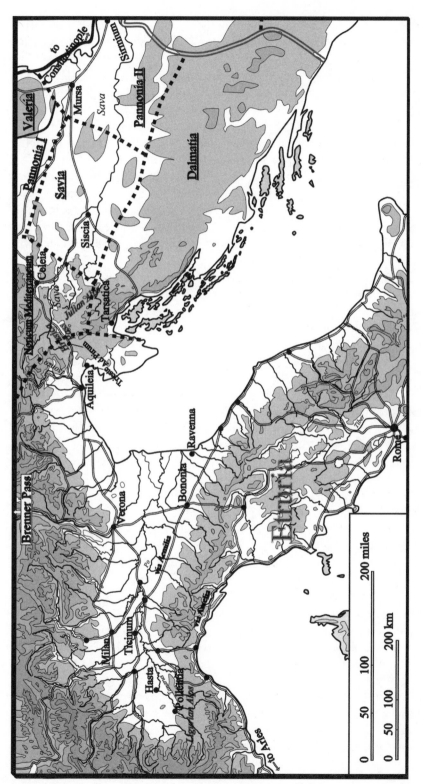

18. Radagaisus' invasion of Italy.

different 'king'. After all, even were they successful, the size of Radagaisus' forces would have ensured that Alaric was subordinate, a situation he is unlikely to have wanted.

As a further incentive, it is likely that at this point Stilicho, realizing that should Alaric join Radagaisus they would be unbeatable with the forces he had at his command, arranged for an exchange of hostages with Alaric.[39] One of these hostages was Aetius, who was later to have such a great influence on events in his own right. Secure in his position, Alaric remained quiet and defended Noricum and Pannonia against further incursions from across the Danube.

Finally, the suggestion that Radagaisus had 400,000 men is a patent exaggeration. Even the figure of 200,000 suggested by Orosius is far too high and probably owed more to the fears of the Italians and Stilicho's later propaganda than to an attempt to estimate the actual numbers.[40] It is more likely that his forces numbered not much more than 20,000 fighting men at the most, although the number of non-combatants will have pushed the number of people he led much higher.[41]

Despite the fact that the figures are exaggerated, the large number of dependents did have an effect upon Radagaisus' strategy. Once in Italy he made the decision to split his forces into three.[42] This was probably forced upon him: with a large number of people to feed over winter, he had no option but to split his forces if they were to avoid the dangers of famine. Unfortunately, the decision would be his undoing.

In Rome the news of the invasion caused a crisis so great that disturbances broke out. These concerned the belief in pagan circles that the disaster had been caused by the abandonment of the old gods, with the ensuing desire to renew the festivals and regain their protection. Obviously, this was opposed by the Christians. Furthermore, the panic was greater than that caused by the invasion of Alaric since in Christian circles it was accepted that, although a heretic, as an Arian Alaric was at least a Christian. Radagaisus, as a barbarian pagan who worshipped half-known, evil deities, was the 'most savage by far' of the two.[43]

Over winter Radagaisus and his forces appear to have roamed over large areas at will, plundering the villages and towns and devastating 'many cities'.[44] Even Rome appears to have been under threat, though this may have been the reaction of the citizens rather than a real possibility.[45] Stilicho was outnumbered and remained with his army at Ticinum.[46] However, he sent orders for troops from the Rhine frontier to move to Italy to reinforce his army, and ordered all of the available Huns and Alans to also meet him in the new year, as well as ordering a recruitment programme to swell his forces in Italy.[47] Furthermore, two edicts, dated 17 April and 19 April 406 (and so at the height of the invasion), called on the inhabitants of Gaul to arm themselves for the peace of their country; it was being made clear that any further invasion, this time from across the Rhine, would have to be dealt with locally until the war against Radagaisus was over.[48]

Once the campaigning season began the two Gothic forces not under Radagaisus' personal command moved separately into Italy to continue their attacks. Radagaisus, with the largest force, moved to besiege Florentia. Once Stilicho had received his reinforcements and his army had reached its maximum size, he advanced on

Radagaisus as the Goth continued his siege operations. According to Zosimus Stilicho's force mustered, 'thirty *numeri* (units) and as many auxiliaries as he could get from the Alans and the Huns', the latter possibly led in person by Uldin.[49] No doubt Uldin was keen to help the Romans, since he wanted to maintain his authority over his subjects. A successful joint campaign with the Romans would demonstrate the futility of attempting to escape from his power.[50] Included in the Western army at this time were the Goths enrolled after the victory at Verona, led by Sarus, and it is interesting to note that they seem to have had little difficulty in facing their 'cousins' in battle.

The defeat of Radagaisus

It is likely that, aside from having the largest army he could muster to hand, Stilicho also wanted to move fast and catch Radagaisus whilst his forces were divided and before he could summon the other two groups of Goths to his aid. Stilicho crossed the Arno and quickly advanced to the relief of Florentia.[51]

The city was in dire straits and on the point of starvation when Stilicho arrived.[52] Following his victory over Alaric Stilicho now had confidence in his own abilities and did not hesitate to launch an attack. It is probable that Radagaisus' forces were encamped at strategic points around the city as part of the siege. Taken by surprise, Radagaisus was unable to gather his troops and respond to the attack. The Goths were driven back and forced to take refuge on the heights around Faesulae. So precipitous was his flight that 'not even one Roman was wounded, much less slain'.[53]

Here the tables were turned, since although Radagaisus and his men were in too strong a position for Stilicho to assault, they were now surrounded and in turn quickly reduced to the point of starvation. Furthermore, trapped on the hill Radagaisus was unable to summon the other two groups to his aid. In these desperate straits Radagaisus decided to abandon his men and make an attempt to escape, although in his defence it is possible that he was making a personal attempt to reach the other two Gothic forces and lead them in an attempt to raise the siege. The attempt was unsuccessful and he was captured by Roman troops. Stilicho felt no need to treat softly with the defeated Goth. He was executed together with his sons on 23 August 406 outside the gates of the city he had tried to capture.[54] With his 'defection' and capture his troops on the hills surrendered. Some 12,000 men were taken into Roman service.[55]

The size of the opposing forces[56]

Much has been made of the number of troops given by Zosimus as being mustered by Stilicho. With thirty *numeri* it should, in theory, be possible to calculate the number of Roman troops at the battle, although the number of federates would still remain open to doubt. Yet the attempt is fraught with danger. Firstly, the exact number of troops in any specific unit is unknown. Secondly, we may be right in assuming that Stilicho's recruitment drive had helped to fill gaps in the ranks, but whether this was the case or not is completely unknown. As a result, many of the *numeri* may have been greatly under strength.

It is probably safe to assume that each of the *numeri* will have mustered at the most

500 men. As a result the maximum size for Stilicho's 'native' forces would be 15,000 men, although the number is likely to have been lower than this in reality due, amongst other causes, to desertion, illness, and an inability to recruit enough troops. With the supporting federates the number may be estimated at a maximum of somewhere around 20,000 men, which at any time in the life of the Empire was a sizeable force. This would explain why Stilicho was prepared to move fast and confront Radagaisus in the open.

Estimating the size of Radagaisus' forces poses an even greater difficulty, since the numbers given in our sources are far too high. As has already been noted, Zosimus claims that Radagaisus had 400,000 men and Olympiodorus claims 200,000.[57] Although the numbers will have included large numbers of dependents rather than simply able-bodied men, it is clear that the figures owe more to the fear of the Italians at having been invaded again than they do to a sober attempt to calculate the forces Radagaisus had at his disposal.

Most modern commentators have – understandably – not attempted to calculate the size of Radagaisus' forces, mainly due no doubt to any estimate being based solely upon guesswork.[58] However, if the invasion was an attempt to escape from Hunnic dominance, then it should not be seen simply as a military operation. A large proportion of Radagaisus' followers would have been non-combatants: the families and dependents of the warriors spearheading the invasion. Given the context, the numbers crossing into Italy would indeed be very large.

The only real clue we have as to the forces Radagaisus had at his disposal is the figure of 12,000 men taken into Roman service after the execution of Radagaisus.[59] It has plausibly been suggested that Olympiodorus had two reports of the campaign, one based on wild rumours and the other upon an official account of the recruitment figures. In order to accept the reported total of Radagaisus' troops as 400,000 he classed the 12,000 that were enrolled in the army as 'leaders'.[60] This allowed for the rest to be captured as slaves.

It is likely that this is not the whole story and close analysis can give a different interpretation. When Radagaisus invaded Italy he soon split his forces into three.[61] It is probable, though impossible to prove, that he retained the largest group under his personal command. When he was defeated at Faesulae there were 12,000 men who were taken into the Roman army and their dependents treated as military families.

The other two groups may have been smaller, numbering only a few thousand warriors each at the most, plus attendant families. It would not seem unreasonable, therefore, if the total invasion force that entered Italy numbered around 50,000. This extremely large number would help to explain the grossly inflated figures quoted in the ancient sources.

The end of the invasion

Once word spread that the main force under Radagaisus had been defeated, the other two groups appear to have quickly lost heart. It is possible that the two groups suffered different fates. Stilicho gave orders to the Huns to attack at least one of them and they were quickly defeated or chased from Italy, with some possibly escaping across the Alps into Gaul.[62] However, there was a later rumour that he had negotiated with the other group, so it is possible that at least one of them was persuaded to leave Italy, although the truth of the claim is open to doubt.[63] So many people were captured and sold into slavery that the slave markets in Rome were flooded with new slaves and prices collapsed due to the sheer number available.[64] Although the invasion had lasted into a second year, the scale of the victory and the speed with which all three groups had been defeated elevated Stilicho to the highest military position he was ever to achieve. Monuments, including a triumphal arch, were erected in his honour by the order of the Senate.[65] Unfortunately, the victory also gave him, for the first time, an army capable of offensive, not just defensive action.

Chapter Twelve

Stilicho and the Invasion of Illyricum, 406–407

Following the defeat of Radagaisus, Stilicho's reputation had reached its peak. The almost bloodless victory and the assimilation of 12,000 new recruits into the army meant that his position was practically unassailable. Yet paradoxically, it is probably at this time that opposition towards his regime gained increasing momentum.

The Roman political elite continued to adhere to the outdated standards of a bygone era. Rome was to be defended by Roman citizens and battles against barbarians were to be crushing victories in which the dead enemy were piled high as a symbol of Rome's supremacy. Although Radagaisus was executed, the sparing of any of his followers ran counter to senatorial beliefs. Furthermore, once beaten the opposition was to be either killed or sold as slaves. They were particularly not to be taken into the Roman army in large numbers.

By taking 12,000 Goths into Roman service Stilicho made a dual mistake that began to tell against him. Firstly, the senatorial elite resented the fact that he was not conducting wars in the manner which Rome expected, especially when it was allied to Alaric's 'escape' in 402. Secondly, and just as importantly, the regular army began to resent the fact that Stilicho was relying more and more on barbarian recruits. By this time his *bucellarii* (bodyguard) was composed of Huns, an honour that no doubt the regular forces felt should have gone to a unit of their own. The tension was greatly exacerbated by the command structure in the Italian army. The regular troops were under regular officers, only the most high-ranking of which would be expected to act in the *consilium*, or 'council' of the *magister peditum*. However, it is likely that a large number of barbarian nobles would expect to be included in military discussions. By this late stage there were probably many such barbarian leaders, all in command of small, independent formations. Stilicho could not afford to alienate these men in case they revolted and either joined an enemy during the course of a battle or simply led their men out of imperial service and into brigandage. With the extremely large number of barbarian 'nobles' in the *consilium*, the Roman commanders and troops began to feel as if they had been displaced by barbarians, and that Stilicho was now deferring to barbarian advice rather than relying on Roman officers.

Events in the East

After the death of Eudoxia in childbirth in 404 her 'corrupt clique' continued to dominate the East until they were overthrown in 405. They were replaced by a broader-based coalition headed by Anthemius, who became the new *praefectus praetorio Orientis*, a post he was to hold until 414.[1] The new regime managed to stop the 'Johannite disorders' (the outbreaks of violence centred around John Chrysostom: see Chapter 11) and so secure peace in the capital. Furthermore, Anthemius had earlier been sent to Persia, possibly in 399, to negotiate a peace treaty with the new Persian ruler, Yezdigerd I.[2] Anthemius was now able to make the most of his previous personal contact with Yezdigerd to secure enduring peaceful relations between Constantinople and Persia. This was a vital breathing space in which the East could order its affairs and regroup – helped by the fact that the new regime remained in place for nine years, ensuring continuity of policy and simple stability for the Empire. However, as a side effect it was obvious that such a stable regime had no need to seek the help of Stilicho, nor to agree to any demands he made. Any claims to be *parens* or to Illyricum were rebuffed.

Stilicho

Thanks to the ensuing tension between East and West, Stilicho refused to acknowledge the East's consul for 405. Relations continued to decline. At the same time, Stilicho's hold upon Honorius was threatened by a personal tragedy; either late in 406 or early in 407 Honorius' wife Maria died. Honorius was no longer Stilicho's son-in-law. Although Serena, Stilicho's wife and Honorius' adopted sister, appears to have quickly arranged for Honorius to marry their other daughter, Thermantia, this would take time and it is clear that such a marriage would be likely to increase opposition to Stilicho's dominance. Stilicho needed to maintain his military supremacy in order to bolster his political superiority.

However, a further incident occurred that helped relations to deteriorate even further. In 407 John Chrysostom died in exile. Honorius, Stilicho and Pope Innocent I had attempted to intervene on his behalf. His death meant that East and West would find it difficult to reconcile their differences over his treatment.

Eventually, Stilicho decided to act. With his claims to the guardianship of Arcadius and to the Prefecture of Illyricum refused, in late 406 he made preparations for an attack upon the East that would take place in 407.[3] This policy had only been made possible by his victory over Radagaisus. With the army bolstered by 12,000 extra men, Stilicho could, for the first time since 397, contemplate taking the initiative and attacking rather than waiting to be attacked. Moreover, the overwhelming defeat of Radagaisus meant that Stilicho's profile abroad would be raised even higher. There was little likelihood of the tribes on the frontiers taking advantage of his absence for a campaign season, as they had heard about Radagaisus' execution.

The claim to Illyricum

The move is usually accepted at face value, being seen as part of a long standing plan to annex Illyricum with little thought for the political implications it had. The primary effect would undoubtedly be the civil war that was almost certain to ensue. Stilicho had seen the armies of the West crushed by Theodosius, so it is certain that this was not an impulsive move, but one whose consequences would have been considered beforehand. Stilicho could not afford to fight a battle against the East; even a victory could be hard-won and leave his army fatally weakened. Therefore, it is reasonable to assume that Stilicho did not expect to fight a large-scale war. This assumption was probably based upon analysis both of the East's recent history of dealing with threats and of the political events taking place in Constantinople.

Since the death of Theodosius, the political leaders in Constantinople had done their best to avoid having powerful generals with large armies free within the Empire to threaten the stability of the regime. The death in 404 of Fravitta had removed the last general in the East with any track record of victory in large battles. Furthermore, the manner of Fravitta's death reveals a deep political divide between those who wanted rapprochement with the West and those opposed to Stilicho's involvement in the East. It is more than likely that Stilicho still had supporters in the East who could inform him that an attempt to take Illyricum for the West would not be opposed by military force. They may also have suggested that, as the prefecture was not vital to the East's survival, its loss would be seen as a small price to pay for the removal of Stilicho from Eastern politics; having declared war, there would be no possibility of him later claiming a role as *parens principum* should circumstances change in Constantinople.

Moreover, it would have been obvious to Stilicho that the East was likely to take any measure possible other than declaring war. The East had a record of avoiding war, since a victory for the East would raise the profile of the victorious general, who could then go on to threaten the stability of the regime. Overall, Stilicho may have felt that giving up the claim to *parens* – which he had no way of making a reality – was a small price to pay for the acquisition of Illyricum.

Modern commentators have suggested that Stilicho's desire to obtain control of Illyricum was flawed, since the prefecture was in a poor condition following decades of being plundered and fought over by barbarians and Romans alike. However, this evades any recognition of the desperate condition of the West. It also ignores conditions in those areas of the prefecture under the control of the East.

The West was becoming increasingly nervous about events in Illyricum. It was now clear that enemies would be free to roam the prefecture, since the East did not take valid measures to stop them. It was also clear from the letter from Honorius to Arcadius that the West would not automatically be warned of these attacks.[4] The result was that a surprise attack on Pannonia from inside the Empire had become a real possibility. This was the main reason why Stilicho had decided to maintain Alaric and his forces in Pannonia. They were to protect the area against attack from any quarter. It had finally become clear to Stilicho that Italy was vulnerable without Illyricum and that he would never gain the confidence of Arcadius in Constantinople.[5]

Furthermore, according to Sozomen after the ejection of John Chrysostom the 'Huns crossed the Ister and devastated Thrace'.[6] Although this may have occurred after Stilicho had made his decision to annex Illyricum, it does add weight to one further reason for his activities. It was clear that the focus of the Eastern government was elsewhere, and that the people of Illyricum were not going to receive any protection from Constantinople. It is also obvious from the sources that this situation had been ongoing since at least the time of Alaric's invasion of Italy, when the army meant to protect Illyricum had left for the West. Stilicho's duty was clear and he was obsessive about doing his duty. He had to control the entire prefecture and bring the population back under the protective wing of the Empire. No doubt he also hoped that by doing so he would gain the thanks of the population, who would repay him by willingly paying taxes and joining the army.

Conditions in Illyricum

Most historians attempting to evaluate the condition of Illyricum have concentrated upon the historical sources, and so painted the prefecture as being a war-torn, oft-ravaged area of little military or financial use. However, recent work on the archaeology of the region has shown that this is not the case.[7] Although in some areas the frequent attacks may have had an effect on conditions, in many this was not the case. The written record may have tended to over-dramatize the effect of the Gothic invasions and the long-term effects may have been less than previously envisioned.

The upland regions that were close to the border seem to have suffered the most. Here there was a low density of cities which were, by-and-large, self-supporting communities based upon agriculture.[8] From the early fourth century many of these cities declined, being replaced by more defensible hilltop settlements. A number of these were founded on strategic high ground covering ancient routeways, which now began to come back into use.[9] This is probably due to the fact that the main Roman roads were the routes most commonly followed by invading armies.

Yet in some areas this was not the case. In Epirus and Macedonia there had been a large-scale reorganization in the early fourth century, connected with the building of the new city at Constantinople between 324 and 330. The building of a new imperial capital had acted in a similar fashion on the region to that of the establishment of Trier and Milan as imperial capitals in the West. The growth of the new city had encouraged agriculture, and ports in the region as well, as towns on the Via Egnatia had rapidly grown in response to the new-found demand for goods.

Due to the troubles of the third and fourth centuries many of these towns had been fortified and so had been able to resist the attacks of the Goths after Adrianople. Theodosius' policy of sending garrisons to important towns ensured that not only were they kept safe from Gothic attack, but the citizens maintained their confidence and loyalty to the Empire. This and the nearby market at Constantinople ensured that, for some areas at least, the late fourth and early fifth centuries were times of economic success. This is, to some degree, reinforced by the presence of imported pottery from Africa.[10] Although these matters are only just becoming clear to modern archaeologists and historians the fact that large areas of the Prefecture were thriving would certainly be clear to Stilicho. By conquering Illyricum Stilicho would be able to tap directly into the Eastern coffers by taxing the goods taken from the diocese to Constantinople.

The tax revenues from Illyricum would be a welcome boost to the imperial treasury. Since the West already had to pay to maintain Alaric and his troops in Pannonia to protect against attack, the annexation of Illyricum would add little to the financial burden. Alaric could be promoted to *magister militum per Illyricum* and simply move with his men to act as a garrison for the whole prefecture rather than just the Diocese of Illyricum (Pannonia). The small extra expense of his promotion and the cost of the expansion of his forces to a more suitable size would be more than covered by the taxes raised in the prefecture.

The move would also allow for recruitment of men for the army from the area, which was of vital importance to Stilicho. The other areas in the West from which he could recruit were Africa, Italy, Sicily and southern Gaul. Although the possibility of recruiting from northern Gaul and Britain should not be discounted, by this late date it is more than likely that attempts to recruit in these areas were either ignored or avoided, since the population would rather fight to defend their homes than be taken to defend Italy, so leaving their homes unprotected.

Yet the main sources of available manpower in Africa, Italy, Sicily and southern Gaul were the vast estates of the senators who did all in their power to stop their people being taken into the army. Illyricum offered a manpower resource not dominated by the Senate. In this way Stilicho could fulfil the Senate's desire to be defended by Romans and not barbarians without coming into conflict with them over the need to conscript men from their lands. The Illyrian and Thracian provinces remained good recruiting grounds and the army of the West was becoming increasingly difficult to maintain. One of the major differences between East and West in these years was that, whilst the West slowly sank under the financial and military pressure, in the East the shortfall in revenues would be made up by Asia Minor, Syria and Egypt, whereas the recruits lost from the Balkans would be found in Eastern Asia Minor.[11]

There is one further commodity that would have interested Stilicho and for which Thrace was later renowned: horses. Procopius notes in his history of the Vandalic War that Belisarius waited on the coast of Thrace, where 'the general received as a present from the emperor an exceedingly great number of horses from the royal pastures, which are kept for him in the territory of Thrace'.[12] Although it is uncertain whether the province could have maintained large herds of horses in the late-fourth and early-fifth centuries, mainly due to the constant warfare in the region, it remains a distinct possibility and is a further reason for Stilicho's desperation to seize the Prefecture of Illyricum. Alaric had escaped from Pollentia thanks to his large cavalry force and Stilicho will have wanted to extend his own mounted arm so that this situation would never arise again.

Once the army had been expanded, and especially the cavalry arm, then Stilicho could begin to make more of a presence in Gaul, and possibly even in Britain. An expanded army in the hands of a general who had proved his competence against Alaric and Radagaisus would cause the enemies of the West to pause and reconsider before attacking.

Finally, there is one further reason for Stilicho's desire to take control of Illyricum.[13] It was clear to everybody that his position as *magister* was unassailable, yet whilst Alaric remained only a *comes* and was confined to a small part of Illyricum, he was likely to remain a problem, always on the lookout for weaknesses with which to gain more power from the government. The only solution was to give him the post of *magister* of a specific prefecture. However, all of the prefectures in the West were taken, and giving him one of these was unacceptable, as it would give him too much power and make him practically uncontrollable. In the circumstances, it is feasible that Stilicho believed that giving him his old post of *magister militum per Illyricum* would satisfy his desires, since between 397 and 401 he had remained quiescent in the post for four years until events in the East forced him to move. At the same time such a post would confine him to the margins of Western politics, again in a similar way to his earlier position at the Eastern court.

With these considerations in mind, there is little doubt that the acquisition of Illyricum was vital for the West. It would provide the manpower to allow the West to become proactive, rather than remaining reactive and so allowing enemies to gain confidence and increase their attacks. It would also remove Alaric as a political nuisance whilst retaining his service for the West should the need arise. Politically, it would relieve Stilicho of much senatorial pressure by removing their main bargaining counters: the supply of money and recruits. The invasion was to proceed.

Yet the decision almost certainly caused further unrest in the Senate. Stilicho, the actual head of the Western government, had failed to deal with barbarians in the traditional manner, instead recruiting them into the army. Now he had decided to lead these same barbarians against his fellow Romans in the East, who had earlier behaved as Romans should and massacred the barbarians who were at large in Constantinople. Stilicho's standing in the Senate continued to decline. Yet it remained an undercurrent, since as yet there was no individual who could act as a focus for all of the people now opposed to Stilicho.

As part of the preparations, Honorius now gave Alaric the rank of *magister militum per Illyricum* and he was ordered to advance into Epirus when the campaign season started. Once there, he was to wait until Stilicho arrived with troops from the Italian army.[14] The combined force would then forcibly annex the whole of the prefecture of Illyricum for the West. It is likely that Stilicho believed that such a show of force would provide a sufficient display of military strength to force the East to give the prefecture to the West without a fight.[15] It should be remembered that in the years following his defeat in 402 there is no doubt that Alaric had recovered at least some of the losses suffered at Pollentia and Verona. In this he had no doubt been helped by the fact that despite the defeat he had remained powerful enough to obtain an official position within the Western army.[16] The combined armies would be a formidable force.

To ensure the smooth running of the newly regained province, Jovius was made *praefectus praetoriano Illyrici* and set out to join Alaric. Finally, possibly in order to prevent news of his activities reaching the East, Stilicho ordered that all ports in Italy were to be closed to Eastern traders; much of the information gained about other peoples was garnered from listening to the reports of merchants, as well as from spies posing as merchants.[17]

The events of 401 and 402 may have played on Stilicho's mind. It was clear that once he was engaged in Illyricum there was a danger that the Vandals, Alans and other tribesmen that had been settled in Raetia and Pannonia after their defeat in 402 may seize upon Stilicho's absence to invade Italy. With this in mind, it is possible that it was now that Stilicho created the last *comes rei militaris* that he was to appoint, that of Italy.[18]

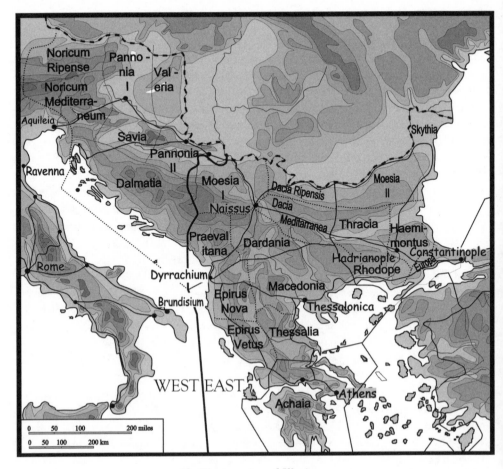

19. The invasion of Illyricum.

This individual would be in control of a large force to deter a revolt of the settled barbarians or attacks from across the Danube.

But not everything went smoothly. There appears to have been a reaction in Rome to his demands. An edict was issued by Honorius on 22 March 407 exempting those who had risen to the rank of military tribune or provost of the liability of supplying military recruits.[19] This edict was issued as a direct response to political pressure on Honorius; it was almost certainly a reaction to Stilicho bringing pressure to bear on military officers in an attempt to enlarge the army prior to the Illyricum campaign.[20]

As a final note, it is certain that Stilicho had learned from his previous experiences. Unlike in 397, this time he would have a large fleet ready to transport the troops across the Adriatic. Furthermore, the campaign against Alaric had ended in embarrassment, partly due to the speed with which it was launched. This time, enough supplies to maintain the army for as long as necessary would be gathered, ready to be shipped across at the start of the invasion.

The army would need a place to embark and a suitable place to land. Although it is not stated in the sources, it is probable that the army for the expedition was gathered at Ravenna, although Brundisium remains a possibility. The aim was almost certainly to sail across the Adriatic to land at Dyrrachium.

Alaric had been ordered to march south, and it will have been expected that his forces would have taken control of the city early in the campaign. Furthermore, as he continued to march south, he would have acted as a decoy to any Eastern resistance. Hopefully, the Italian army would have an unopposed landing in a captured city.

There can be little doubt that the political stance of Stilicho early in the year, and the growing rift that was growing between East and West, alarmed the Eastern court. Even more so as this rift encompassed not just the senior officials but also the two emperors. The danger of conflict was great. They made immediate provision for the defence of Illyricum. A law was issued in Constantinople. Addressed to Herculius, the (Eastern) *praefectus praetoriano Illyrici*, it orders him to construct defences in Illyricum (that is, the Dioceses of Macedonia and Dacia, which were in Eastern hands), obviously in the belief that the East was in danger of attack from the West.[21]

The invasion of Illyricum

According to his orders, in early 407 Alaric marched with his troops to Epirus, so declaring war on the East, and there awaited the arrival of Stilicho with the Western army. It was the end of a remarkable phase in the life of Alaric; he had gone from *magister militum per Illyricum* with the East, to invader of the West, to defeat by the West, to *comes* of Pannonia and by sheer endurance he had been raised, although this time by the Western government, to be *magister militum per Illyricum* once more. However, his tenure of the post was to be short lived. Prior to his departure for Illyricum, and whilst based in Ravenna, Stilicho was dismayed to receive the information that Alaric had died.[22] It has been suggested – probably correctly – that this was a ruse by Stilicho's opponents to delay, if not postpone, the attack on the East.[23] The subterfuge was at least partially successful. Unsure if, in the circumstances, he should carry on with the invasion, Stilicho delayed and only then received a letter from Honorius forbidding him to go.[24]

The nature of the letter is clearly stated by Zosimus when discussing later events. According to this passage Serena had caused the letter to be written, 'since she wished to maintain the accord between the two emperors'.[25] Although in some respects a reasonable request, since the two emperors were her adoptive brothers, one aspect of this does not ring true. Surely both the emperor and Serena had known the plans long before sending the letter. It is more likely that the letter was, at least in part, a political manoeuvre. Stilicho had declared war on the East by sending Alaric to Epirus. The fact that Honorius, under the promptings of Serena, sent orders to Stilicho cancelling that attack suggests that the move was intended both to halt the war and appease the East. In effect, the order implied that Stilicho had overstepped his authority and declared war without the emperor's consent; therefore, the war had stopped before it had begun and the West was relieved of the need to fight in Illyricum. The real message, also reported by Zosimus, appears to have been transmitted in a separate letter received at the same time and this conveyed a completely different message: barbarians had crossed the Rhine into Gaul.[26]

Chapter Thirteen

The British Revolt and the Invasion of Gaul, 406–407

Nowhere do we miss the loss of Claudian's poetry more than in the period from 406 to 408. We are forced to rely mainly on the fragments of Olympiodorus, the *Chronicle of Prosper*, and the histories of Sozomen and Zosimus for events. Unfortunately these accounts do not give many secure dates for events and where these are given doubt and controversy have arisen amongst modern commentators. As a result, it should be noted that none of the reconstructions given below are definitive, and that the sources can be used to support many different variations. Where appropriate, some of these alternatives are discussed, but it is impossible in a book of this size to completely cover all of the possibilities inherent in the sources.

Revolt

In 406, before the invasion of Gaul, unrest in Britain broke into open revolt. The precise causes are unknown, although the claim by Zosimus that this was due to the barbarian invasion of Gaul and a perceived threat to Britain is unlikely, as will be shown.[1] Instead, it is probable that the revolt was caused mainly by feelings of insecurity and frustration.[2] During the supremacy of Stilicho the imperial government had focused upon Italy and the East, largely ignoring the needs and problems of the provincials in the furthest reaches of the Empire. Despite the repulse of the Picts at the turn of the century, by 407 imperial concerns over Britain seem to have taken a back seat. As an example, it is possible that by this date the government was no longer paying the troops in Britain. Although an argument from absence, it is noteworthy that the last Roman coins to occur in large numbers in Britain date no later than 402.[3] Furthermore, it would appear that Irish raids into Britain had resumed, especially if the association of the attacks of the Irish under Niall of the Nine Hostages can be dated to 405, as is usually claimed.[4]

It should also be noted that the Empire appeared to be withdrawing from north-Western Europe; the movement of the *praefectus praetorio Galliarum* from Trier to Lyon in 402 illustrated that northern Gaul was no longer as important as it once was. Furthermore, this would likely have a domino effect on the British, who were further away and already feeling as if they were no longer relevant to the policy makers in Italy.

The British finally decided to act. In the tradition of the island that had promoted Constantine the Great and Magnus Maximus as pretenders to the throne, an individual named Marcus was declared emperor in Britain.[5] Unfortunately, we know nothing else about him. He was quickly assassinated and replaced by Gratian, a British native.[6] The concept that he was a civilian, as is usually claimed, is based upon the word '*municeps*', which has recently been noted as being used as early as Cicero to denote an indigenous native rather than a civilian.[7] Therefore, he may in fact have been a member of the military establishment.

However, due to the speed at which these events occurred and the fact that they happened so close to winter, when a crossing of the English Channel could be dangerous, it is possible that no official word was sent to Italy to declare that Britain was in revolt. In fact, several ancient writers took no notice of Marcus and Gratian, implying that the first they knew of a revolt was the arrival on the coast of Gaul of Constantine III and the British army. In point of fact it is possible that actual news of the revolt of Marcus and Gratian never reached Italy, with only rumours of a rebellion arriving at court – and it was not the custom of the court to react to mere rumours.[8] Instead of sending messengers to announce the defection of the island, the local inhabitants appear to have concentrated upon securing their own situation prior to openly declaring their revolt. Before that could happen, a major event took place. On 31 December 406 a mixed force of Asding Vandals, Siling Vandals, Alans and Sueves crossed the Rhine and entered Gaul.

Asding Vandals, Siling Vandals, Alans and Sueves

Origins

The origin of the Asding Vandals is unknown. There are two plausible theories. One is that the forces that crossed into Gaul are the remnants of one of the three groups of 'Goths' that Radagaisus led in Italy in 405–6. In this proposition, one of these groups escaped over the Julian Alps and crossed the Danube before travelling through Germany and finally arriving at the Rhine.[9] Furthermore, it is proposed that the remnants of the third of Radagiasus' contingents crossed the Cottian Alps into Gaul and later rejoined their compatriots.[10] Although plausible, this is a very complicated course of events.

The second theory is probably the correct version of events. This hypothesis accepts the claim of Procopius that the trans-Danubian lands of the Asding Vandals (see Map 2) became insufficient to support their growing numbers, and that, furthermore, the Vandals and their neighbours were unhappy at being dominated by the growing power of the Huns.[11] As a result of this pressure the Asdings, probably led by Godigisel, invaded Raetia in 401, where they were defeated by Stilicho.[12] Some of these men were then forced to accept service in the Roman army and helped to defeat Alaric's invasion of Italy in 402. The balance of the Asdings and Alans were either settled just inside the imperial borders or were forced to remain on the far side of the Danube. These men decided to migrate further West, forming the core of the Asding Vandals and Alans who appeared on the banks of the Rhine in 406.

Size of the forces

We have no clear idea of the size of the tribes that invaded Gaul. Earlier historians followed Jerome in claiming that the tribes crossing the Rhine were innumerable hordes bent on the destruction of the Empire.[13] More recent historians have drastically reduced the numbers involved in the invasion, although some still refer to the invaders as a 'vast horde'.[14] However, most historians are – understandably – unwilling to put actual numbers to the invading 'hordes', with many simply avoiding the problem and others simply noting that the numbers of the invaders should probably be in the 'tens' rather than the 'hundreds' of thousands.[15]

Yet there is a compelling argument that the initial invasion forces were not very large, instead being composed mainly of men of military age prepared to risk all to find a new life within the Empire.[16] In this model the core of the invading tribes was relatively small. Only later were they swollen by new recruits and dependents joining them whilst they were in Gaul. This explanation receives some support from the Chronicle of Prosper. A close reading of this gives the impression that Prosper, writing in the mid–late fifth century, believed that little had changed between 406 and 418.[17] This is hardly likely had vast numbers of barbarians swept through Gaul and Spain, pillaging as they went. Instead, Prosper sees the collapse of imperial rule as coming after 422.

Although there is no need to see the invaders as beginning with a vast number of people, it is clear that they later grew in size and there is a need to identify where their reinforcements may have originated. The invaders had crossed large areas of border territory, including regions controlled by Franks, Alamanni and Burgundians; the only hint in any of the sources that these tribesmen were tempted to join the invasion in large numbers is the letter already referred to by Jerome. In this instance it is possible that it is only the invasion of their territory that forced the Burgundians to cross the frontier.[18] Although the main tribal bodies did not join the invasion, separate cantons certainly did. These are the 'Alamanni' attested to in Jerome, along with one tribe at least from either the Marcomanni or the Quadi.[19] When joined together, these tribes were referred to collectively as the Sueves in Roman sources.

The joining of small numbers of individuals does not account for the tribal figures that were later needed to control large areas of Spain. The tribes needed to gain recruits from within the Empire in order to survive. Yet the size of their forces remained relatively small; when later they were settled in Spain they were attacked by the Goths originally led by Alaric and decimated. Although no doubt by that late date they were more numerous, it would appear that they were still not the vast hordes claimed in the sources.

Aims

The aims of the invading tribes are unknown, but as has already been noted it is likely that their leaders were attempting to acquire a position similar to Alaric, with a military post and sufficient revenues to support their followers. It is likely that this prompted the attempt to invade Raetia and Pannonia in 401, and when news arrived in 406 of the defeat of Radagiasus and the assimilation of 12,000 Gothic warriors into the Roman army, it became clear that an assault on Italy was doomed to failure.

With his people being trapped in the no–man's land between Rome and the Huns in Raetia, Godigisel decided to lead his people to relatively-undefended Gaul in a second attempt to gain the Roman military position he needed. Again they were accompanied by the Alans, who were by now led by two kings, Goar and Respendial.[20] They too will have realized that they had very little chance of playing an important part in imperial politics unless they took drastic action.

The final group to invade the Empire is the Sueves. Their identity is usually ignored, since they are classed as being a contemporary tribal group living beyond the frontier. Yet this is not the case. 'Sueves' appears to be a label for a composite collection of tribes that incorporated sections of the Marcomanni, the Alamanni and the Quadi. It would appear that in their migration across the rear of the frontier zone the Vandals and Alans managed to attract support from at least two of these tribes; if only one tribal group was included, that group would have been identified by its own name, not that of the composite group. Given the route of the tribes, it is likely that the 'Sueves' consisted of distinct groupings of all three of the aforementioned tribes, joining with the hope of making careers in the West. This would explain why only the Franks are recorded as resisting the invasion; the Burgundians were too weak to fight and the Alamanni were unwilling to attack members of their own tribes. This interpretation of events allows for the inclusion of all of the ancient sources, whilst explaining the possible motives of the tribes and their leaders in wanting to enter the Empire. Finally, the four tribes approached the Rhine, ready to make a second attempt to enter the Empire.

The combined army forced its way across Europe to the river Main, where they were joined by Siling Vandals. It is possible that, like the Asdings, the Siling Vandals who united with the coalition were either wary of the spread of the power of the Huns or were no longer capable of supporting themselves on the land. It is probable that their leaders also wanted to enter the Empire in order to carve out a glorious future for themselves.

The invasion of Gaul

The events surrounding the invasion across the Rhine are some of the hardest to unravel in the story of Stilicho, with one historian even placing the date in December 405 rather than December 406. This is based upon the claim in Zosimus that the revolt in Britain, which is firmly attested to 406, broke out due to the barbarian invasion of Gaul.[21] As will be shown, the original date of 406 is still to be preferred, mainly due to the following interpretation of events.

Confusion over the course of events is equally prevalent. The renowned report that the Rhine was frozen is not upheld by any of our ancient sources. It would appear to be a theory proposed by Gibbon, possibly to account for the lack of a Roman defence at any of the bridges and crossings that should have been defended, and to be based on the ancient sources that do say that the Rhine could freeze in bad winters.[22] This has been repeated so often that it is now accepted as fact, rather than as theory.

As the invaders arrived on the Rhine the four groups faced different dilemmas. Although their arrival was a surprise, which reinforces the concept that the original invading forces were small and relatively mobile, they faced resistance from the start. This was not helped by the fact that they were not working to a unified plan and so marched as separate tribes.[23]

The independent groups arrived at different times on the banks of the Rhine, and straight away different attitudes appeared as to the goals of the march. Goar, one of the Alanic kings, immediately offered his services to the Romans and along with the people he led appears to have crossed into the Empire unhindered. He is later attested as serving Aetius during his tenure as leader of the West.[24] Faced with Goar's defection, Respendial decided to retire from the frontier and join the Asding Vandal forces under Godigisel.

The federate tribes on the border also faced difficult choices. The Burgundians appear to have been either swept aside or forced into the Empire.[25] There is no record of whether the Alamanni opposed the movement of the invaders, although this may simply be an omission in our admittedly poor sources for the event. The Franks, however, were unwilling to let the invaders pass without a fight.

On the far bank of the Rhine there was a fierce battle between the Franks and the Asding Vandals.[26] Given the approach route of the Vandals (see Map 20) it is probable that many Burgundians took part in the battle, however there is no surviving evidence to corroborate this. King Godigisel was killed and the Asdings on the point of being overwhelmed when the Alans under Respendial, retiring from the Rhine, arrived on the scene and the Franks were defeated.[27] Godigisel was succeeded by his son Gunderic, who was to lead the Asding Vandals for the next twenty-two years.[28] It is interesting that the sources for the battle only write that the Franks fought the Vandals, nowhere giving them 'federate' status.[29] Therefore, claims in modern works that the Franks were allied to Rome are not conclusive. However, the fact that these events were reported in Rome suggest that the Franks were indeed those federates who had agreed to defend the Empire. Having overcome the Frankish and Burgundian defences, the way was now clear for the Vandals, Sueves and remaining Alans to cross into the Empire.

Gaul

Since the frontier had remained quiet for the previous ten years – ever since Stilicho had led his lightning campaign in 396 – surprise appears to have been almost complete. Probably the first news that Gaul received of the invasion was that the Franks had been defeated and that the barbarians had already crossed into the Empire.

The sudden arrival and 'frightening mobility' of the invaders, coupled with the neglect of the Gallic frontier, the focus upon Italy and the East, and the demoralizing effect these policies had had on the Gallic army, now had a major impact.[30] There is no need to assume, as some have done, that the invasion was made easier due to troops being moved to the coast to face the British revolt.[31] The frontier in this sector was defended by the Franks, who had been defeated. Furthermore, there is no evidence that tells us when the British rebellion came to the notice of the government in Italy. Instead, once the invaders had crossed the frontier there appears to have been a complete collapse of morale amongst the army in the affected areas, especially when they received news of the defeat of the Franks.[32] It is likely that it was only at this point that information that the Rhine had been crossed was sent to Stilicho.

Stilicho

The news arriving in Italy would have been alarming, confusing, but also slightly heartening and suggesting that there was no real need for panic. Although Gaul had been invaded, the Franks, unaided, had almost defeated the enemy and had actually killed their king. However, the battle had still been a defeat and reinforcements were needed.

Unaware of the nature of the invaders, and assuming that the invasion was composed of tribes from along the Rhine, Stilicho ordered those Vandals serving in Pannonia to go to the assistance of Gaul. As an aside, this implies that the Vandal forces that invaded Gaul may have been those peoples earlier (401) forced to remain outside the Empire.[33] This may in part be supported by Jerome. In one of his letters he declares that the invasion was composed of Quadi, Vandals, Sarmatians, Alans, Gepids, Herulians, Saxons, Burgundians, Alamanni and 'even the Pannonians'.[34] Although usually believed to be a rhetorical flourish by Jerome, the support in Jordanes that the Pannonians were involved implies that the story may be true that Vandal reinforcements were sent by Stilicho to Gaul.

Given the apparently small numbers of the attackers and the fact that they had allegedly lost 20,000 men in battle with the Franks, it was a reasonable response to send a few contingents to simply shore up the defences and defeat the invaders in Gaul.[35] Stilicho's dispatch of the Pannonian Vandals was likely due to reports of separate, small invasions of separate barbarian tribes that could easily be defeated. As this is the only action Stilicho appears to have taken, it is possible that he believed that the invasion could be held by the troops in situ with minimal reinforcements.[36] Despite the earlier removal of troops to reinforce the army of Italy, with the inclusion of the Germanic allies in the area there should still have been enough forces to deal with the crossing of the Rhine.

The move was to be a mistake. As yet Stilicho would have had little information concerning the nature of the attackers. He was not to realize that sending the Pannonians would cause more problems for Gaul. Upon their arrival in Gaul the Pannonians found that the Gallic cities refused to acknowledge that they were serving Stilicho, deciding instead that they were simply a section of the Vandals already terrorising northern Gaul. It is almost certain that these Vandals had transferred to Gaul at short notice and that as a consequence they carried only the provisions needed for the journey. Quickly running out of food, as a last resort they were reduced to plundering the countryside for supplies.[37] Realizing that these actions would be resented in Italy, they joined forces with the invaders, who thus received a welcome boost of recruits.

As a further aside, the fact that the Pannonian Vandals joined the invaders may have confused Orosius. In his account he suggests that Stilicho ordered the Vandals settled in Pannonia to invade Gaul so that he could strip Honorius of the crown and give it to Eucherius.[38] It would seem that Orosius had found evidence of Stilicho's orders to the Pannonian Vandals to travel to Gaul. As they had joined in with the invasion, he then conflated the Vandals defeated and settled in Pannonia with the 'free' Vandals who had invaded Gaul. As a result, he assumed that the whole invasion was of Stilicho's making.

The course of the invasion

Before the reinforcements could arrive, the Vandals, Alans and Sueves began to attack the cities of northern Gaul. It would appear that, although the Franks, Alamanni and Burgundians were not prepared to join the assault on Gaul, the Saxons had no such scruples. According to Prosper they mounted a raid into Gaul that coincided with the invasion.[39]

20. The barbarian invasions of Gaul.

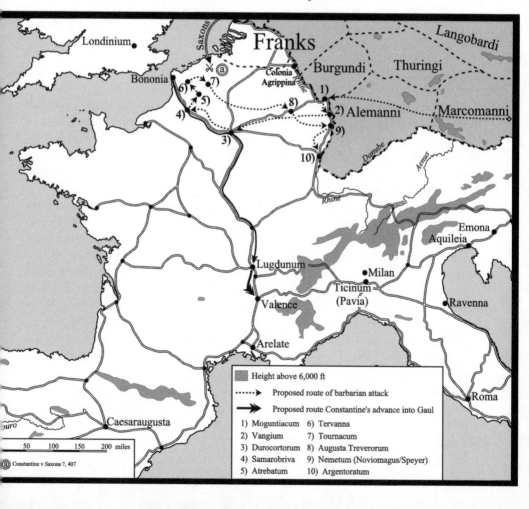

By taking the list of cities given by Jerome in order, and adding information found in Salvian, it is possible to set an itinerary to the invaders' movements (see Map 20).[40] However, it should be acknowledged that attempts to trace the movements of the invading peoples is open to doubt, since it cannot be decided with certainty that Jerome placed his list in chronological order, or that it is extensive. The first city to fall was Moguntiacum (Mainz), after which they moved south to Vangium (Augusta Vangionum: Worms), before heading West and attacking Durocortorum (Reims). They then moved north-west, taking Samarobriva (Amiens), Atrebatum (Arras), and Tervanna (Therouanne), before heading east and sacking Tornacum (Tournai).

However, at this point they changed direction, marching south around the Ardennes forest to attack Augusta Treverorum (Trier). This city is not mentioned by Jerome, probably because it successfully resisted the invaders and so avoided being sacked, but by Salvian.[41] Finally, the invaders continued on to Nemetum (Speyer) and Argentoratum (Strasbourg).[42] As a last piece of detail to the attacks of 407, Paulinus of Nola writes of an attack on one of his houses, though we are not given a precise location.[43]

Although, as has already been noted, this account relies heavily on the accuracy of Jerome's letter, it does give a valid course of events. However, there is still the need to account for their sudden reversal of direction and their possible failure to capture Trier. This would appear to be the result of events in the north of Gaul.

Constantine[44]

We are not told when the news of the invasion of Gaul arrived in Britain. Although traversing the channel could be difficult in the winter months, suggesting a date in spring, the experience of traders travelling between Gaul and the Rhine may have allowed the news to reach Britain early in the new year.[45] There was now a delay of up to several weeks before it was realized that Gratian was not going to cross to Gaul to defend the provinces and make the attempt to take control of the West.

As a result, after a reign of four months in Britain – possibly from November 406 to March 407 – Gratian was overthrown because of his 'refusal to go on the offensive' and he was replaced by the more aggressive Flavius Claudius Constantinus, better known as Constantine III.[46] Apparently a seasoned soldier, according to Orosius he had no merit other than his name, but according to Procopius he was a 'not obscure man'.[47] His actions once in control of the army suggests that the latter view is more likely; it would be surprising if a common soldier without experience of rank would have been able to devise and implement the strategic and political plans that Constantine applied.

However, 'Flavius Claudius Constantine' was not elevated simply due to his aggressive stance. He was chosen in part at least because of his name.[48] It appears that there was a superstitious link back to Constantine I, who less than one hundred years before had also been elevated in Britain and had gone on to become sole ruler of the whole Empire.[49] In order to reinforce this perception he appears to have changed the names of his sons to Constans and Julian, who had both been members of the Flavian (Constantinian) dynasty that had ruled in the West.[50]

The above chronology helps to explain the confusion in Zosimus regarding the date of the barbarian invasion of Gaul. Constantine was certainly elevated due to the invasion of Gaul. Zosimus knew that Constantine had been elevated due to the invasion across the Rhine and naturally assumed that the previous two incumbents had been promoted for the same reason. Zosimus, and modern historians who have followed him, are confused by the chronology of events.[51] There is no need to move the invasion of Gaul back to 405 to allow for it to influence events in Britain.

Constantine quickly collected an army together and crossed to Gaul, landing at Bononia (Boulogne). The dating of his crossing is unknown but it was probably as late as April 407; when Honorius issued an edict on 22 March 407 (exempting those who had risen to the rank of military tribune or provost from the liability of supplying military recruits) there was no sign of panic.[52] By the middle of March the news of his landing had yet to reach Italy.

It is possible that he appointed a colleague before he sailed, as may be suggested by the numismatic evidence, but the attribution is insecure.[53] What is certain is that he appointed Justinianus, a Briton, and Nebiogast (sometimes spelt Nebeogast), a Frank, as *magistri militum* before he crossed.[54]

The size of the forces mustered by Constantine is also unclear. The army in Britain will have been weakened by Stilicho's request for troops to fight Alaric in 401 and Radagaisus in 405. As a result, modern historians have estimated that the forces with Constantine numbered around or slightly below 6,000 men and comprised the whole of the 'field army' of Britain.[55]

Having set up his headquarters at Bononia (Boulogne), he appears to have quickly won the support of the local garrisons that remained in the area. This is hardly surprising; given the disregard they had received from Italy, the troops in Gaul were more than willing to follow a local leader. It seems that the rest of the army in northern Gaul quickly followed suit. Having secured their loyalty, Constantine now reorganized his forces to meet his own needs.[56]

At this point, we are told by Zosimus that Constantine defeated an enemy that later reorganized itself ready for a second attack.[57] This is usually accepted as either a doublet for the battle of Pollentia or as possibly referring to an attack on the remnant of the third Gothic group that had invaded Italy under Radagaisus and appears to have left Italy via the Cottian Alps.[58] Given the confused nature of Zosimus' account, either of these remains a possibility. However, there is a third alternative. When Constantine arrived in the north of Gaul he quickly defeated the bands of invading Saxons that Prosper states had previously invaded and it is likely that this is the conflict referred to in the sources.[59] Although the theory must be classed only as a possibility, the fact that Zosimus claims that Constantine quickly made the Rhine completely secure adds weight to the speculation.[60] The speed with which Constantine – or more likely one of his two *magistri* – defeated the invading Saxons would further help to explain why the Gallic army was quick to change their allegiance. This leader was prepared to fight to protect Gaul, and he had either personal military ability or was served by men who did.

There is little doubt that Constantine would need to establish a relationship with the Germanic tribes on the border, and especially the Franks. In this he may have been helped by the fact that his *magister militum*, Nebiogast, was a Frank. This clearly illustrated that he was willing to use men of ability, no matter their origin, and would have given hope to any Franks who were thinking of a career in the Roman army. Furthermore, the Franks had only just been defeated by the invading tribes and so any strong forces arriving in their support would no doubt have been welcome. The Franks appear to have quickly changed allegiance from Stilicho to Constantine.

The arrival of Constantine and the swift defeat of the Saxon invaders help explain one dilemma. Prior to his arrival the Vandals, Alans and Sueves who had invaded Gaul were heading towards the northern coast. After reaching Tournai they heard of his arrival at Bononia and the inroads of the Saxons in the north. Consequently, they immediately reversed direction, heading back towards the Rhine; if the worst should happen, they might be able to cross the river and escape into the German interior. Unfortunately for them, Constantine appeared to be ready to follow them (see Map 20).

Having secured the northern Rhine frontier for at least a short period, Constantine now moved deeper into Gaul. The barbarians could wait; first, he needed to secure his position in Gaul against the emperor in Italy. He sent Nebiogast and Justinianus to secure the new capital of the *praefectus praetoriano Galliarum* at Lyon. These actions were of direct benefit to the inhabitants of Trier (Augusta Treverorum). Discovering that Constantine was fighting the Saxons, the Vandals, Alans and Sueves had laid siege to the city. Hearing of Constantine's advance, they raised the siege and moved further to the south-east.

Constantine and his troops completely ignored them, instead continuing south and capturing the city of Lyon. At the same time, Nebiogast and Justinianus also secured the passes from Italy to the Rhone valley, so restricting any potential counter-attack launched by the government in Italy.[61] With the defection of the Gallic army the ministers who were loyal to Stilicho appear to have had no means of defence. The *praefectus praetoriano Galliarum* (either Petronius or Limenius) vacated the new capital and the governor of Viennensis (whose name is unknown) left Vienne and established a new capital at Arelate (Arles).[62] Constantine moved his headquarters to the newly conquered seat of government in Lyon, where he was strategically placed to maintain contact with his armies in the south whilst still being in a position to supervise the continuing restoration of the Rhine frontier.[63]

Furthermore, he immediately began to mint coins.[64] The minting of these coins offers a valuable clue both to one of the reasons for his success and an insight into his political policy towards the government in Ravenna. Firstly, Constantine clearly had a reserve of gold – possibly including money found during the capture of Lyon – and so he had a means of subsidising the tribes on the Rhine frontier, so ensuring their cooperation. These reserves of gold would also give him the means to pay for German mercenaries to supplement his forces.[65]

Far more importantly, Constantine followed the traditional method of using his coins to make political statements. The coins that he minted at Lyon in the first year of his reign are extremely interesting. Some bear the title '*Restitutor Rei Publicae*' (Restorer of the Republic) and they and others bear on the reverse a female figure symbolizing the Empire with her foot on a defeated foe – no doubt in this case representing the Saxons.[66] However, on some at least of the earliest coins the reverse bears the legend 'VICTORIA AAAUGGGG' (see Plate 15). The four 'Gs' illustrate that the coin designated the rule of four separate emperors. The four emperors represented were Constantine himself and Honorius in the West, and Arcadius and Theodosius II in the East. It is clear that at this early date Constantine was not setting himself up as a rival; he was aiming to achieve partnership with Honorius and he will have sent ambassadors to the court at Ravenna in an attempt to reach an agreement with the emperor.

Yet at the same time he could not guarantee acceptance of his position in the West. Accordingly, he needed to strengthen his position militarily. His main problem, apart from uncertainty concerning the reaction of Honorius, was the activities of the Vandals, Alans and Sueves in Gaul. Although that part of the Alans who were ruled by Goar had doubtless pledged their loyalty by this time, the other tribes remained at large, plundering and causing unrest wherever they went. Obviously, this could not be allowed to continue; not only would the disruption undermine his financial viability, since his money was bound to run out at some point, but any failure to destroy or at least control the invaders could easily lead to discontent and his own downfall – the death of Gratian had shown just how tenuous loyalties could be in the West.

With these practicalities in mind, Constantine opened negotiations with the barbarian intruders.[67] Still in the region around Argentoratum (Strasbourg), they had obviously been scared of the large military forces passing through Gaul and bypassing them on the way south. Unsure of where to go, after sacking Argentoratum they appear to have remained relatively stationary for a short time.

It is interesting to note that the letter earlier referred to in which Jerome listed the cities overrun by the barbarians breaks off after the fall of Argentoratum.[68] The letter appears to be dated 409 or 410.[69] After specifically attesting the sack of Argentoratum Jerome only vaguely describes their attacks in the south of Gaul except for acknowledging an attack on Toulouse. This implies that he had specific information on the earlier devastation, but had only just received news of the renewed barbarian attacks.[70] This suggests that the invaders were relatively inactive from mid-late 407 until late 408 to early 409. In fact, all of the more reliable evidence suggests that their presence in southern Gaul at the later date may be in association with later events, which will be covered in due course.[71]

It is almost certain that by a combination of force and diplomacy Constantine brought the invaders under control and used them to swell his own ranks – although the sources suggest that not all of the tribes involved adhered to their agreements or were happy to serve in Constantine's army.[72] The fact that Constantine was able to quickly restore Roman administration in the north and that the mint at Trier began to strike coins in Constantine's name suggests that the invaders had ceased to be a major problem.[73]

There is no doubt that Constantine used diplomacy rather than force to overcome the invaders. The reasons for this are easy to understand. The major factor was that he badly needed recruits and the invaders were a ready supply of manpower. It was cheaper and quicker to enrol the barbarians than face the need to collect, train and equip raw recruits. Furthermore, by recruiting them and giving them a position in the army he stopped their attacks. His success at stopping their attacks enabled him to secure the loyalty of the Gallic administration and he was able to bring it under his own control. This allowed him to collect taxes from the region. It would also mean that it was no longer necessary to detach troops from his limited resources to counter the barbarians' movements. Finally, it gave relief to the frightened citizens of Gaul, helping to add to his military reputation and so lessen the chances of a revolt against his own administration. As a consequence, after the sack of Argentoratum the three tribes halted their predatory attacks and became part of the army of Constantine. In this way too it is probable that the wishes of at least some of the barbarian leaders to attain high rank in the imperial armies were met.

But apart from these factors, it is likely that even at this early stage there was a further aspect to be borne in mind; the invaders were increasingly becoming a force to be reckoned with.

Barbarian recruitment

The activities of the *bacaudae* strongly suggests that the inhabitants of Gaul were no longer unswervingly loyal to the Empire. The presence in their midst of a strong force of warriors must have tempted many to switch their allegiance, either in return for protection from the newcomers or simply in order to join them in their plundering. Yet this will have been a relatively slow process, as the invaders did not have everything their own way. Some towns, such as Trier, successfully resisted their attacks and the activities of the armies under Constantine no doubt acted to hinder their movements.

Despite this the size of their forces grew. It is only after their entry into the Empire that they began to assume the size reported by popular myth. Alongside the *bacaudae*, there are indications that they may have been joined by those refugees from Radagaisus' attack on Italy that crossed into Gaul.[74] As they grew in size, so their effects on districts they passed through grew to be ever more serious. A large army, with dependents, requires a large amount of provisions to survive.

Once the invaders became allies of Constantine the situation in Gaul calmed down and Constantine was allowed to focus upon his attempts at reconciliation with Honorius. One measure that he took in order to assure the emperor of his good will was that he left the south-east of Gaul in imperial hands. This was an astute move, since control of this area would have caused panic in Italy, as it was the natural springboard for an assault upon Milan and Ravenna from the West.[75]

Spain

To add to the woes of the Western government, the governors of Spain had recognized Constantine before he had gone far into Gaul.[76] This is understandable; after all, Gaul was the only land route through to Spain and the Spanish governors would have been alarmed at the news that a large number of barbarians had entered Gaul and that the government in Italy seemed paralyzed. Constantine's response was to dispatch *iudices* (judges) to take control of Spain, where, according to Orosius, they were obediently received.[77]

Conclusions

The rapidity with which Constantine took control of Gaul and Spain demonstrates that Stilicho's policies towards the Empire, focused as they were on the need to maintain the goodwill of the Senate, alienated the peoples of those provinces as much as they had the people of Britain. In reality, the barbarian attack on Gaul should have been repulsed with relative ease, especially when the fact that Radagaisus' invasion had been defeated so quickly and his men used to bolster the army is taken into account. Yet in the end the invasion turned into a disaster for Stilicho. His failure to provide instant imperial support in strength to repel the invaders – as had been the case with Radagaisus – resulted in the Gallic army feeling that they had been deserted.[78] Yet credit must be given to Constantine III. Unlike Gratian, he was willing to gamble on the support of the Gallic army and, when Stilicho failed to act, he seized the opportunity with both hands. The question of why Stilicho failed to react remains to be answered.

Chapter Fourteen

Stilicho Responds to the Invasions, 407–408[1]

Stilicho

These events could not have occurred at a worse time for Stilicho. Poised for the invasion of Illyricum, he had sent Alaric into Epirus. This, in itself, was a declaration of war. Before he could sail to join the Gothic forces, news had arrived that Alaric was dead. Unsure of whether the invasion would be feasible without the support of Alaric's Goths, and uncertain as to who would take control of them now, Stilicho received news of the invasion of Gaul. News of the barbarian invasion caused worry, but the situation was not yet critical.

Having dispatched the Pannonian Vandals to help secure Gaul, Stilicho was probably either still awaiting news from Epirus or had just learnt that Alaric was still alive when the letters arrived from Honorius.[2] The letter cancelling the attack on Illyricum was allegedly sent under the promptings of Serena. This was a clever political move. It absolved Honorius from all responsibility for the attack, laying it squarely at Stilicho's feet. In effect, it declared that the war against the East was not official and that Stilicho had overstepped his responsibilities. This gave room for negotiation with the East and the possibility of averting conflict. This was critical. Stilicho could not afford to fight a war on two fronts, since he only had enough forces for one offensive. There can be little doubt that messengers were sent to Constantinople to apologize for the invasion and that their main purpose was to ensure that the East did not continue the war.

Yet included within the dispatches for Stilicho was the news that a usurper had arisen in Britain and landed with an army in Gaul.[3] News of Constantine's landing caused a crisis.[4] No Roman emperor could admit that an upstart could call themselves *Augustus*, since this would merely encourage others to challenge his own position.[5] Moreover, Stilicho was, in effect, a fourth-century general who realized that the usurpation was the most important thing.[6] Stilicho now had no option but to postpone the proposed campaign in Illyricum. Moreover, political considerations in the Senate also caused concern. Opposition to Stilicho's policies was growing, especially as the defence of Gaul – and especially the senators' large estates there – was seen as one of the over-riding responsibilities of the Western emperor. Stilicho needed to remain in Italy to maintain the cooperation of the emperor and nullify political opposition in court.[7] There is little doubt that he believed that the army in Gaul would have no difficulty in repelling Constantine's invasion – especially when reinforced with the Pannonian Vandals. Yet the Gauls quickly transferred their

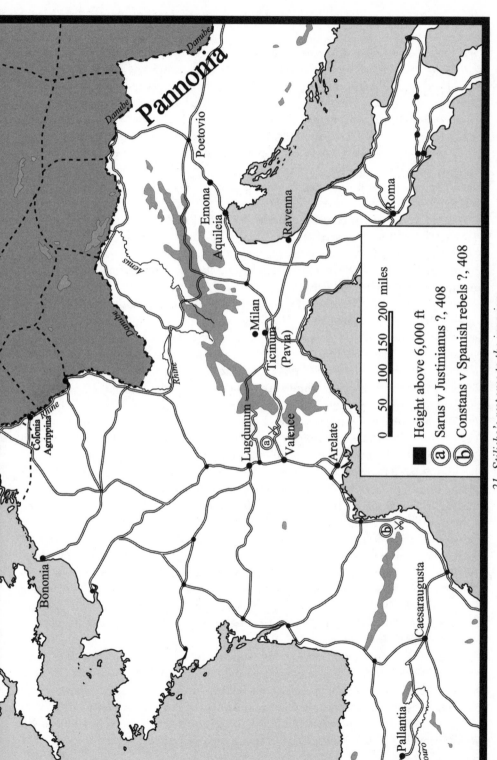

21. Stilicho's response to the invasions.

allegiance to Constantine and the Gallic army suddenly swelled the ranks of the usurper's armies.

It is probable, given the nature of communications and the delays caused by waiting for rumours to be confirmed as facts, that the campaign season was nearing its end before Stilicho and the Italian army were in any position to strike at Constantine. Taking advantage of the hesitation, Constantine had taken control of the north and centre of Gaul, basing himself in Lyon. No doubt by this time also the news of the defection of Spain had arrived, but this may not have been seen as a major factor yet. After all, Spain was the home of the Theodosian dynasty and there will have been long-standing loyalty to the house in at least some of the peninsula. The main concern still remained Constantine's actions in Gaul and potential action in Italy.

Despite having taken control of most of Gaul, Constantine made no attempt to conquer Arles. The Honorian administration of Gaul had retreated to there and founded an emergency headquarters for the *praefectus praetoriano Galliarum*. Instead, Constantine remained in Lyon and began to mint coins stressing his desire to be a colleague of Honorius, not a rival.

Stilicho was ordered to meet Honorius in Rome to decide upon what course of action to take. At the same time, Honorius issued a series of laws concerning the invasion.[8] In desperation Honorius, probably in agreement with Stilicho, sent conciliatory messages to the East. Although this has been interpreted as Stilicho breaking his treaty with Alaric, this is not the case; Alaric was a member of the Roman armed forces and had simply been doing as ordered. Although his orders had changed, there is no evidence that his agreement to serve Stilicho was affected.[9]

With the entire army in Italy geared towards the invasion of Illyricum, Stilicho was in no position to move quickly to face the threat in Gaul. The army on the Adriatic was ordered to move to north-west Italy in preparation for hostilities. The fleet was ordered to disperse and return to its normal duties, where appropriate being used to carry a proportion of the large amount of supplies up the River Po to the new rendezvous. In this, Stilicho made an excellent choice.

By choosing Pavia, on the River Ticinus, a branch of the River Po, Stilicho made it easier to move supplies by sea and river from the Adriatic to the new mustering point. Furthermore, Pavia is in an ideal position both to monitor the crossings over the Alps from Gaul and from which to launch an attack into Gaul from Italy. Furthermore, it was ideally placed to launch an attack on the flank or rear of any troops heading for Milan or Ravenna (see Map 21). In this manner Stilicho could guard against an attack from Constantine whilst at the same time keep his options open as to where to strike into Gaul.

These moves took time. In the event, Stilicho decided to wait for the new year's campaign season to open before opposing Constantine. This was a sensible decision, since unless the campaign was successful in an incredibly short time, communications with an army in Gaul would be difficult in the winter months, with the passes over the Alps either blocked or at least extremely hazardous, making a detour necessary. Furthermore, what action to take remained unclear.

Stilicho remained with the emperor and his advisors into early 408, debating what should be done and countering the recriminations that were no doubt being raised against him.[10] These will have included the anger of the emperor, as it is unlikely that he would have been happy with the decision to declare war on the East over the control of Illyricum, an action which had removed the army from northern Italy and easy access to Gaul, so making Constantine's conquest of Gaul easier.[11] Although no record of these talks remains, it is more than likely that they centred upon a few main facts. The most important of these was that Stilicho had been so engrossed in his preparations to go to war with the East, itself with little justification, that he had neglected two of the main duties of a Roman leader: defence against invasion and the prevention of usurpation. Despite the fact that the invasion of Roman territory by barbarians was unbearable, the Empire would eventually win. But the rise of a usurper threatened the survival of the emperor himself. No doubt these arguments and recriminations mainly revolved around the fact that Gaul and Spain had been lost and that the emperor was close to losing his throne. Added to these factors was the economic one. The emperor in Italy now had no taxes from Spain, Britain and most of Gaul. Additionally, the lands owned by the senators in the south of Gaul had now either been conquered by Constantine or were under direct threat of annexation. For Stilicho, speed was essential before the coffers were emptied and yet more support was lost; troops who are unpaid tend to find excuses not to fight.

Yet as was just noted, little appears to have been done during the remainder of 407. Along with concerns over the weather, it is almost certain that one of the reasons for delay was political. Without doubt, placatory envoys were sent to the East and early in 408 the Eastern nominee as consul was officially recognized in the West.[12] Moreover, as has already been noted, Spain was a stronghold for the Theodosian house. The Theodosian family in Spain would have wanted to support Honorius in his time of need, but have been uncertain as to which course to take. Consequently, it is likely that during the winter months messengers were passing between Italy and Spain, coordinating a revolt of those members of the family in the peninsula willing to act. Plans may also have been made to coordinate their actions with an attack across the Alps from Italy.

It would appear that two members of the family, Didymus and Verinianus, agreed to act. Although they were on bad terms with each other, they agreed to forget their differences and join against the common foe Constantine, and set about raising an army from their dependents.[13] Two further members of the Theodosian house, Theodosiolus and Lagodius, did not take part in the revolt.[14]

The revolt led by Didymus and Verinianus and planned for early 408 was of inestimable value to Stilicho. Forcing Constantine to divide his forces would deprive him of troops in Gaul and so help any forces sent to attack him from Italy. It is also sometimes claimed that Stilicho was sending messengers into Gaul to incite barbarians already there to cause further chaos and so weaken Constantine's position.[15] There is no evidence for such a claim and it is far more likely that these disturbances were caused by later events in Spain.[16]

Alaric

Prior to his attempt to cross to Illyricum, Stilicho had heard a rumour that Alaric was dead. However, this was proved to be a false report when news arrived that Alaric was alive and well and waiting with his troops in Epirus. Yet the planned invasion was now impossible. Furthermore, to ensure victory, Stilicho would need to muster all of his available resources to deal with the uprising. As part of the process it has been proposed that Stilicho ordered Alaric to leave Epirus.[17] This interpretation goes against the accepted theory, based on Zosimus, that from the moment Stilicho heard of the rebellion of Constantine Alaric was left to his own devices.[18] Nonetheless, Stilicho ordering Alaric to move is almost certainly true. The idea that during the political crisis, when Stilicho and Honorius were desperately trying to repair the rift with the East, Alaric would be left in Epirus is hard to believe. Taking into account the need to avoid conflict with the East, and the need to muster all available forces, it is more likely that Stilicho ordered Alaric to withdraw to Noricum, and, whilst garrisoning the province against attack, await further instructions.[19] The concept is further reinforced by Zosimus, who later notes that Alaric sent his brother-in-law Athaulf with a group of Goths and Huns to defend Pannonia from attack.[20] The news reported by Zosimus was simply confirmation that Alaric had done as ordered. The reason for the manner of the report by Zosimus is that he knew the end result and all of his account is twisted by his knowledge of the conclusion.

There remained the question of who to appoint as the military commander for the upcoming war. Stilicho could not afford to go himself. Apart from the danger of being killed, he would also lose the political domination of Honorius, a factor becoming increasingly vital to his survival. Furthermore, a defeat would lose him much of the prestige gained by his recent victories, allowing the opposition to grow and coalesce.

The attack on Gaul

In the end the Goth Sarus, who had changed allegiance from Alaric to Stilicho after the Battle of Pollentia in 402, was appointed to the command in Gaul, probably as *comes rei militaris*, with the specific brief of defeating Constantine.[21] At this time the two main representatives of the emperor in Gaul were Limenius, the *praefectus praetoriano Galliarum*, and Chariobaudes, the *magister militum per Gallias*.[22] It may be thought odd that Chariobaudes was not given command of the force, but since he had lost the trust of the Gallic army, which had deserted to Constantine, it may have been thought that he did not have the prestige to win them back. He may also have lacked Sarus' military ability as well as Sarus' political connections at court.

Stilicho has sometimes been criticized for not dealing with the barbarians devastating Gaul, instead focusing on Constantine's usurpation.[23] This is unfair. The fact that Constantine quickly reached the south of Gaul shows that Stilicho did not have the time necessary to react to the depredations of the barbarians in the north of Gaul (see Map 21). Furthermore, the line of Constantine's advance precluded actions in the north. Any such manoeuvres would have to detour around Constantine, who would thus be in position to threaten their lines of communication. Stilicho was never in a position to deal with the barbarian invaders.

For the attack in Gaul the new *comes rei militaris* Sarus was given a relatively small but highly mobile force with which to oppose Constantine, probably composed of his own Gothic followers and picked elements of the Italian field army.[24] It is possible that Stilicho was hoping that Sarus' campaign would mirror that of Mascezel against Gildo: a quick assault that would take Constantine by surprise and allow him to be defeated heavily, so overthrowing his regime before it was able to fully establish itself. Furthermore, as noted above, it is likely that Didymus and Verinianus also declared their revolt early in the year, possibly coordinating their rebellion with Sarus' planned assault.

In early 408, the counter-attack by Sarus was launched.[25] After crossing the Alps, Sarus advanced towards Lyon. Constantine was aware of his movements and sent Justinianus against him. Sarus won a complete victory, killing Justinianus, many of his men and capturing a 'vast amount of booty'.[26] Learning that Constantine was at Valentia (Valence) Sarus quickly advanced and managed to catch Constantine while he was still in Valence. Sarus laid siege to the city in the knowledge that capturing Constantine would almost certainly end the rebellion.

Constantine's other *magister*, Nebiogast, now arrived on the scene and entered negotiations with Sarus. We are unsure about the nature of these talks. It is usually assumed that Nebiogast was attempting to change allegiance, but he may have been attempting to negotiate a truce on behalf of Constantine; the wording of the source does not specify which.[27] Having come to an agreement with Sarus, Nebiogast was treacherously killed.

The time that Constantine had spent in the north of Gaul now saved him. Following the victory over the Saxons and his time spent reforming the Rhine frontiers, he had sent Edobich, a Frank, and Gerontius, a Briton, to raise troops. After he had been besieged by Sarus for only seven days they led their newly recruited force south, relieving the siege. Constantine's move to Valence and the swift arrival of a large relief force is usually ignored by historians, yet they are vital to an understanding of the course of events.

It is clear that Constantine expected an attack over the Alps, hence his move south to Valence and the swift dispatch of Justinianus to fight Sarus. Yet the speed of his actions suggests that Constantine was confident of victory. If he was convinced that Justinianus would win, then there was no need for him to arrange the large-scale reinforcements that now arrived on the scene.

Therefore, there must have been a separate reason to amass large numbers of Franks and Romans. Since he was still attempting to convince the court at Ravenna that he wished to be a colleague, and not a rival, these troops are unlikely to have been raised for an invasion of southern Gaul. Given the timescale, neither were they raised specifically to raise the siege of Valence. It is hard to believe that troops could have been raised, organized and then led to relieve the siege in less than two weeks.

As a consequence, they must have been required for a separate task. This can only have been to go to Spain. Early in 408 news must have reached Constantine of the rebellion of Didymus and Verinianus. They probably declared their intentions before the beginning of the campaign season, to allow them to amass troops before Constantine could take any action. It must be that the new troops in Gaul were raised specifically with the aim of a reconquest of Spain. After assembling in the north they marched south to join Constantine, who no doubt was planning to send them to Spain under one of the *magistri* – probably Nebiogast as Justinianus was obviously to be retained for the defence of Gaul. It was simply coincidence that as they approached the south of Gaul they found that they had a major crisis to deal with; Constantine was besieged in Valence.

It would appear that Constantine had managed to send messengers through the lines of the siege to request help, and it would also appear that he had appointed Edobich and Gerontius as the new *magistri* following the death of Justinianus and Nebiogast. This implies that these two men were already well known to Constantine and high in his esteem. They now led the recently raised troops to the rescue.

There was no battle fought outside the city. It would appear that as they moved to the attack Sarus retired in the face of overwhelming numbers and in fear of the military skill of Gerontius and Edobich. It also seems that he was forced to retire at speed, since he lost a large amount of his baggage train to the enemy. Although strategically a defeat, the fact that Sarus had managed to win a battle and kill both of Constantine's *magistri* no doubt considerably heartened the court in Italy. However, humiliation ensued for Sarus: when he attempted to retreat across the Alps his crossing was opposed by local *bacaudae*. With the enemy in hot pursuit, he was forced to buy a crossing by giving the *bacaudae* the remains of his baggage train.[28]

When news of Sarus' return was announced, although the ease of Sarus' first victory gave cause for hope, there can be little doubt that the later defeat damaged Stilicho's reputation. Yet Sarus had not been defeated in battle, and had actually won a significant victory. The Senate, rather than being downhearted, may have actually gained confidence by the news that a small expeditionary force had come so close to success. However, the attack had made it clear to Constantine that he was not going to be accepted as a fellow *Augustus* by Honorius and in late spring, believing that Constantine would now launch an attack of his own, the remnant of the imperial government in Gaul followed Limenius and Chariobaudes as they returned in haste to Italy.

The second marriage of Honorius

Earlier, at approximately the same time as Constantine first conquered Arles, some time in May 408 Stilicho married his second daughter, Aemilia Materna Thermantia (commonly known as Thermantia), to the Emperor Honorius, who was now aged twenty-three. Unfortunately, as is usual in the story of Stilicho, the circumstances surrounding the marriage are unclear and open to interpretation.

We do know that Honorius was earlier married to Stilicho's eldest daughter Maria. We know that prior to the second marriage Maria had died, but we do not know the date of her death. Nor do we know for certain whether Honorius, Stilicho or Serena were the moving force behind the second marriage. It is commonly accepted that it was

Stilicho who arranged the marriage in an attempt to bolster his weakening position by ensuring that he remained the father-in-law of the emperor. It is a lot easier simply to accept the statement of Zosimus that Honorius wanted to marry Thermantia, and in this was supported by Serena who was fearful of losing her power and prestige.[29] In the same passage Zosimus claims that Stilicho was against the match. This is probably more feasible. Although the marriage would reunite Stilicho and Honorius as father- and son-in-law, it was politically dangerous.

The first marriage was probably accepted by the Senate out of necessity, since Stilicho at that time was far too powerful to resist. This second marriage would be opposed, both by Christians, who would see it as incest and so against scriptures, and by Stilicho's opponents, who would be able to interpret it as the action of a desperate man. The latter would be able to use it for propaganda purposes to help persuade potential opponents to join their cause. In fact, it has been proposed that the unrest surrounding events in 407 and 408 was made worse by the marriage of Honorius and Thermantia for just this reason.[30]

Gaul

Following the aborted attack by Sarus, Constantine had no qualms about his reaction. He advanced south with his armies and by early summer had established his seat of government in Arles.[31] Using some of the booty captured from Sarus (although it must be remembered that a proportion of this had earlier been captured by Sarus from Justinianus) Constantine began to mint new coins at Arles.

These coins are useful in providing a date for Constantine's setting up of the new mint. Both Sozomen and Zosimus imply that Constantine had only just reached Arles when the news arrived from the East that Arcadius had died.[32] Unlike the earlier coins, which were minted with the legend AUGGGG in the hope that Constantine would be accepted as *Augustus* alongside Honorius, Arcadius and Theodosius II, these coins bore the imprint AUGGG. The loss of the fourth '*Augustus*' dates the production of the coins to after the death of Arcadius in May. However, the coins also show that Constantine was willing to forget about the recent attack from Italy and still wanted to be accepted as an imperial colleague alongside Honorius and Theodosius.

Spain[33]

In spite of the defeat of Sarus, and the lukewarm reception to Thermantia's marriage to Honorius, Stilicho, Honorius and even the Senate may have taken heart from events in Spain. In the spring of 408, as the army of Italy began to gather at Pavia ready for the war in Gaul, Didymus and Verinianus, relatives of Honorius, raised a rebellion in Spain.[34] Although usually interpreted as a spontaneous reaction to Constantine's occupation, it is more likely that they had been in contact with Honorius and Stilicho throughout 407 and had agreed to act in early 408. They may have been further encouraged by the news that the Italian army was collecting at Pavia prior to intervention in Gaul.[35] They quickly succeeded in establishing themselves in Spain and set about attempting to seal the passes over the Pyrenees.

In response Constantine ordered fresh troops to be raised from the Rhine frontier, as outlined above. After the attack by Sarus, Constantine established himself at Arles. Once settled, Constantine promoted his eldest son Constans as *Caesar* and sent him with an army to Spain, along with the *magister militum* Gerontius.[36] Didymus and Verinianus resisted and won a victory in the Pyrenees. However, Constans called for reinforcements from Gaul and with these succeeded in forcing a crossing of the Pyrenees. Whilst Gerontius continued in command of the troops, Constans moved to Caesaraugusta with the newly appointed *praefectus praetoriano*, Apollinaris, and the *magister officiorum*, Decimius Rusticus, who were probably sent to reorganize the newly recaptured provinces.[37] After stiff resistance, Gerontius defeated and captured the two rebels in Lusitania.[38] In an attempt to cow resistance, Constans now allowed one unit, the *Honoriaci*, to sack the *campi Pallentini*.[39] Although of uncertain location, this was possibly in the region of Pallantia (Palencia) in Spain, in the Castilian *meseta* along the middle course of the Duero (Douro). The area contains many sumptuous residential villas and was most likely the centre of Didymus' and Verinianus' estates. Once the territory was pacified, Constans left Gerontius in Spain with Gallic troops to cover the passes over the Pyrenees, and returned to his father in Arles with Didymus and Verinianus as captives.[40] Strangely, he also left his wife in Spain with Gerontius.[41] Despite not having taken part in the uprising, Lagodius and Theodosiolus fled, with Lagodius travelling to Constantinople and Theodosiolus seeking sanctuary at Ravenna.

Italy

It was during his time at Ravenna that Stilicho first received the envoys from Alaric, informing him that Alaric had moved to Emona.[42] There has been debate concerning whether Emona was in Italy or Noricum, and so whether Alaric actually declared war on the Empire by leaving the boundaries of Illyricum (Pannonia).[43] This is not claimed by the ancient sources, and in fact in the confused passage in Zosimus Alaric specifically sends envoys from Noricum.[44] This implies that whether Emona was in Noricum or Italy was unimportant. What may have been important was that Emona was at the head of the pass across the Alps which led to the River Frigidus, the implications of which would not have been lost on either Alaric or Stilicho, since they had both served in the army that had crossed the pass in 394 under Theodosius to win the Battle of the Frigidus.

The envoys also conveyed that Alaric had a grievance, which was that he had been forced to support his men from his own pocket during the stay in Epirus. Accordingly, Alaric was demanding that he be paid 4,000 pounds of gold to cover his expenses for the invasion of Epirus.[45] This may have been enough to keep 72,000 men for a year, and it was twice the cost of the praetorian games that Symmachus produced for his son.[46] Although the payment for the praetorian games was probably the result of senators' saving for many years, the fact that one senator could amass such a sum implies that the gathering of 4,000 pounds of gold was still a viable prospect for the Senate as a whole.[47]

There is no doubt that Alaric's forces did not amount to 72,000 men. Zosimus later gives his forces the total of 40,000 men.[48] However, this total is arrived at after he had been joined by 30,000 men from the army of Italy, and by fugitive slaves from Rome, and also by another large band of Gothic warriors under his brother-in-law Athaulf.[49] This means that his army in early 408 probably mustered a maximum of 5–6,000 men. Yet Stilicho had no choice but to support the payment to Alaric. Stilicho needed the whole army to suppress Constantine's rebellion, so it was vital that Alaric be kept on side. As with the decision to seek peace with the East, Stilicho knew that a war on two fronts – this time against Alaric – would be impossible to win. Conversely, should Alaric's men fight alongside the Romans against Constantine there would be a good chance of victory.

Although Alaric's demand is usually interpreted as him being willing to manipulate Stilicho's troubles to his own advantage, there are valid reasons for the ultimatum. First, as the defection of many Goths during the Italian campaign had shown, Alaric did not have complete control of his forces. As a result, he needed to maintain his standing in order to remain their leader. Second, he had actually spent a large amount of his financial reserves on the project and needed more money, again in order to maintain his status at the head of the Goths. For the campaign in Epirus it is almost certain that the Empire had provided provisions, but they had not provided pay.[50] Finally, he had been ordered by Stilicho to march to Epirus to take part in what became a fictitious operation. In order not to lose face with his men, who could easily think of the whole episode as a waste of time and which had only served to make their leader look foolish, he needed a political concession to re-establish his standing. As a consequence, it is possible to see his actions as motivated, not by a desire to injure Stilicho politically, but as a need to maintain his own position at the head of his forces.[51]

The debate in the Senate[52]

Obviously, Stilicho would need clearance from the emperor to pay such a large sum and would need the cooperation of the Senate to gather the money. Leaving the envoys at Ravenna, Stilicho travelled to Rome and participated in the most crucial senatorial session of his career. The fact that Honorius and Stilicho needed to be present in person at the ensuing senatorial debate shows that the prestige of the imperial government had declined. They now needed the agreement of the Senate before they could act, a necessity that would have been anathema to many earlier emperors. The Senate had returned to a position of importance vital to the conduct of foreign policy.[53]

Buoyed by the report that a small force had almost encompassed Constantine's downfall, the news of the rebellion against Constantine in Spain, and further reinforced by their traditional views of barbarians and how they should be treated, the Senate was in no mood to be conciliatory. When Stilicho announced Alaric's demands, there was a debate. This showed that there was a split in the Senate over whether Alaric or Constantine, who was still attempting to become a colleague of Honorius, was the major threat to Italy. Stilicho and his supporters wanted to employ Alaric against the usurper in Gaul, but the majority believed that Alaric posed the greater danger and so the Senate voted for a declaration of war on Alaric.[54] Probably in angry and accusatory tones, Stilicho was then asked for his reasons for wanting to pay Alaric and so shame the reputation of the Romans.[55] He replied that Alaric's presence in Epirus had been following orders from the emperor and so the expenses were a reasonable request. At this some of the senators relented and a second vote was called. The vote split the Senate. Although Alaric was voted 4,000 pounds of gold to cover his losses, the result hardened opposition to Stilicho's dominance.[56] In due course the gold was sent to Alaric.[57]

Lampadius

Nowhere is the growth of opposition more apparent than in the comment of Lampadius after the second vote. At the end of the vote he made the acidic aside '*non est ista pax sed pactio servitutis*' ('this is slavery rather than peace'), probably quoting Appius Claudius' phrase arguing against peace with Pyrrhus in the third century BC.[58] At the end of the session, aware that he had spoken out of turn, he sought sanctuary in a nearby church.

Lampadius was the brother of Flavius Manlius Theodorus, who had been made *praefectus praetorio Italiae* in 397, and himself had been made *praefectus urbis Romae* by Stilicho in 398 to force through the demands for recruits during the African crisis. It would appear that Lampadius was a senator who believed that Rome should be defended by her own forces, but was realistic enough to realize that to ensure this the senators should be forced to supply recruits from their own estates to build the army to the necessary strength. His early support for Stilicho had now been eroded and he had joined the opposition. The most likely cause is Stilicho's continuous addition of barbarians to the ranks of the army over the preceding eight years, a persistence that offended Lampadius' aristocratic beliefs beyond endurance.

The growth of opposition may have begun to disturb Stilicho, but to become effective the disparate groups, including the army, the Senate and the Catholics who opposed Stilicho's employment of pagans, needed a figure who could act as the focus for their resistance.[59] Out of the shadows there emerged such a man: Olympius. During either late 407 or early 408 Olympius slowly came to the forefront and began to orchestrate the opposition.

Olympius

At this time serving as the *magister scrinii* (master of the imperial secretaries), Olympius was ideally placed to influence the emperor when Stilicho was not present. Ironically, he had been advanced thanks to Stilicho's patronage.[60] He worked on the emperor's suspicions to widen the rift that was growing between Honorius and Stilicho, especially concerning Stilicho's attempt to conquer Illyricum and his continued dominance of Western politics, despite Honorius being the emperor. As time passed Olympius' influence over Honorius grew.

For the moment, however, Stilicho had been victorious in the Senate and he prepared to leave for Ravenna. Honorius, apparently encouraged by Serena, who feared for his safety if Alaric broke the peace and again invaded Italy, also set out for Ravenna. Zosimus claims that Serena's advice was more out of fear of losing her own position than worry over the safety of Honorius for his own sake.[61] In this she may have been encouraged by Stilicho, who may have feared a repetition of the situation during the siege of Milan during Alaric's first invasion, when Honorius had been besieged by Alaric.

It is unlikely, despite Zosimus' claims to the contrary, that on the way from Rome to Ravenna Honorius stopped at Pavia to collect troops to suppress Stilicho.[62] It is possible, as has been claimed elsewhere, that Olympius did collect some forces, although it might not have been to suppress Stilicho; it may be that they were simply reinforcements for the garrison at Ravenna.[63]

Shortly before they left Rome rumours arrived in Italy of the death of Arcadius. The two men continued their journeys, but at different speeds. When the news arrived that Arcadius had definitely died, Stilicho was already in Ravenna but Honorius had only reached as far as Bononia. The situation would now turn on the decisions of the emperor and his senior advisor upon receipt of the sad news.

Chapter Fifteen

The Fall of Stilicho

When confirmation that Arcadius had died reached Italy Honorius sent a message for Stilicho to meet him at Bononia. One reason for the recall is that there appears to have been some unrest in the army at Bononia and Stilicho's presence was needed to calm the troops.[1] The disturbances were probably over the uncertainty caused by Arcadius' death. The army would have known that Stilicho would take some form of action, but the nature of his response was unclear. All that is certain is that opposition to Stilicho within the army was continuing to mount and that the army was reaching the point where it was unwilling to follow Stilicho's orders. Upon his arrival Stilicho reprimanded the troops and declared that Honorius had decreed that they should be punished and that those most guilty of stirring up trouble would be decimated. Terrified at the prospect, the troops begged Stilicho to intercede with the emperor. Stilicho announced that he would speak on their behalf and the unrest collapsed.[2]

After he had calmed the troops Stilicho entered long discussions with the emperor concerning what action to take regarding the accession of Honorius' nephew, Theodosius II. Aged only seven, it was clear that his future was in jeopardy should unscrupulous ministers manage to seize control in the East. Anthemius was an unknown quantity in this situation. He had occupied the post of *praefectus praetoriano Orientis* continuously since 405, and had opposed Stilicho's claims as *parens* in the East. Yet at the same time he had engineered an enduring peace with Persia, showing that he had political ability. It was possible that he would survive the political chaos that usually surrounded the accession of a minor, but his loyalty to Theodosius was unknown. However, Honorius was now the senior emperor and decided that, as such, he would be able to exert influence upon the appointments and policies in Constantinople.

He resolved that the best course of action was for him to travel East and personally oversee the installation of his nephew as emperor. In that way, he could ensure that Theodosius received guardians who would look after his welfare. According to the sources, and unfortunately for Honorius, Stilicho saw the death of Arcadius as an opportunity – and probably the last – of gaining the role of *parens principum* of the whole Empire. He will have been encouraged by the knowledge that, with the additional resources of the East at his disposal, he would be able to defeat Constantine in Gaul and at the same time unite the disparate halves of the Empire.[3] He too wanted to travel to Constantinople to impose his will on the Eastern government.

Still following Zosimus' account, there followed an intensive argument over which of the two was to go to Constantinople. Honorius could claim to the superior political

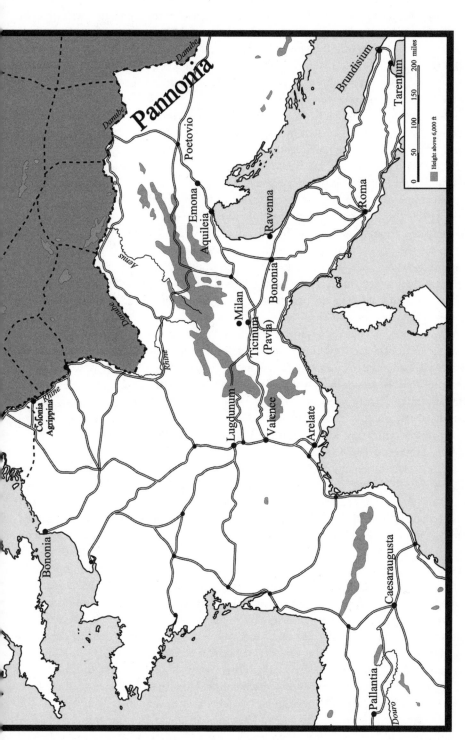

22. The fall of Stilicho.

position, since he was the senior emperor and so, at least in theory, could give orders in the East. Stilicho, on the other hand, realized that if Honorius went and succeeded, then his own position would be seriously weakened. Honorius would gain confidence with the success of the mission. The new-found self-belief, coupled with the biased political advice he was certain to be given in the East, would weaken Stilicho's position in the West. Stilicho could not afford to risk Honorius travelling to the East.

There is considerable merit to the reconstruction. Honorius was relatively weak-willed and his arrival in Constantinople would leave him open to manipulation by the Eastern ministers. This included Anthemius, who had been in power since 404 and was Stilicho's main opponent in the East. Obviously, Honorius could not be allowed to go. Fortunately for Stilicho, in the debate he had the upper hand due to circumstances in the West. The main difficulty with Honorius travelling East was the cost.[4] Emperors were expected to travel in comfort and to have the splendour of the court mirrored in their baggage train. The fact that Stilicho could have used such an argument reveals how grave the financial situation was in Italy. With the loss of the revenues of Gaul, Spain and Britain, the West had to rely on the taxes from Italy, Africa, Sicily and Illyricum (Pannonia). The reality that the largest estates in these provinces were held by senators who would use any excuse to avoid paying taxes only added to the dilemma faced by Honorius and Stilicho.

An even more persuasive argument concerned the presence on the Italian border of the usurper Constantine.[5] Should Honorius travel to Constantinople, the way would be open for Constantine to enter Italy. If he managed to cross the Alps, there would be no guarantee that the troops in Italy would remain loyal – as witnessed by the near-mutiny that had only recently been suppressed. Honorius needed to remain in Italy as the figurehead to promote and maintain the loyalty of the army. Furthermore, it was expected that emperors be accompanied by a large number of troops when they travelled, and these could not be spared from the upcoming campaign in Gaul.

There is also the claim in Zosimus that Honorius was needed in Italy as a counter to the presence of Alaric, since Alaric was a 'faithless barbarian' and he too might see Honorius' absence as the opportunity to revolt and lead an attack on Italy.[6] This last claim remains doubtful, not least because during the same discussion Stilicho proposed sending Alaric at the head of a combined army into Gaul.[7] It is clear that Stilicho actually trusted Alaric to follow his commands. Furthermore, Stilicho had already arranged for the payment of 4,000 pounds of gold to Alaric, reinforcing the impression that Alaric was better off loyally serving the emperor. The claim was probably made by Zosimus as it emphasized the desperation felt by Stilicho; further, Zosimus knew the outcome and used the suggestion simply to build tension in his account. Despite that observation, it remained obvious that Honorius was safest in Italy, and Stilicho was unwilling to put the emperor at unnecessary risk. The events of 402, when Honorius was besieged in Milan by Alaric, was a fear that remained with Stilicho to the end.

The weight of the arguments was overwhelming: Honorius, with an 'understandable lack of enthusiasm', acceded to Stilicho's request that he stay in Italy and act as the focus for those troops loyal to his court.[8] Honorius dictated letters for Stilicho to carry to Constantinople, and also drafted orders for Alaric to travel to Pavia and take control of the army in Italy.[9] The title he was to be given is unclear; the likelihood is that it was either *magister militum vacans* or *magister militum per Gallias*. The claim that he was to be made *magister equitum* is not stated in any of the sources and is actually negated by another piece of evidence.[10] It would appear that at this time Vincentius, who is otherwise unknown, was made *magister equitum*.[11] His appointment would have fulfilled several functions at the same time. First, he would be Stilicho's representative whilst Stilicho was in Constantinople. Second, such an appointment was probably forced on Stilicho by the emperor and Senate, who would have otherwise been extremely annoyed at having Alaric as the second in command of the Western army. Finally, his appointment would act as a counter to Alaric whilst Stilicho was absent.

According to Zosimus, Stilicho was to go to Constantinople and take control of matters supported by a force of only four legions.[12] However, he was also to carry letters of authorization from Honorius, plus a *labarum*, a standard carrying the image of Christ which was specifically associated with the emperor and attested that the carrier had the emperor's trust.[13] The small force may have been a political necessity. Any more and the expense involved would have weakened Stilicho's claim that Honorius could not go in person due to the poor state of the treasury and the need for troops in the West. It may also have been decided that this was the optimum force to show that Honorius and Stilicho were serious in their claims, but still weak enough not to suggest that they were prepared to use force to achieve them.

Yet it is difficult to believe that Stilicho could seriously expect a positive welcome in Constantinople. Not only were the laws still in place barring Eastern traders from entering Italian ports, but the East was also attempting to repair the damage caused by Alaric's invasion of Epirus. The idea that Stilicho could expect that his reception in Constantinople would be anything less than hostile remains dubious. Yet there was no one else who he could trust to go in his stead. Sending another minister at a time of such unrest was, like sending Honorius, courting disaster. Furthermore, nobody had his political authority. If anyone was to go it had to be Stilicho.

What may also have become apparent was the level of the repercussions in the West should Stilicho travel East. Stilicho would be leaving Honorius in the hands of politicians now becoming more vocal in their opposition to Stilicho's regime. Stilicho must have realized that he was in grave danger. If he remained in Italy to maintain his hold on Honorius, he gave the lie to his claim to be needed in the East. This would lead to accusations that Honorius should have gone and weaken Stilicho's position. If Stilicho travelled to Constantinople and left Honorius in the care of his enemies, it was clear that Honorius would in all likelihood be turned against him by his opponents. The situation would become even worse if he travelled East and was opposed by the court at Constantinople. Whatever he did, he was likely to lose.

It would appear that all of these considerations weighed heavily on Stilicho. Unable to make up his mind, he failed to move from Bononia, even after receiving the orders to go East. By contrast, Honorius moved to fulfil his duties. Despite being urged by Serena to travel direct to Ravenna, he decided that his first duty was to travel to Pavia so that he could review the troops before their dispatch to Gaul.[14] It is not known where Serena herself went. She may have taken her own advice and travelled directly to

Ravenna. The only certainty is that she did not accompany the emperor or remain with Stilicho.

Backlash

Olympius was no doubt aware of Honorius' unhappiness with the decision that Stilicho should go East. It is clear that from now on he was able to dominate Honorius in the same way that Stilicho had previously done, especially as Honorius travelled to Pavia and Stilicho remained at Bononia, so losing intimate contact with the emperor. Olympius knew how to employ Stilicho's mistake and Honorius was too weak to control matters.

A strong emperor would have been able to neutralize the opposition, using the opposition to Stilicho to strengthen his own position and break free from Stilicho's domination. With luck and judgement, he could have achieved a balance between the opposing parties where he held the upper hand. In this way, Honorius could have retained the services of Stilicho in a suitably subordinate position. Unfortunately, Honorius was not strong. Although it was clear that Honorius wanted to rule in his own right, he was too weak and insecure and so uncertain of Stilicho's motives. Olympius was able to play on the suspicions of the emperor, ensuring that the rift between the two men grew.

Moreover, Honorius was a terrible judge of character. He was made to believe that Stilicho had ulterior motives, but did not realize that the men telling him these things had political aims of their own. However, he did have a certain amount of low cunning, so continued to allow Stilicho's enemies at court to undermine the general's position.[15]

As a further dilemma, Stilicho's plan to send Alaric into Gaul at the head of a combined army was sensible but fatally weakened his position and was the greatest mistake of his career.[16] The decision was extremely unpopular with the Roman forces, who would have preferred to serve under a Roman figure, especially either Stilicho or Honorius. The appointment of a man they had memories of fighting in Italy itself ensured that discontent in the army reached new levels. They did not want to serve under a barbarian whose loyalty to Rome was extremely suspect and they did not have the same level of trust towards Alaric as had Stilicho.

Dissatisfaction will not have remained confined to the regular army. Many leaders of the Germanic forces serving under Stilicho had previously served with Alaric and deserted him for Rome. Alaric could easily use his position to exact revenge on the men who had deserted him. The Germanic federates too would have been unhappy with the new proposals.[17]

The same level of opposition certainly appeared in the Senate. For many years they had opposed the employment of barbarians in the army. They now had the humiliation of having Alaric appointed to one of the highest ranks in the army, subordinate only to Stilicho, Vincentius, and in theory the emperor. This same man had recently demanded a vast amount of money on threat of invasion, and will have known that many of the senators had opposed him in the Senate meeting to discuss his demands. As a high-ranking official, he might be prepared to use his new-found power to extract vengeance. The deal whereby Alaric was sent against Constantine was interpreted as a betrayal by the Senate and was seen as giving a valid motive for a conspiracy against Stilicho.[18]

At the same time as Honorius was listening to the whisperings of court officials, discontents were spreading rumours amongst both the troops and the general populace that Stilicho was actually in league with the barbarians – especially Alaric and the 12,000 Goths that had joined Stilicho after Radagaisus' defeat. As evidence of this he had failed in his duty, allowed a usurper to rise in the Prefecture of Gaul and when it was imperative that he focus on the West, instead he was intending to head East.[19] His place as *magister utriusque militiae* was at the head of the army defeating Constantine III in Gaul. The fact that he was ignoring his responsibilities meant that he had an ulterior motive behind his convoluted schemes. The one that was advanced was that he wanted to replace Theodosius II in the East with his own son Eucherius. Like Theodosius II, Eucherius was a member of the imperial family and was the adoptive grandson of Theodosius I, who had publicly recognized Eucherius before his death in 395. Dissatisfaction with Stilicho's policies was now becoming increasingly widespread.

Stilicho

Eventually, the level of opposition grew to such an extent that it became obvious that a crisis was looming. The victories of 402 (Alaric) and 406 (Radagaisus) were forgotten.[20] As has already been noted, it is probable that, allied to the dawning realization that he would not be welcome in the East, Stilicho's inactivity was a reaction to the growing enmity. It is possible that by now accusations that he wanted to crown Eucherius in Constantinople had reached even his own ears. He dared not head East, since then it was certain that his opponents would use it as proof that he wanted to elevate Eucherius to emperor of the East. If he returned to Honorius, his opponents could claim that he was failing to follow Honorius' orders to go to the Eastern court, so setting himself above the emperor. Nor could he travel to Pavia to regain the loyalty of the army, since this could be interpreted as an attempt to wrest their loyalty away from Honorius and so be the precursor to an attempt to place Eucherius on the throne in the West. The summer was spent devising plans but not implementing them.[21]

Pavia

Whilst Stilicho delayed in taking any concrete action, Honorius left Bononia and travelled to Pavia to fulfil his duties as emperor and leader of the armed forces. Once Honorius and the rest of the court had separated from Stilicho, Olympius decided to make his move. He approached Honorius and made the claim that Stilicho wanted to travel to Constantinople to fulfil his aim of removing Theodosius II and replacing him with Eucherius.[22] He continued to make these claims to the emperor until after their arrival at Pavia on 13 August.

Once there, Olympius made several visits to a hospital in which sick soldiers were recovering and began to voice the same claim in their hearing.[23] Understandably, the rumour caused widespread alarm, especially since the troops already felt ill-disposed to Stilicho thanks to his apparent preference for 'barbarians' over the regular forces.

On the fourth day after the arrival of the emperor, the troops were ordered to muster for inspection prior to departure for the war against Constantine.[24] At a signal from Olympius a mutiny broke out in the army. The troops broke ranks, seized and then killed Limenius, the *praefectus praetorio Galliarum* who had earlier (401) been *comes sacrarum largitionem*, and Chariobaudes, the *magister militum per Gallias*, who had recently fled from Arles in the face of Constantine's advance. Alongside them Vincentius, the new *magister equitum*, and Salvius, the *comes domesticorum*, were also killed.[25] As the mutiny spread Honorius retreated to the palace and the remainder of the magistrates dispersed in flight. The mutiny quickly exceeded Olympius' ability to control it. The soldiers spread throughout the city, seizing and killing any officials that they could find who were classed as supporters of Stilicho.

Finally, the emperor put on a simple tunic and advanced into the centre of the city, from where he slowly managed to exert some control over the mutineers. Yet his control remained minimal; when the *quaestor*, another Salvius, clasped at the emperor's feet and begged for mercy, the soldiers simply dragged him away and killed him. Fearful for his safety the emperor once again withdrew to the palace.

In the late afternoon the troops began to calm down and a death toll of the magistrates was taken. Alongside those already named, Naimorius the *magister officiorum*, Patroinus the *comes sacrarum largitionum*, possibly Ursicinus the *comes rerum privatarum*, and Longinianus the *praefectus praetorio Italiae* were found to be dead.[26] Alongside these distinguished people were 'a host of ordinary people not easy to calculate'.[27]

News of the mutiny was quickly carried to Stilicho in Bononia. However, it was as yet unclear whether Honorius was amongst the fallen magistrates. The only troops Stilicho had with him appear to have been federates. During the course of a hasty council Stilicho and the barbarian leaders decided upon one of two courses of action. If Honorius had been killed, it was decided to unleash the federates on the Roman troops at Pavia, so sending a clear message of what to expect to any other troops in Italy thinking of mutiny. However, if the emperor was safe then only the ringleaders of the mutiny should be punished, despite the fact that many of Stilicho's leading supporters had been killed. When news was received that the emperor was still alive, Stilicho unaccountably reneged on the decision to punish the ringleaders, instead heading for Ravenna.[28]

In the circumstances, this is entirely understandable. With the only information being gathered from confused reports, Stilicho was unsure of whether the 'mutiny' was indeed a mutiny. It may have been the first sign that Honorius had lost patience with him. In that circumstance, setting the barbarians under his control on the troops under the emperor was tantamount to a declaration of rebellion against Honorius.

Whatever the cause, the decision was not supported by his federate allies, who still wanted to attack the Roman troops at Pavia. When it became clear that this was not going to happen, the majority of the federates decided to leave and set themselves apart from Stilicho until the political situation became clearer, and especially until they knew whether Stilicho was still the leading magistrate in the West. Sarus, however, the Goth who had led the attack on Constantine, waited until everyone was asleep and then led his men in an attack on Stilicho's *bucellarii*, his Hunnic bodyguard. Whilst they slept the Goths crept up and killed them all, before taking control of the entire baggage train, after which Sarus retired to his tent.[29] Shortly afterwards he left the scene and roamed Italy before once again taking service with Honorius.

Not knowing who to trust, even amongst his own federates, Stilicho fled to Ravenna and sent orders to all of the cities which had families of the barbarians in their midst, telling them that on no account should they admit federate forces into their cities.[30] There he awaited developments.

He did not have long to wait. It was now clear to Honorius that the troops at Pavia were no longer serving Stilicho, instead being loyal to Olympius. It was also clear, as demonstrated by the execution at his feet of the *quaestor* Salvius, that they did not serve Honorius. Fearful for his safety, the young emperor – who was not yet twenty-four – decided that the only way of guaranteeing his own safety was to obey the requests of Olympius. Olympius, having now gained control over the emperor, sent imperial decrees to Ravenna, ordering the troops there to put Stilicho under house arrest. It is unclear how Honorius felt about this state of affairs. Although usually accepted as grateful to be free of Stilicho's dominance, the circumstances surrounding the events suggest that he might instead have had little choice but to do as ordered and had been forced to recognize that he was now under the domination of Olympius. It was unclear yet as to whether or not he would escape with his life, since so many leading members of the previous regime had been killed.

Apparently, news reached Stilicho of his impending arrest and he quickly sought sanctuary in a nearby church. His servants and those federates still loyal to him armed themselves and waited upon events. At daybreak on 22 August the soldiers, led by one Heraclianus, entered the church and swore an oath before the bishop that they had been ordered by the emperor not to kill but to arrest Stilicho.[31] Forming a military guard, the soldiers led Stilicho out of the church. At this point Heraclianus produced a second letter, condemning Stilicho to death for his 'crimes against the state'.[32] Eucherius, who at this point was not mentioned in the dispatches, fled towards Rome. Stilicho was prepared for his execution. At this point Stilicho's servants and loyal federates made to rescue him from execution. Stilicho stopped them with 'terrible threats and submitted his neck to the sword'.[33] On his death, chaos and anarchy broke out in Italy.

Conclusion

Honorius usually emerges from the mutiny at Pavia as a weak emperor who was unsure of what to do, sending Stilicho to his death in a fit of petulance at not being allowed to rule on his own initiative. Yet prior to Pavia, there are signs that Honorius was his own man who was willing to listen to advice from Stilicho – for example in his desire to go to Constantinople to support Theodosius II. However, in one respect he was a political realist. When Olympius took control of the mutiny it was clear that Olympius now had the support of the army. The army which had just mutinied had shown itself capable of ignoring the emperor's presence by killing Salvius when he clung to the emperor's knees and asked for shelter. The episode would not have filled Honorius with confidence and demonstrated that whoever controlled the army could – in effect – force the emperor to do his bidding. When Honorius sent the letters for Stilicho's arrest and execution, there is a good chance that this was under duress and that he only sent them because he did not know what would happen if he defied Olympius.

When the news arrived that Stilicho was dead, Olympius took control of the situation. Stilicho's property was confiscated, his adherents arrested and tortured to secure proof of his treasonable conspiracy and Eucherius, Stilicho's son, was arrested and executed. Olympius also promulgated laws damning Stilicho and his supporters.[34] As part of the *damnatio memoriae* inscriptions dedicated to Stilicho were located and his name erased from them (see Plate 2).

Events after the death of Stilicho

> After the death of Stilicho, all court affairs were controlled by Olympius …
> and the emperor distributed the other offices to Olympius' nominees. A
> widespread search was made for Stilicho's friends and supporters. Deuterius,
> the *Praepositus Sacri Cubiculi*, and Petrus, the *Primicerius Notarium* were
> brought to trial and public torture was used to make them inform against
> Stilicho. When, however, they revealed nothing against either themselves or
> him and Olympius had wasted his efforts, he had them clubbed to death.
>
> Zosimus, 5.36.1–2

Other supporters of Stilicho were similarly treated in an attempt to prove that he had had designs on the throne, but all of them failed, hence the edict issued on 22 November 408, which solely alleged that Stilicho was charged with encouraging the barbarians to make trouble, not with having designs upon the throne, either for himself or for Eucherius.[35] The only 'success' that Olympius had was in arranging that Thermantia, Honorius' second wife and Stilicho's daughter, was dismissed from court and returned to her mother in Rome.

Ironically, Stilicho's domination of the Western military had a disastrous knock-on effect after his fall. When he was killed, the government was assumed by civil politicians. There was no outstanding successor to Stilicho to lead the army against Alaric.

Yet it was Stilicho's close relations with the federates which was to have the greatest bearing on events. The federates were unlike the other units in the Roman army. In the regular forces the appointment as officer to a regular unit was part of the normal process of promotion. Therefore, these officers were usually prepared to take orders from 'legitimate authority' without too much discussion. Stilicho had been executed, but the regular officers still owed their loyalty to Honorius and whoever he 'appointed', whether willingly or not.

The federates, on the other hand, had distinct political leaders with aims that did not necessarily mirror those of regular officers. Their first loyalty was to themselves and their men. Their second loyalty was to the man they had agreed to serve; in this case, Stilicho. They had little or no loyalty to either the emperor or the Empire. They now waited to see what happened next.

What happened next will have exceeded their wildest fears. In an orgy of reprisal and bloodlust the regular Roman troops in Italy turned upon the federates. However, as the actual federate troops were not at hand, the wrath of the Romans focused upon their families, who were located in nearby cities. All of the families were either killed or enslaved.[36]

The reasons for the attacks are unclear. They were probably the result of anger at Stilicho's employment of barbarian troops, and the resultant power of barbarian leaders in Stilicho's councils. It is also likely that, in some minds at least, there was an attempt to emulate the earlier elimination of Gothic power in the East in the events surrounding the fall of Gainas in 400. It is possible that Stilicho's earlier order that the towns and cities of Italy should not allow federate troops to enter them helped to inflame the anti-barbarian feeling amongst both the troops and the population. Since it implies that Stilicho himself did not trust his own allies, it would only inflame the mistrust of the general population of Italy concerning the federates.

Whatever the cause, the massacre was a massive blunder. The federates immediately joined their forces to Alaric, swelling his army and enhancing his power. Zosimus claims that over 30,000 men now joined Alaric, although he later claims that after being joined by 10,000 slaves Alaric's forces still only numbered 40,000 men.[37] It is probable that Alaric was actually joined by troops mainly composed of the 12,000 men who joined Stilicho after the defeat of Radagaisus, and that the slaves who later joined him were the remnants of Radagaisus' forces that had been sold into slavery after his defeat.[38] Alaric was once again in a position to invade Italy, this time in the knowledge that there was no military commander of Stilicho's standing to stop him.

Italy and the invasion of Alaric

Surprisingly, Alaric did not simply invade Italy as he had in 401. Instead, he released the hostages he had been given in 405. Aetius and his fellow hostages were allowed to return home. The reasons for this act are unknown, but it is likely that, since the hostages that Alaric had given to Stilicho either escaped or were released after his death, as an act of faith Alaric unilaterally released the hostages that Stilicho had given him in 405. Alaric still wanted a position within the Empire.

The theory that Alaric was attempting to prove his sincerity and loyalty is strengthened by his subsequent actions. According to Zosimus, after releasing the hostages Alaric sent embassies to Ravenna asking for a new exchange of hostages, again including Aetius, and the payment of a small sum of money, after which he would lead his forces back to Pannonia.[39] Honorius refused, but instead of taking steps to counter Alaric by appointing an energetic new *magister militum* (Zosimus proposed Sarus for the post) and gathering an army to fight Alaric, Honorius appointed Turpilio as *magister equitum*, Varanes as *magister peditum* and Vigilantius as *comes domesticorum equitum*, all of whom are described as being only able to 'inspire contempt in the enemy'.[40]

Frustrated by Honorius' refusal to agree terms, for the second time in his career Alaric decided to invade Italy. He recalled Athaulf from his defence of Pannonia, but before Athaulf could join him Alaric invaded Italy.[41] Realizing that Honorius in Ravenna was safe, Alaric marched straight to Rome and laid the city under siege. Fear that Serena, out of grief for her husband, would attempt to aid the Goths led to the Senate ordering her execution. Surprisingly, Galla Placidia, the sister of Honorius who had been raised by Stilicho and Serena, encouraged the Senate in their decision to execute Serena.

As Athaulf hurried to join Alaric, Olympius despatched a party of 300 Huns who defeated Athualf in a short battle.[42] Undeterred, Athualf joined Alaric with the remainder of his forces. The siege continued over the winter of 408–409 but, rather than being seen as a serious attempt to capture Rome, should be seen as an attempt by Alaric to put political pressure on Honorius to grant Alaric concessions.[43] Eventually, the Roman citizens came to terms, agreeing to supply the Gothic forces with 'gifts' and at the same time sending an embassy to Honorius to promote Alaric's cause. Alaric withdrew to Ariminum.[44]

Olympius refused to meet Alaric's demands, but in a curious reversal of fortune those concessions which he did make during the ensuing negotiations caused him to lose face. Rather than accept the consequences, Olympius fled into exile. His replacement was Jovius, the same who had been appointed as *praefectus praetorio Illyrici* by Stilicho in 407. He had retained close ties with Alaric and now began negotiations in an attempt to prevent war.[45]

Jovius reached an agreement with Alaric wherein the Goths would receive an annual supply of gold and corn, and that the Goths should be allowed to settle in Venetia, Noricum and Dalmatia. Jovius sent the agreement to Honorius for ratification, along with the recommendation that Alaric be given the post of *magister utriusque militiae* in the hope that the flattery would make him renounce at least some of his claims.[46] When the proposal was put to Honorius, the emperor refused to ratify any of it, declaring that he would never have a Goth as *magister militum*.[47] Honorius was clearly feeling safer than when Olympius had been in control. Alaric immediately made a more moderate offer, but again Honorius rejected it.[48]

Unimpressed, Alaric returned to Rome and once again placed the city under siege. However, in a strange twist, in December 409 Alaric persuaded the *praefectus urbis Romae*, Attalus, to become the new emperor. A pagan senator, Attalus quickly had himself baptised as a Christian in order to be acceptable to the vast majority of the population. It is probable that it was at this time that Galla Placidia was taken captive by the Goths, as it was only now that she is mentioned by Zosimus as being a hostage of Alaric, not before.[49]

When news of the usurpation reached Africa, the province decided to remain loyal to Honorius. Realizing that their position was reliant on the grain supplies from Africa being maintained, Alaric proposed an invasion of the province by Gothic troops. Strangely, at this point Attalus showed that he was more than a mere puppet emperor, refusing permission for Alaric to send Goths to Africa and instead organizing a campaign using Roman forces. Unfortunately for Attalus, the campaign was a failure and the province remained loyal to Honorius.

Yet as the pressure on Honorius mounted he made one major concession. However, this was not to either Alaric or to Attalus; at some point in 409 Honorius recognized Constantine III as his colleague in the West. Constantine now attempted to invade Italy with his forces in an attempt to subdue Alaric but the attempt failed, probably due to events in Spain (see below). However, the recognition of the usurper had illustrated that Honorius was not going to come to terms with Alaric and Attalus except by force.

As a consequence, Attalus and Alaric now moved to Ariminum, from where they hoped to put pressure on Honorius. Talks began but at this vital moment 4,000 troops arrived from Constantinople to help Honorius. Gaining confidence from their unexpected arrival, Honorius stood firm and the talks broke down.[50]

With Honorius now secure, in summer 410 Alaric deposed Attalus in the hope that the concession would encourage further negotiations.[51] He was advancing towards Ravenna in preparation for the opening of talks when he was unexpectedly attacked by Sarus. Although the attack was quickly defeated and was almost certainly on Sarus' own initiative, being an attempt to continue the vendetta that existed between the two Goths, Alaric saw it as being endorsed by Honorius. Furious, Alaric returned to Rome. On 24 August 410 his troops were allowed to enter the city at the Salarian Gate and, for the first time in 800 years, the eternal city was sacked by barbarians.[52]

Rather than being seen as a sign of strength, the sack should be interpreted as Alaric's recognition of failure. There was now no way that he could negotiate a treaty with Honorius, as Honorius could not negotiate with the man who had sacked Rome. Instead, after the sack Alaric marched his troops south and began to gather ships for an attempt to attack and conquer Africa. Unfortunately for Alaric, storms then destroyed the ships he had gathered. It was to be his last act; possibly even as he was gathering the ships Alaric became ill with an unknown disease. Before he could decide upon another course of action he died. His successor was his brother-in-law Athaulf.

Gaul and Spain

Earlier, in 408, Didymus and Verinianus had rebelled against Constantine III's rule. Once Constans, Constantine's son, and Gerontius, the *magister militum*, had retaken control of Spain, Constans returned with his captives to Gaul. However, in early 409 Gerontius rebelled, proclaiming his *domesticus* Maximus as emperor at Tarraco, before gaining the support of the Spanish army. Gerontius then incited the barbarians in Gaul to rebel against Constantine.[53] According to Jerome, they devastated large parts of Gaul including Aquitaine, Narbonensis and Novempopulum, and Jerome notes that when he wrote Toulouse had not yet fallen.[54]

It is usually accepted that the policy backfired on Gerontius, as in early autumn 409 the Vandals, Alans and Sueves, finding the passes of the Pyrenees either weakly guarded or by bribing the guards, crossed the Pyrenees and entered Spain. Although Gerontius managed to subdue them, and enforced treaties where they would provide him with military support, in effect a large part of Spain was lost to Rome.

However, it is also possible that as part of their agreement with Gerontius they had devastated Gaul in an attempt to weaken Constantine's political position before crossing into Spain to serve with Gerontius. It is also possible that as part of the agreement they were allocated land by Gerontius, deciding which tribe received which area by the means of lot when they could not reach an amicable agreement. In this way, the Asding Vandals received the southern parts of the province of Gallaecia with the Sueves gaining the northern parts. The Siling Vandals were granted lands in Baetica whilst the Alans received territory in Lusitania. Gerontius himself retained Tarraconensis and Carthaginiensis (see Map 1).

Once affairs in Spain had settled, in 411 Gerontius attacked Constantine and Constans in Gaul. He quickly defeated and killed Constans at Vienne and then moved his army to Arles, where he placed Constantine III under siege. Unfortunately for him, the new *magister militum* of Honorius' army was an energetic and capable soldier by the name of Constantius, who had been a supporter of Stilicho. Constantius took an army across the Alps and advanced on Arles. Gerontius' troops deserted him and he fled back to Spain, where shortly afterwards his troops mutinied and he was executed, with Maximus being deposed and sent into exile. In the meantime, Constantius continued the siege of Arles. Eventually, the city surrendered and Constantine III was arrested and beheaded; there was no room in the imperial family for a failure.

The East

Soon after Alaric had moved to Italy in 408 the Eastern government took steps to take military control of Illyricum, securing it against attack both from the West and from across the Danube.[55] However, once it became clear that Stilicho was dead there was an immediate thawing of relations between East and West, as both recognized that the survival of Honorius depended upon having only one front on which to fight. Despite the tension between the two emperors, it is unlikely that the government in the East would want Constantine III, an unknown entity, taking control in the West. As a result of the thaw in relations, during 408 the Eastern nominee for consul was recognized in the West.

Furthermore, on 10 December of the same year the barriers that Stilicho had imposed in Italy to trade with the East were removed.[56] The improvement in relations between the two was so rapid that as early as 409, when Alaric was personally threatening Honorius in Ravenna, the East dispatched 4,000 troops to his aid (see above). The change in relations would continue into the new decade.

Athaulf

Athaulf remained in Italy throughout 411, but, under pressure from Honorius' new *magister militum* Constantius, in 412 Athaulf led his men over the Alps into Gaul, taking with them the emperor's sister Galla Placidia. Thus they arrived in Gaul shortly after the defeat and execution of Constantine III. Unfortunately for Honorius, at the same time a new usurper by the name of Jovinus declared himself emperor in Gaul, supported by tribes along the Rhine. Athaulf declared his support for the new emperor.

Having fallen out with Honorius, the Goth Sarus also travelled to Gaul and declared himself a supporter of the new regime. En route, he was attacked by the Goths under Athaulf and killed; the long feud was finally over.

Athaulf's support for Jovinus was to be short-lived. The defeat and death of Sarus was against Jovinus' wishes – obviously, he did not want his commanders fighting each other – so he did not bother to consult Athaulf when he decided to elevate his brother Sebastianus to be co-emperor. The breach allowed Dardanus, appointed by Honorius to be the new *praefectus praetorio Galliarum*, to convince Athaulf that he should abandon his allegiance to Jovinus. Athaulf captured the two 'emperors' and they were quickly beheaded, their heads being sent to Honorius at Ravenna.

However, the main stumbling block between Athaulf and Honorius remained the captivity of Galla Placidia. When the Romans failed to supply the Goths with necessary supplies of grain, Athaulf refused to release her. Consequently, Constantius began to put military pressure on the Goths. Notwithstanding this, in January 414 Athaulf married Galla Placidia.[57] She quickly bore him a son, named Theodosius. Unfortunately, Theodosius died soon after and Athaulf himself was assassinated in 415.

Athaulf was succeeded by Sarus' brother, who humiliated Galla Placidia by making her walk in front of his horse. Fortunately for her, he was quickly assassinated and the new king, Wallia, soon came to an agreement with Honorius and Galla Placidia returned to Italy – where she was forced to marry Constantius although she loathed him intensely. The Goths were ordered to attack the Vandals in Spain, which they did to such good effect that the Vandals left Spain in search of safer territory. In return, the Goths were allowed to settle in Aquitania in Gaul. Their long wanderings were finally over.

Chapter Sixteen

Stilicho: The Vandal Who Saved Rome?

Legacy

In the years following his death for the majority of the time the real rulers of the Western Empire were military men who followed the example set by Stilicho. Stilicho's accepted rule as simply '*magister militum*' was used as an exemplar by later Western generals and also by many barbarian kings; the Visigoths (Alaric and Athaulf), the Burgundians (Gundobad), the Ostrogoths (Thiudimir and Theodoric), and the Franks (Childeric) all traced the genealogy of their royal families back to individuals who had been given the title '*magister militum*' during the twilight of the Western Empire.[1]

Yet the net result was instability. An emperor on the frontier could be seen to be fulfilling his duty, was available to the local elites petitioning for advancement, and was able to distribute and redistribute his patronage at will, so reducing the threat of disaffection. Stilicho suffered from a 'legitimacy gap', which meant that he could not fulfil the same function as an emperor. As a result, he was forced to turn away from the traditional forms of government in an attempt to find methods suitable for his own purposes.[2] The actions of Olympius proved that individuals wanting power could now exploit the 'legitimacy gap' between the individual who was the *magister militum* and the emperor.[3] It was no longer necessary to overthrow the emperor, only to control him. Stilicho's example may have indirectly helped to cause the Fall of the Western Empire later in the fifth century.

Reputation

Despite recent works challenging accepted opinions, Stilicho is still perceived as the Vandal who, for a short period, took control of Rome and defended it against other barbarians – hence the title of this book.[4] This fact underlines the major difficulty with studying the career of Stilicho; although revision has been attempted, in many cases the biases of previous authorities, both ancient and modern, still influence the interpretation of how Stilicho reacted to events.

Obviously, as has already been noted, immediately after Stilicho's overthrow Olympius and his followers issued a *damnatio memoriae* against Stilicho, condemning the man and his memory to oblivion. As Olympius' attempts to find evidence that Stilicho was attempting to overthrow the emperor had failed, the only avenue left open for Olympiodorus was personal attack. Orosius, Jerome and Rutilius followed the official line emanating from Ravenna and damned Stilicho as the man who had sold the

Empire to the barbarians: 'Wherefore more bitter is the crime of cursed Stilicho in that he was betrayer of the Empire's secret.'[5] In fact, the only ancient sources which both support the official line and mention the fact that Stilicho's father was a Vandal, are Jerome and Orosius, both of whom followed Olympius in damning Stilicho's memory.[6]

Although Gibbon in his *Decline and Fall of the Roman Empire* described him as 'the great Stilicho', later historians similarly followed Olympius' official policy and condemned Stilicho for his actions. More recently, however, there has been a swing of opinion, probably influenced by attention being focused upon Olympiodorus, who praised Stilicho and blamed his downfall on the 'inhuman plotting' of Olympius.[7] The result has culminated in a more sympathetic perception of Stilicho's plight, although many still believe that Stilicho and Alaric reached an agreement early in their careers. However, the latest historians have attempted to rehabilitate Stilicho, claiming that his only fault was that of 'idealism'.[8] Yet the change is not complete; he is still seen as a barbarian general more concerned with doing deals with other barbarians than with defending the Roman frontiers.[9]

Alongside the recognition of Olympiodorus' viewpoint has been an increased analysis of all of the other relevant sources. One major example of this is the still-repeated comment that following the invasion of Gaul by the Vandals, Alans and Sueves in 407 the Rhine frontier collapsed due to Stilicho's neglect.[10] Yet a comparison of the *Chronicle of Prosper* and that known as the *Gallic Chronicle of 452* shows that this is not the whole story. The *Chronicle of 452* damns Stilicho as a traitor for allowing the destruction of Gaul. However, Prosper, who was writing earlier and may have suffered personally from the barbarian attacks, did not perceive the invasion of 406 in such apocalyptic terms. Unlike the later chronicler, he does not see the invasion as 'events that had transformed the world'.[11] This implies that contemporaries did not perceive the invasion across the Rhine as a major event, and so Stilicho's failure to deal with it is not a major fault. Only later were attitudes to Stilicho to change, probably influenced by the rhetoric and propaganda emerging from Ravenna.

This opinion is supported by a close scrutiny of the events. Shortly after the invasion across the Rhine Constantine III crossed to Gaul and quickly re-established control using only the readily available British and local Gallic troops. If there had been no revolt in Britain, there can be little doubt that Stilicho also would have quickly overcome the invaders. Furthermore, there is no evidence that any other major invasions occurred in the West until the attack of Attila the Hun in 451. The expansion of the Franks, Burgundians and other tribes into the vacuum left by the withdrawal of Roman forces later in the century is a different phenomenon and should not be interpreted as a collapse of the frontier under Stilicho.

As a consequence of this hypothesis, it is clear that Stilicho was simply following well-established imperial priorities by first attempting to eliminate the usurper before deploying the combined army to defeat the barbarian invaders. However, it must be accepted that in part at least this was forced upon him by the swiftness of Constantine's movement to Lyon. In effect, Constantine protected the invaders from Stilicho's intervention.

As a result of these reinterpretations, attention has been focused on more large-scale issues, with the resultant conclusion that 'the accumulation of pressure meant that Italy itself fell under direct and indirect threat which coincided with usurpations and civil conquest to produce internal instability'.[12] The whole situation was made worse by Stilicho's ambiguous position as second-in-command. Stilicho's subordinate position resulted in the opposition being able to focus on controlling Honorius rather than the more momentous decision to depose a ruling emperor; whilst many may have balked at eliminating Honorius himself, Stilicho remained a viable target for their animosity.

These examples are a clear indication of why, to the vast majority of his contemporaries, Stilicho was no different to any other Roman politician in that his outlook was wholly Roman. In stark contrast to the commonly accepted opinion, it is clear from studying his life that Stilicho was neither a 'Vandal' nor a 'barbarian'. In large part the confusion concerning Stilicho's conduct is caused by three factors: the perceived political division between East and West caused by Stilicho's alleged obsession with Illyricum; his claim to be *parens principum* of the East as well as the West; and his conduct as a general, especially when fighting Alaric.

Illyricum

The most prominent atypical quality that Stilicho displayed as a traditional Roman aristocrat was his loyalty to Honorius and the House of Theodosius. Both prior to and following his domination the leading generals of the West tended to be loyal only to themselves, not to the emperor sitting on the throne.[13] From his assuming the role of *parens principum* in 395 until the invasion of Radagaisus in 405 Stilicho's main aim remained that of preserving an Empire united against foreign attack and internal unrest. Although his methods provoked opposition and at times even threatened to create a civil war, his motives always revolved around his personal view of what was best for the Empire.

After 405 the situation changed. It was only following the invasion of Radagaisus that Stilicho slowly came to realize that the East would never accept his claim to be guardian of Arcadius or give him any support in his defence of the West. Furthermore, it was only at this point that he finally recognized that the needs of the West were being hindered by the East's control of Illyricum.

The decision to invade Illyricum is interpreted as a long-standing plan and Stilicho is usually criticized for it, yet there is no hard evidence to support such a claim. The plan only materialized after Radagaisus' invasion in 406, and was the major turning point in Stilicho's life. The fact that such large barbarian forces were again able to penetrate Italy came as a shock both to Stilicho and the Senate in Rome. However, it was almost certainly the defeat of Radagaisus and the absorbtion of 12,000 Goths into imperial service that tipped the balance. Stilicho must have been disheartened by the news that the Senate was unhappy with the enrolment of so many barbarians into the army. As a result, Stilicho was forced to accept that, without the whole-hearted cooperation of the East, the West was doomed as the opposition of the Roman Senate to conscription and taxes resulted in an army that was not strong enough to meet the demands being placed upon it.

For the first time he was forced to make a choice; his decision was to switch his patronage from the 'House of Theodosius' and instead gave his full support to the regime of Honorius in the West. This was signalled by his plan to annex Illyricum from the East by force. This represents a major sacrifice on the part of Stilicho; in effect, he was abandoning his dream of uniting the whole of the Empire under his personal guidance.

Parens principum

Stilicho's decision in 406–7 to invade Illyricum despite his claim to be *parens principum* is usually interpreted by modern historians within the context of the permanent division of the East and West; indeed, it is often seen as a major cause in that divide. Yet this is not strictly accurate. Only one year after his death the East sent troops to aid Honorius in his conflict with Alaric. The division in Stilicho's lifetime was not based upon divergent political aims between East and West, but was caused by the personal political strife between Stilicho in the West and his opponents in the East. In reality, the permanent division of East and West took place later, with the dominance of German generals who were determined to eliminate Eastern interference in their 'rule'.

Stilicho's years of conflict with the Eastern court should not be understood in terms of permanent political division, but in terms of the political intrigue attendant on a royal minority – or in this case two – which broke out the moment Theodosius was dead.[14] It is not a result of him being a Vandal, nor is it a result of him maintaining an unrealistic dream of political unity between East and West. The dream was feasible, but was halted by the strength of opposition in the East, led by three individuals – Rufinus, Eutropius and Aurelian – who refused to allow their own power to be constrained by an outside force.

It should also be noted that his claims revolved solely upon his family ties to Arcadius. When it became clear that Eudoxia, herself a family member, was in effective control in the East Stilicho allowed his claim to lapse. Up until 406 it should be acknowledged that Stilicho was only concerned with the safety of his 'brother-in-law' in Constantinople.

After 406, Stilicho focused solely upon Honorius and at this point the unity of the Empire and peace with the East became secondary to his perception of what was vital to the survival of the West: the taxes and recruiting grounds of Illyricum. That is the reason why he put aside all of his preconceptions and recognized that, far from becoming the guardian of Arcadius, he would have to invade territories claimed by the East in order to give the West a chance of survival. It is certain that Stilicho and his supporters were emotionally attached to a 'united Empire', but finally he was forced to the realization that unless he took control of Illyricum the chances were that the West would slowly dwindle away and become dominated by barbarian tribes.[15]

Yet this was not the only reason for the decision to invade Illyricum. In part at least it was an attempt by Stilicho to break his reliance upon the Senate in Rome. As long as they maintained their hold on the supply of taxes and recruits, their influence would be strong. With the recruits and taxes of Illyricum Stilicho could finally break free of their domination and so be free to follow his own policies without continually having to refer them for ratification to the Senate.

Unfortunately, he came to that conclusion too late; before he could absorb the resources of Illyricum and so strengthen both his own position and the condition of the army, usurpers had arisen in Britain and the Vandals, Alans and Sueves had crossed the Rhine. However, although the emergence of a rival in Britain in effect marked the beginning of the end for Stilicho, the barbarian invasion across the Rhine was not seen as vital to the defence of the Empire by contemporaries. Only after the event did historians mistakenly look back and interpret the crossing of the Rhine as an event of imperial significance.

Yet his focus upon Eastern affairs, which was forced upon him both by his political and especially by his military weaknesses, made him neglect the peoples of Gaul, Britain and Spain. Had he ensured the loyalty of Britain he would have had the resources necessary to defeat the invasion of 406 with ease; with only the armies of Britain and Gaul, Constantine III quickly forced the invaders to come to terms. However, Stilicho would still have had to cope with the narrow outlook of the Western Senate, which resulted in him lacking total political control.

Generalship

Yet it is not the decision to invade Illyricum or the invasion across the Rhine or the outbreak of a revolt in Britain that are the main sources of antagonism towards Stilicho. Instead, criticism focuses mainly upon his failure as a general, specifically in his battles against and subsequent dealings with Alaric. There can be little doubt that if Stilicho had displayed the military ability of a Caesar or a Trajan then events would have turned out differently. Unfortunately, he did not: he was trained in a period when such leadership was no longer accepted as the norm in military circles.

The anachronistic belief of the Roman Senate that all Roman victories should be complete and end in the annihilation of the enemy has been continued by modern authors up until very recently. This has resulted in the mistaken conclusion that from a very early date Stilicho and Alaric had reached a secret agreement.

The claim is unfounded. Shortly after the Battle of Adrianople, in 380 Theodosius made a single attempt to defeat the Goths in combat. He was heavily defeated, losing many men that it was becoming ever-more difficult to replace. Thereafter, he reverted to the accepted military policy of the era: strategy and blockade. This policy was to be followed almost universally after Theodosius, and, with only two exceptions (the Battles of Pollentia and Verona), Stilicho adhered to the method.

Saul's attack on Alaric's forces at Pollentia opened Stilicho's eyes to the possibility of using aggressive tactics if circumstances allowed. Furthermore, his own conduct following Saul's death in the battle gave him much-needed self-confidence in his own martial abilities.

In spite of this, an analysis of Stilicho's battles reveals that Stilicho was never realistically in a position where he could have eliminated Alaric without the risk of severe military and political consequences.[16] The loss of even low levels of manpower would have greatly reduced the army's efficiency as Stilicho could no longer guarantee reinforcements. Alaric was saved at Pollentia by the survival of his mounted arm, which acted as a threat to halt pursuit of the defeated infantry. After the Battle of Verona, Stilicho could not attempt to destroy Alaric. Due to the speed of his victory, many of Alaric's troops had defected to Stilicho, as a result of which the 'Roman' army instantly had a large proportion of Goths in its ranks. Stilicho was quite rightly unwilling to risk sending these men against their former comrades.

As a consequence, it is clear that Alaric's survival had more to do with luck and his own military and political ability, especially with regard to the maintainence of the cohesion of his forces, than with Stilicho's generalship.[17] Where Alaric was concerned Stilicho made only one fatal flaw, which was political; in 408 he failed to recognize how feared and hated Alaric was in Italy. As a result, his attempt to promote Alaric to the command in Gaul proved the final straw in breaking the support of the army. After that there was no chance that Stilicho would survive.

The army itself was a double-edged weapon. The Roman nucleus of the army was loyal to the emperor and to Rome. They saw themselves as the heirs of the army that had conquered the Empire. Despite Vegetius' comments, it is clear that when they were led by strong officers who demanded high standards the army was still effective and capable of defeating invading barbarians; although the army suffered a disaster at Adrianople, it is often forgotten that during the battle the troops doggedly fought on even after it was clear that they had lost.

Although the Roman troops could still be effective in battle, the lack of recruits meant that their numbers were always low. No longer could a Roman commander lead his troops into battle secure in the knowledge that any losses suffered could easily be replaced. The army had become a precious treasure that needed to be preserved and only used when defeat was deemed impossible.

Politics

The Senate

The lack of conscripts was mainly due to the Senate being unwilling to supply the recruits the army needed. There is no doubt that the inhabitants of Italy who supplied legion after legion to face Hannibal in the third-century BC would have found it inconceivable that six hundred years later the same peninsula would be unable to supply the troops with which to defeat Alaric's forces. The situation severely restricted the options open to the commander of the army.

Alongside refusing to supply recruits, at every opportunity the Senate avoided paying the taxes needed to train and equip the army. This resulted in the small revenue that was available being used to recruit barbarian mercenaries that were already equipped with the basic equipment and had some experience of fighting. The vicious cycle this created would ultimately lead to Stilicho's downfall.

The situation was exacerbated by Stilicho's own political position. Normally, an emperor would be able to distribute many ranks and titles amongst his supporters in order to encourage loyalty. This included the two posts of *magister peditum* and *magister equitum*. However, Stilicho himself occupied these two posts, with the exception of a short period when he appointed a *magister equitum* to command alongside him, but the experiment does not appear to have been a success and was never repeated. In effect, Stilicho's position removed the highest level of reward from the aristocracy.

Coupled with his monopoly of the highest rewards for service to the emperor, Stilicho retained a tight control of appointments and ensured that either they were given to his own supporters, or, where this was impossible such as in the military sphere, he appointed his supporters to the staff of the individual in order to maintain a close watch on their activities. Although this ensured their 'loyalty', it also encouraged opposition and it is noticeable that in his final years he was forced to give positions of rank and influence to an ever-decreasing circle of intimates. The narrowing of his support showed that he was losing control of the West.

The federates

Apart from his loyalty to the House of Theodosius, the other major atypical quality that Stilicho possessed was his more flexible and pragmatic approach to the problems he faced. He realized that he had no choice but to pay mercenaries to augment his meagre force of regular troops. He also came to understand that he would be unable to protect the West without recruits from Illyricum, but the majority of people in the West did not realize this. Unfortunately, the employment of large numbers of barbarians alienated the Senate and drove many of his early supporters into opposition, including the army.[18] At least part of the motive for the uprisings against Stilicho was a desire in the West to emulate the Eastern response against the growth of barbarian power.[19]

The attack on the families of the federates was too late and went against political reality. Without the support of barbarian troops, the West simply did not have the ability to deal with barbarian invasions. He must have realized that his policy of using Germanic troops was losing him support, but it may be that he believed that his moral claims were so strong that Honorius could never turn against him.[20] In this he was almost correct; only when his own safety was in doubt did Honorius bow to the demands of both the army and the politicians by ordering Stilicho's arrest and execution.

Catholic opposition

The new Catholic majority that had appeared following Constantine the Great's conversion in the early fourth century was still wary of the pagan minority and heretics such as Germanic Arians. They strongly objected to Stilicho's employment of such people in positions of power. This was because Stilicho was determined to make use of any able men who would support his policies regardless of their personal beliefs. This was unacceptable to the more militant Catholics and they formed a core around which opposition to Stilicho was able to build. The death of the Catholic Mascezel after his successful campaign against his brother Gildo in 398 no doubt further alienated the Catholic 'hard core'. There is little doubt that the existence of this opposition group helped to encourage others, such as Olympius, in the belief that surviving the overthrow of Stilicho was a real possibility.

Conclusion

Stilicho was an able, if not gifted, general. Unfortunately, he was born into an age where offensive tactics were no longer feasible due to severe manpower shortages, and as a result he had little training or confidence in offensive rather than defensive warfare. Towards the end of his life he appears to have gained in confidence and become more willing to take the initiative and launch attacks when circumstances were favourable. Unfortunately, this was too little and too late. Moreover, he was forced to rely on barbarian troops, the employment of which caused opposition in both the Roman army itself and amongst the politicians at court.

Politically, he was wise enough to ally himself with two of the most gifted men of the age: the politician Symmachus and the orator and poet Claudian. Stilicho was extremely unfortunate that these two influential figures died within two years of each other (Symmachus in 402 and Claudian in 404) and there were no individuals of like stature with which to replace them. Without their support political opposition to Stilicho began to unite, eventually leading to the rise and short-lived dominance of Olympius. Yet the fact that Olympius was overthrown so quickly, particularly when compared with Stilicho's longevity, highlights the fact that Stilicho had a high degree of political ability. This was especially with regards to his political image. He made the most of having Symmachus representing him in the Senate and having Claudian as his mouthpiece to the wider Roman world. In this manner he ensured that those facts and interpretations which he wanted to promote gained the widest audience possible. Politically, Stilicho was master of the West until after the influence of Symmachus and the poems of Claudian began to fade.

Throughout the period 395 to 406 Stilicho defended the West to the best of his abilities. There can be little doubt that it was only the pressure from the Senate in Rome that compelled him to put the defence of Italy before that of Gaul or Britain, and that this political pressure resulted in his reluctant declaration of war on the East when he sent Alaric into Epirus. On the whole, his record is one of an honourable man whose support was given to the family into which he had married, and that this was only compromised when he recognized the irreconcilable need of the West to be put before the unity of the Empire. Overall, the time of his dominance was one in which the West was allowed to recover a little from the ravages of civil war. Unfortunately, circumstances dictated that he would not be allowed the time or resources to complete his vision for the West.

Yet in one aspect of his dominance he failed. Although it is possible to see Stilicho's survival as the result of his mastery of propaganda, maybe Stilicho's greatest failure of all was his inability to convince others of the military realities in the West and the need to either allow him to collect the recruits necessary to rebuild the army or the taxes to allow him to recruit and deploy large numbers of mercenaries.[21] In this he failed and so ensured his own downfall.

Notes

Introduction

1 Salway, 1993, 291.
2 O'Flynn, 1983, 57.
3 Cameron, 1974, 135–6.
4 Heather, 1994, 5f.
5 Honoré, 1987, passim.
6 Deferrari, 1981, xx.
7 Deferrari, 1981, xx.

Chapter 1

1 For a more detailed examination of the changes in the Roman Army, see Nicasie, 1998, passim.
2 Possibly during the reign of Galerius or Diocletian.
3 For example, in 306 Crocus (a king of the Alamanni serving under Constantine I), and after 316 Bonitus (a Frank, possibly *praepositus legionis*, also under Constantine).
4 Soc. 4.33.1–4; Soz. 6.37.6f: 12f.
5 Amm. Marc. 16.12.23f; Burns, 2003, 336.
6 Heather, 1994, pp. 12–33.
7 For a more detailed discussion of the issues, especially concerning the Sântana-de-Mureş/ Černjachov culture, see Kulikowski, 2007, Chapter 3 (43–70).
8 Examples of recent research re-appraising the Huns include Heather 1991 and Randers-Pehrson 1983; for a more traditional view, E A Thompson 1948.
9 Heather, 1991, 135.
10 Heather, 1998, 98.
11 See Heather, 1994, 182, for the view that the Goths adopted Arianism only as part of the condition of their entry into the Empire.
12 Or maybe had been deployed in a concealed position ready for a swift attack – a tactic much used by the Goths; Todd, 2004, 43.
13 For example, see Eunapius of Sardis, fr. 60. 1.
14 The commonplace idea that Theodosius was recalled from Spain after the Battle of Adrianople is probably mistaken. The small amount of time between the Battle of Adrianople and Theodosius' acclamation as emperor suggests that Theodosius was already in the vicinity when the battle took place. Instead, Errington proposed (Errington, R M, 'The Accession of Theodosius I', *Klio* 28 (1996), 438–53) that Theodosius was sent for before the battle and was thus a strong, readily available candidate for the throne following the death of Valens: Mitchell, 2007, 85.
15 Cameron, 1993, 138.

Chapter 2

1 Claud., *de Cons. Stil. I*.
2 Father a Vandal, Oros. VII 38; father a cavalry officer, Claud. *de Cons. Stil. I*: his mother Roman, Jer. *Ep*. 123. 16. Ferrill claims that he fought at Adrianople, although the veracity of the claim is uncertain.
3 For a summary of current thinking, O'Flynn, 1983, 15.

4 Claud., *de Cons. Stil. I.*

5 Lydus, *Mag.* 3. 53.

6 Claud., *Laus Serenae*, 179f.

7 O'Flynn, 1983, 16.

8 Kulikowski, 2007, 164.

9 *comes sacri stabuli*, Claud. *Laus Serenae*, 190–3: *comes domesticorum, CIL VI.* 1731 (http://compute-in.ku-eichstaett.de:8888/pls/epigr/epiklergebnis_en), where he is styled *comiti domesticorum et stabuli sacri.* It should be noted that opinion differs as to whether these titles were held separately or jointly. See O'Flynn, 1983, 16 f and 157–8, note 14.

10 Zos., 5.34: for discussion see O'Flynn, 1983, 17 and 157, note 13.

11 Burns, 1994, 148.

12 On the proposals, Zos. 4.37.

13 Zos., 4.38–9.

14 Philos., *HE*, 10.8.

15 Zos., 4.45.3; Amm. Marc. 25.6.13; 31.10.18. It should be noted that Halsall, 2007, 190. n.17 accepts the 'rebellion' of 391 as a possibility, but notes that it is no means a certainty due to the 'garbled' nature of the sources.

16 Zos., 4.45–8.

17 Liebeschuetz, 2004, 54.

18 Liebeschuetz, 2005, 263. n. 1.

19 Theoderet, V. 18.

20 On the dating of Claudian's account, Kulikowski, 2007, 161.

21 Claud., *Get.* 524–5; VI. *Cons. Hon.* 104–8.

22 On the turmoil, Halsall, 2007, 194.

23 Claud., *VI. Cons Hon.* 105.

24 Jordanes, 29.146

25 On Jordanes' claims, see Heather, 1991, 31, n.47: Halsall, 2007, 189.

26 For a full discussion of these topics, see Heather, 1994, 187–98.

27 Zos., 4.53.4.

28 Zos., 4.53.3–4.

29 Examples of sources that claim he was murdered: Zos. 4.54.3; Soc. 5.25; and Oros. 7.35. Uncertain about events: Soz. 7.22.

30 A more detailed discussion on the army and its ranks is included in Chapter 4.

31 CIL VI 1730 (*comiti divi Theodosi Augusti in omnibus bellis atque victoriis*) and CIL VI 1731 (*socio bellorum omnium et victoriarum, adfini etiam divi Theodosi Augusti*): PLRE I, 854.

32 Zos., 4.51.

33 *Cod. Th.* 7.9.3.

34 Claud., *de Cons. Stil. I.* 94–6; *in Ruf.* 1. 314–22; 350–1; *III Cons. Hon.* 147–50.

35 E.g., Cameron, 1970, 55, where Stilicho's martial abilities are downplayed because he did not fight and win a major battle.

36 Liebeschuetz, 1998, 52.

37 Zos., 5.5.4: Kulikowski, 2007, 164.

38 Liebeschuetz, 1998, 54.

39 For a detailed account of the arrangements, Zos. 4.55f.

40 The use of different titles suggests that there was no structure to the Roman military hierarchy, as claimed by some modern commentators. See Chapter 4.

41 Eun. fr. 59; Zos. 4.56.1: see also Liebeschuetz, 2004, 54.

42 20,000 men, Jordanes, *Getica*, 28.145: 'a large number', Soc. 5.25.

43 Zos., 4.57.3; Joh. Ant. fr. 187.

44 For example, Socrates (5.25) does not enter into detail and is an extremely simplified account, with the battle being decided very quickly in one day. Zosimus (4.55f) gives a more detailed account, but even this is comparatively brief and does not include detail we should like.

45 Williams and Friell, 1995, 132.

46 Sozomen, 7.24.

47 Zos., 4.58.2; Soz. 7.24.

48 Zos., 4.58.3.

49 Or. 7.35.

50 Following Zosimus, 4.58: Oros. 7.35.19. This is usually compared to Tacitus, *Agr.* 53. 2, where at the Battle of Mons Graupius Agricola allegedly placed the non-Roman *auxilia* to bear the brunt of the battle and so save Roman lives.

51 Sozimus' claim (7.24) that it was Theodosius' vanguard that attacked the opposition supports the theory that Theodosius was compelled to use the troops at the front of the column, without regard to strategical or tactical niceties.

52 Soz., 7.24 'he fell prone upon the earth, and prayed with tears'. Soc. 5.25, 'he cast himself in great agony upon the ground, and invoked the help of God in this emergency'.

53 Oros., 7.35.16; Soz. *HE.* 7.24.5.

54 Zos., 4.58.

55 Zos., 4.58; *Fasti Vindobonenses priores* no. 522.

56 For example, Paulinus, *Vita sancti Ambrosii*, 31; Oros. 7.35; cf. a pagan perspective, Zos. 4.58. See also Oros. 7.35.

57 Amb., *Ep, Ex Coll. 2, 6: Ex. Coll 3. 3.*

Chapter 3

1 On invasions, Cameron 1970, 38.

2 Eun. fr. 70; quoted in PLRE I, 914.

3 On the dating of the appointment, Cameron, 1970, 38. On his titles, see below.

4 cf. Liebeschuetz, 1994, 150.

5 Cameron, 1970, 31–2.

6 O'Flynn, 1983, 46.

7 O'Flynn, 1983, 45–6.

8 Bequest made without other witnesses; Claud, *Cos III Hon*, 142 160: deathbed bequest; Zos. 5.4.3; Olymp. fr.2.

9 O'Flynn, 1983, 16.

10 For example, O'Flynn (1983, 15) neatly sidesteps the issue, merely noting that the claim was questionable but that the support of Ambrose 'lent it an air of respectability'. Ferrill (1991, 90) states that Stilicho was hoping that Arcadius would acquiesce in his becoming guardian for the East thanks to the family ties, and suggests that Stilicho would have been surprised by Rufinus' challenge to his authority. Ferrill (1991, 89) also claims that Stilicho's control of the combined armies – since both armies were now in the West after the battle of the Frigidus – ensured his claim would succeed in the West, and further implies that a similar claim would be expected to succeed in the East. Williams and Friell (1994, 143) postulate that Stilicho 'took the wish for the deed and, in effect, sensibly seized power', suggesting that they don't believe the bequest to be real and that Stilicho was not the legitimate guardian of the West; a better phrase might have been 'assumed the position to which he had been appointed'. Finally, in the *Cambridge Ancient History* (2004, 113) although the claim is 'undocumented and unofficial', it remains 'plausible' as it was obvious that Theodosius wanted a united empire under his dynasty.

11 Claud., *Cos III Hon.* 142 160

12 Cameron, 1970, 42–4.

13 Although it should be noted that Ferrill suggests that Stilicho hoped for Arcadius' acquiescence and that Rufinus was not expected to challenge his authority (Ferrill, 1991, 90).

14 In 397, *Ruf. II.* 4–6; in 398, *IV Cons. Hon.* 437–8 and *Nupt.* 307-8; and in 399, *Eut. II.* 599f; 400, *Stil.* II. 53f. See Cameron, 1990, 49–50.

15 Cameron, 1974, 134–5.

16 O'Flynn, 1983, 19.

17 O'Flynn, 1983, 18-23.

18 O'Flynn, 1983, 23.

19 Norwich, 1988, 116–17.

20 On the dates, Oost, 1965, 1–3.

21 Chron. Pasch. 385.

22 Liebeschuetz, 1998, 93–4.

23 E.g., Helio, *magister officiorum*, 414 and following; Eutropius, *praepositus sacri cubiculum* from 395.

24 For more on the meanings of these terms, see the discussion on titles and treaties in Chapter 4.

25 Amm. Marc. 17.8.3–4. For this use of the term, see Goldsworthy, 2000, 215. See also Burns, 2003, 321.

26 O'Flynn, 1983, 16.

27 Matthews, 1998, 254–5.

28 Matthews, 1998, 255.

29 For a discussion and evaluation of the letters, see Matthews, 1975, passim.

30 Olymp., fr.44; Soc. 5.14.5.

31 PLRE I, 868.

32 Matthews, 1998, 268. However there is little, if any, evidence to support his view that Symmachus had any resentment towards the 'half-Vandal generalissimo'.

33 Marcianus, PLRE I 555-6; Symm, *Ep. III.* 33: Flavianus, PLRE I, 345-6; Symm. *Ep. IV*, 19; V37. Flavianus was reinstalled as *praefectus urbis Romae* (prefect of Rome) by June 399.

34 Matthews, 1998, 265–6.

35 Matthews, 1998, 253.

36 cf. Matthews, 1998, 268.

37 Matthews, 1974, 73f. – esp. 75.

38 Matthews, 1974, 68–9.

39 cf. Matthews, 1998, 270.

40 See Williams and Friell, 1994, 143; Claud., *de Bello Gild.* 305–6.

41 PLRE I, 251.

42 Matthews, 1998, 259.

43 PLRE I, 149.

44 PLRE I, 671–2

45 Claud, *Panegyricus de Consulatu Flavii Manlii Theodori* (Panegyric on the Consulship of Flavius Manlius Theodorus).

46 Claud., *de Bello Gild.* 305–6.

47 Jones, 1966, 208.

48 Matthews, 1998, 255–6.

49 Matthews, 1998, 264: *Cod Th.* VIII. 5.54 (April 395).

50 see Chapter 5.

51 Cameron, Av. 1993, 126.

52 O'Flynn (1983, 14–15) claims that Theodosius held Rufinus in higher esteem than Stilicho, based largely upon the fact that Rufinus was given a consulship in 392. However, this may simply have been a matter of seniority, since in 392 Stilicho had only just arrived within the higher echelons of rank and prestige.

53 PLRE I, 746–7, 778–9, 876–8.

54 Liebeschuetz, 1998, 52: 338, n. 8.

55 Claud., *in Ruf II*, 76; Chron. Minor, 650. 34.

56 PLRE I, 778–81; Joh. Ant. fr.188, 190; Eun. fr.62, and 63; Oros. 7.37.1.

57 Zos. 4.51.1–3.

58 PLRE II. 440-444; CAH 113.

59 PLRE II, 410; Zos. 5.3.2.

60 Chron. Pasch. The marriage appears to have been relatively happy, since they had five children between the marriage and her death in October 404.

61 Zos. 5.3.

Chapter 4

1 For a full discussion on the size of units and the problems of dating any changes, see for example Nicasie 1998, 23f. and Southern and Dixon, 1996, 29–33.

2 As an earlier example, in Alexandria Caesar's Legio VI had less than 1,000 men left of its original 'paper' strength of approximately 5,000 men (Caesar, *Alexandrian War*, 69), and in the Civil Wars his legions average less than 3,000 men (Caesar, *Civil Wars*, 3.6 and 3.89).

3 There is still dispute over the strength of the Roman army, both before and after the reforms of Diocletian and Constantine. Jones (1966) sees the pre-Tetrarchy army as c. 300,000 strong (p. 32) and the post Tetrarchy army as 435,000 strong, (p. 266), following John Lydus (p. 213). Agathias, writing in the sixth century, gives the figure of 645,000 for the fourth century army, which is probably far too high: Cameron (1993) accepts the figure of c.400,000 (p. 34–5). Heather (2005) leaves the question open (pp. 63–4).

4 Jones, 1966, p. 32.

5 Annual conscription Southern and Dixon, 1996, pp. 43–4; deserters and enlistment *Cod. Th.* 7.18.1f.

6 There appears to be some confusion over the use of *riparienses/ripenses* and *limitanei*: see Nicasie (1998, p. 19–22) and Southern and Dixon (1996, p. 36) for a clarification. For the sake of simplicity the traditional separation into river- and land- frontier forces respectively has been used.

7 Elton, 2004, 204f.

8 Elton, 2004, 216.

9 *palatina*: from *palatium*, 'palace'.

10 E.g., the Balkan campaigns of Valentinian I against the Alamanni; Southern and Dixon, 1996, p. 41.

11 See Southern and Dixon, 1996, p. 57.

12 Southern and Dixon, 1996, p. 47.

13 Southern and Dixon, 1996, p. 47: *Not. Dig. Or* . XI. 6. 10; *Oc* . XI. 7.

14 *Not. Dig. Oc* . XLII. 46–70.

15 Elton, 2004, 131.

16 Southern and Dixon, 1996, p. 48: Liebeschuetz, 1991, p. 9.

17 Elton, 2004, 135.

18 Olymp. fr.7.4.

19 Proportion, Elton, 2004, 152.

20 c.f. Elton, 2004, 138–40.

21 Christie, 2007, 569.

22 Southern and Dixon, 1996, p. 14

23 E.g. Jones, 1966, p. 32; Southern and Dixon, 1996, p. 14.

24 It is possible to compare these ideas with several passages in Procopius, which, although of a later date, may have a bearing on the matter. Procopius gives numerous examples of both Justinian and his generals giving commands of units to members of their bodyguard – primarily, of course, Belisarius. In this way Belisarius could gauge the effectiveness of the individuals as well as giving them command experience in situations where inefficiency would not necessarily lead to disaster. This was especially the case during the siege of Rome, when Belisarius rotated command of sallies against the Goths between members of his personal bodyguard: e.g. Proc. 5.27.4; 5.27.11.

25 E.g. Cowardice, Amm. Marc. 24.3.1–2 and 27.2.6–7; Proc. 8.16.19–20. Generals unable to fulfil duties and only serving for status and money, Lib *Or.* 47.28-9. Valens unhappy with his subordinates, Zos. 4.22.4. See further Southern and Dixon, 1996, pp. 174–5. It should be noted, however, that modern 'staff colleges' have had similar experiences of producing low-quality officers.

26 Hoffmann, D, 'Der Oberbefehl des spätrömischen Heeres im 4. Jahrhundert n. Chr.', in D M Pippidi (ed.), *Actes des IXe Congrès International d'études sur les frontières romains*, Cologne, 381–97, as referenced in Liebeschuetz, 2004, 54, n.8.

27 This situation is similar to the command structure of the German army in the Second World War, where Hitler appears to have shared power around in order to discourage opposition, since his generals were too busy politicking against each other.

28 Southern and Dixon, 1996, p. 57.

29 Amm Marc. 39.3.7

30 O'Flynn, 1983, 17–22.

31 *Scholae, Cod. Th.* 6. 13. 1: *legionis, Cod. Th.* 7. 20.10.

32 Elton, 2004, 129.

33 Liebeschuetz, 1991, p. 20.

34 See Southern and Dixon, 1996, p. 69.

35 Amm. Marc. 15.12.3.

36 *Cod. Th.* 7. 13. 5.

37 Amm. Marc. 15.12.3: Elton, 2004, 115..

38 Elton, 2004, 129.

39 *Cod. Th.* 7.13.7.

40 *Cod. Th.* 15.1.13.

41 Zos., 4.23.2–4.

42 Amm. Marc., 27.2.2–8

43 Amm. Marc., 22.7.7

44 Tomlin, 1990, 117.

45 Zos., 4.23.2–4.

46 Hamstringing, Amm. 23.5.21; Parading in women's clothes, Zos. 3.3.4–5; Hand-loss, Amm. 29.2.22–4.

47 E.g. decimation; 471 BC (Livy, 2.59), 71BC (Appian, Civil Wars, 1.118) and AD 20 (Tacitus, *Annals*, 3).

48 Amm. Marc., 16.12.37.

49 E.g., Southern and Dixon, 1996, p. 170.

50 E.g., the defeat of the combined force of both Germanic provinces under Charietto, *comes per*

    utramque Germaniam: Amm. Marc. 27.1.2–3

51 Amm. Marc., 14.10.4.

52 Amm. Marc., 19.11.2.

53 Southern and Dixon, 1996, pp. 62–3: Burns, 2003, 183.

54 Burns, 2003, 184: *Cod. Th.* 7.4.28.

55 E.g., Southern and Dixon, 1996, 38, simply mirror the disaster for the East at Adrianople and the West at Frigidus.

56 Burns, 1994, 113 and 149.

57 Soc., 7.10

58 Zos., 5.34.

59 *Cod Th.* 7.13.16 (406).

60 Milner, *Vegetius*, 1996, 19, n.6.

61 Bishop and Coulston, 2006, 208: AM. 16.10.8; 19.8.8; 24.6.9; 25.1.16 etc.

62 Veg., 2.15 and 4.21.

63 Veg., 4.22.

64 No examples of the *plumbatae tribolatae* have been found, so the weapon must still remain a possibility rather than a certainty.

65 Elton, 2004, 108.

66 Veg., 2.15.

67 Veg., 2.15.

68 Elton, 2004, 108.

69 Elton, 2004, 108.

70 Bishop and Coulston, 2006, 205.

71 Amm. Marc., 19.6.7; Proc. 2.21.7.

72 Theoph., *Hist.* 8.4.13.

73 Lasso, Elton, 2004, 108.

74 Bishop and Coulston, 2006, 213–14.

75 Bishop and Coulston, 2006, 213.

76 Attaching of crests, Bishop and Coulston, 2006, 214.

77 Earlier claims, e.g. James, 1986, cited in Bishop and Coulston, 2006, 230, n.43.

78 I would like to thank the members of www.romanarmytalk.com for their in-depth discussions on these topics: for example at www.romanarmytalk.com/rat/view topic.php?f=17&t=25150 &p=224574&hilit=spangenhelm#p224574 (December 2008 – July 2009).

79 Elton, 2004, 110f.

80 Bishop and Coulston, 2006, 216.

81 For more detailed analysis of mail manufacture, see Bishop and Coulston, 2006, 241–2 and associated bibliography.

82 The exact nature of '*cuir boulli*' as used from the ancient to the medieval period is unknown. It may have been made by using hot wax, or boiling oil or water. Unfortunately, until a piece from the period is found and examined, the process – and therefore the protection offered as armour – will remain a mystery.

83 For example, Pliny the Elder dismisses hippopotamus armour as useless when wet: NH. 8.9.5.

84 Coulston, 1990, 143.

85 For example, Bishop and Coulston, 2006, 208.

86 Germanic influence, Bishop and Coulston, 2006, 217; guardsmen using round shields, Elton, 2004, 115.

87 Amm. Marc., 16.12.6

Chapter 5

1 For example the Goths, Wolfram, 1990, 145.
2 Elton, 2004, 22.
3 Elton, 2004, 72.
4 Elton, 2004, 72.
5 Proc., 3.5.18.
6 Elton, 2004, 58.
7 Veg, 1.20.
8 Elton, 2004, 58.
9 Todd, 2004, 35.
10 Aur. Vic., *Caes.* 21.2.
11 Todd, 2004, 41–2.
12 Todd, 2004, 39.
13 Although usually dismissed as poor in comparison to the composite bow, it should be noted that the English longbow of the Middle Ages was made from a single piece of wood, utilising the differences in compression and flexibility between the heartwood and the outer layers.
14 Agathias, *Hist.*, 2.5.4.
15 Elton, 2004, 68.
16 E.g., Vandals 3.8.15–28, Goths 5.27.1f.
17 Isidore, 6.9. http://penelope.uchicago.edu/Thayer/L/Roman/Texts/Isidore/18*. html#6 (June 2009).
18 Greg. Tur., *securis* e.g. 2.27; 8.30: *bipennis* e.g. 8.19; 10.27.
19 Elton, 2004, 65.
20 Elton, 2004, 108.
21 Bishop and Coulston, 2006, 200.
22 Elton, 2004, 65.
23 Elton, 2004, 67.
24 Defined by the Bosworth-Toller dictionary as a short-sword or dagger http://beowulf.engl.uky.edu/~kiernan/BT/bosworth.htm, p. 853 (June 2009).
25 Elton, 2004, 65.
26 Elton, 2004, 67.
27 Elton, 2004, 67; Amm. Marc., 16.12.24. Unfortunately, the claim does not seem to be attested by the reference.
28 Elton, 2004, 70.
29 Elton, 2004, 69.
30 Elton, 2004, 45.
31 Elton, 2004, 45.
32 Elton, 2004, 74.
33 Amm. Marc. 16.12.21–2 and 37–42.
34 Elton, 2004, 81.

Chapter 6

1 Zos., 4.59.
2 Claud., *Stil II*. 88f; cf Cameron, 1970, 121.
3 E.g. Zos., 4.58.2.
4 Liebeschuetz, 1998, 56.
5 Alaric's reward; Soc. 7.10 where he is 'honoured with Roman dignities', the most obvious is being given the title *comes rei militaris*; wanting regular forces to command, Zos. 5.5.4.
6 Liebeschuetz, 1998, 56–7; Heather, 1998, 141, especially footnote 12. Burns, 1994, suggests

that the army comprised barbarian troops that had been serving as regulars in new units within the Roman army, although this must remain doubtful.

7 Kulikowski, 2002, 164f.

8 Halsall, 2007, 191–2.

9 It should be noted, however, that Kulikowski is correct in noting that there is no ancient source that supports the assumption that Alaric was followed by a large number of the Goths from the treaty of 382 (2007, 165). Unfortunately, this is somewhat negated by the fact that there is no alternative, since the sources fail to mention *any* origins for Alaric's troops.

10 Halsall, 2007, 190–95.

11 Liebeschuetz, 1998, 27, esp. n. 12.

12 Eun., fr. 59: Zos. 4.56.1.

13 Halsall, 2007, 190.

14 Jord., *Get.* 267; Liebeschuetz, 1998, 56; Kulikowski, 2007, 154.

15 This concept is reinforced by the deduction that the force did not contain many family groups, since between 395 and 400, when Alaric was given a post in Illyricum, he and his troops were likely billeted on the towns of the region and there would have been great difficulty in maintaining coherence if large numbers of families were involved

16 Liebeschuetz, 2004, 49.

17 Zos., 5.5.4. see also, Claud. *In Ruf. II*, 75–85

18 Liebeschuetz claims that Alaric and Rufinus came to an agreement and that Alaric and his followers were settled in Thessaly prior to the arrival of Stilicho with the army (1998, 58).

19 Ferrill, 1991, 92.

20 Claud., *de IV Cons. Hon.* 439–59: cf Priscus *fr.* 48.1; Malchus *fr.* 2. 20. 222–5. Elton, 2004, 183.

21 See for example, O'Flynn, 1983, 28; Jones, 1966, 74; Halsall, 2007, 195.

22 Cameron, 1970, 59.

23 Cameron, 1970, 59–60.

24 E.g., this is often given as one of the major factors behind Claudius' decision to invade Britain in AD 43.

25 Matthews, 1998, 269; Burns, 2003, 327.

26 O'Flynn, 1983, 22.

27 Cameron, 1970, 60.

28 Claud., *In Ruf.* II. 186–96.

29 Ferrill, 1991, 91.

30 Zos., 5.4.

31 Liebeschuetz, 1994, 135.

32 Cameron, 1970, 89 and especially 159f.

33 E.g., see Williams and Friell 1994, 144.

34 Cameron, 1970, 159f.

35 Cameron, 1970, 89 and especially 159f.

36 Claud., *de Cons. Stil. I.* 94–6; *In Ruf. I.* 314–22, 350–1; *III Cons. Hon.* 147–50.

37 Zos., V. 7. 3.

38 Frigidus, being a civil war, was a different matter; Theodosius had to fight and had to win. The chances of using blockade as he had against the Goths were small, as the armies of the West could match his own forces.

39 E.g. Halsall, 2007, 195.

40 Claud., *In Ruf. II.* 275f, esp. 340–5; 402–3. See also Cameron, 1970, 90–91.

41 Phil., *EH*, 11.3. 507–8.

42 For example, Phil., *EH*, 11.3. 507–8.

43 Burns, 1994, 155.

Chapter 7

1 Christie, 2007, 547.

2 Christie, 2007, 548.

3 For information on these defences and associated bibliography, see Potocnik, A J, Claustra Alpium Iuliarum at http://www.ars-cartae.com/claustra/claustra.htm (May 2009).

4 For more on these considerations, see Chapter 12.

5 Heather, 1994, 202.

6 On the condition of the defences over the Alps, see the discussion in Burns, 1994, 164.

7 *Cod. Th.* 11.16.21 (January 397); 11.30.58 (January or June 399).

8 PLRE II, 83: *Cod. Th.* 11.14.3 (June 397): *Cod. Th.* 6.28.6. (November 399).

9 E.g., Burns, 1994, 159f.

10 See below.

11 See, for example, Liebeschuetz, 1994, 159–61.

12 Burns, 1994, 159f.

13 Liebeschuetz, 1998, 94–5.

14 The vast majority of historians have placed Eutropius' negotiations with Alaric in the small period of time between Stilicho's campaign and Eutropius' campaign against the Huns, which took place towards the end of 397. For further analysis, see the remainder of the chapter.

15 Zos. 5.5.5–6 blames Antiochus and Gerontius for Alaric's being allowed to pass Thermopylae. cf. Claud, *in Ruf II*, 187f. Eunapius in his *Lives of the Sophists* attributes the treachery to Christian monks, Eun, *LS*, 439. See also, Jerome, *Ep.* 60.16.

16 This list and the suggestion that the author of the *Historia Augusta* was here commenting on events that were occurring during his own era, see Cherf, 1993. The troops described as being deployed by Claudius are more likely to have been those given to Gerontius, since the level of detail in the passage is unlikely to have been possible to an event in the previous century.

17 Liebeschuetz, 2004, 57.

18 CAH, 2004, 115.

19 Paulinus., *Vita Amb.* 34.

20 See Chapter 3.

21 As evidenced by his laws concerning provisions for the army. *Cod. Th.* 7.4.22–3.

22 Gregory of Tours, *History of the Franks*, 2,9. (Medieval Sourcebook: http//www.fordham. edu). In this section he is quoting from Sulpicius Alexander, Book 3. It is likely that this is the 'disaster' suffered when fighting against Marcomeres and Sunno described by Renatus Profuturus Frigeridus (LH 2.9) referenced by Halsall (2007, 199).

23 Gregory of Tours, *History of the Franks*, 2,9. (Medieval Sourcebook: http//www.fordham. edu). In this section he is quoting from Sulpicius Alexander, Book 4.

24 Claud., *Stil I* 218–20.

25 Gregory of Tours, *History of the Franks* 2.9; quoting from Orosius, Book 7.

26 Claud., *Stil I*. 241–45; cf. Elton, 2004, 39.

27 Claud., *Stil I*, 210–13; cf. *IV Con Hon.* 439f.

28 Claud., *Stil I*. 232–40; *IV Cons Hon.* 439–58.

29 *Cod. Th.* 7.18.9.

30 Jones, 1966, 377f.

31 Williams and Friell, 1994, 144.

32 Burrell, 2004, 252.

33 Paulinus, *Vita Amb.* 45.

34 There is no historical evidence for Liebeschuetz's claim that Stilicho was en route to Constantinople, 1994, 157.

35 For example, Halsall, 2007, 200.

36 Baynes, 1922, 214.

37 Claud., *IV Cons. Hon.* , 459f.

38 E.g. Claud., *IV Cons. Hon.* 479f.

39 Cameron, 1970, 86.

40 Claud. *IV Cons. Hon.* 459f, cf. *de Bello Get.* 513–17.

41 Zos., 5.7.2.

42 E.g., Cameron dismisses Claudian's version of events whilst Mazzarino, Grumel and Bury dismiss that of Zosimus. (Cameron, 1970, 169f; Mazzarino's, 'La politica religiosa di Stilicone', *Rendiconti dell'Istituto Lombardo* (Cl. di Lettere) lxxi (1938), 235f, esp. 262, and Grumel, V. 'L'Illyricum de la mort de Valentinien Ier (375) a la mort de Stilicon (408)', *Rev. et. Byz.* ix (1952) 5046, esp. 36) as discussed by Cameron, 1970, 175.

43 Claud., *de Bello Get.* 516f.

44 Cameron sees the declaration as caused by a suspicion in Constantinople that Stilicho was in league with Alaric and so let him escape (Cameron, 1970, 86). This is not attested in our sources and, as the chronology is insecure, doubt remains as to the exact dating of events. On the insecure dating of the *hostis publicus*, see CAH, 2004, 115.

45 Claudian later attempted to annul the declaration by claiming that Stilicho had gone to Greece on the orders of Honorius: *IV Cons. Hon.*, 459f. See also, Cameron, 1990, 96f.

46 Claud., *Cons. Stil. I*, 297–8.

47 Williams and Friell, 1994, 149; Liebeschuetz, 1997, 397.

48 Claud., *de Bello Get.* 87–8, plausibly dated by Cameron to 397 rather than 395: Cameron, 1970, 170–71.

49 Zos., 5.7.2, as quoted above.

50 John of Antioch, *fr.* 190 quoting Eunapius 64. 1.10–15; Zos., 5.7.2–3.

51 Claud., *Stil. I.* 277–8.

52 For the declaration being interpreted as an attempt to subvert the loyalty of the troops, Cameron, 1970, 113.

53 Zos., 5.7.3.

54 Claud., *IV Cons Hon* 479–83. On escape to Epirus, *Claud In Eut. II.* 214–5. On keeping the booty from Greece, *In Eut. II.* 199f. This is reaffirmed by Claudian when he states that the booty was recaptured by Stilicho after the victory at Pollentia in 402, *de Bello Get.* 611f.

55 cf. Cameron, 1970, 172 for a full discussion, where he notes that Stilicho had little to offer Alaric as a return for a treaty of alliance. In favour of an agreement, e.g. Norwich, 1988, 128–9.

56 Lifted the blockade and returned to Italy as heard of Gildo's rebellion, e.g. Stein, E, *Histoire du Bas-Empire i*, 1959, 231 as referenced by Cameron, 1970, 173.

57 Zos., 5.6.4.

58 Liebeschuetz, 1998, 59.

59 Heather, 1994, 205, although the lack of detailed information concerning the agreement reached between Eutropius and Alaric leaves the matter open to doubt. Liebeschuetz has stated, probably rightly, that throughout his career Alaric was not interested in obtaining farmland for his men; he wanted a senior post for himself – including command over Roman regular troops – and pay and billets for his men as *foederati* (1998, 57).

60 Liebeschuetz, 1998, 95.

Chapter 8

1 Amm. Marc., 29.5.2.6: PLRE I, 633–4.

2 Matthews, 1990, 179.

3 He was certainly a 'prince', due to his father being a 'king', yet it is unclear which of Nubel's sons – if any – inherited their father's position.

4 St Jerome, *Ep*, 79 (to Salvina).

5 The exact dating is problematical.

6 Millar, 1982, 7.

7 For discussion on the speed of information, Millar, 1982, passim; Elton, 2004, 177–8.

8 Millar, 1982, 10.

9 Josephus, *BJ* 2.10.5 (203); Josephus, *Ant.* 8.9 (305), quoted in Millar, 1982, 10. Caligula died in January, 41.

10 Pliny, *NH*, 19.3, quoted in Millar, 1982, 10.

11 Millar, 1982, 10.

12 Millar, 1982, 10, and referencing Starr, C G, *The Roman Imperial Navy*, 1941, 177–8.

13 Compare with the revolt of Firmus already mentioned.

14 There are two possible interpretations at this point. The difficulty lies with Claudian. In his early poems he states that Gildo approached Eutropius (e.g. *de Bello Gild.* 276f), whereas in his later poems he states that Eutropius approached Gildo (e.g. *Stil. I.* 269f.). However, even in this later poem he early states that 'Gildo had transferred the nominal rule of Libya to the Eastern empire', only then alleging that 'From Byzantium came edicts to subvert the loyalty of governors' (271–7). Accordingly, it is more plausible that the initiative came from Gildo, with Claudian later changing the blame to Eutropius only as a means of further damaging Eutropius' reputation. Although support for Eutropius' guilt can also be found in Zosimus, this is likely to be a result of Eutropius' equally poor reputation in the East after his fall from power; he was the first eunuch to assume the consulship, which resulted in both his downfall and his low standing (Zos., 5.11.2). For an alternative version, see Cameron, 1970, 92f, and especially 110.

15 For the dating, Claud., *de Bello Gild.* 16.

16 Earlier in the empire, Egypt had supplied Rome with grain. Later, both Egypt and Africa supplied the capital, but when Constantine founded Constantinople he decreed that Egypt would supply his new city, whilst Africa would continue to supply the city of Rome.

17 Cameron suggests that Eutropius would have had a similar motive in attempting to limit Stilicho's responses (1970, 93–4).

18 E.g. Matthews, 1998, 272–3 and Cameron, 1970, 92f. Matthews approves of Gildo's 'choice' and claims that he was 'constitutionally quite correct in supporting Arcadius' whilst Cameron suggests that Gildo's 'rebellion' was because allegiance to 'distant' Constantinople was preferable to being under the constant scrutiny of nearby Rome (Cameron, 1970, 93).

19 Zos., 4.59.

20 For the opposite view, see Cameron, 1970, 93.

21 The claim that Stilicho retired from Greece due to reports that Gildo had rebelled, e.g. Burrell, 2004, 254f., relies upon a clear chronology, which is inferred, and an extremely efficient series of communications between Africa, Constantinople and Italy, which is unlikely.

22 Cameron suggests that the timescale was too tight and that Eutropius was not given time to support Gildo before the rebellion was crushed (1970, 95).

23 cf Cameron, 1970, 95.

24 Cameron proposes that the rebellion was an attempt by Gildo to free Africa from the

crippling obligation of supplying Rome (Cameron, 1970, 93), although this would seem extremely unlikely given the likely ramifications.

25 Claud., *de Cons. Stil I*, 314f: *II*, 393f: *III*, 91f: and *in Eut. I*. 401f.

26 For a detailed description of the earlier form of *senatus consultum*, see *Smith's Dictionary of Greek and Roman Antiquities*, at http://penelope.uchicago.edu/ Thayer/E/Roman/Texts/ secondary/SMIGRA*/Senatusconsultum.html.

27 cf. Millar, 1982, 4f.

28 Symm., *Epp* 7.38, 6.72 and 9.48 for examples of the movement and billeting of troops in Italy; Matthews, 1998, 268, footnote 1.

29 For example, the wars of Jugurtha (c.112–104 BC) and Tacfarinas (AD 17–24), as noted by Cameron, 1990, 94: and especially that of *comes* Theodosius (c.372–5)

30 Claud., in *Stil. II*, 86f. Claudian admits that Gildo's action had brought the empire to the verge of civil war.

31 Claud., *de Bello Gild.*, 333f.

32 *Cod. Th* 7.13.12.

33 Seeck, Symmachus, p. LXIX; Matthews, 1998, 268–9, footnote 2.

34 *Cod. Th.* 7.13.13 (repeal for the petitioners); 7.13.14 (repeal for imperial estates).

35 For a full discussion, see Matthews, 1998, 267f.

36 Claud., *Stil I*, 291f.

37 cf Cameron, 1970, 119.

38 The claim by Cameron that Stilicho could not lead an expedition against a 'legitimately appointed' servant of Arcadius does not stand up to scrutiny (1970, 94).

39 Some Christian bishops and other leaders had cooperated with the persecutions ordered between 303 and 305 by the Emperor Diocletian. They had renounced their faith and surrendered the scriptures to the authorities. Although many had later been reinstated, Donatists believed that these individuals had lost their authority and refused to accept their legitimacy. In this they had come into conflict with the Catholic Church and been declared heretics.

40 cf Amm. Marc., 29.5.14.

41 Orosius, 7.36.6.

42 For the names of the units, Claud., *de Bello Gild*. 418–23.

43 Elton, 2004, 97–8.

44 Claud., *Cons Stil. I*. 314f notes the gathering of ships and the deployment of a new army with new recruits. On specialist ships for horses, Elton, 2004, 97–8: Menander, fr.23.1.

45 Claud., *de Cons. Stil I*, 333f.

46 Cameron, 1970, 116.

47 Liguria and Etruria, Claud., *de Bello Gild*. 504–6: Capraria, Oros. 7.36.5.

48 Markus, 1974, 9.

49 Symm., *Ep* I.52.

50 Claud., *de Bello Gild*. 483

51 Oros., 7.36.5.

52 Claud., *de Bello Gild*. 504f.

53 Claud., *de Bell Gild*. 516f.

54 Over a century later, during the campaign to retake Africa from the Vandals, Belisarius received news of Gelimer's whereabouts from an individual in Syracuse.

55 Paulinus, *Vita Ambr.* 51.

56 Zos., 5.11.4.

57 Williams and Friell, 1995, 150, claim that Gildo was deserted by his troops, whilst Cameron

argues that these would have been Catholics forced to fight for Gildo, 1970, 117: 151.

58 Claud., *In Eut. II*, 70f.

59 In some respects this is a faint echo of the actions of Augustus when he became the first Roman emperor.

60 On the date, Cameron, 1970, 109.

61 Cameron, 1970, 96. Allusions, Claud., *IV Cons. Hon.* 22–9.

62 Claud., *Epith*, 333. An 'Epithalamium' (from the Greek; *epi-* 'upon' and *thalamium* 'nuptial chamber') refers to a form of poem that is written for the bride.

63 Cameron, 1970, 101.

64 *Not. Dig.* Oc XII 5; Jones, 1966, 156; Matthews, 1998, 273.

65 Zos., 5.11.4.

66 e.g. Claud., *de Bello Gild.*, 387f

67 Claud., *Stil. I*. 269f.

68 Mann, 1979, 182.

69 For a different view, see Cameron, 1970, 118.

70 This is the view promoted by, for example, Cameron: 1970, 120.

Chapter 9

1 See Burns, 1994, 112 for a more detailed account of the discussions.

2 O'Flynn, 1983, 20.

3 E.g. *Not Dig. Oc.* VII 34 and 35. For a full discussion of these changes and their effects on two provinces (Raetia I and II) see Burns, 1994, 114.

4 E.g., the *Honoriani Mauri Seniores* and *Honoriani Mauri Iuniores* (*Oc.* V. 203, 204). Other examples can be found at *Oc.* V. 215, 216, and 220. See Liebeschuetz, 1986, 466; Hoffmann, 1969, 358–67; Jones, 1964, App. II, table 1, 5–7; Burns, 1994, 112.

5 Liebeschuetz, 1994, 149f.

6 The *magister peditum* had supplanted the *magister equitum* as the senior position in the Western army during the course of the previous fifty years. As a note of caution, the officer actually recruiting individuals, or possibly even whole units, did not necessarily need to be the *magister militum*. As time passed individual generals in the provinces began to recruit troops from outside the borders. On the whole, however, such recruitment practices seem to become common after the period under discussion.

7 Burns, 1994, 112; Jones, 1964, 1426.

8 Williams and Friell, 1994, 143; Burns, 1994, 112.

9 *Cod. Th.* 7.20.12, dated January 400, issued to Stilicho: Burns, 2003, 186.

10 Burns, 1994, 143–4.

11 Wolfram, 1997, 95.

12 Claud., *In Iacobum magistrum equitum*, Carmina Minora 50, http://penelope.uchicago.edu/Thayer/E/Roman/Texts/Claudian/Carmina_Minora*/50.html, (May 2009).

13 PLRE II, Iacobus 1, 581–2.

14 Mann, 1979, 182.

15 Mann, 1979, 182.

16 Burns, 1994, 149.

17 For a more detailed analysis, Hoffmann, D *Das spätromische Bewegungsheer und die Notitia Dignitatum* (Düsseldorf 1969–70).

18 Williams and Friell, 1994, 146.

19 Liebeschuetz, 1986, 465.

20 Olymp., *fr.* 7.4.

21 Liebeschuetz notes that after Adrianople in 378 most sources divide the army into 'Roman'

and 'barbarian': 1986, 463. This suggests that new terminology was needed and that this only came into force under Stilicho.

22 Compare the superiority of Roman arms except when faced with the revolt of Germans who had previously served in the army, e.g. Arminius in AD 9 and Civilis' Batavian revolt AD 69–70, both led by ex-Roman soldiers.

23 See also Burns, 1994, p. 113.

24 Wolfram, 1997, 95.

25 Williams and Friell, 1994, 148.

26 Burns, 1994, Chapter 5.

27 Burns, 1994, 123. It is possible that this is also the model followed in at least parts of the British provinces.

28 Burns, 1994, 123.

29 Liebeschuetz, 1986, 468–9.

30 Government decree, *Cod Iust.* 12.10 (AD 468); Redistribution, Proc. *Hist.* IV. 17; *Bucellarius* alone, *Leges Visigothorum*, 18. fr. 310, n. 25; see Liebeschuetz, 1986, 468–9.

31 O'Flynn, 1983, 23.

32 *Cod. Th.* 7.13.16; O'Flynn, 1983.

33 O'Flynn, 1983, 21–2.

34 cf Williams and Friell, 1994, 148.

35 Claud., *Stil. I.* 291f; Cameron, 1970, 134.

36 On the date, Cameron, 1970, xv.

37 Claud., *de Cons. Stil. II.* 354f.

38 O'Flynn, 1982, 60.

39 For events and claims in this section, see Miller, 1975, based on a comparison of Gildas and Claudian. As he notes, there is no archaeological evidence for these claims but this is not surprising as archaeology has usually been limited to forts or the settlements around forts which are likely to have been avoided by invading armies and it is notoriously difficult to tie historical information to archaeological data. See also, Elton, 2004, 8: Salway, 1993, 297f.

40 On the (ambiguous) archaeological evidence, see Halsall, 2007, 196.

41 Claud., *In Eut. II.* 196–201

42 Claud., *In Eut. II.* 214–18.

43 *Not. Dig., Or* xi 35–9. Horreum Margi, possibly to be identified as Požarevac in Serbia.

44 On the Thracian herds, and the emperor's control of them, see Procopius, 3, 12, 6.

45 Williams and Friell, 1994, 147.

46 Cameron, 1970, 101.

47 Claud., *de Bello Gild.* 465–6

48 Cameron, 1970, 124.

49 In a continuation of earlier practice, there were still two annual consuls 'elected' each year. Usually, one was nominated from the East, one from the West.

50 Arcadius' affection for Eutropius, Cameron, 1970, 128.

51 Cameron, 1970, 133.

52 Cameron, 1970, 126.

53 Cameron, 1970, 127.

54 Williams and Friell, 1994, 151.

55 Williams and Friell, 1994, 152.

56 Williams and Friell, 1994, 223, n. 44.

57 Soz., *HE.* 8.4.1.

58 Zos., 5.13.2; Liebeschuetz, 1994, 168.

59 Claud., *In Eut. II.* 176f; Cameron, 1970, 134.

60 Zos., 5.13.3: Claudian calls him a '"dux" ("tribune") of the Getic squadron'; *In Eut. II*, 176.

61 Zos., 5.15.5; 16.1–3.

62 All referenced in Zosimus; Lydia, 5.13.4; Pisidia, 5.14.3; Pamphylia, 5.25.2; cf. Philost. 11.8.

63 Claud., *In Eut.* 320–1.

64 Zos., 5.13.4.

65 Soc., *HE*, 6.6.1.

66 PLRE II, 661

67 Liebeschuetz, 1994, 155; cf Gainas sent to Thrace when news of the revolt arrived.

68 Liebeschuetz, 1994, 170.

69 Zos., 5.17.2.

70 For a discussion of the different views, see Cameron, 1970, 134–5.

71 Cameron, 1970, 134.

72 See Cameron, 1970, 134.

73 This section is based mainly upon Cameron, 1970, 128f.

74 Cameron, 1970, 130.

75 PLRE I, 128–9.

76 CAH, 116.

77 Philost. 11.8.

78 Liebeschuetz, 1994, 170–1.

79 Zosimus states that 7,000 were killed in Constantinople, but that these were only one-fifth of Gainas' whole force: Zos. 5.19.4: Synesius gives a more detailed account in *On Providence*, II.2.

80 Zos., 5.21.6.

81 Zos., 5.22.

82 CAH, 116–117.

83 CAH, 117.

84 Elton, 2004, 142–3, citing Synesius, *Ep.* 38.

Chapter 10

1 Eun. 66.2 reports on the confusion in the West surrounding the course of events in the East, due both to the long voyage making the information out of date and to the large number of differing reports, dependent upon the viewpoint of the reporters.

2 On the dating of the poems, see Cameron, 1970, xv.

3 Either as a result of the declaration itself being declared annulled, or, more likely, as a result of all of Eutropius' legislation being declared void, *Cod. Th.* 9.40.17.

4 Matthews, 1974, 77.

5 Heather, 1991, 210.

6 Date Eudoxia elevated as *Augusta, Chron. Pasch,* 400.

7 For example, Burns, 1994, 166–78.

8 In an attempt to avoid confusion, the Diocese of Pannonia/Illyricum will from now on be titled Illyricum (Pannonia) whereas the prefecture will still be called simply Illyricum.

9 Eunapius. 71. 3; Burns, 1994, 174.

10 Halsall, 2007, 203 states that Fravitta was killed some time in 400–401. However, as he was consul in 401 it is likely that an event such as the arrest and execution of the consul would have been noted. 404 is much more likely.

11 Cf. Liebeschuetz, 1998, 62.

12 Synesius of Cyrene, *De Regno,* at http://www.livius.org/su-sz/synesius/synesius_monarchy_14.html (December 2008). The use of 'Skythians' for 'Goths' is a literary *topos*

common throughout this period.

13 Eunapius is especially complimentary of Fravitta: 69. 1–3.

14 Jordanes, *Getica*, 146. cf. Liebeschuetz who proposes that there was a shortage of food due to the flight of Gainas and the presence of Fravitta and the Eastern army: 1998, 61.

15 Liebeschuetz, 1998, 61 n. 103. quoting Cameron, Long and Sherry, 1990; cf. Zos. V. 22.

16 Wolfram, 1990, 145; Olymp. 3 and 36 calls Sarus an *'eparchos'*.

17 Liebeschuetz, 1998, 62; Claud., *de Bello Get.*, 568: Soz. 9. 6.

18 The concept is reinforced by later events following the settlement of the Goths in Aquitaine in 418.

19 Jordanes, *Getica*, 29. Halsall (2007) argues – convincingly – that Alaric and his successors used the title intermittently, but with increasing regularity, from 400/401 onwards in response to 'specific political developments'.

20 Prud., *Contra Symm.* II 695f; Wolfram, 1990, 145.

21 Wolfram, 1990, 144; cf Claud, *de Bello Get.* 488–551.

22 Wolfram, 1990, Chapter 3, passim.

23 Some historians date the invasion to 400, following the ancient chronicles such as Prosper, *Prosperi Tironis epitome chronicon* (*Chronicon Minores I*, 341–485) and Cassiodorus, *Cassiodori Senatoris Chronica* (*Chronicon Minores II*, 111–61). This assumes that the chronicles are correct concerning the date of the Raetian invasion, but are incorrect in assuming that Alaric was involved. It is clear that Stilicho led a winter campaign against the Vandals and it is also certain that Alaric invaded in late autumn 401. Yet the sources claim that the passes into Italy were unguarded and this is most likely the result of troops being withdrawn for the Raetian campaign. If Stilicho's campaign in Raetia had been in 400–401, it is likely that by autumn of 401 at least some of the troops will have been returned to guard the passes into Italy. Therefore, it is more likely that Stilicho's campaign began in early autumn 401 and that Alaric's invasion was partly based on the knowledge that Stilicho had been called away with the army. This assumes that the sources have confused the date by one year and at the same time assumed that Alaric was involved in any barbarian invasion of the West.

24 On the campaign being in winter, Claud., *de Bello Get.*, 348–9.

25 Claud., *de Bello Get.*, 279–80; 363-5; 400f.

26 This is acknowledged by Claudian, for example at *de Bello Get.*, 321f: 'Next he ascended those mountains, inaccessible in winter, with no thought for the season or the weather'.

27 Cameron, 1970, 375–6: Claud., *de Bello Get.*, 400f.

28 Claud., *de Bello Get.*, 151–3 (in Italy one winter prior to the Battle of Pollentia in 402); Chron. Min. I 299.

29 Claud., *de Bello Get.*, 278f.

30 For a full discussion of the topic, see Bayliss, 'The Visigothic Invasion of Italy in 401'; Cameron, 1970, 178f. Claimed by an ancient source: Olympiodorus, 1, 2.

31 Williams and Friell, 1994, 151.

32 Jordanes, *Get*, 147

33 Chron. Min. I 299

34 Claims that Jordanes in his *Getica* (147) has the Pannonian Goths joining Alaric are not supported by the text.

35 Claud., *de Bello Get.* 562: see Wolfram, 1990, 436, n. 200 for more detail on the sites of resistance.

36 Jerome, *Apologeticum adversus Rufinum*: at 'http://www.newadvent.org/fathers/ 27103.htm' (December 2008)

37 Claudian, *de Bello Get.*, 60f; 227f.

38 Gaudentius, '*Tract.*' 17. 1f. cf. 13. 21 (CSEL LXVIII, pp. 141, 120) referenced in Matthews, 1974, 59: Symm. *Epp.* 4.9: 7.13–14.

39 Cf. Claud., *de Bello Get.*, 416f.

40 *Cod. Th.* 7.16.1.

41 Claud., *de VI Cons. Hon*, 454f.

42 Claud., *de Bello Get.*, 450f.

43 The first law issued from Ravenna is dated 6 December 402. *Cod. Th.* 7.13.15.

44 CAH, 2004, 120.

45 CAH 120. The suggestion that Arelate (Arles) would have been a strategically better choice does not bear close scrutiny.

46 Capturing Tuscany and Rome, Prudentius, *Contra Symmachum*, II 702. Claud. *de Bello Get.* 430; 531f. Jordanes claims (*Get.* 152–3) that Alaric wanted to integrate the Goths with the inhabitants of Italy, but the accuracy of this is open to question.

47 Claud., *de VI Con. Hon*, 201–3.

48 Unfortunately, we are not told the name of the commander of the town.

49 The prophecy is also mentioned by Sozomen. 9.6

50 Oros., 7.37.

51 See also, Ferrill, 1991, 96.

52 Orosius, 7,37.2.

53 On Saul, see esp. PLRE II 981. Escape in flight, Zos. 4.58.2-3. On the allegations, see Cameron (1970, 181) who in this instance may be mistaken as to the intent of Claudian's poetry.

54 PLRE II, 981.

55 Orosius, 7.37.2.

56 Claud., *de Bello Get.*, 623f. Retiring with the majority of his cavalry intact, Claud, *VI Cons. Hon*, 274f; Camp and booty captured, *de Bello Get.*, 605f; 624f.

57 *de Bello Get.*, 124f.

58 On the negotiations, Claud. *VI Cons. Hon.* 210; abandoning Italy, *de Bello Get.* 144; *VI Cons. Hon.* 138. The passage at *de Bello Get.* 646–8 implies that the invasion is now over. See Liebeschuetz, 2004, 63. I disagree with Cameron (1970, 181) and Wolfram (1990, 152) who see the claim as fictitious and an attempt by Claudian to protect Stilicho from claims of treason and incompetence, and suggest instead that he was in an alliance with Alaric.

59 Claud., *VI Cons. Hon.*, 285f; cf *de Bello Get.* 144; *VI Cons Hon*, 211–12.

60 Claud., *VI Cons. Hon.*, 193f.

61 Cf. Claud., *de VI Cons. Hon.*, 238f.

62 Alaric attempting to cross the Alps, Claud. *de VI Cons. Hon.* 229–33. Stilicho's response to Alaric's attempts to cross the Alps, CAH. 120; for a discussion and comparison, Wolfram, 1990, 152.

63 Claud., *de VI Cons Hon.* 230f; Liebeschuetz, 1998, 63.

64 Claud., *de VI Cons. Hon.* 210f and 301f. See also Cameron, 1970, 184.

65 O'Flynn, 1983, 40.

66 Claud., *de VI Con. Hon.* 123-6. This is most probably a device used by Claudian to pacify those members of the Senate who simply expected and desired that Alaric be defeated before being captured or killed.

67 O'Flynn, 1983, 41.

68 Claud., *de VI Cons. Hon.* 239–44.

69 Sarus, PLRE II 978: Segericus PLRE II 987.

70 Wolfram, 1990, 34; 152.

71 Claud., *de VI Cons Hon.* 251f.

72 On Alaric being given territory in the West, see Liebeschuetz, 1998, 64.

73 Halsall, 2007, 202.

74 Soz. 8.25.3–4: 9.4.2–4.

75 On dating the hostage exchange, which included Aetius, later *magister militum* himself, to 402 rather than 405, Liebeschuetz, 1998, 63–4: Halsall, 2007, 202.

76 *Dux Pannoniae secundae* = *Not. Dig.* Oc I. 40. On location of settlement, Soz. 8.25.3–4; IX 4.4. On title of 'King of the Goths' and 'Count of the Romans', Or. 2.3.3. See Cameron, 1970, 185, for a discussion of these events. On the earlier appointments of a *comes rei militaris* of Africa see Chapter 8 and of Britain see Chapter 9.

77 Claud., *de Bello Get.* 624f. and *VI Cons. Hon.* 297–8: Prudentius, *Contra Symmachus*, II. 696–744. Modern agreement, e.g. Liebeschuetz, 1998, 63.

78 Cassiodorus, *Chron. a* 402: Jordanes, *Getica*, 154–55.

79 Prosper, *Chron. a.* 402; Orosius, 7.37.2; and Jerome *Ep.* 107.2.3. Modern agreement, e.g. Wolfram, 1990, 152.

80 For example, Wolfram suggests that Stilicho was able to stand his ground but was forced to let Alaric go due to the Gothic cavalry arm remaining intact (1997, 96). Halsall suggests the battles were indecisive, although Stilicho had the better of them (2007, 201).

81 Veg., *Epit. Rei Mil.* 3.9.

82 Maur., *Strat.* 8.2.4.

83 Maur., *Strat*, 10.2. The passage rewards careful reading by illuminating the profound shift in emphasis that the Roman army had undergone from the times of the Early Empire.

84 These are the tactics idealized by Vegetius in his *Epitoma rei Militaris*: 3.9f.

85 E.g., O'Flynn, 1983, 40.

86 E.g., O'Flynn, 1983, 40.

87 Claud., *de Bello Get.*, 580f.

88 Claud., *VI Cons. Hon.* 223f.

89 O'Flynn, 1983, 54.

90 Burns, 1994, 193.

91 Christie, 2007, 547f.

92 Ferrill, 1988, 97.

Chapter 11

1 Matthews, 1998, 309 n.3.

2 Amm. Marc., 17.8: 20.10.2.

3 Burns, 2003, 325

4 Burns, 2003, 357

5 Drinkwater, 1998, 273.

6 It is probable that, along with recruiting barbarians for their armies, both Maximus (383–8) and Arbogast (388–95) made treaties with the tribes on the frontiers to defend the same frontiers against attack, so allowing them to withdraw the troops usually stationed there to face Theodosius in the ensuing civil wars.

7 Burns, 2003, 353.

8 For a more detailed discussion, see Halsall, 2007, 207–10.

9 For a more in-depth discussion of the date and references to related literature, see Halsall, 2007, 209f. See also Wolfram, 1997, 95.

10 cf. Drinkwater, 1998, 274 and 277.

11 Drinkwater, 1998, 277.

12 Burns, 2003, 361.

13 Halsall, 2007, 347f.

14 Matthews, 1998, 256

15 This section is heavily indebted to the works of E A Thompson, especially 'Peasant Revolts in Late Roman Gaul and Spain', *Past and Present*, No. 2. (Nov., 1952), pp. 11–23.

16 Thompson sees the revolt of Maternus during the reign of Septimius Severus (193–211) as the earliest known example of an uprising that would later be known as *bacaudae* (1952, 12).

17 Thompson, 1952, 1506.

18 Burns, 2003, 359. Poulter, 2007, 67f. and Heather, 2007, 170–71, describe the process in more detail with reference to the extensive ongoing archaeological investigations.

19 Matthews, 1998, 264.

20 Gaudentius, '*Tract.*' 17.1f. cf. 13.21 (CSEL LXVIII, pp. 141, 120) referenced in Matthews, 1974, 59: Symm. *Epp.* 4.9: 7.13–14.

21 Matthews, 1975, 281, n.4.

22 *Collectio Avellana*, No.38. p. 85 (ref. Wolfram, 1990, 153): '*Etiam super excidio pereuntis Illyrici pio apud vos prodiderimus affectu esse nobis dolori, cur ista nos detrimenta rei publicae nolueritis agnoscere et aliis potuis indicibus quam pietatis vestrae litteris fuerint nuntiata.*'.

23 Honorius apologizing, Wolfram, 1990, 153; Honorius accusing Arcadius, Halsall, 2007, 202 n.69; Heather suggests Honorius is complaining that Arcadius has not informed the West of Alaric's attacks after he was evicted from Italy in 402; Liebeschuetz, 1991, 65, avoids the issue of the meaning of the letter, only commenting upon the nature of the barbarians.

24 Williams and Friell, 1994, 155: On the dating, see the previous chapter.

25 This section is based mainly on Liebeschuetz, 2004, 167f. See also Norwich, 1988, 125f.

26 This is the letter *Collectio Avellana*, No. 38. p. 85, mentioned above.

27 For the complexities surrounding this event, Williams and Friell, 1994, 155; on the date, 223, note 52; see also Heather, 1994, 221.

28 Soz., *HE* 8.25.3; 9.4.2-4. Kulikowski, 2007, 171; Williams and Friell, 223, note 52. Zos. 5.26.

29 405, Seeck, Stein, Schmidt and Mazzarino; 406, Demougeot: source *Zosimus: New History*, Trans. Ridley, p. 215, n. 84.

30 Heather, 1991, 77–78.

31 PLRE II, Iovius 3, 623.

32 It is possible that Stilicho 'revived or manufactured a claim' that Theodosius had ordered that the Prefecture of Illyricum be attached to the West: CAH, 2004, 121.

33 Rutilius Namatianus, *de Reditu suo*, 41f: http://penelope.uchicago.edu/ Thayer/E/Roman/ Texts/Rutilius_Namatianus/text*.html (July 2009).

34 'seeing that Arcadius' ministers were alienated from him': Zosimus, New History, VIII. 26. 1–2:

35 'King of the Goths', for example: Aug., *Civ. Dei.*, 5.23; Oros. 7.37.4; Prosp. Tiro. s.a. 400; Chron. Gall. 452 no. 50.

36 E.g., Williams and Friell, 1995, 155: Wolfram, 1997, 97.

37 Burns, 1994, 198 believes that Radagaisus entered Italy via the Brenner Pass: Kulikowski, 2007, 171 also implies the same when he notes that Radagaisus invaded via Raetia. For the alternative, see e.g. Wolfram, 1997, 97, who believes that Radagaisus entered the empire via Pannonia.

38 This obviates the need to understand why Alaric did not join the forces passing through 'his' territory; cf. Williams and Friell, 1994, 155, who claim that Alaric was still too weak to join in.

39 This is the traditional date for the exchange of those hostages including Aetius which may have instead taken place in 402; cf., Liebeschuetz, 1998, 63–4; Halsall, 2007, 202.

40 Oros., 7.37.4.

41 For a more detailed discussion of the numbers, see below.

42 *Chron. Gall.* 452 no. 52: Paulin. *Vita Amb.* 50.

43 Oros. 7.37f.

44 *Chron. Gall.*, 452. No. 52.

45 Aug., *Civ. Dei.* 5.23; Oros. 7.37.6.; Zos. 5.26.4.

46 Zos., 5.26.4.

47 Williams and Friell, 1995, 155.

48 *Cod. Th*, 7.13.16: 7.13.17. Interestingly, Freeman (1886, 54) saw this as a measure to counter the invasion of the Vandals, Alans and Sueves, which didn't happen until the end of the year.

49 Zos., 5.26.4; Huns led by Uldin, Wolfram, 1997, 97.

50 Williams and Friell, 1995, 155.

51 Zos. 5.26.4 claims the Danube, but see Ridley's translation, p 215, n.87 for clarification.

52 Paulin. *Vita Amb.* 50.

53 Aug., *Civ. Dei.* 5.23 (http://www.ccel.org/ccel/schaff/npnf102.iv.V.23.html). Orosius 7.37.14 also notes that the Romans suffered few casualties.

54 Captured and executed, Oros. 37.13–15; with his sons, Aug. *Civ. Dei.* 5.23.(http://www.ccel.org/ccel/schaff/npnf102.iv.V.23.html); date, *Addit. ad Prosp. Hann. Ad. A.* 405 (Radagaisus, PLRE II, 934). Possibly in Rome, rather than at Faesulae, Paul. Nola. *Carm.* 21. 1–34.

55 Olymp. fr. 9.

56 For additional information and clarification on detailed aspects of the Roman army, refer to Chapter 4. See also Burns, 1994, 356, n.53 for an outline of the problems surrounding the size of Stilicho's forces.

57 Zos., 5.26.3: Oros. 7.37.4.

58 For example, Wolfram simply states that the army was 'many tens of thousands' (1997, 96–7). Others simply bypass the problem: for example, Liebeschuetz declares it was a 'vast war band' (2004, 65), Williams and Friell describe it as 'a massive invasion' (1995, 155), and the CAH has Radagaisus leading 'a large force of barbarians' (2004, 120–21)

59 Olymp. fr. 9.

60 Burns, 1994, 198.

61 *Chron. Gall.* 452 no. 52; Paulin. *Vita Amb.* 50.

62 Zos., 6.3. Zosimus may have confused events, with the last remnants of Radagaisus' forces that escaped by crossing the Alps turning into Vandals, Sueves and Alans. However, this may actually represent a historical tradition, as discussed during the events of 406 below.

63 O'Flynn, 1983, 41.

64 Oros., 7.37.16; Zos. 5.26.4.

65 Paul. Nola, *Carm.* 21.1–34.

Chapter 12

1 CAH, 2004, 123.

2 CAH, 2004, 123.

3 For the possibility of Stilicho laying claim to the guardianship and Illyricum, see Chapter 11.

4 *Collectio Avellana*, No.38. For a full discussion, see Chapter 11.

5 Baynes, 1922, 216.

6 Soz., 25.1–2.

7 This section has been based mainly upon Sodini, 2007, who has demonstrated that the large-scale decline of Illyricum may have begun only after the attacks of the Huns in the 440s, since they had siege techniques that could capture Roman cities.

8 Poulter, 2007, 18.

9 Sodini, 2007, 315–16.

10 Sodini, 2007, 328f.

11 Jones, 1966, 82

12 Proc. III. 12.6–7.

13 Heather, 2005, 219–20.

14 Soz. *HE* 8.25. Compare this to Kulikowski's claim (2007, 171) that there is no evidence that Stilicho was going to join Alaric in Epirus.

15 Heather, 2005, 220.

16 Kulikowski, 2007, 172.

17 *Cod. Th.* 7.16.1.

18 This should be compared with the appointment of *comes rei militaris* in Africa (Chapter 8), Britain (Chapter 9), Spain (Chapter 9) and Illyricum (Chapter 10). Mann, 1979, 182.

19 *Cod. Th.* 7.13.18.

20 Burns, 1994, 205.

21 *Cod. Th.* 11.7.14 (April 9, 407).

22 Zos. 5.27.2f. Stilicho was in Ravenna and Honorius in Rome when news of the death of Alaric reached them. Bury, 1923, 60.

23 *Zosimus*, Ridley, 1982, 216, n.91.

24 Soz., *HE* 8.25: Zos., 5.27.2.

25 Zos., 5.29.8.

26 Zos., 5.27.2.

Chapter 13

1 Zos., 6.3.1.

2 Drinkwater, 1998, 271.

3 Salway, 1993, 300. This can be compared to the often repeated complaint concerning lack of pay to be found throughout Procopius, for example during the reconquest of Africa and Belisarius' campaigns in Italy.

4 E.g. Salway, 1993, 300: Bury, 1923, 188.

5 Olymp., fr. 12, perhaps giving the date as late 406, cf. PLRE II. Marcus 2, 719: Zos. 6.2.1, giving the date as 407; cf. Soz. 9.11.2.

6 '*municeps eiusdem insulae*', Oros. 7.40.4.

7 Kulikowski, 2000, 332 and note 44, as opposed to e.g. Burns, 1994, and Matthews, 1998, 308.

8 Freeman, 1886, 55, 60.

9 Drinkwater, 1998, 273; Gibbon, 1861, II, 249.

10 Possibly adding to the anger of the Gauls and British at the lack of protection from the emperor.

11 Lands becoming insufficient, Bury, 1923, 186, quoting Proc. III.22–3. Threatened by Huns, Bury, 1923, 186

12 Godigisel, Greg. Tur. *HF* 2.9.

13 Jer. *Ep*. 123.16: early modern historians appear to have followed Gibbon, who claims that the tribes that crossed the Danube comprised at least one third of the forces that Radagaisus led into Italy. These were numbered at 200,000 warriors and 400,000 overall, so leading to an estimate of around 60,000 warriors and 130,000 people overall (Gibbon, 1861, II, 246): cf. Freeman, 1904, 19f.

14 Liebeschuetz, 1990, 13–14.

15 Matthews, 1998, 275f: Kulikowski, 2007, 171f: Williams and Friell, 1994, 84.

16 Drinkwater, 1998, 273f.

17 Muhlberger, 2002, 29–30.

18 Jer., *Ep.* 123.15.

19 Jer., *Ep.* 123.15.

20 Greg. Tur., *HF* 2.9.

21 Kulikowski prefers to date the invasion to 405 rather than 406, based upon a preference for Zosimus' dating at 6.3.1 rather than Prosper's chronicle at 1230 (2000, 326f). Unfortunately, he weakens his own argument by later noting that Book 6 of Zosimus, upon which he bases the theory, is 'the deeply unreliable Book VI of Zosimus' (2000, 332, n.40, 41).

22 Gibbon, 1861, II, 250: 'The victorious confederates pursued their march, and on the last day of the year, in a season when the waters of the Rhine were most probably frozen, they entered, without opposition, the defenceless provinces of Gaul'; based on, for example, Herodian, 6.7.6–7

23 Elton, 2004, 40, suggests that the invasion was not coordinated. The events surrounding the nature of the invasion, with the tribes arriving separately, to some degree supports this theory. However, the retreat of that section of the Alans under Respendial and their participation in the battle with the Franks (see below) implies that a low level of coordination existed.

24 *Chron. Gall. 452*, No. 127 (s.a. 442).

25 Once inside any further Burgundian movement was only permitted with Roman agreement: Oros. 7.38.3.

26 Oros., 7.40.3.

27 Bury, 1923, 186.

28 Succession, Greg. Tur. *HE* 2.9; duration of Gunderic's rule, PLRE II 522.

29 Kulikowski, 2000, 326 and n.8; Greg. Tur. 2.9; Oros. 7.40.3.

30 Drinkwater, 1998, 273–4.

31 Drinkwater, 1998, 273.

32 Drinkwater, 1998, 274.

33 Jord., *Get.* 22 (115); Jer. Ep. 123.15.

34 Jer., *Ep.* 123.15.

35 Greg. Tur., 2.9.

36 cf. Drinkwater, 1998, 271.

37 Jord., *Get.* 22 (115).

38 Oros., 7.38.

39 Freeman, 1886, 54 and n.2.

40 For further details and bibliography on the proposed itineraries, see Kulikowski, 2000, 331.

41 Salvian, *de Gub. Dei.* 6.82–4. However, it should be noted that this episode is not clearly dated by Salvian and so could have occurred at any time during the period 406–9.

42 Jer., *Ep.* 123.15.

43 Paul., Euch. 239.

44 The section covering the advance of Constantine into the heart of Gaul is in very large part based upon the analysis made by Drinkwater (1998), since his study clearly explains many issues which before then remained in doubt.

45 Paschoud 1989, 20, on Zos. 5.27.1–2, suggests a date in February (Kulikowski, 2000, n.48); Burns, 1994, 210, suggests the date of 1 March.

46 Dating, Burns, 1994, 210; reason for overthrow, Kulikowski, 2000, 332.

47 Oros. 7.40.4; Proc. III. 2. 31. Burns argues that he was of a relatively high rank, 1994, 213.

48 Soz., 9.11.

49 Drinkwater, 1998, 272.

50 For a discussion of the changes, see Drinkwater, 1998, 272.

51 Kulikowski, 2000, 328, following Paschoud, 1989, 20 and Zos. V. 27. 1–2.

52 *Cod. Th.* 7.13.18.

53 Bury, 1923, 188, referencing Evans, A.J *Num. Chron.* 3rd Series VII, 191.

54 Justinianus in Zosimus, Justinus in Olympiodorus; PLRE II Justinianus 1, 644; Nebiogastes in Zosimus, Neobigastes in Olympiodorus; PLRE II, Nebiogastes, 773–4.

55 E.g., Burns, 1994, suggests 5,500 men, and Drinkwater, 1998, 275 6,000 men.

56 Drinkwater, 1998, 275, n.42 referencing Hoffmann, 1973, 15–17.

57 Zos., 6.3.

58 Pollentia, Ridley, 'Zosimus', 1982, 227.n. 19; Goths, ibid; Freeman, 1886, 57.

59 Freeman, 1886, 54 and n.2.

60 Zos., 6.3.

61 Drinkwater, 1998, 277.

62 Drinkwater, 1998, 277–8.

63 Drinkwater, 1998, 277.

64 Drinkwater, 1998, 277.

65 Drinkwater, 1998, 275.

66 Coins: Kulikowski, 2000, 332 and footnote 51. Kulikowski links the coins to alleged victories over the invaders, whilst suggesting that they may instead proclaim 'Constantine's intention of fighting the barbarians and restoring the respublica'.

67 We are not informed directly that Constantine attempted to ally himself with the Vandals, Sueves and Alans. However, Oros. 7.40.4 and 7. 28. describes 'unreliable alliances' with barbarians and how these treaties were 'not strictly kept'. This can only relate to treaties with the invaders.

68 Jer., *Ep.* 123.15.

69 Cavallera 1922, 2:52, referenced in Kulikowski, 2000, 331, n.38.

70 Kulikowski, 2000, 331.

71 On the reliability of the various sources: Kulikowski, 2000, 331, footnote 39; 'Apart from Jerome's letter, Sozomen and three more or less contemporary poems (the *Ad uxorem*, the *Carmen de diuinaprovidentia*, and the *Epigramma* of Paulinus ...) attest to a barbarian presence in southern Gaul. Soz. 9.12.3 explicitly ties that presence to the rebellion of Gerontius against Constantine III in 409. Oros. 7.40.3 condenses more than three years of events into a single sentence which tells us nothing about chronology'.

72 Oros., 7.28

73 Kulikowski, 2000, 332.

74 Drinkwater, 1998, 276.

75 Drinkwater, 1998, 278.

76 Oros., 7.40.5.

77 Oros., 7.40.5.

78 Drinkwater, 1998, 275.

Chapter 14

1 The exact chronology for this section is extremely confusing, especially taking into account the speed of messengers carrying news and orders. The majority of this section is derived from Drinkwater, 1998, passim. Although this interpretation is viable, others can be constructed that differ in large part from this one yet remain valid. See, for example, Heather, 2005, 220f and Liebeschuetz, 2004, 66f plus accompanying footnotes and bibliographies.

2 The attempt to date these events by Burns using the *Codex Theodosianus* are, at the very least, unconvincing. All that is certain is that news arrived very quickly that Alaric was still alive:

Zos. 5.27.3.

3 Zos., 5.27.2.

4 Zos., 5.27.2.

5 Elton, 2004, 193.

6 Halsall, 2007, 213.

7 Honoré interprets passages in the *Scriptor Historiae Augustae* as evidence of some of the natural assumptions of the Western Senate: 1987, 156f.

8 *Cod. Th.*, 7.13.8: 7. 20.13.

9 Wolfram, 1997, 97.

10 Bury, 1923, 61.

11 Possible rift between Honorius and Stilicho; Matthews, 1975, 279.

12 Williams and Friell, 1994, 157. The two consuls were Bassus and Philippus.

13 Soz., 9.11.4: Or. 7.40.6.

14 Soz., 9.12.1.

15 For example, Salway, 1993, 304.

16 See Chapter 13.

17 Liebeschuetz, 1990, 66. His claim is based upon the concept that Stilicho needed Alaric's forces to make good the losses suffered by Sarus, but the chronology seems to work against him.

18 Zos 5.29.1; cf. for example Kulikowski, 2007, 172.

19 Possibility of Alaric acting to defend Noricum, Burns, 1994, 215.

20 Zos., 5.37.1f.

21 Drinkwater avoids having to make a decision on Sarus' appointment, leaving it open as to whether Sarus was *comes rei militaris* or *magister militum vacans*. For a discussion and further bibliography, see Drinkwater, 1998, 279. n. 63.

22 cf. Zos, 5.32.4.

23 e.g. CAH, 2004, 122; Liebeschuetz, 2004, 66.

24 *Comes rei militaris magister militum vacans* Burns; Drinkwater, 1998, 278 and note 63.

25 Drinkwater, 1998, 275–6 and 278.

26 Zos., 6.2.4.

27 Kulikowski, 2000, 334. Zos. 6.2.4; 'Nebiogastes, the surviving magister, made overtures of peace to Sarus and was amicably received by him.'

28 Zos., 6. 5.

29 Zos., 5.28. It is also interesting to note that after Stilicho's fall, and the death of the rest of her family, Thermantia was allowed to live in peace until she died in 415. Obviously, Honorius had either a deep respect or still retained some feelings for Thermantia.

30 Kulikowski, 2007, 172.

31 Ausonius, *Ordo Nobilium*, VIII.

32 Soz. 9.4, Zos. 5.34.1.

33 This section is largely reliant on the observations of Drinkwater, 1998, especially 279–80.

34 Zos., 6.4.1–2.

35 Drinkwater, 1998, 279.

36 Both Sozomen (9.11.4) and Zosimus (6.4.1) imply that Constans was promoted specifically for the campaign in Spain. cf. Kulikowski, 2005, 335.

37 On the appointments, Greg. Tur. 2.9.

38 It is difficult to reconcile the different accounts given in the sources. This reconstruction is based on Kulikowski, 2000, 335 and n. 67, using Soz. 9.11.4 – 12.1; Or. 7.40.6–8; and Zos. 6.4.

39 Or. 7.40.78; Soz. 9.12.1.

40 Zos. 6.5.1; 6.13.1; Greg. Tur. HF. II.9.

41 Or. 7.40.9–10; Soz. 9.12.3.

42 Zos., 5.29.1. It should be noted that this chapter is actually rather confusing and has Alaric crossing the Apennines, which was as yet an impossibility.

43 For example, Burns, 1994, 215 claims that it was not whereas Matthews, 1975, 46–7 claims that it was. Soz. HE 8.25.4 claims that Alaric returned to Italy, which may merely be a simple error given the context.

44 Zos., 5.29.5.

45 Zos., 5.29. 5.

46 Enough to keep 72,000 men, Liebeschuetz, 2004, 67 n. 155 quoting Wolfram; cost of the praetorian games, Matthews, 1975, 277 derived from Olymp. fr. 44.

47 For an alternative viewpoint, Matthews, 1975, 277–8.

48 Zos., 5.42.3.

49 30,000 men, Zos. 5.35–6; slaves from Rome, Zos. 5.42; large band under Athaulf, Zos. 5.37.1.

50 Liebeschuetz suggests that Stilicho was expecting the 'pay' to be in the form of booty, but this is not really valid, since he would need the goodwill of the people in Illyricum to ease the transition of government and, more importantly, have them volunteer to serve in the army and willingly pay their taxes.

51 This analysis is counter to that proposed, for example, by Heather, 2005, 221.

52 This section is heavily reliant on the account given by Zosimus: 5.29.

53 Salway, 1993, 295.

54 Zos., 5.29.6.

55 Zos., 5.29.7.

56 Zos. 5.29,9, following Olymp. fr. 5.

57 Burns, 1994, 361.n. 129; Olym. fr. 7.2. (from Photius).

58 Quotation, Zos. 5.29. 9; comparison to Claudius, Ridley, Zosimus, 217, n.105.

59 For the growth of Catholic opposition see Chapter 7.

60 Olymp. fr. 2.

61 Zos., 5.30.2.

62 Zos., 5.30.1.

63 Burns, 1994, 361, n. 129.

Chapter 15

1 Zos., 5.31.

2 Zos., 5.31.2.

3 Zos., 5.31.3.

4 Zos., 5.31.4.

5 Zos., 5.31.4.

6 Zos., 5.31.5.

7 Zos., 5.31, perhaps also Jord. 153; Liebeschuetz, 1990, 67

8 Drinkwater, 1998, 281.

9 Zos., 5.31.6.

10 See discussion in Wolfram, 1990, and 237 n.438 concerning contradictions between Zosimus (5, 42.1; 44.1; and 50.3) and Olym. fr.5 and the claim that Alaric was created *magister equitum*.

11 Zos., 5.32.4.

12 Zos., 5.30.3.

13 Soz., 9.4.6. On the significance of the *labarum*, Burns, 2004, 216.

14 Urged to travel to Ravenna by Serena, Zos. 5.30.

15 Kulikowski, 2007, 172.

16 Kulikowski, 2007, 172.

17 Williams and Friell, 1994, 157.

18 Interpreted as a betrayal, Zos. 5.29; motive for conspiracy, Zos. 5.32–4: 30.1.

19 cf Ferrill, 1988, 101.

20 Jones, 1966, 76.

21 Heather, 2005, 222.

22 Zos., 5.32.1.

23 Zos., 5.32.2.

24 Zos., 5.32.3.

25 Zos., 5.32.4.

26 Zos., 5.32.6f.

27 Zos., 5.32.7.

28 Zos., 5.33.

29 Zos., 5.34.1.

30 Zos., 5.34.2.

31 As a reward for his service, Heraclianus was made *comes Africae*: Zos. 5.37.6; PLRE II, p. 539. He remained loyal to Honorius, and was granted the consulship in 413. In the same year he rebelled, aiming to become emperor, before being murdered.

32 Zos., 5.34.4. For the date of the execution, *Consularia Italica* p. 300, as referenced by Burns, 1994, 216.

33 Zos., 5.34.5. Stilicho was allegedly buried in the Sarcophagus preserved beneath the pulpit of the Sant'Ambrogio Basilica in Milan, Italy.

34 *Cod. Th.* 9.42.21–1; cf. Zos. 5.35.

35 *Cod. Th.* 9.42.22.

36 Zos., 5.37.6.

37 Zos., 5.35.6; 40,000 men, 5.42.3.

38 See Chapter 11; Heather, 1994, 213f.

39 Zos., 5.36.1.

40 Zos., 5.36.3. Turpilio and Vigilantius were both killed following a mutiny of the troops in March 409, but Varanes was made consul in the East in 410: Ridley, 1983, 220, n. 132–134.

41 Zos., 5.37.1.

42 Zos., 5.35–7 and 45.

43 Heather, 1994, 215.

44 Zos., 5.38–44.

45 Jovius retained close ties with Alaric, Soz. 9.4.4.

46 Zos., 48.3.

47 Zos., 48.4.

48 Zos., 5.45–52: Soz. 9.7.

49 Zos., 6.12.3.

50 Zos., 6.8.

51 Zos., 6.6–12: Soz. 9.7.

52 Zos., 6.13; Soz. 9.9.

53 Zos., 6.5.2.

54 Jer., *Ep.* 123.16: Kulikowski, 2000, 331.

55 Poulter, 2007, 38.

56 *Cod. Th.* 7.16.1.

57 Goldsworthy, 2009, 303.

Chapter 16

1 Burns, 2003, 376.

2 cf. Halsall, 2007, 213–4.

3 Halsall, 2007, 188.

4 'The indecisive outcome of no less than five head-on confrontations between Stilicho and Alaric (392/3, 395, 397, and two in 402) implies a sense of solidarity between barbarians in the armies of the empire, and is a more likely explanation than the need to recruit barbarians.' Liebeschuetz, 2004, 53.

5 Rut. *de Reditu suo*, 40f: http://penelope.uchicago.edu/Thayer/E/Roman/Texts/Rutilius_Namatianus/home.html, referenced May 2009. See also Williams and Friell, 1994, 224. n.64.

6 Elton, 2004, 141–2, noting that only Jerome and Orosius highlight his Vandal origins, and that even the extremely hostile Rutilius Namatianus makes no mention of it.

7 Olymp., 5.1.

8 Williams and Friell, 1994, 158; 224, n.64.

9 Williams and Friell, 1994, 156.

10 Williams and Friell, 1994, 156.

11 Muhlberger, 2006, 89–91.

12 Christie, 2007, 553.

13 For example, prior to Stilicho, Arbogast; after Stilicho, Orestes.

14 Kulikowski, 2007, 164.

15 'United empire', Liebeschuetz, 2004, 67.

16 See Chapters 6, 7 and 10 for a more detailed analysis.

17 cf. Elton, 2004, 266.

18 cf. Matthews, 1975, 278.

19 Liebeschuetz, 2004, 68.

20 O'Flynn, 1983, 43–4.

21 'Propagandist', O'Flynn, 1983, 43.

Appendix I

Glossary

A glossary of some of the Latin titles and phrases used in the book.

Angon	Germanic heavy javelin with a long iron shank and a barbed head. The equivalent of the earlier Roman *pilum*.
Annona	Subsidies paid to barbarian kings in return for their cooperation.
Arcuballista	Roman crossbow (see also *Cheiroballista*).
Aurem tironicum	'Gold for recruits': the tax paid in lieu of supplying men for the army.
Auxilia palatina	'Auxilia of the palace': auxiliaries (theoretically non-Roman troops) serving directly under the emperor and of suitable high status within the army.
Bipennis (Francisca)	Name given to the throwing-axe later known as the *francisca* in texts contemporary to Stilicho.
Bucellarii	'Biscuit eaters': nickname originally applied to (some) Roman troops but during the time of Stilicho applied to the new bodyguards recruited by generals and high-ranking officials.
Carroballista	Artillery piece mounted on a wagon for ease of transport.
Cheiroballista	Roman crossbow (see also *Arcuballista*).
Claustra Alpium Iuliarum	'Fortifications of the Julian Alps': defensive fortifications in the Julian Alps to protect northern Italy from invasion.
Comes Africae	'Count (Commander) of Africa': military leader in Africa.
Comes Britanniarum	'Count (Commander) of Britain': military leader in Britain.
Comes domesticorum	'Count (Commander) of the household bodyguards': military leader of the imperial guard.
Comes et magister utriusque militiae per Africam	'Count (Commander) and Master (General) of all of the troops in Africa': title given to Gildo by Theodosius.
Comes Gildoniaci patrimonii	'Count (Commander) of the patrimony of Gildo':

	person in control of the lands confiscated by the emperor from Gildo after his revolt.
Comes rei militaris	'Count (commander) of things military': title of military commanders below the *magistri* in seniority.
Comes rei militaris per Aegyptum	'Count (commander) of things military in Egypt': sometimes title of military commander in Egypt.
Comes rei privatae	'Count (commander) of things private': personal secretary to the emperor.
Comes sacrarum largitionem	'Count (commander) of the sacred largesse': Imperial Chamberlain.
Comes sacri stabuli	'Count of the sacred stables': cavalry commander of the imperial guard.
Comes/comites	'Count' (commander): deriving from the 'companions' of the earlier emperors, by the time of Stilicho it was a rank given to men trusted by the emperor with specific duties (see above).
Comitatenses	'Companions': the second tier of the army, the troops so designated were stationed in the interior and could expect to serve in the emperor's armies in the field.
Commentariensis	'Registrar of public documents': imperial functionary with considerable power.
Dediticii	Army units of unclear derivation and status, tending towards the lower end of the army hierarchy.
Dux Aegyptae	'Duke of Egypt': military leader of the frontier forces stationed in the province of Egypt.
Dux Pannonia Secunda	'Duke of Pannonia Secunda': military leader of the frontier.
Dux/duces	'Duke': military commander of forces stationed on the frontier of provinces on the borders of the Empire.
Foederati	'Federates': troops recruited from barbarian tribes, each one probably following a separate treaty and under different conditions. In this book, the term *foederati* is usually used of those men serving under Alaric in order to differentiate between them and other federates serving under different leaders and conditions.
Fabrica/fabricae	'Factories': the imperial factories making equipment for the army on a large scale.
Francisca	Germanic throwing-axe, later associated with the Franks. At this time known as either the *securis* or the *bipennis*.
Fundae	Sling.
Gentiles	Army units of unclear derivation and status, tending towards the lower end of the army hierarchy.

Gladius hispaniensis	'Spanish sword': the sword used by the Roman legions earlier in the Empire.
Gothi minores	'Little Goths': name given to those Goths who, after the treaty of 382, chose to remain in Moesia rather than follow Alaric in another attempt to fight the Empire.
Hostis publicus	'Public enemy': name given by the emperor to any individual who is an 'enemy of the state'.
Iacula	A Roman spear or javelin.
Laetus/laeti	'Allies': name given to the Franks (and others) who had been defeated after entering the Empire, but had then been allowed to settle inside the Empire on condition that they guard the borders against attack.
Limitanei	Roman troops assigned to defend the land frontiers of the Empire. For a more in-depth discussion on these troops, see Nicasie (1998, p. 19–22) and Southern and Dixon (1996, p. 36). See also *riparienses*.
Magister militum	'Master of the soldiers': Roman general. Without any additional title, it is assumed that the individual has been assigned the rank with duties under the emperor, rather than in a specific area (see *magister militum per Illyricum* etc. and the discussion of military titles in Chapter 4).
Magister equitum	'Master of the cavalry': the second-highest military post in the West after the *magister peditum*. See also *Magister militum*.
Magister equitum et peditum	'Master of the cavalry and infantry': title taken by Stilicho to denote his sole control of the Western military machine.
Magister militum per Illyricum	'Master of the soldiers of Illyricum': military commander in the Prefecture of Illyricum.
Magister militum per Orientem	'Master of the soldiers of the East': military commander in the Prefecture of the East.
Magister militum per Thracias	'Master of the soldiers of Thrace': military commander in the Prefecture of Illyricum.
Magister officiorum	'Master of ceremonies': personal secretary to the emperor.
Magister peditum	'Master of the infantry': highest ranking military officer in the West.
Magister scrinii	'Master of the Imperial Secretaries': high-ranking official in the immediate entourage of the emperor.
Magister utriusque militiae	'Master of all the troops': see *Magister militum*.
Magister utriusque militiae praesentalis	'Master of all the troops in the presence (of the emperor': one of two military officials serving directly

	underneath the emperor. In the West more normally called the *magister equitum* and the *magister peditum*.
Manuballista	Roman torsion artillery firing a heavy bolt. Equivalent to the earlier *scorpio*.
Martiobarbuli	Type of Roman throwing dart used by the army. See also *Mattiobarbuli*.
Mattiobarbuli	Type of Roman throwing dart used by the army. See also *Martiobarbuli*.
Numerarii	Financial officer on the staff of high-ranking officials charged with maintaining financial records.
Numerus/numeri	Barbarian units serving within the Roman army earlier in the Empire. The word is used by later writers for any unit or groups thereof in the army.
Praefectus urbis Romae	'Prefect of the city of Rome': individual in charge of the running of the city.
Parens principum	'Parental guardianship': claim to 'guardianship' made by Stilicho over Honorius and Arcadius.
Pilleus Pannonicus	'Pannonian Hat': hat, probably made of felt and starting as headgear worn under a helmet. This later became a garment worn in its own right by soldiers to distinguish them from civilians when they did not need to wear a helmet.
Plumbatae mamillatae	Throwing dart with a heavy lead weight to increase penetration.
Plumbatae tribolatae	Throwing dart with a heavy lead weight to increase penetration and three spikes to form a caltrop, with one of the spikes always pointing upwards if it landed without hitting a target.
Praefectus praetorio Galliarum	'Praetorian prefect of Gaul': one of the four praetorian prefects in the Empire with responsibility for the civil administration of approximately one-quarter of the Empire under the emperor.
Praefectus praetorio Illyrici	'Praetorian prefect of Illyricum': see *Praefectus praetorio Galliarum*.
Praefectus praetorio Italiae	'Praetorian prefect of Italy': see *Praefectus praetorio Galliarum*.
Praefectus praetorio Orientis	'Praetorian prefect of the East': see *Praefectus praetorio Galliarum*.
Praepositus sacri cubiculi	'Head of the Sacred Chambers': high-ranking imperial functionary on the emperor's staff.
Princeps	'Chief clerk': high-ranking imperial functionary on the emperor's staff.
Proconsul Achaiae	'Proconsul of (the province of) Achaea': high-ranking official responsible for the administration of Achaea

	(see Map 1).
Proconsul Africae	'Proconsul of (the province of) Africa': high-ranking official responsible for the administration of Africa (see Map 1).
Protectores divini lateris	'Observed guards of the divine emperor'?): founded (possibly) during the reign of Gallienus (253–68). The precursors of the *protectors domestici*.
Protectores domestici	'Household guards': a group of individuals of relatively high rank who served under the emperor in the belief/hope that they could be trained and become high-ranking field officers in the army.
Pseudocomitatensis/ pseudocomitatenses	'Almost-*comitatenses*': *limitanei/riparienses* (q.v.).
Pteruges/pteryges	Leather or fabric strips attached to garments worn under armour which protected the hips/groin and/or shoulders of Roman troops.
Pugio	Earlier Roman dagger.
Reiks	Gothic word for 'king'. See also *Thiudans*.
Rex Gothorum	'King of the Goths': name taken by Alaric as a means of establishing his ascendancy amongst the Goths and as a political statement of intent in 400.
Ripariensis/riparienses	Roman troops assigned to defend the river frontiers of the Empire. For a more in-depth discussion on these troops, see Nicasie (1998, p. 19–22) and Southern and Dixon (1996, p. 36). See also *Limitanei*.
Sax/seax	Long dagger/short sword carried by many Germanic warriors.
Scholae	'Bodyguard': cavalry units serving directly under the emperor.
Scorpio	'Scorpion': early type of Roman catapult, later known as the *manuballista*.
Secures (francisca)	Earlier name for the *francisca* (q.v.).
Semispatha	'Half-spatha': short version of the longsword known as the *spatha* (q.v.)
Spatha	A long sword, probably of Germanic origin, that by the end of the fourth century was in common use in the Roman army.
Spicula	A heavy javelin, possibly the equivalent of the earlier *pilum*.
Tela	Name given to a variety of Roman javelin.
Thiudans	Gothic, the highest possible rank in Gothic society, this was normally only applied to a ruling Roman emperor.
Thusundifath	'Thousand-leader': later rank in Germanic armies given to leaders of 1,000 men.

Tribunus et notarius	'Tribune and notary': dignitary in the late Roman Empire.
Tribunus praetorianus militaris	'Praetorian military tribune': tribune and notary on the military general staff.
Tributarii	'Tributaries': low-ranking military units possibly composed of barbarians serving in the army after defeat in battle.
Verruta	Name given to a variety of Roman javelin.
Vicarius per Hispania	'Vicar of Spain': civil official serving under the Praetorian Prefect of Gaul administrating the provinces of Spain.

Outline Chronology

235	Death of Severus Alexander: beginning of 'Third Century crisis'.
260	Valerian defeated and captured by Persians: Antioch sacked.
284	Diocletian becomes emperor.
305	Diocletian and Maximianus resign: Galerius made *Augustus* of the East, Constantius of the West. Severus made *Caesar* of the West, Maximinus Daia *Caesar* of the East.
306	Constantius dies in York: the 'British' army proclaims Constantine as *Augustus*. Galerius proclaims Severus as *Augustus*. Constantine accepts junior post of Caesar. Maxentius, son of Maximianus, proclaimed *Augustus* in Rome: takes control of South Italy, Sardinia Corsica and Africa. Galerius refuses to recognize him.
307	Severus maintains control of North Italy, and early in the year leads invasion in attempt to defeat Maxentius. Maxentius asks his father Maximianus to come out of retirement. Maximianus appeals to Severus' troops, who served under him before his abdication. They renounce Severus and join Maximianus and Maxentius. Severus surrenders but is later killed. As there is now a vacancy for the post of *Augustus* in the West, Maxentius declares himself *Augustus*. In summer, Galerius invades Italy, but as many of his men desert to join the old *Augustus* Maximianus, he retires to the East. In order to cement an alliance, Constantine marries Fausta, daughter of Maximianus.
308	Maximianus appeals to the troops in an attempt to depose his son; surprisingly, the attempt fails. Maximianus flees to Constantinople. The Congress of Carnuntum: Galerius continues in control of the East, with Maximinus Daia as his Caesar. Licinius made *Augustus* of the West, in place of the deceased Severus, with Constantine as Caesar. Maximinus Daia and Constantine now referred to as *filii augustorum*.

Late in the year, Domitius Alexander acclaimed at Carthage. Maxentius loses control of Africa.

309/310 Death of Maximianus: relations between Constantine and Maxentius deteriorate. Constantine cements alliance with Licinius. In an attempt to counter this, Maxentius approaches Maximinus Daia with an alliance proposal. Maximinus Daia assumes title of *Augustus*.

310/311 Maxentius sends an army to Africa. It topples Alexander and reclaims the provinces for Maxentius.

311 Death of Galerius. Maximinus Daia seizes control of his territories. In summer, a meeting between Maximinus Daia and Licinius see the two sharing Galerius' lands.

312 Constantine invades Italy and, after winning several battles, defeats Maxentius at the Battle of the Milvian Bridge. Death of Maxentius.

313 February: marriage alliance between Licinius and Constantine signals end of Maximinus Daia's treaty with Licinius. Daia crosses the Bosporus, takes Constantinople and begins the siege of Heracleia. Licinius arrives and defeats Daia, who retreats East. Licinius pursues and wins a battle at the Cilician Gates. Daia dies July/August.

314 Battle of Cibalae: Constantine narrowly defeats Licinius.

317 Battle of Campus Ardiensis: Constantine again narrowly defeats Licinius – possible peace treaty/agreement.

324 Battle of the Hebrus River: Constantine's army defeats and routs Licinius. Battle of Chrysopolis: Constantine's army again defeats and routs Licinius. Licinius abdicates.

325? Licinius executed.

332 Constantine I defeats the Goths and agrees a treaty.

337 Death of Constantine I. His three sons eliminate all other rivals except Gallus and Julian. They accept Constantine's division of the Empire into three. Constantine II, the eldest, takes Gaul, Britain and Spain; Constantius II, the second son, takes the East, and Constans, the youngest, takes Italy, Pannonia and Africa.

340 Constantine II invades Italy, but is defeated by Constans at Aquileia and dies.

Constans becomes Augustus of the West.

341   Constans bans pagan sacrifices in the West.

341–2   Constans campaigns against the Franks.

350   The general Magnentius, commanding on the Rhine, declares himself emperor. Constans' troops defect to the usurper. He flees but is captured and killed.

350-1   Constantius II campaigns against Magnentius. Defeats Magnentius at Battle of Mursa and becomes sole ruler of the Empire. Deciding that the Empire is too big to be ruled by one man, he appoints his cousin Gallus as Caesar in the East.

354   Gallus executed: Constantius II attempts to withdraw the order for the execution, but this is ignored by the *praepositus cubiculi*, the eunuch Eusebius.

355   Germanic invasions of the West and the revolt of Claudius Silvanus in Gaul cause Constantius II to elevate his last remaining cousin, Julian, to the rank of Caesar. Silvanus' revolt quickly collapses.

357   Battle of Strasbourg (Argentoratum): Julian defeats Alamanni.

361   Constantius II orders Julian to send troops East. The troops refuse to go, instead elevating Julian to *Augustus*. Preparing for war, Constantius II dies in October: Julian becomes sole emperor.

361–3   Julian attempts to eliminate Christianity and impose a form of Neo-Platonism on the Empire. Begins major reforms of the bureaucracy.

Julian invades Persia, where he is killed. Jovian is elevated to *Augustus*.

363-4   Jovian cedes territory to Persia in return for peace. He re-establishes Christianity as the official religion of the Empire.

364   Death of Jovian, cause unknown. Valentinian I becomes emperor. He names his brother Valens as colleague. Valentinian I takes the West (Italy, Illyricum, Spain, Gaul, Britain and Africa) and Valens receives the East (Balkans, Greece, Egypt, Syria and Asia Minor).

365   Valentinian I defeats invading tribes and ejects them from Roman territory.

366   Procopius, last relative of Julian, proclaims himself emperor in the East. Battle of Thyatira and death of Procopius.

367   German tribes cross the Rhine and sack Moguntiacum (Mainz). Valentinian I attacks and defeats them with heavy losses.
The barbarian 'coalition' of Saxons, Picts and Scots invades Britain.
Valens leads campaign against Goths, the first since that of Constantine I in 332. War breaks out with Persia.

368   Valentinian I sends the *comes* Theodosius to Britain. Theodosius defeats the invaders and frees the provinces from occupation. As a reward, he is promoted to *magister equitum praesentalis*.
Floods in the East prevent a second year of campaigning against the Goths. Romans invade Armenia in an attempt to put the Armenian prince Pap on the throne. The Persians counter-attack.

369   Valens defeats the Goths and a treaty is signed.

370   Second Roman invasion of Armenia.

371   Shapur invades but is defeated and a truce is agreed.

372   Firmus rebels in Africa. Theodosius sent to deal with the rebellion. Eventually, Firmus is betrayed and the rebellion is crushed.

374   Treaty between Valentinian I and Macrianus, King of the Bucinobantes.
The Quadi invade and devastate Pannonia. Valentinian I leads an army to face them.
Theodosius, the son of the *magister equitum praesentalis* made *Dux Moesia*.

375   Theodosius is arrested and executed. His son retires to his estates, possibly as a result of losing two legions fighting against the Sarmatians.
Valentinian I agrees to meet embassy from the Quadi, during which he goes into a rage and dies. His sons (Valens' nephews), Gratian and Valentinian II, are made *Augusti*. Gratian is allotted Gaul, Spain and Britain; Valentinian II Italy, Illyricum and Africa.
Revolt in Isauria.

376   A large force of Goths appears on the border and requests admission to the Empire. Eventually, they are allowed to cross the Danube.

377   The Goths rebel, possibly due to maltreatment: the Battle of Ad Salices. Saracen attacks devastate Phoenicia and Palestine. The attacks are defeated and the Isaurian revolt brought under control.

378 With affairs in the East stable, Valens advances to face the Goths. Battle of Adrianople, defeat and death of Valens. Gratian orders Theodosius out of retirement and sends him to the East.

379 Theodosius made *Augustus* by Gratian with orders to command in the East.

382 After years of campaigning, Theodosius signs treaty with Goths, who are given land in the Balkans.

383 Magnus Maximus declares himself emperor. He takes control of Britain, Gaul and Spain. Gratian dies while attempting to escape. Agreement reached between Maximus, Valentinian II and Theodosius to share the Empire.

387 Maximus invades Italy; Valentinian II flees East.

388 Theodosius defeats Maximus at the Battles of Siscia and Poetovio. Maximus is killed.

388–92 Valentinian II rules Gaul from Vienne, supported by Theodosius' appointee Arbogast.

390 Theodosius orders the 'massacre at Thessalonica'. Bishop Ambrose of Milan demands that Theodosius acts as a true penitent before granting him pardon for the act.

391 Theodosius ambushed by Goths, ostensibly under Alaric, as he returns East.

392 Valentinian II found hanged. Unknown whether suicide or murder.
Arbogast elevates Eugenius to *Augustus* in the West
Theodosius tolerates the appointment until troops can be gathered.

393 Theodosius elevates son Honorius, aged eight, as *Augustus* in the West.

393–4 Stilicho blockades Alaric into submission in the Balkans. Alaric forced to serve Theodosius in his upcoming campaign against Arbogast and Eugenius.

394 Theodosius defeats Arbogast and Eugenius at the Battle of the Frigidus. Arbogast commits suicide, Eugenius is executed.

395 Death of Theodosius. Honorius remains emperor of the West, Theodosius' younger son Arcadius made emperor of the East. Stilicho guardian of the West.
Hunnic raids across Caucasus Mountains.

Alaric raises 'rebellion' in Balkans and Stilicho leads combined East/West armies to confront him. Stilicho is baulked by the order from Arcadius to return the Eastern troops to Constantinople and retires from Illyricum.

396   Alaric moves into Greece. Stilicho leads a lightning campaign along the Rhine.

397   Stilicho's second campaign in Illyricum against Alaric. Stilicho is declared *hostis publicus* by Arcadius and again retires without defeating Alaric. Alaric made *magister militum* per Illyricum.

398   Revolt of Gildo in Africa. Gildo defeated by his brother Mascezel and Africa returns its loyalty to Rome.

400   Citizens of Constantinople rebel against the rule of Gainas. Thousands of Gainas' troops are killed as they attempt to leave the city.

401   Stilicho leads the army of Italy against Vandals and Alans in Rhaetia and Pannonia. Simultaneously, Alaric invades Italy.

402   Stilicho returns to Italy and defeats Alaric at the Battles of Pollentia and Verona.
Alaric accepts minor post in Pannonia.

405-6   Radagaisus leads his Goths across the Alps into Italy. Stilicho defeats the main force at Faesulae and the others retreat from Italy.

406-7   Stilicho plans the invasion of Illyricum. Alaric is sent to Epirus. Rebellion of Constantine III in Britain: Vandals, Alans and Sueves cross Rhine into Gaul. Constantine accepts service of Vandals, Alans and Sueves. Invasion of Illyricum cancelled.

408   Sarus defeats forces of Constantine III but is forced to flee back to Italy. Didymus and Verinianus revolt against Constantine III in Spain but are defeated and killed. Death of the (Eastern) Emperor Arcadius. Honorius and Stilicho argue about the correct course of action to take. It is agreed that Stilicho will go to Constantinople to assume control of the new young Emperor Theodosius II. As Honorius inspects his troops at Pavia, they rebel and kill as many of Stilicho's supporters as they can. Honorius gives the order for the arrest and execution of Stilicho. Stilicho's son Eucherius is also killed. The troops kill the families of the German federates and the German troops flock to Alaric. First siege of Rome by Alaric. Serena, wife of Stilicho, executed in Rome.

409   Vandals, Alans and Sueves cross into Spain. Second siege of Rome.

410   Third siege and sack of Rome by Alaric.

Appendix III

Select Personalities

A brief summary of some of the major characters appearing in the story of Stilicho.

Alaric (c.370–410): Leader of a large group of warriors, mainly Goths, from their revolt against Roman rule in 395 until his death in 410. The main opponent of Stilicho, he was an able politician and general. Led the Goths in their sack of Rome in 410.

Ambrose (c.340–397): Bishop of Milan, now a saint. Came to the bishopric unwillingly, but was then steadfast in his support of Catholicism. When in 390 Theodosius I ordered a massacre in Thessalonica, Ambrose excommunicated him and forced the emperor to serve several months of penance before allowing him to return to the fold. Following Theodosius' death in 395 Ambrose supported Stilicho until his own death in 397.

Anthemius (*praefectus praetorio Orientis* 405–414): From his appointment in 405 Anthemius was the leader of a political coalition that guided the East through the minority of Theodosius II. He refused to accept Stilicho as *parens principum* from 405 until Stilicho's death in 408.

Arbogast (d.394): A Frank, he was placed in charge of Valentinian II in 388. His refusal to accept the young emperor's orders may have resulted in Valentinian committing suicide in 392. Arbogast then promoted Eugenius as the new emperor in the West. Theodosius refused to accept this and in 394 led an army into Italy. At the hard-fought Battle of the Frigidus Theodosius was victorious and Arbogast fled before committing suicide.

Arcadius (emperor 383–408): Weak-willed, his court was dominated by a succession of strong individuals until the rise of Anthemius, after which Anthemius and his allies dominated the East and stabilized the situation until Arcadius' death in 408.

Aurelian (*praefectus praetorio Orientis* 399 and 414–416): He was consul alongside Stilicho in 400, but was arrested and exiled under Gainas. After the fall of Gainas he returned and remained a powerful political figure until late in his life.

Claudian (Claudian Claudianus (died c.404)): Was an Egyptian poet. Under the patronage of Stilicho he wrote, amongst others, panegyrics both for Stilicho and the

Emperor Honorius (see Introduction for more information).

Constantine III (d.411): Declared emperor in Britain in 407, he crossed the English Channel and took control of Gaul and Spain. Although at first opposed by Honorius, when Alaric invaded Italy Honorius recognized him as co-emperor. Due to political intrigues at his own court, in Spain and in Italy, Constantine led an abortive invasion of Italy before retreating and being besieged in Arles by his own rebel general Gerontius. Finally Constantius, the new *magister militum* in Italy, drove off Gerontius and himself laid siege to Constantine. He eventually surrendered and was executed in 411.

Eucherius (c.388–408): The son of Stilicho, he was betrothed to Galla Placidia but they never married. He was killed in Rome in 408.

Eudoxia (*Augusta* 400–404): Daughter of the Frank Bauto, she married the Emperor Arcadius in 395 as arranged by Eutropius. She was declared *Augusta* in Constantinople in 400, to the disgust of the West, and died in 404.

Eugenius (*Augustus* 392–394): A teacher of Latin Grammar and Rhetoric, he was raised to the purple by Arbogast following the 'suicide' of Valentinian II. Defeated at the Battle of the Frigidus, he was then executed.

Eutropius (*praepositus sacri cubiculum* 395–9): A eunuch, he was *praepositus sacri cubiculum* in Constantinople. He was the great rival of Rufinus. He arranged the marriage of Eudoxia to Arcadius to thwart Rufinus' plans, and then took both Rufinus' power and wealth when Rufinus was killed by the troops in 395. Instigated the declaration of Stilicho as *hostis publicus* to safeguard his own position. Led a military expedition against the Huns but then alienated the court by assuming the consulship for 399, which was never accepted in the West. Overthrown by Gainas following the political intrigues of Tribigild. He was exiled before being recalled and executed for treason.

Eutychianus (*praefectus praetorio Orientis* 397–399, 399–400 and 404–405): After the fall of Rufinus in 397 he was the *praefectus praetorio Orientis* until 399, being consul in 398. With the fall of Eutropius in 399 he was replaced before being reinstated following the coup of Gainas. With the fall of Gainas he was once again replaced before being restored for a brief period in 404–405, after which the domination of Anthemius ensured he made no further returns to power.

Flavia Galla (second wife of Theodosius I, 387–394): Daughter of Valentinian I, sister of Valentinian II, and mother of Galla Placidia, she married Theodosius as part of the political arrangements for Theodosius' support for her brother against Magnus Maximus. Died in childbirth in 394.

Fravitta (d.404): A Goth, leader of the pro-Roman party of the Goths settled by

Theodosius in 382. Killed Eriulph, leader of the anti-Roman faction, prior to Theodosius' campaign against Eugenius, after which he served Theodosius and then Arcadius. Appointed *magister militum* in 400 to quell the revolt of Gainas, his success earned him the consulship in 401. A supporter of Stilicho and the unity of the Empire, he was executed after accusing John of sowing dissension between East and West.

Gainas (d.400): A Goth, he was given joint-command of the federate troops during Theodosius' campaign against Eugenius in 394. After Theodosius' death he assumed command of the Eastern troops serving under Stilicho before leading his men back to Constantinople. Probably responsible for the death of Rufinus at the hands of the troops on their return. Angered by not receiving high honours under Rufinus' successor Eutropius, took advantage of Tribigild's revolt to oust Eutropius from power before assuming command himself. Unfortunately, he was not up to the task. Realizing he was under threat, he left Constantinople but many of his men were massacred by the inhabitants as they attempted to join him. He attempted to cross to Asia Minor, being stopped by Fravitta, before crossing the Danube. Once across he was defeated and killed by the Hun Uldin.

Galla Placidia (c.388–450): Daughter of Theodosius I, she was brought up in the household of Stilicho and Serena. In 408 she approved of the execution of Serena. In 410 she was taken prisoner by the Goths and married the Gothic king Athaulf in 414. After the murder of Athaulf she returned to court and was forced to marry Constantius III. She bore him two children, one of whom was the future emperor Valentinian III.

Gildo (*comes et magister utriusque militiae per Africam*, 386–398): Son of King Nubel of Mauretania, he served under Theodosius, father of Theodosius I, in the campaign against Gildo's brother Firmus. As a reward he was given titles in Africa, culminating in being appointed *magister militum* of the province. In 394 he did not send help to Theodosius against Firmus and in 397 he revolted against Stilicho and the West and pledged his allegiance to Eutropius and the East. He was defeated and killed in 398 by his brother Mascezel.

Honorius (384–423, *Augustus* 393–423): Younger son of Theodosius I, on the death of his father assumed the rule of the Western Roman Empire. He was dominated by Stilicho, marrying two of Stilicho's daughters, Maria (398) and on her death Thermantia (408), though neither marriage produced children. He based his court in Milan until the invasion of Alaric in 401–402. After this, he moved the court to Ravenna. Allegedly a weak ruler and easily dominated, at least part of this reputation may be ascribed to the army being loyal to his generals rather than him, producing a high level of paranoia and insecurity. Ruled until 423, when he followed in his father's footsteps by dying of oedema (dropsy).

John: Trusted advisor to Arcadius, and rumoured to be the father of Theodosius II, he was exiled during the dominance of Gainas before returning to court. He was accused by Fravitta of fostering discord between East and West, for which Fravitta was later executed.

John Chrysostom (c.347–407): Against his will, John was made Bishop of Constantinople in 398. His epithet *Chrysostom* (golden-mouthed) was given due to his blistering attacks upon the wealthy, including Eudoxia. She took advantage of his dispute with Theophilus of Alexandria to have him sent into exile, where he died. The event was one of the causes of the quarrel between East and West, as Pope Innocent I, Honorius and Stilicho attempted to intervene on Chrysostom's behalf. Eudoxia and her ministers were understandably angry at Western interference in Eastern affairs.

Lampadius: Brother of Theodorus, he was an early supporter of Stilicho, being appointed *praefectus urbis Romae* by Stilicho to vigorously enforce conscription for the war with Gildo in 398. Later changed his allegiance, becoming an opponent of Stilicho, especially after the Senate had been convinced of the need to pay Alaric 4,000 pounds of gold in 408.

Magnus Maximus (c.335–388): Was proclaimed emperor by his troops in Britain in 383, following which he crossed to Gaul. The Western emperor Gratian was defeated and fled before him but was killed. Ruled Britain, Gaul, Spain and Africa until 387. In that year he invaded Italy and forced Valentinian II to flee to the East. In 388 Theodosius invaded the West and defeated Maximus, who surrendered and was executed.

Maria (married to Honorius 398–407/8): Daughter of Stilicho and Serena, she married Honorius but died childless in either 407 or 408.

Mascezel (d.398): Brother of Gildo, he followed his elder brother Firmus in his revolt against Rome in 373–375. Retained in Africa, possibly as a counterbalance to Gildo, in 397 Gildo attempted to kill him but he fled to Stilicho. His two sons were killed by Gildo. In 398 he was sent by Stilicho to Africa with an army and easily defeated Gildo. On his triumphant return to Rome, he drowned, possibly on Stilicho's orders. He was a Catholic and may have been associated with the Catholic opposition to Stilicho.

Radagaisus (d.406): A Goth, led an invasion of Italy in 405. In 406 he was defeated and captured by Stilicho before being executed.

Richomeres (d.393/4): A Frank who served as a military commander to both the East and West. An able general, he was appointed by Theodosius to command the cavalry against Eugenius but died of illness before the start of the campaign. Praised as an able commander.

Rufinus (*praefectus praetorio Orientis* 392–395): A Gaul, served Theodosius from c.388 and was left in charge of Arcadius and the East when Theodosius left to campaign against Eugenius in 394. He opposed Stilicho's claims to be *parens principum* of both East and West on the death of Theodosius, and was then (probably falsely) accused of colluding with Alaric during the latter's invasion of Illyricum and Greece. He was killed by the Eastern army as it returned from Italy in 395, probably under the instigation of Gainas.

Sarus (d.412): A Goth, probably deserted Alaric following Alaric's defeat at Verona in 402, after which he served under Stilicho until the latter's death in 408. Following the invasion of Gaul by Constantine III, he defeated and killed Constantine's *magister militum* Justinianus but was forced to retire to Italy on the approach of Constantine's reinforcements, losing his baggage to the *bacaudae* in the Alps on the way. He was the obvious choice as Stilicho's replacement as *magister militum* in 408, but Honorius refused to give him the post. He had a vendetta against Alaric and his family, so when Alaric's successor Athaulf captured him he was quickly executed. He was a strong, brave and experienced commander.

Saul: A barbarian, possibly an Alan, he was joint commander of the federates serving Theodosius at the Battle of the Frigidus in 394 before serving under Stilicho in the West. He commanded the first attack on Alaric at the Battle of Pollentia, where he was killed.

Serena: Daughter of Honorius (died before 379), elder brother of Theodosius I, and so Theodosius' niece. When her father died Theodosius adopted her as his own daughter. Married Stilicho sometime around 384, with whom she bore two daughters, Maria and Thermantia, who both married the Emperor Honorius. She also gave birth to a son, Eucherius. A devoted Christian, she built the shrine of Nazarius at Milan. She was killed in 408 when the Goths laid siege to Rome, as it was thought that, after the execution of her husband and son and the deaths of the families of the federates, she would support Alaric in his assault on the city.

Stilicho (c.360–408).

Symmachus (?–c.402): An accomplished orator and writer, he served the Western emperors from at least 365 until his death in c.402. Although he supported Magnus Maximus when the usurper invaded Italy in 388, after a prolonged period of estrangement and public disgrace, he was reconciled with Honorius after writing a panegyric and full apology to the emperor. As the senior member of the Senate, his support during Stilicho's regime was invaluable in that it helped to control opposition, as well as giving Stilicho an accomplished orator to speak on his behalf in the Senate. His death in c.402 must be seen as one of the turning points in Stilicho's 'rule'.

Theodorus (senior): Made *praefectus praetorio Italiae* in 397 by Stilicho, he held the post until 399 when he was awarded with the consulship for his loyalty and service to

Stilicho. Father of Theodorus (junior).

Theodorus (junior): Son of Theodorus (senior), he was made *praefectus praetorio Galliarum* by Stilicho. It would appear that towards the end of Stilicho's rule he changed allegiance, since in 408 he is recorded as having been made *praefectus praetorio Italiae* by Olympius.

Theodosius I (Emperor of the East 379–395): After a shaky start, in 382 he concluded peace with the Goths who had revolted and won the Battle of Adrianople in 378. In 388 he invaded Italy in support of Valentinian II when that young emperor had been forced to flee by Magnus Maximus. Magnus Maximus was defeated and killed. After the death of Valentinian II, Arbogast declared Eugenius the new Western emperor. In response in 394 Theodosius again invaded Italy, defeating and killing Eugenius. Arbogast committed suicide. Shortly after his victory in early 395 he died.

Theodosius II (401–450): Son of Arcadius (or possibly John) and Eudoxia he assumed the throne in Constantinople in 408. Coming early to the throne, he was dominated by others, in the early years especially by Anthemius (408–414) and Theodosius' sister Pulcheria (414–416).

Thermantia (d.415): Second daughter of Stilicho and Serena. In 408 after Maria's death she too married Honorius. After Stilicho's death she was repudiated and sent back to her mother in Rome. She died in 415.

Timasius: An experienced and capable soldier, he served under Theodosius against both Magnus Maximus in 388 and Eugenius in 394. Despite (or more likely because of) his successful career in 396 he was falsely accused of treason and exiled. He attempted to escape and was never heard of again.

Tribigild: A Goth, although a Roman commander in 399 he revolted against the command of Eutropius, possibly in collusion with Gainas. Although Gainas was successful in ousting Eutropius and assuming his power, Tribigild died shortly afterwards.

Valentinian II (371–392): Proclaimed *Augustus* in 375, he was still only a child during the Gothic War of 378–382 and so took no part. After the attempt by Magnus Maximus to evict him from power was foiled by Theodosius in 388, he was placed in the care of the general Arbogast. Unfortunately, Arbogast treated him with contempt and after the general had torn Valentinian's orders to pieces in front of him the young emperor appears to have committed suicide at the age of twenty-one.

Select Bibliography

Primary sources

Ammianus Marcellinus, *The Histories*, trans. Rolfe, J C (Harvard, 1986)

Blockley, R C, *The Fragmentary Classicising Historians of the Later Roman Empire: Eunapius, Olympiodorus, Priscus and Malchus Vol 2* (Liverpool, 1983)

Chronicon Paschale 264–628 AD, trans. Whitby, M and Whitby, M (Liverpool, 1989)

Claudian, *The Complete Works*, trans. Platnauer, M (Harvard, 1922),http://penelope.uchicago.edu/Thayer/E/Roman/Texts/Claudian/home.html

Codex Theodosianus, http://ancientrome.ru/ius/library/codex/theod/tituli.htm

Codex Theodosianus, http://webu2.upmf-grenoble.fr/Haiti/Cours/Ak/Constitutiones/codtheod1.htm

Codex Theodosianus, trans. Pharr, C (New York, 1952)

Collectio Avellana, see *Corpus Scriptorum Ecclesiasticorum Latinorum*

Corpus Scriptorum Ecclesiasticorum Latinorum, http://www.fourthcentury.com/index.php/the-collectio-avellana/

Eugippius, *Life of Saint Severinus*, trans. Robinson, G W (Harvard, 1914)

Eunapius, *Lives of the Philosophers and Sophists*, trans. Wright, W C, (1921), http://www.tertullian.org/fathers/index.htm

Gregory of Tours, *History of the Franks*, trans. Brehaut, E (Columbia UP, 1916), http://www.fordham.edu/halsall/basis/gregory-hist.html

Jordanes, *The Origin and Deeds of the Goths*, trans. Mierow, C C (Lenox, MA, 2006)

Latin Epigraphy, http://www.manfredclauss.de/gb/index.html

Marcellinus Comes, *Chronicon* in *Chronica Minora II*, Mommsen,T (Berlin, 1894), http://www.thelatinlibrary.com/marcellinus1.html

Notitia Dignitatum: accident Notitia Urbis Constantinopolitanae et latercula provinciarum, Seeck, O (Frankfurt am Main, 1962)

Olympiodorus, see Blockley, R C, *The Fragmentary Classicising Historians of the Later Roman Empire: Eunapius, Olympiodorus, Priscus and Malchus Vol 2*

Orosius, *Historiarum Adversum Paganos*, Zangemeister, C (ed) (1889), http://www.attalus.org/latin/orosius.html

Paulinus of Pella, *Eucharisticon Deo sub ephemeridis meae textu*, trans. Evelyn White, H G (1921), http://penelope.uchicago.edu/Thayer/E/Roman/Texts/Paulinus_Pellaeus/home.html

Paulus Orosius, *The Seven Books of History Against the Pagans*, trans. Deferrari, R J (Washington DC, 2001)

Philostorgius, *Epitome of Ecclesiastical History*, trans. Walford, E (London, 1855), http://www.tertullian.org/fathers/philostorgius.htm

Philostorgius, *Church History*, trans. Amidon, P R (Atlanta, 2007)

Priscus, see, Blockley, R C *The Fragmentary Classicising Historians of the Later Roman Empire: Eunapius, Olympiodorus, Priscus and Malchus Vol 2*

Rutilius Namatianus, *de Reditu suo*, in *Minor Latin Poets*, Volume II, pp. 753–829, Wight Duff, J and Duff, Arnold M (Harvard, 1935), http://penelope.uchicago.edu/Thayer/E/Roman/Texts/Rutilius_Namatianus/home.html

St Jerome, *Letters and Select Works: Vol VI*, Schaff, P (ed.) (Edinburgh), http://www.ccel.org/ccel/schaff/npnf206.toc.html

Salvian, *On the Government of God*, trans. Sanford, Eva M (Columbia, 1930), http://www.tertullian.org/fathers/index

Seeck, O *Notitia Dignitatum*, (Berlin, 1876)

Socrates, *Socrates and Sozomenus: Ecclesiastical Histories*, trans. Schaff, P (New York, 1886), http://www.ccel.org/ccel/schaff/npnf202.iii.xiii.iv.html

Sozomen, *Socrates and Sozomenus: Ecclesiastical Histories*, trans. Schaff, P (New York, 1886), http://www.ccel.org/ccel/schaff/npnf202.iii.xiii.iv.html

Synesius, *The Egyptian Tale or On Providence*, trans. Fitzgerald, A (Oxford UP, 1926),http://www.livius.org/su-sz/synesius/synesius_providence1_00.html

Tacitus, *The Histories*, trans. Hamilton Fyfe, W (Oxford, 1912), http://www.gutenberg.org

Theoderet, *The Ecclesiastical History*, Schaff, P and Wace, H (eds.) (New York, 1892), http://www.ccel.org/ccel/schaff/npnf203.iv.html

Zosimus, *New History*, trans. Ridley, R T, (Sydney, 1982)

Secondary sources

Barnes, T D, 'The Victims of Rufinus', *The Classical Quarterly*, New Series, Vol. 34, No. 1. (1984), pp. 227–230.

Barnish, S J and Marazzi, F, *The Ostrogoths from the Migration Period to the Sixth Century* (San Marino, 2007).

Barrett, J C et al, *Barbarians and Romans in North-West Europe* (Oxford, 1989).

Bayless, W N, 'The Visigothic Invasion of Italy in 401', *The Classical Journal*, Vol. 72, No. 1 (Oct. – Nov., 1976) pp. 65–7.

Baynes, N H, 'A Note on Professor Bury's "History of the Later Roman Empire."', *The Journal of Roman Studies*, Vol. 12. (1922), pp. 207–229.

van Berchem, D, 'On Some Chapters of the Notitia Dignitatum Relating to the Defence of Gaul and Britain',*The American Journal of Philology*, Vol. 76, No. 2. (1955), pp. 138–147.

Binns, J W (ed.), *Latin Literature of the Fourth Century*, (London, 1975).

Bishop, M C and Coulston, J C N, *Roman Military Equipment: From the Punic Wars to the Fall of Rome*, (Oxford, 2006).

Bloomers, J H F, 'Acculturation in the Rhine/Meuse Basin in the Roman Period: Demographic Considerations', in Barrett, J C et al, 1989.

Breeze, D J and Dobson, B, 'Roman Military Deployment in North England', *Britannia*, Vol. 16 (1985), pp. 1–19.

Burns, T S, *Barbarians Within the Gates of Rome*, (Indiana, 1994).

Burns, T, *Rome and the Barbarians 100 BC – AD 400*, (Baltimore, 2003).

Burrell, E, 'A re-examination of why Stilicho abandoned his pursuit of Alaric in 397',

Historia, Band LIII/2 (2004) pp. 251–56.

Bury, J B, 'The Notitia Dignitatum', *The Journal of Roman Studies*, Vol. 10 (1920), pp. 131–154.

Bury, J B, *History of the Later Roman Empire*, (London, 1923) http://penelope.uchicago.edu/Thayer/E/Roman/Texts/secondary/BURLAT/home.html

Cameron, A, *Claudian: Poetry and Propaganda at the Court of Honorius* (Oxford, 1970).

Cameron, A, 'Claudian' in Binns, J W (ed) *Latin Literature of the Fourth Century* (London, 1975) pp. 134–59.

Cameron, A, *The Later Roman Empire*, (London, 1993).

Cameron, A and Garnsey, P (eds), *The Cambridge Ancient History: Volume XIII The Late Empire, A.D. 337–425*, (Cambridge, 2004).

Cherf, W J, 'The Thermopylae Garrison of "Vita Claudii" 16', *Classical Philology*, Vol. 88, No. 3 (Jul. 1993), pp. 230–236.

Christiansen, P G, 'Claudian versus the Opposition', *Transactions and Proceedings of the American Philological Association*, Vol. 97 (1996), pp. 45–54.

Christie, N, 'From the Danube to the Po: The Defence of Pannonia and Italy in the Fourth and Fifth Centuries A.D.', *Proceedings of the British Academy*, 141 (2007), pp. 547–578.

Coulston, J C N, 'Later Roman Armour, 3rd – 6th Centuries AD', *Journal of Roman Military Equipment Studies 1* (1990), pp. 139–60.

Dewar, M, 'The Fall of Eutropius', *The Classical Quarterly*, New Series, Vol. 40, No. 2 (1990), pp. 582–584.

Donnelly, P, 'What Happened at Adrianople?', http://mysite.verizon.net/res1bup4/adrianople.htm, 2008.

Drinkwater, J F, 'The Usurpers Constantine III (407–411) and Jovinus (411–13)' *Britannia* 29 (1998), pp. 269–98.

Drinkwater, J and Elton, H (eds), *Fifth-Century Gaul: A Crisis of Identity?* (Cambridge, 2002).

Elton, H, *Warfare in Roman Europe AD 350–425* (Oxford University Press, 1997).

Ferrill, A, *The Fall of the Roman Empire: the Military Explanation* (London, 1991).

Freeman, E A, 'The Tyrants of Britain, Gaul and Spain A.D. 406–411', *English Historical Review*, Vol. 1 (1886), pp. 53–85,
http://penelope.uchicago.edu/Thayer/E/Roman/Texts/secondary/journals/EHR/1/Tyrants*.html (April, 2009).

Freeman, E A, *Western Europe in the Fifth Century* (London, 1904).

Freeman, P and Kennedy, D (eds), *The Defence of the Roman and Byzantine East, Parts I and II* (Oxford, 1986).

Gibbon, E, *The Decline and Fall of the Roman Empire*, in 4 volumes (Liverpool, 1861).

Goldsworthy, A, *The Fall of the West: the Death of the Roman Superpower* (London, 2009).

Halsall, G, *Barbarian Migrations and the Roman West 376 – 568* (Cambridge, 2007).

Hanson, R P C, 'The Reaction of the Church to the Collapse of the Western Roman Empire in the Fifth Century', *Vigiliae Christianae*, Vol. 26, No. 4 (Dec. 1972), pp. 272–287.

Heather, P, *Goths and Romans: 332–489* (Oxford, 1994).

Heather, P, *The Goths* (Oxford, 1998).

Heather, P, *The Fall of the Roman Empire: A New History* (London, 2005).

Heather, P, 'Goths in the Roman Balkans c.350–500', *Proceedings of the British Academy* 141 (2007), pp. 163–90.

Heather, P and Matthews, J, *The Goths in the Fourth Century* (Liverpool, 1991).

Honoré, T, 'Scriptor Historiae Augustae', *The Journal of Roman Studies*, Vol. 77 (1987), pp. 156–76.

Jones, A H M, *The Decline of the Ancient World* (Harlow, 1966).

Jones, A H, Martindale, J R and Morris, J, *The Prosopography of the Later Roman Empire Vol. I, AD 260–395* (Cambridge, 2006).

Kulikowski, M, 'Barbarians in Gaul, Usurpers in Britain', *Britannia* 31 (2000), pp. 325–45.

Kulikowski, M, *Rome's Gothic Wars* (New York, 2007).

Ladner, G B, 'On Roman Attitudes Towards Barbarians in Late Antiquity', *Viator* 7 (1976), pp. 1–26.

Lenski, N, *Failure of Empire: Valens and the Roman State in the Fourth Century AD* (California, 2002).

Liebeschuetz, J H W, 'Generals, Federates and Bucellarii in Roman Armies around AD 400' in Freeman, P and Kennedy, D, 1986, pp. 463–74.

Liebeschuetz, J H W, *Barbarians and Bishops: Army, Church and State in the Age of Arcadius and Chrysostom* (Oxford, 1992).

MacMullen, R, *Corruption and the Decline of Rome* (Yale, 1990).

Mann, J C, 'Power, Force and the Frontiers of Empire', *Journal of Roman Studies*, Vol. 69 (1979), pp. 175–183.

Mann, J C, 'The Notitia Dignitatum – Dating and Survival', *Britannia*, Vol. 22. (1991), pp. 215–219.

Markus, R, A, 'Paganism, Christianity and the Latin Classics in the Fourth Century' in Binns, J W (ed) *Latin Literature of the Fourth Century* (London, 1975).

Martindale, J R, *The Prosopography of the Later Roman Empire, Vol. II, AD 395–527* (Cambridge, 2006).

Matthews, J F, 'The Letters of Symmachus', in Binns, J W (ed) *Latin Literature of the Fourth Century* (London, 1975).

Matthews, J, *Western Aristocracies and Imperial Court AD 364–425* (Oxford, 1998).

Millar, Fergus, *The Roman Empire and its Neighbours* (London, 1993).

Millar, F, 'Emperors, Frontiers and Foreign Relations, 31 B.C. to A.D. 378', *Britannia*, Vol. 13 (1982), pp. 1–23.

Miller, M, 'Stilicho's Pictish War', *Britannia*, Vol. 6 (1975), pp. 141–5.

Mitchell, S, *A History of the Later Roman Empire AD 284–641* (Oxford, 2007).

Muhlberger, S, *The Fifth-Century Chroniclers: Prosper, Hydatius and the Gallic Chronicler of 452* (Cambridge, 2006).

Murray, A C (ed. and trans.), *From Roman to Merovingian Gaul* (Toronto, 2000).

Musset, L, *The Germanic Invasions: the Making of Europe AD 400–600* (trans. E and C James) (London, 1975).

Nicasie, M J, *Twilight of Empire: The Roman Army From the Reign of Diocletian until the Battle of Adrianople* (Lieden, 1998).

Norwich, J J, *Byzantium: The Early Centuries* (London, 1988).

O'Flynn, J, *Generalissimos of the Western Roman Empire* (University of Alberta Press, 1981).

Oost, S I, 'Count Gildo and Theodosius the Great', *Classical Philology*, Vol. 57, No. 1. (Jan. 1962), pp. 27–30.

Oost, S I, 'Some Problems in the History of Galla Placidia', *Classical Philology*, Vol. 60, No. 1. (Jan. 1965), pp. 1–10.

Poulter, A G, 'The Transition to Late Antiquity', *Proceedings of the British Academy* 141 (2007), pp. 1–50.

Randers-Pehrson, J D, *Barbarians and Romans: the Birth Struggle of Europe, AD 400–700* (London, 1983).

Salway, P, *The Oxford Illustrated History of Roman Britain* (Oxford, 1993).

Sodini, J-P, 'The Transformation of Cities in Late Antiquity Within the Provinces of Macedonia and Epirus', *Proceedings of the British Academy 141 (2007), pp. 311–366.*

Southern, P and Dixon, K R, *The Late Roman Army* (London, 1996).

Stephenson, I P, *Romano-Byzantine Infantry Equipment* (Stroud, 2006).

Thompson, E A, 'Peasant Revolts in Late Roman Gaul and Spain', *Past and Present*, No. 2 (Nov. 1952), pp. 11–23.

Todd, M, *The Early Germans* (Oxford, 2004).

Tomlin, R S O, 'Army of the Late Empire', in Wacher, J (1990), pp. 107–120.

Treadgold, W, *Byzantium and its Army 284–1081* (Stanford, 1995).

Trout, D E, 'The Years 394 and 395 in the "Epitoma Chronicon": Prosper, Augustine, and Claudian', *Classical Philology*, Vol. 86, No. 1 (Jan. 1991), pp. 43–47.

Vogt, J, *The Decline of Rome* (London, 1993).

Wacher, J, *The Roman World* (London, 1990).

Ward, J H, 'The British Sections of the "Notitia Dignitatum": An Alternative Interpretation', *Britannia*, Vol. 4 (1973), pp. 253–263.

Whitby, M, 'The Late Roman Army and the Defence of the Balkans', *Proceedings of the British Academy* 141 (2007), pp. 135–61.

Williams, S and Friell, G, *Theodosius: The Empire at Bay* (London, 1994).

Wolfram, H, *History of the Goths* (trans. T Dunlap) (Berkeley and Los Angeles, 1990).

Wolfram, H, *The Roman Empire and its Germanic Peoples* (trans. T Dunlap) (California, 2005).

Woods, D, 'Arbazacius, Fravitta, and the Government of Isauria ca AD 396–404', *Phoenix*, Vol. 52 (1998), pp. 109–19.

Index